The Impact of the Market

Jürgen von Hagen | Michael Welker
John Witte | Stephen Pickard (Eds.)

The Impact of the Market

on Character Formation, Ethical Education,
and the Communication of Values
in Late Modern Pluralistic Societies

WIPF & STOCK · Eugene, Oregon

Wipf and Stock Publishers
199 W 8th Ave, Suite 3
Eugene, OR 97401

The Impact of the Market
On Character Formation, Ethical Education, and the Communication
of Values in Late Modern Pluralistic Societies
By von Hagen, Jürgen and Welker, Michael
Copyright © 2020 Evangelische Verlagsanstalt GmbH All rights reserved.
Softcover ISBN-13: 978-1-6667-5058-4
Hardcover ISBN-13: 978-1-6667-5059-1
Publication date 6/14/2022
Previously published by Evangelische Verlagsanstalt GmbH, 2020

INHALT

Acknowledgments 9

Michael Welker, John Witte Jr., Jürgen von Hagen, and Stephen Pickard
Preface to the Series 11

Jürgen von Hagen
Introduction 15

PART ONE: SYSTEMATIC CONTRIBUTIONS

Jürgen von Hagen
Markets and the Human Character 23

Frank J. Lechner
Commercial Society and its Values 39
The Merits of the Market in Social Theory

Ginny Seung Choi and Virgil Henry Storr
Growing up in the Market 51
The Character Traits that Markets Reward and Punish

Jason Brennan
How Market Society Affects Character 73

Paul Oslington
Understanding the Economic Impacts on Virtue and the Pursuit of Good 93

PART TWO: BIBLICAL AND HISTORICAL IMPULSES

Michael J. Broyde
Law, Economy, and Charity 115
Formations in Torah and Talmud

Jürgen von Hagen
Old Testament Principles of Economic Ethics 133

Kaja Wieczorek
Economic Conditions Impacting Luke's Concept of Economic Solidarity 147

Peter Lampe
Christian-Apocalyptic Protest from the First-Century 90s as a Reaction to Economic Conditions 161

Samuel Gregg
Commerce, Finance, and Morality in the Thought of Early Modern Catholic Scholastics 171

John Witte Jr.
Oikos and Oikonomika 187
The Early Modern Family as a Matrix of Modern Economics

Part Three: Contemporary Perspectives

Katrin Gülden Le Maire
Pushing New Frontiers 211
The (Im)Possibility of Character Formation through ICT Products and Services

William Schweiker
Can Character Formation Survive the Digital Economy? 223

Steven Pickard
Rational Choice Theory and Virtuous Economics? 233
Problems and Possibilities

Piet Naudé
A Conceptual Analysis of "Value" in Select Business Literature and Its Implications for Ethical Educations 247

Part Four: Applications and Explanations

Manfred Lautenschläger
Economics, Character, and Values 263
Vital Questions in Society

Klaus Leisinger
Nice Words Are Fine, But Hens Lay Eggs 271
Communication about Values Leads to Expectations of Practical
Consequences

Michael Welker
Entrepreneurs' Ethics in South East Asia 285
Some Insights from Expert Interviews
Contributors 295

Acknowledgments

The consultation leading to this volume took place at the Forschungszentrum Internationale und Interdisziplinäre Theologie (FIIT) at the University of Heidelberg, October 5-6, 2018. We thank the Karl Schlecht Foundation and the University of Heidelberg for their generous support.

Jürgen von Hagen, Michael Welker, John Witte Jr., Stephen Pickard

Preface to the Series
Character Formation and Ethical Education in Late Modern Pluralistic Societies

An Interdisciplinary and International Research Project

Five hundred years ago, Protestant reformer Martin Luther argued that "three estates" (*drei Stände*) lie at the foundation of a just and orderly society—marital families, religious communities, and political authorities. Parents in the home; pastors in the church; magistrates in the state—these, said Luther, are the three authorities whom God appointed to represent divine justice and mercy in the world, to protect peace and liberty in earthly life. Household, church, and state —these are the three institutional pillars on which to build social systems of education and schooling, charity and social welfare, economy and architecture, art and publication. Family, faith, and freedom—these are the three things that people will die for.

In the half millennium since Luther, historians have uncovered various classical and Christian antecedents to these early Protestant views. And numerous later theorists have propounded all manner of variations and applications of this three-estates theory, many increasingly abstracted from Luther's overtly Christian worldview. Early modern covenant theologians, both Christian and Jewish, described the marital, confessional, and political covenants that God calls human beings to form, each directed to interrelated personal and public ends. Social-contract theorists differentiated the three contracts that humans enter as they move from the state of nature to an organized society protective of their natural rights— the marital contract of husband and wife; the government contract of rulers and citizens; and, for some, the religious contracts of preachers and parishioners. Early anthropologists posited three stages of development of civilization—from family-based tribes and clans, to priest-run theocracies, to fully organized states that embraced all three institutions. Sociologists distinguished three main forms of authority in an organized community: "traditional" authority that begins in the home, "charismatic" authority that is exemplified in the church, and "legal" authority that is rooted in the state. Legal historians outlined three stages of development of legal norms—from the habits and rules of the family, to the customs and canons of religion, to the statutes and codes of the state.

Already a century ago, however, scholars in different fields began to flatten out this hierarchical theory of social institutions and to emphasize the foundational role of other social institutions alongside the family, church, and state in shaping private and public life and character. Sociologists like Max Weber and Talcott Parsons emphasized the shaping powers of "technical rationality" exemplified especially in new industry, scientific education, and market economies. Legal scholars like Otto von Gierke and F.W. Maitland emphasized the critical roles of non-state legal associations (*Genossenschaften*) in maintaining a just social, political, and legal order historically and today. Catholic subsidiarity theories of Popes Leo XIII and Pius XI emphasized the essential task of mediating social units between the individual and the state to cater the full range of needs, interests, rights, and duties of individuals. Protestant theories of sphere sovereignty, inspired by Abraham Kuyper, argued that not only churches, states, and families but also the social spheres of art, labor, education, economics, agriculture, recreation, and more should enjoy a level of independence from others, especially an overreaching church or state. Various theories of social or structural pluralism, civil society, voluntary associations, the independent sector, multiculturalism, multinormativity, and other such labels have now come to the fore in the ensuing decades—both liberal and conservative, religious and secular, and featuring all manner of methods and logics.

Pluralism of all sorts is now a commonplace of late modern societies. At minimum, this means a multitude of free and equal individuals and a multitude of groups and institutions, each with very different political, moral, religious, and professional interests and orientations. It includes the sundry associations, interest groups, parties, lobbies, and social movements that often rapidly flourish and fade around a common cause, especially when aided by modern technology and various social media. Some see in this texture of plurality an enormous potential for colorful and creative development and a robust expression of human and cultural freedom. Others see a chaotic individualism and radical relativism, which endangers normative education, moral character formation, and effective cultivation of enduring values or virtues.

Pluralism viewed as vague plurality, however, focuses on only one aspect of late modern societies—the equality of individuals, and their almost unlimited freedom to participate peaceably at any time as a respected voice in the moral reasoning and civil interactions of a society. But this view does not adequately recognize that, beneath the shifting cacophony of social forms and norms that constitute modernity, pluralistic societies have heavy normative codes that shape their individual and collective values and morals, preferences and prejudices.

The sources of much of this normative coding and moral education in late modern pluralistic societies are the deep and powerful social systems that are the pillars of every advanced culture. The most powerful and pervasive of these are the social systems of law, religion, politics, science/academy, market, media, family, education, medicine, and national defense. The actual empirical forms of each of these powerful social systems can and do vary greatly, even in the relatively homogeneous societies of the late modern West. But these deeper social systems in one form or another are structurally essential and often normatively decisive in individual and communal lives.

Every advanced society has a comprehensive legal system of justice and order, religious systems of ritual and doctrine, a family system of procreation and love, an economic system of trade and value, a media system of communication and dissemination of news and information, and an educational system of preservation, application, and creation of knowledge and scientific advance. Many advanced societies also have massive systems of science, technology, health care, and national defense with vast influence over and through all of these other social systems. These pervasive social systems lie at the foundation of modern advanced societies, and they anchor the vast pluralities of associations and social interactions that might happen to exist at any given time.

Each of these social systems has internal value systems, institutionalized rationalities, and normative expectations that together help to shape each individual's morality and character. Each of these social spheres, moreover, has its own professionals and experts who shape and implement its internal structures and processes. The normative network created by these social spheres is often harder to grasp today, since late modern pluralistic societies usually do not bring these different value systems to light under the dominance of just one organization, institution, and power. And this normative network has also become more shifting and fragile, especially since traditional social systems like religion and the family have eroded in their durability and power, and other social systems like science, the market, healthcare, defense, and the media have become more powerful.

The aim of this project on "Character Formation and Moral Education in Late Modern Pluralistic Societies" is to identify the realities and potentials of these core social systems to provide moral orientation and character formation in our day. What can and should these social spheres, separately and together, do in shaping the moral character of late modern individuals who, by nature, culture, and constitutional norms, are free and equal in dignity and rights? What are and should be the core educational functions and moral responsibilities of each of these social spheres? How can we better understand and better influence the complex interactions among individualism, the normative binding powers of these social systems, and the creativity of civil groups and institutions? How can we map and measure the different hierarchies of values that govern each of these social systems, and that are also interwoven and interconnected in various ways in shaping late modern understandings of the common good? How do we negotiate the boundaries and conflicts between and among these social systems when one encroaches on the other, or imposes its values and rationalities on individuals at the cost of the other social spheres or of the common good? What and where are the intrinsic strengths of each social sphere that should be made more overt in character formation, public education, and the shaping of minds and mentalities?

These are some of the guiding questions at work in this project and in this volume. Our project aims to provide a systematic account of the role of these powerful normative codes operating in the social spheres of law, religion, the family, the market, the media, science and technology, the academy, health care, and defense in the late modern liberal West. Our focus is on selected examples and case studies drawn from Western Europe, North America, South Africa, and Australia, which together provide just enough diversity to test out broader theories of character formation and moral education. Our scholars are drawn from across the academy, with representative voices from the humanities, social sciences, and natural sciences as well as the professions of theology, law, business, medicine, and more. While most of our scholars come from the Protestant and Catholic worlds, our endeavor is to offer comparative insights that will help scholars from any profession or confession. While our laboratory is principally Western liberal societies, the modern forces of globalization will soon make these issues of moral character formation a concern for every culture and region of the world—given the power of global social media, entertainment, and sports; the pervasiveness of global finance, business, trade, and law; and the perennial global worries over food, health care, environmental degradation, and natural disasters.

In this volume, we focus in on the role of the economic market in shaping character development, ethical education, and the communication of values in late modern pluralistic societies.

Michael Welker, University of Heidelberg
John Witte Jr., Emory University
Jürgen von Hagen, University of Bonn
Stephen Pickard, Charles Sturt University

Introduction

Jürgen von Hagen

The chapters in this volume focus on the role of "the market" as a key subsystem of modern societies. The authors understand the market as an economic mechanism for the exchange of goods and services in societies with a very large degree of division of labor and, more generally, as a term representing a society largely shaped and driven by commerce and private economic interests. The authors show that the role of the market in shaping the human character, ethical education, and the communication of values in late modern pluralistic societies is not a one-way street. The market shapes human character, ethical education, and the communication of values, while, at the same time, human character, ethical education, and the communication of values shape markets and their performance. The chapters in this volume explore this dialectical relationship.

We have grouped the contributions to this volume into four parts. Part one deals with general and conceptual relationships among markets, character formation, and values. Part two brings pertinent biblical considerations into the debate. Part three discusses some contemporary aspects of our topic. Finally, part four reports on some ways that markets, character formation, and values interact.

In the opening chapter, "Markets and the Human Character," *Jürgen von Hagen* provides a brief introduction to the economics of markets. Markets provide opportunities not only for voluntary exchange of goods and services generating welfare benefits for the participants, but also for fraud and deceit. Markets are embedded in legal and regulatory environments that determine the quality of economic results. The chapter goes on to present two contrary positions regarding the impact of markets on character formation. The "doux commerce" hypothesis, which goes back to the seventeenth century, claims that markets promote virtues like prudence, honesty, and care for others. The "markets-make-villains" hypothesis, which has been popular since the nineteenth century, argues the opposite, namely, that markets promote vices like greed, deception, and selfishness. The subsequent chapters frequently come back to contrasting these two positions.

Frank J. Lechner ("Commercial Society and Its Values: The Merits of the Market in Social Theory") continues the discussion by noting that modern societies exhibit significant moral divisions. Such divisions might be overcome when people from different moral positions participate in common practices that unite them. Lechner discusses the potential merits of the market in this regard. While the market does promote certain virtues, Lechner concludes that its unifying potential is limited, because the relevant moral disagreements often concern the nature and purposes of market activities themselves.

Ginny Seung Choi and *Virgil Henry Storr* ("Growing up in the Market: The Character Traits That Markets Reward and Punish") explore the question of what kind of character traits markets teach. They review empirical evidence from cross-national studies along a number of moral dimensions: selfishness versus selflessness, honesty versus dishonesty, loyalty versus disloyalty. Overall, they find that market economies tend to perform better in fostering positive traits than nonmarket economies do. This does not, of course, exclude the existence of morally bad persons in market economies, nor does it prove that markets have a positive influence on the human character. But it does suggest at least that markets do not promote morally inferior behavior in societies.

"How Market Society Affects Character," by *Jason Brennan*, complements this discussion by bringing in additional evidence. Brennan reviews some famous case studies of the question whether markets promote selfishness, and he reports microeconomic evidence concerning the effect of markets on the levels of trust, tolerance, and honesty in societies. This evidence also leads to the conclusion that markets do not corrupt morals. Why, then, do so many philosophers and others hold the opposite view? Brennan suggests two answers: first, that empirical evidence does not much impress the philosophers and, second, that they grossly misunderstand the economist's rhetoric of utility as saying that monetary values are all that counts in market societies.

The final chapter in this section, "Understanding the Economic Impacts on Virtue and the Pursuit of Good," by *Paul Oslington*, begins by noting that the rise of the market economy in modern societies has been accompanied by a rise of economic thought in modern culture. The core of economic thought is the concept of rational and maximizing behavior. It has replaced the concepts of virtue and the pursuit of general goods that are worthy of attainment in themselves and cannot be traded off against each other. As a result, virtue and general goods have lost their former power in guiding individual and societal behavior. Oslington proposes a natural-law approach to economics as an alternative. Yet he remains skeptical of the potential of such an approach, so long as it remains unclear how to cast it in the kind of formal model structures that economists are used to working with.

Part two begins with "Law, Economy, and Charity: Formations in Torah and Talmud," by *Michael J. Broyde*. He studies how the Torah laws of charity have evolved in Jewish communities over time. He shows how the understanding of charity-giving as an obligation to help the poor gradually changed into an obligation to support the general good of modern Jewish society with its many different institutions. This movement away from charity as supporting the poor has been facilitated by the development of the modern welfare state in Western countries. Contrary to what one might expect, government-provided care for the poor has not crowded out private charity altogether.

Jürgen von Hagen ("Old Testament Principles of Economic Ethics") explains how the two fundamental principles of economic ethics found in the Old Testament—stewardship and charity—relate to four basic economic issues, namely, work, property, exchange, and solidarity. Human beings are obliged by the economic order of creation to live and work as stewards of their divine creator and to pursue the well-being of other human beings. These two fundamental principles are reflected in the Torah's laws concerning human work, private property, the exchange of goods, and the performance of acts of solidarity. Living according to Old Testament Law requires freedom. Von Hagen concludes that a market economy can provide that freedom better than systems of central planning.

In "Economic Conditions Impacting Luke's Concept of Economic Solidarity," *Kaja Wieczorek* argues that the Gospel of Luke, with its many economic motifs, can be interpreted as a critique of the economic and social realities of the first-century Roman Empire. Wieczorek shows how Luke seems to take up some of these motifs from contemporary Roman literature to unmask it as economic propaganda. Some of Luke's parables criticize the dire economic situation that the poor and dependent classes of the empire found themselves in. Luke calls on Christians to make the world one of greater solidarity founded on the hope that God will act to make his kingdom come.

Peter Lampe continues this discussion in "Christian-Apocalyptic Protest from the First-Century 90 s as a Reaction to Economic Conditions." He proposes a reading of the book of Revelation as a protest against the barbarous political and economic conditions of the lower classes of the Roman Empire. Characteristically, Revelation is not a book of hope but a call for patient suffering and upholding of Christian identity in the face of hardship and persecution.

The next two chapters study the relationship between the emerging market economy and religious and moral thinking in medieval and early modern Europe. *Samuel Gregg*, in "Commerce, Finance, and Morality in the Thought of Early Modern Catholic Scholastics," traces the development of some key economic concepts in the scholastic writings from St. Thomas Aquinas to the second half of the sixteenth century. These writings were a response to the emergence of far-ranging trade relations and markets for capital and credit and the concomitant moral concerns of what it meant to be righteous in this new environment in view of the ethical demands of the Bible discussed in chapter 7. Gregg shows how the discussion of moral issues led to the discovery of important insights into the economics of capital and financial markets.

In "*Oikos* and *Oikonomika:* The Early Modern Family as a Matrix of Modern Economics," *John Witte Jr.* studies the interaction between the economy and the family in shaping moral character as reflected in the early household manuals of the sixteenth and early seventeenth centuries. These manuals idealize the Protestant household as a family church, business, and school. They teach the moral values of industry, discipline, frugality, and mutual care which Max Weber later identified as the "spirit of capitalism."

Part three begins with two chapters that reflect on the power of information and communications technologies (ICT) and their markets to shape human character. In "Pushing New Frontiers—The (Im)Possibility of Character Formation Through ICT Products and Services," *Katrin Gülden Le Maire* argues for the need to study the impact of these new technologies on character formation. Studies have shown that their use has significant effects on brain formation and structures, especially in children and young adults. As ICT continues to spread though all parts of society, this could change societal perceptions of morals and values.

William Schweiker discusses the implications of one particular feature of the ICT economy—the way human attention has become a valuable economic commodity in "Can Character Formation Survive the Digital Economy?." He fears that ICT causes people to lose sight of their own moral values to the point of losing their souls for the benefit of increased economic wealth. Educating conscience and an understanding of individual responsibility might be an appropriate antidote.

Stephen Pickard ("Rational Choice Theory and Virtuous Economics? Problems and Possibilities") returns to Paul Oslington's theme, that is, the relationship between moral thinking and economic rationality as exemplified by the (in)famous *homo oeconomicus*. Pickard argues that there is an appropriate and legitimate place for economic activities such as trade, distribution, and consumption of goods within the economy of God. However, economic activities and rationality must not be separated from other spheres and practices of society. Through the Eucharist, the church can display what a renewed economic logic might look like.

"A Conceptual Analysis of 'Value' in Select Business Literature and Its Implications for Ethical Education" is devoted to a discussion of value concepts in contemporary business. *Piet Naudé* presents four current views of what value means in business: shareholder value (Milton Friedman), shared value (Michael Porter and Mark Kramer), strategic stakeholder value (Edward Freeman), and collective value (Thomas Donaldson and James Walsh). Going from the first to the last is a move from a very narrow understanding of the value of a business as the financial return to its owners to a comprehensive economic and moral valuation of all those who participate in its activities. In this move, financial returns gradually lose importance while intrinsic values gradually gain. Moral education of business managers becomes more important along the way.

Part four begins with a speech by *Manfred Lautenschläger* to the participants of the October 2018 consultation at Heidelberg that formed the basis of this volume. In "Economics, Character, and Values: Vital Questions in Society," Lautenschläger gives an account of his own experiences with the ethical side of business and the economy and calls for continued interdisciplinary research into the intersection of theology, economics, and moral philosophy.

In "Nice Words Are Fine, but Hens Lay Eggs: Communication about Values Leads to Expectations of Practical Consequences," *Klaus M. Leisinger* reflects on his experience in consulting with businesses about the communication of values, which has become quite fashionable recently. Leisinger argues that it is possible to base successful management on moral values, but it is dangerous when actions do not follow pronouncements. Value-based management is difficult, because it requires a redefinition of what a business organization regards as normal behavior. Such management is, therefore, a long-term project that needs careful planning and perseverance to succeed.

Michael Welker ("Entrepreneurs' Ethics in South East Asia: Some Insights from Expert Interviews") presents summaries of interviews with business owners and managers focusing on the relationship between their religious beliefs and their business practices. The interviewees come from different religious backgrounds—Daoist, Confucian, Buddhist, and Christian. Despite these differences, the interviews reveal two commonalities, namely, that religious beliefs impact how these individuals interpret their role and place in business, but that these beliefs do not take preeminence over core business principles.

Altogether, the contributions to this volume span a large range of topics and issues. The authors have benefitted greatly from the discursive culture of the venerable University of Heidelberg, and we hope that this volume will stimulate further fruitful debate of and research into the interrelationship among the spheres of the market, human character formation, and thinking about values and virtues.

Part One:
Systematic Contributions

Markets and the Human Character

Jürgen von Hagen

Modern societies are market societies. *The market* is the predominant economic institution and has pervaded all spheres of life. If institutions generally shape the human character, it is obvious that the market does. This chapter begins with a general discussion of the nature and functioning of markets.

Markets

The market is a place where people exchange goods and services in commodity mode. The word "market" reminds us of places such as the village square or the central square of a city, where farmers and artisans of all kinds offer their products for sale with the purpose of buying the products of other farmers and artisans later on. While this was the predominant form of the market in times past, it has long since ceased to be the case. Some markets still exist physically and geographically, while others are purely fictitious and exist only virtually. They may still have physical manifestations, such as the delivery of the goods bought and the making of payments, but the market in its entirety is an abstraction which exists only in the minds of those who speak about it, feel constrained by it, design policies to influence it, and do research trying to understand it. For example, we can visit websites where we purchase the right to listen to music online and pay for that online. There is a market for such services, but it has no physical manifestation. We may also buy books online, pay for them online, and have the books delivered to our homes. The delivery of the book then is the only material manifestation of the online book market. The US stock market and other global financial markets today extend beyond the trading floors of exchange buildings and are essentially online trading platforms where financial claims and liabilities are traded that never take physical form.

The essence of a market is the interaction between potential buyers and sellers of the objects traded—commodities for commodities or commodities for money. The extent of the market is the scope of the interaction between potential buyers and sellers. It is limited by the cost of transportation of the objects traded and the cost of communication among the potential buyers and sellers, including the effects of national borders, differences in tax systems, customs regulations, and differences in product regulations.

Potential buyers and sellers in a market engage in *voluntary exchange.* The word "voluntary" has two aspects here. First, no market participant is obliged to buy or sell a commodity at a certain price unless he desires to do so. This has important consequences for interpreting what is going on in a market. If we observe two or more individuals voluntarily exchanging goods (or goods for money), each one must be better off as a result: the seller, since he would not accept the exchange if what he receives was of inferior value in his own eyes than what he gives; the buyer, since he would not give what he pays if what he receives was not of superior value to him. Voluntary exchange entails what economists call a Pareto improvement: no party to the exchange can be worse off, and at least one party must be better off as a result of the exchange. The proof is simple: an individual who would be worse off would just withdraw from trading.

Voluntary exchange involves a certain kind of reciprocity: one partner of the exchange achieves a welfare gain from the exchange by making another realize a welfare gain as well.[1] Thus, voluntary exchange is necessarily a positive-sum game, a notion developed and emphasized by the sixteenth-century French political philosopher Jean Bodin and the seventeenth-century French lawmaker Pierre de Boisguilbert.[2] Note that the principle of voluntary exchange says nothing about the distribution of the welfare gains between the two individuals. One may gain very little, the other very much. Still, to say that an exchange between two individuals leaves one worse off is the same as saying that that individual did not trade voluntarily, and that where the exchange took place was not a market.

More generally, then, every market trade generates a surplus of economic welfare to be shared among the participants. The price paid by the buyer determines how much of the surplus he receives and how much goes to the seller. The question then is, at what price will the buyer and the seller agree to trade? There is no general answer to that question. Much of it depends on how the exchange between the two individuals is organized. If the two bargain over the price, the result depends on their relative bargaining power. The more power one individual has, the larger the welfare gain he can secure for himself. This is where competition comes into play: the more competition there is among traders, the less power each

---

[1] Wilhelm Röpke, in *The Moral Foundation and the Impact of Keynesianism* (New York: National Association of Manufacturers, 1963), called voluntary exchange the "method of solidarity" to alleviate economic scarcity.

[2] On Bodin, see Henri Baudrillart, *J. Bodin et son temps* (Paris: Librairie de Guillaumins et Cie., 1853), 176 ff.; on de Boisguilbert, see Félix Cadet, *Pierre de Boisguilbert: Précurseur des Economistes* (Paris: Institut Coppet, 2014), 167 ff.

individual has to determine the terms of trade in his favor, and the more equitable will be the outcome.³ It is on these grounds that the medieval scholastics, among them Thomas Aquinas, argued that the just—that is, morally justified—price of a commodity would be the one that can be obtained in a competitive market.⁴ Martin Luther later agreed with them.⁵ Competition requires transparency, in the sense that the participants on both sides of the market know what market conditions prevail, what is the going market price, and what kind of exchanges are possible.

The view of market exchange as a positive-sum game stands in stark contrast to another tradition, one that holds that one man's gain from trade can be realized only by another man's loss and that, therefore, market exchange is necessarily a zero-sum game. Félix Cadet traces the history of this idea to Francis Bacon and Michel de Montaigne.⁶ According to this view, a nation's government should strictly regulate and even suppress trade with other nations to assure that the nation suffers no losses. Economic policies from Colbert's mercantilism to modern forms of protectionism have rested on the notion of trade as a zero-sum game pitting nations against each other as rivals. The positive-sum view, in contrast, regards trade between nations as promoting international solidarity and peace.⁷ Even today, Donald Trump's call to "make America great again" rests on the zero-sum-game view, while the awarding of the Nobel Peace Prize to the European Union in 2012 is impregnated with the positive-sum-game view.

The second aspect of voluntary trade is that every trader in a market has a choice of whom to trade with. An individual buyer is not obliged to buy from a certain seller. He can search for better opportunities. Similarly, an individual seller is not obliged to accept the price offered by a certain buyer. He can search for

---

3   There is a long tradition of discussing what is a "fair" price, reaching all the way from Aristotle through Roman law to the scholastics (including Thomas Aquinus) and Martin Luther to today's "fair-trade" movement. We will not enter into this debate here.
4   See Odd Langholm, *The Legacy of Scholasticism for Economic Thought* (Cambridge: Cambridge University Press, 1998) for an extensive survey of the scholastic debate on commerce, prices, and markets.
5   See Martin Luther, "Von der Kaufshandlung und Wucher," 1524.
6   Cadet, *Pierre de Boisguilbert.* For Francis Bacon, see *Essays or Councils Civil and Moral with Introduction and Illustrations by Samuel Harvey Reynolds* (Oxford: Clarendon Press, 1890), Essay 15, 99, available at www.archive.org. For Montaigne, see "Le Profit de l'Un est Dommage de l'Autre," in *Les Essais de Michel de Montaigne* (Paris: Michel Sonnius, 1595), Book 1, 53 ff.
7   This had been argued already by Jean Bodin and Pierre de Boisguilbert and, almost a century later, by Immanuel Kant, *Zum ewigen Frieden: Ein philosophischer Entwurf,* 1st ed. (Königsberg: F. Nicolovius, 1795), available at: https://archive.org/details/zumewigen frieden00kant.

another buyer offering a better price. Market exchange, therefore, stands in contrast to economic transactions within closely knit communities like the family, the clan, the village, the church, or the tribe, where customs and hierarchies determine who can make exchanges with whom, and at what terms. While such exchanges involve lasting and stable personal relationships, market exchanges typically do not. In fact, many market exchanges are anonymous, in the sense that the buyer does not know the seller and vice versa, and the two interact through the veil of a trading business or platform. The mark of the market is that potential buyers and sellers interact for no other purpose than to buy and sell. From the point of view of a buyer, all sellers are equivalent as long as they sell the same commodity at the same price. Similarly, from the point of view of the seller, all buyers are equivalent, as long as they buy their commodity at the same price. Market exchange is characterized by cold, impersonal relationships among the participants, in which each participant seeks only his own advantage.

Market transactions are contracts between buyers and sellers. Market exchange requires that all potential exchange partners regard and accept each other as autonomous individuals, that is, individuals who are able to enter into such contracts, understand and agree on the terms, and fulfill them. Private property is, therefore, a prerequisite of market; where property rights do not exist or are not properly defined and enforced, markets will not function.[8]

Every market has a set of rules governing the contracts market participants enter into. These rules are defined by the legal system of the economy. "Free" markets, in the sense of a total absence of legal rules, cannot exist. Aristotle argued in the *Politics* that the principal office in a state is the office that watches over the market and the contracts concluded in market exchanges.[9] Not all possible contracts and transactions are in the interest of society, and therefore the government must ensure that those that are not, are illegal and invalid. Moreover, since the very notion of a market presupposes that contracts are enforceable, a market system can function only when the government provides legal security. Adam Smith

---

[8] Fyodor Dostoevsky reports that, in the Siberian prison where he was being held, the buying and selling of things including vodka and, hence, the existence of any markets was suppressed by the guards on the argument that prisoners were not allowed to have private property. The purpose was to deprive the prisoners of their human qualities and turn them into brutes. See Dostoevsky, *Notes from a Dead House* (New York: Alfred E. Knopf, 2015), kindle edition pos. 489.

[9] Aristotle, *Politics*, translated by Benjamin Howitt (Oxford: Clarendon, 1808), book 6, section 8, 251–52. The text reads: "First among the necessary offices is that which has the care of the market; a magistrate should be appointed to inspect contracts and maintain order. For in every state there must inevitably be buyers and sellers who will supply one another's wants; this is the readiest way to make a state self-sufficing and so fulfill the purpose for which men came together into one state."

emphasized the importance of a well-functioning legal system for a market economy:

> That security which the laws in Great Britain give to every man that he shall enjoy the fruits of his own labour is alone sufficient to make any country flourish, notwithstanding these and twenty other absurd regulations of commerce; and this security was perfected by the revolution much about the same time that the bounty was established. The natural effort of every individual to better his own condition, when suffered to exert itself with freedom and security is so powerful a principle that it is alone, and without any assistance, not only capable of carrying on the society to wealth and prosperity, but of surmounting a hundred impertinent obstructions with which the folly of human laws too often encumbers its operations; though the effect of these obstructions is always more or less either to encroach upon its freedom, or to diminish its security.[10]

Laws and government regulations thus shape a market and the way it functions and, therefore, the outcomes it produces. Smith was also very aware that competitive markets are likely to be suppressed by the efforts of some market participants to engage in collusion, and that a high degree of competition needs to be protected by the state.[11]

The mode of exchange in the market is *commodity mode*. That is, the objects bought and sold in a market are characterized by a relation of equivalence. To the buyer, an apple is an apple, a cow is a cow, a worker is a worker, etc.—all worth the same price as any other apple, cow, or worker. This characteristic of market exchange has long been criticized by philosophers as morally despicable. Immanuel Kant argued that any object can have either *dignity* or a *price*.[12] Dignity requires uniqueness. An object with dignity cannot be compared to any other object. If an object has a price, there are other objects equivalent to it. Treating an object as a commodity, therefore, has the moral consequence of depriving it of its dignity.

---

[10] Adam Smith, *An Inquiry into the Nature and Causes of the Wealth of Nations* (London: Methuen, 1904), online at https://archive.org/details/AdamSmithAnInquiry, IV.5.b.43, 540. For a discussion, see Friedrich A. von Hayek, *Die Verfassung der Freiheit* (Tübingen: J. C. B. Mohr, 1983), 75.

[11] Smith, *Wealth of Nations*, I.10.c.27, 145: "People of the same trade seldom meet together, even for merriment and diversion, but the conversation ends in a conspiracy against the public, or in some contrivance to raise prices. It is impossible indeed to prevent such meetings, by any law which either could be executed, or would be consistent with liberty and justice. But though the law cannot hinder people of the same trade from sometimes assembling together, it ought to do nothing to facilitate such assemblies; much less to render them necessary."

[12] Immanuel Kant, *Grundlegung zur Metaphysik der Sitten* (Stuttgart: Reclam, 2008).

Such dignity of an object may not concern us much when we think about apples, but it must concern us when we think about human beings treated as commodities, as in slave labor or prostitution. Alvin Roth notes that societies generally deem a range of exchanges as repugnant because treating the objects exchanged as commodities is regarded as morally reprehensible. Among such objects are human body parts, adoption, human eggs and sperm, religious services, votes, and horse meat. Such repugnance varies with cultural context.[13]

Before I enter into the following discussion, I wish to clarify that markets are not the same as capitalism. Markets existed long before capitalism and, as the economic history of the twentieth century has shown, capitalists were often eager to suppress markets and cooperate with political movements that favored state planning and administration of the supply of goods and services to the general population. It is perfectly conceivable to have a capitalist system without markets —in fact, that would be the dream of all capitalists. Therefore, Max Weber's *The Protestant Ethic and the Spirit of Capitalism* and the huge literature that developed from it are not the focus of my discussion here. Similarly, markets are not the same as consumerism or economic materialism, a life devoted to the acquisition of ever-increasing amounts of things. The ethical debate concerning economic materialism is not the topic of this chapter, either.

Markets and Human Character

Since markets are (fictitious, perhaps) places of a certain type of exchange between human beings, it is clear that there must be a relationship between markets and the character of those who interact with one another. It is therefore no surprise that the relationship between markets and human character has been discussed extensively. Economists have invented their own paradigm of the human character, *homo oeconomicus*, a gruesome, despicable type of cold, calculating, rational human being who knows nothing but his own utility.[14] But this was al-

---

[13] Alvin Roth, "Repugnance as a Constraint on Markets," *Journal of Economic Perspectives* 21/3 (2007): 37–38.

[14] According to Joseph Persky ("The Ethology of Homo Oeconomicus," *Journal of Economic Perspectives* 9/2 [1995]: 221–31), the term "economic man" first appeared in John Kells Ingram's *History of Political Economy*, (Cambridge: Cambridge University Press, 1888), where it was used to describe men as "money-making animals" (136) and as people living in a society ruled solely by the law of competition, where all transactions are governed by contracts among equals (86). However, the term was used earlier by Francis Edgeworth in his *Mathematical Psychics: An Essay on the Application of Mathematics to the Moral Sciences* (London: C. Kegan Paul & Co, 1881), e. g., 54. The Latin term *homo oeconomicus* was first used by Vilfredo Pareto in his 1906 *Manual of Political Economy*, edited by Aldo Mon-

ways meant among economists as a modeling device of the theory of markets, not to describe actual human behavior nor to prescribe how it should be.[15] Here, I will focus instead on two lines of argument, one saying that markets promote and strengthen good moral behavior, the other saying the exact opposite. In this chapter, I will concentrate on the history of these traditions and some conceptual aspects. The following chapters by Jason Brennan, Ginny Choy, and Virgil Storr discuss the empirical evidence and policy aspects related to these lines of argument.

DOUX COMMERCE

In his best-selling book *The Advantage: Why Organizational Health Trumps Everything Else in Business*, business consultant Patrick M. Lencioni writes that, when it comes to defining a company's mission, he always asks the CEO: "What does your company do to create a better world?"[16] Why the question? Because, he says, if you do not do anything to make the world better for at least somebody, you will not have any customers, and your company will die. Lencioni hits on a theme that goes back to Bodin, de Boisguilbert, and Montesquieu. In *De L'Esprit des Lois*, Montesquieu argued in his chapter about economics that commerce—and hence markets—promotes the human sense of justice and the understanding that one cannot rigidly pursue one's own interests all the time.[17] Success in commerce requires us to know and serve the interests of others. In a competitive market, buying and selling in one's own interest makes them find out what is in other peoples' interest and do their best to fulfill the needs and desires of those they trade with. The mutual dependence of trade partners on each other and their attempts to sat-

---

tesano, et al. (Oxford: Oxford University Press, 2014), 9. Pareto used the term to study human economic action, abstracting from moral, religious, aesthetic, and other aspects of human behavior, yet without negating their importance for understanding an individual's actual behavior. In his study on ethics, Eduard Spranger (*Lebensformen. Geisteswissenschaftliche Psychologie und Ethik der Persönlichkeit* [Halle: Max Niemeier, 1921]) proposed *homo oeconomicus* as one of six basic "patterns of life" which all persons share to various degrees. Most generally, Spranger explains, *homo oeconomicus* is the one who, in all relationships, pursues what is useful more than anything else. A pure utilitarian, "he economizes on matter, force, space, and time to obtain a maximum of useful effects from them" (ibid., 133). Anything that has no use has no value to *homo oeconomicus*.

[15] Nevertheless, the late Christian economist Paul Heyne concluded that, properly understood, *homo oeconomicus* might be a Christian. See his "Can Homo Oeconomicus be Christian?" in *Are Economists Basically Immoral? and Other Essays on Economics, Ethics, and Religion*, edited by Paul Heyne, Geoffrey Brennan, and Anthony M. C. Waterman, chapter 4 (Indianapolis: Liberty Books, 1998).

[16] Patrick M. Lencioni, *The Advantage: Why Organizational Health Trumps Everything Else in Business* (San Franciso: Jossy-Boss, 2012), 82 f.

[17] Charles-Louis de Montesquieu, *De L'Esprit des Lois. Les grands thèmes* [1748], edited by J. P. Mayer and A. P. Kerr (Paris: Gallimard, 1970), book 20, chapter 2, 236 f.

isfy the wants of the other strengthen social cohesion. Thus, commerce and markets promote the friendly and peaceful aspects of human coexistence—hence the term *doux commerce*.[18]

How commerce and markets shape the human character under this view is succinctly summarized in Samuel Ricard's 1704 *General Treatise on Exchanges and Money*:

> Commerce attaches (men) one to another through mutual utility. Through commerce, the moral and physical passions are superseded by interest. ... It affects the feelings of men so strongly that it makes him who was proud and haughty suddenly turn supple, bending and serviceable. Through commerce, a man learns to deliberate, to be honest, to acquire manners, to be prudent and reserved in both talk and actions. Sensing the necessity to be wise and honest in order to succeed, he flees vice, or at least his demeanor exhibits decency and seriousness so as to not arouse any adverse judgment on the part of present and future acquaintances.[19]

More prominent writers later in the same century—David Hume, Adam Smith, and Thomas Paine—credited the spread of market exchange and industry for teaching human beings such virtues as industriousness, frugality, punctuality, and probity.[20] Modern examples of this view are the work of Deirdre McCloskey and of Bruni and Sugden, who argue that markets promote specific market virtues such as "universality (the willingness to enter into contracts with others without regard to social status), enterprise and alertness, respect for the preferences of one's trading partners, trust and trustworthiness, acceptance of competition, self-help, and stoicism about rewards."[21] The market, one might say, is a practice in the sense of Alasdair MacIntyre, that is, "a coherent and complex form of socially established human activity" through which the virtues specific to commerce are learned and lived and through which their standards of excellence are established and passed on from one generation to the next.[22]

Three points deserve attention here. First, as Ricard points out, having a reputation of being honest, prudent, and reserved is a condition of economic success in market exchange. This is because many market transactions involve time and

---

[18] Samuel Ricard, *A General Treatise of the Reduction of the Exchanges, Moneys, and Real Species of Most Places in Europe* (London: J. Matthews for S. and J. Sprint, 1704). For an extensive discussion, see Albert O. Hirschman, *Rival Views of Market Society and Other Recent Essays* (New York: Penguin Books, 1986), 105 ff.
[19] Quoted in Hirschman, *Rival Views*, 108.
[20] Ibid., 109.
[21] Luigino S. Bruni and Robert Sugden, "Reclaiming Virtue Ethics for Economics," *Journal of Economic Perspectives* 27/4 (2013): 141–64.
[22] Alasdair MacIntyre, *After Virtue* (Notre Dame: Notre Dame Press, 3rd edition 2007), 187.

asymmetric information, exposing the buyer to the risk of being defrauded by the seller. Buyers can protect themselves against that risk by investing in information about the sellers in the market, but this requires the investment of scarce resources. A good reputation is a means of reducing transaction costs and facilitates more mutually advantageous trades.

The second point is the juxtaposition of "passions" and "interest." Montesquieu, Ricard, Hume, Paine, Smith, and other writers of the same period were still historically close to a culture in which the life and the actions of the noble class were dominated by passions, such as the striving for honor, glory, power, and riches, which often produced bad results for society. As explained by Hirschman, the notion of "interest" underwent a change in meaning during the seventeenth and eighteenth centuries and came to be understood as the "methodical pursuit and accumulation of private wealth."[23] In contrast to the unruly and often violent and chaotic passions, interests were regarded as leading to peaceful and rational conduct, making people more predictable and governable. Importantly, Smith argued in a famous passage in *The Wealth of Nations* that the pursuit of one's interest resulted in serving the public good:

> Give me that which I want, and you shall have this which you want, is the meaning of every such offer; and it is in this manner that we obtain from one another the far greater part of those good offices which we stand in need of. It is not from the benevolence of the butcher, the brewer, or the baker, that we expect our dinner, but from their regard to their own interest. We address ourselves, not to their humanity but to their self-love, and never talk to them of our own necessities but of their advantages.[24]

This gives the pursuit of one's interest a moral approval much like the idea of "enlightened self-interest" in modern discussions.[25]

The third point is that, as Ricard points out, market success is promoted by the reputation of being of good character. This is not necessarily the same as actually being of good character. Even a person of bad morals can be successful in the market as long as he or she appears to be of good morals. Of course, one might argue that this distinction, while important for the spiritual state of the individual market participant, does not matter much for market performance and society at large.[26]

---

[23] Ibid., 46. See also Albert O. Hirschman, *The Passions and the Interests: Political Arguments for Capitalism Before its Triumph* (Princeton: Princeton University Press, 1977).

[24] Smith, *Wealth of Nations*, I.2, 26.

[25] David W. Haddorff, "Religion and the Market: Opposition, Absorption, or Ambiguity?," *Review of Social Economy* 58 (2000): 483–504.

[26] In a classic paper shedding light on the issues, David M. Kreps, Paul Milgrom, John Roberts, and Robert Wilson show that in a repeated social interaction characterized by a pris-

The Argument that Markets Make Villains

Naturally, the *doux commerce* hypothesis has not remained uncontested. Montesquieu himself admitted that commerce, while smoothing and polishing the "raw and barbaric customs of men," corrupts their "pure virtues."[27] In the Communist Manifesto of 1848, Karl Marx and Friedrich Engels argued that as the capitalist market system spread through all spheres of society, all human relationships and values would gradually be integrated into it and be degraded to commodities. Their argument is reminiscent of Kant's verdict, mentioned above, that all things can have either dignity or a price. When everything has a price and nothing has dignity, traditional moral values lose their meaning, and the human character is reduced to the making of choices among alternative means to fulfill individual desires.[28] In this view, the market develops and teaches its own "market ethos." According to Alan Wolfe:

> An older generation [in the United States] ... took refuge from the economy in civil society. Long marriages, whether satisfying or not, were combined with relatively stable communities and commitment to the expansion of the public sector, all to create a system in which people could to some degree rely on one another for support. For a younger generation, by contrast, the market, rather than something against which individuals would be protected by civil society, has become more of a model by which relations in civil society can themselves be shaped. Marriage and childbearing are shaped increasingly by considerations of self-interest; communities are organized more by the logic of buying and selling than by principles of solidarity; and services, when no longer satisfactory to the public, are increasingly purchased privately. In a way unprecedented in American experience, the market has become attractive in not only the economic sphere but in the moral and social spheres as well.[29]

Is Wolfe right in his description of the (then) younger American generation? In an important empirical study, Charles Murray casts doubt on this hypothesis.[30] He shows that Wolfe's account of marriages becoming unstable and commitment to

---

oners' dilemma, socially optimal cooperation among the players can be sustained by even a tiny probability that one's opponent in the game always cooperates: "Rational Cooperation in the Finitely Repeated Prisoners' Dilemma Game," *Journal of Economic Theory* 27 (1982): 245–82.

[27] Haddorff, "Religion," 235 f.

[28] Karl Marx and Friedrich Engels, *Manifest der Kommunistischen Partei*, from the text of the 1890 German edition (Heidelberg: vulture-bookz.de, 2000), 3–4.

[29] Alan Wolfe, *Whose Keeper? Social Science and Moral Obligation*, Berkeley: University of California Press, 1989), quote taken from Haddorff, "Religion," 488.

[30] Charles Murray, *Coming Apart: The State of White America 1960-2010* (New York: Random House, 2012).

communities withering away is an issue predominantly among white, lower-class people with little education and unstable employment (called the "people of Fishtown" in his book.) In contrast, stable marriages and commitment to communities still prevail as they did in the past among upper-class people of all colors (called the "people of Belleville." But if both the people of Fishtown and the people of Belleville were raised and live in the same market system, can the difference between them be a result of the market, or must the reason be sought elsewhere?

Market ethos is the ethos of choice purely in one's own interest, always searching for the best opportunity. The fundamental equivalence of all things traded and all partners traded in commodity mode leaves no room for considerations of intrinsic value. Does the market teach participants to ignore the intrinsic value of things?

A recent empirical study by Armin Falk and Nora Szech seeks to shed light on this issue.[31] The authors conducted an experiment in which participants were given an amount of money which they could keep for themselves or spend on buying the life of a mouse. The mice in this experiment were surplus animals from medical labs which would be killed if not bought by the participants; if bought, they would be allowed to live until their natural deaths. All participants got to see mice in a video during the instructions to the experiment. Falk and Szech then let the participants make their decisions in different settings. In an isolated setting, an individual would decide for himself how much money—if any—to spend on the life of the mouse. In a bilateral market setting, the mouse was given to a seller, who would bargain with a buyer with whom he would split the money not spent on the mouse. In a multilateral market setting, seven buyers and nine sellers bargained simultaneously over the price of a mouse and split the remaining amount of money among themselves.

Falk and Szech report that, in the bilateral market setting, the percentage of traders willing to kill their mice for money was substantially higher than in the isolated setting, and that in the multilateral market setting the percentage was even higher. Furthermore, the price paid to save the life of a mouse was higher in the isolated setting than in the market settings. The authors conclude from this that markets indeed erode moral values. Their reasoning is that, first, in market settings there is more than one trader, and the guilt feeling of each trader over a morally bad decision can be shared and is thus perceived to be smaller. Furthermore, market interaction reveals information about moral standards prevailing in a society. By observing that people are willing to trade animal lives at low prices, individuals with greater moral compunctions lose their scruples and converge to the lower moral standards they observe.

This is an interesting argument, and it is reminiscent of popular claims made in the public debate following the 2008 financial crisis that markets teach people

---

[31] Armin Falk and Nora Szech, "Morals and Markets," *Science* 340/ 6133 (2013): 707–11.

to be greedy and irresponsible. But it is not clear how forceful this argument is. On one hand, markets can demonstrate morally good behavior as much as morally bad behavior—think of markets for sustainable investment, Christian media, or Amazon's contributions to charities of its customers' choice with every purchase. On the other hand, markets for morally reprehensible commodities often exist on the sly, hiding the information from people of higher moral standards. Jason Brennan, in chapter 4, below, presents a more general discussion of the strength of experimental evidence in this area.

The idea of a market ethos raises the question of where the scope for choice ends. The expansion of the market into ever more spheres of life implies that ever more spheres of life are open to choice. And since market choices can be changed over time, this creates a kind of fluidity or indeterminacy in peoples' lives. Akerlof and Kranton take this to the extreme, suggesting that, in a market environment, human beings can freely choose and change their own identities.[32] This, of course, would mean that humanity can make and change itself. If "character" transports the idea of something stamped on a body from the outside, it would imply the dissolution of human character, a topic discussed by Katrin Gülden Le Maire in and William Schweiker below.

In the late 1960 s, Fred Hirsch warned that the expansion of the market system would promote excessive individualism and destroy what he deemed precapitalist social values and virtues.[33] In an economic system emphasizing the pursuit of self-interest, it would become more and more difficult to produce collective goods and sustain cooperation for the benefit of society. A recent book by Harvard law professor Michael J. Sandel makes a similar argument.[34] For example, when you can buy your place in line waiting for a bus or a ride on a roller coaster, your social status (in that line) is determined solely by how much money you have. This is in contrast to traditional lines, where all who wait are fundamentally equal, and the feeling of equality fosters social cohesion. Sandel calls for legal rules limiting the domain of the market in society. In the same vein, social conservatives bemoan that markets destroy traditional forms of human community.[35] Ginny Choi and Virgil Storr discuss this topic in more detail.

---

[32] George Akerlof and Rachel E. Kranton, *Identity Economics: How Our Identities Shape our Work, Wages, and Well-Being* (Princeton: Princeton University Press, 2009).

[33] Fred Hirsch, *Social Limits to Growth* (Cambridge, MA: Harvard University Press, 1976).

[34] Michael J. Sandel, *What Money Can't Buy: The Moral Limits of Markets* (New York: Farrar, Straus, and Giroux, 2013).

[35] See, e. g., Stephen A. Marglin, *The Dismal Science: How Thinking Like an Economist Undermines Community* (Cambridge, MA: Harvard University Press, 2008).

Human Character and Markets

If markets can shape the human character, it is clear also that the proper functioning of markets depends on the character of those trading in them. But we need to be precise at this point. As David Gauthier convincingly argues, a *perfect* market is a moral-free zone.[36] Perfect markets are defined by perfect competition, implying that every individual is a price-taker, externalities are absent, perfect and symmetric information is available, all aspects of the future can be included in contracts (completeness), and all trades are executed simultaneously and instantaneously. In this setting, every individual trader takes the actions of all others as parametrically given and chooses his own optimal action. Market outcomes maximize social welfare. There is no necessity here to make moral decisions, and, hence, human character is irrelevant.

Morals and a role for human character enter when real markets deviate from that ideal. As argued above, moral traits can reduce transaction costs and enlarge the scope of potential traders in a market when information is incomplete and asymmetric, and trading takes time. The latter point is illustrated in the fact that, where property rights and contracts are not well enforced, people tend to trade only with others whom they trust on the basis of close social relations, thus reducing the extent of the market. Moral choices also arise in the presence of externalities. With negative externalities, the question is whether the individual undertakes an activity imposing costs on others; with positive externalities, the question is whether the individual undertakes an activity costly to him and beneficial to others. Finally, moral choices arise when contracts are incomplete and allow individuals to cheat. In these settings, trust among market participants becomes a condition for the functioning of markets, and we tend to trust people of good character more easily than people of bad character.

The two lines of thought outlined above lead to two opposing conclusions in this regard. The *doux commerce* hypothesis suggests that trading in markets teaches people the moral traits conducive to the functioning of the market. People are successful in real markets by being honest, prudent, rational, reliable, and so on. By observing the correlation between morality and success, others learn to adopt these traits. In this sense, the market is a system reinforcing itself. Thus, Montesquieu concluded: "It is almost a general rule that commerce prevails where manners are gentle, and that manners are gentle where commerce prevails."[37]

A counterargument to this which is already hinted at in Ricard's statement quoted above is that market success requires only the appearance of being honest, prudent, rational, and reliable. That is, commerce and markets might teach

---

[36] David Gauthier, *Morals by Agreement* (Oxford: Oxford University Press, 1986), chapter 4.
[37] Montesquieu, *L'Esprit des Lois*, 235.

hypocrisy rather than true probity. To the extent that market success teaches that one can get away with hypocrisy, character formation by the market becomes questionable. One may argue that fundamentally honest participants would still learn probity. But less-firm characters may become staunch hypocrites instead.

The "markets-make-villains" hypothesis, in contrast, suggests that markets erode the very moral traits their functioning depends on, and thereby undermine their own existence. This view suggests that high moral standards are grounded somewhere outside the economic sphere of society, such as in religion or traditional culture. Being in the market, in contrast, teaches individuals to be selfish and calculating and to despise traditional values and relationships. The expansion of the market system would then weaken the sway that such external forces have over society.

It is useful to place these two views—the *doux commerce* view and the markets-make-villains view—in their historical perspective. The first emerged in a time when European societies came out of the feudal age with its aristocratic values. This period saw the emerging market system as a mechanism taming human behavior, hence progress. The second view emerged when the market system was already the dominant form of economic interaction, and the rise of capitalism created new forms of social degradation and unrest. Hirschman argues that the first view lost its intellectual appeal precisely because of these later developments.[38] Those who adhered to the second view regarded the moral traits sustaining the market system as an inheritance of the past, and the present as moving towards decline.

Conclusion

The *doux commerce* hypothesis and the markets-make-villains hypothesis start from very different views of the human character. The first assumes that humans are sinful, and their behavior needs to be improved. The second assumes that humans are morally good, and markets deprave them.

Both hypotheses claim that markets shape the character of those who trade in them. Where they differ is in the direction of that shaping. Can we reject one or the other? Certainly, morally good and morally bad behavior exist in market settings and in nonmarket settings of social interaction. Some aspects of market behavior certainly encourage and teach morally good behavior, while other aspects encourage and teach the opposite. What is the net effect of markets on the human character? We need more research on this.

Christian theology teaches that all humans are sinful and need divine instruction and help for moral improvement. The writers of the seventeenth century

---

[38] Hirschman, *Rival Views*, 181 f.

thought that the market was, indeed, God's instrument for improving humanity.[39] That view fell into disrepute in the nineteenth century. But the general point remains. And it implies that the moral decay predicted by "markets make villains" may not be the final verdict on the fate of humanity.

For the Christian economist, another consideration is relevant. The market is a mechanism to allocate scarce resources to productive activities, and the products to the fulfillment of human needs and desires. Even if we find that the market has negative effects on human character, the consequence is not necessarily that we should abolish markets. For as long as scarce resources need to be allocated and human needs and desires fulfilled, society needs some mechanism to do that. Apart from anarchy, the alternatives to the market system are command-control and tradition. It seems highly doubtful that the impact of these alternatives on human character would be better than the impact of the market.

---

[39] See Paul Oslington, *Political Economy as Natural Theology: Smith, Malthus, and Their Followers* (Abingdon, UK/New York: Routledge, 2018).

Commercial Society and its Values
The Merits of the Market in Social Theory

Frank J. Lechner

Introduction

Modern societies are morally divided. In the United States, religious and nonreligious citizens hold different views on so-called social issues, residents of urban and rural communities vary along many lines, blacks and whites tend to disagree on matters of justice, and adherents of "materialist" and "postmaterialist" values oppose each other both philosophically and politically–divisions that result in the polarization evident in reporting on American affairs.[1] Famous American sociological studies stress the theme of division; in the 1980 s, for example, Robert Bellah and his colleagues diagnosed Americans' "habits of the heart" as both at odds and confused.[2] Europe is not exempt. In recent decades, the European Values Study (EVS) has found that, within countries, different kinds of individuals and demographic groups show considerable value divergence, and that, across countries, modernization in the form of industrialization and economic growth did not lead to the convergence they expected but that, instead, "cross-national variation of value patterns was larger than predicted."[3] The differences shift over time, owing, for example, to population changes. In the case of Europe, the greater tolerance of younger cohorts on a range of issues has introduced generational divi-

---

[1] Robert D. Putnam and David E. Campbell, *American Grace: How Religion Divides and Unites Us* (New York: Simon and Schuster, 2010); Pew Research Center, *What Unites and Divides Urban, Suburban and Rural Communities* (Washington DC, 2018), https://www.pewsocialtrends.org; Ronald Inglehart, *Cultural Evolution: People's Motivations Are Changing, and Reshaping the World* (Cambridge: Cambridge University Press, 2018).

[2] Robert N. Bellah, Richard Madsen, William M. Sullivan, Ann Swidler, and Steven M. Tipton, *Habits of the Heart: Individualism and Commitment in American Life* (New York: Harper & Row, 1986).

[3] Wil Arts and Loek Halman, "Cross-National Values in Europe Today: Facts and Explanations," in Wil Arts and Loek Halman, *Value Contrasts and Consensus in Present-Day Europe: Painting Europe's Moral Landscapes* (Leiden: Brill, 2014), 3.

sions, and new fissures by religious or ethnic background have also emerged, as the influx of Muslims has created "worlds of difference" on several dimensions, including a number of morally sensitive issues.[4]

Such division has long been a theme in social theory, the scholarly effort to make sense of "modernity." In philosophy and in what became sociology, intellectuals often construed such division as a problem, at least implicitly assuming that a real society needs shared values. Of course, they typically had solutions handy, deriving moral guidance from their "scientific" analysis.[5] Sociology got its start with these very issues: Auguste Comte diagnosed the crisis of his time as the fruitless confrontation of two faulty worldviews and kindly offered his positivist program and religion of humanity, designed to foster a new common spirit, as a way to transcend that predicament. New rituals of his own design aimed to sensitize members of the positive polity to the feminine virtues represented by his "angel," Clotilde de Vaux, and instill in them a proper sense of "altruism" (a term he invented). The discipline he envisioned eventually took off, but, after briefly enchanting a group of followers, his proposals failed to take root. So it went with rival solutions. Charting the divides has proved easier than bridging them.

Not everyone joined in the jeremiads from Comte to Bellah. After all, two strands of Enlightenment thought, derived from Spinoza and Herder, had already endorsed the intrinsic value of pluralism, the possibility of different people and different groups finding different ways to think and live, and deserving the space to develop them fully. Various social scientists have also studied practical ways to manage and channel deep divisions; Arend Lijphart's study of the Dutch "politics accommodation," which enabled ideologically divided "pillars" to coexist, is a classic case in point.[6] A more direct challenge to the jeremiads comes from work showing that, at least in the West, many people tend to share basic values as well—after all, democracy and personal freedom are widely affirmed. Even on issues that provoke disagreement, rather large majorities favor a particular position, as the EVS showed in the case of support for two-parent families raising children and for the acceptance of same-sex marriage in Europe. Some population trends point to an emerging consensus or at least new moral centers of gravity. Ron Inglehart has made the case that postmaterialism really is in the evolutionary cards, stu-

---

[4] Willem Huijnk, Jaco Dagevos, Mérove Gijsberts, and Iris Andriessen, eds. *Werelden van Verschil: Over de Sociaal-Culturele Afstand en Positie van Migrantengroepen in Nederland*. (The Hague: Sociaal en Cultureel Planbureau, 2015); Ruud Koopmans, "Religious Fundamentalism and Hostility against Out-Groups: A Comparison of Muslims and Christians in Western Europe," *Journal of Ethnic and Migration Studies* 41 (2015): 33–57.

[5] Levine, Donald N., *Visions of the Sociological Tradition* (Chicago: University of Chicago Press, 1995).

[6] Arend Lijphart, *The Politics of Accommodation: Pluralism and Democracy in the Netherlands* (Berkeley: University of California Press, 1968).

dents of secularization have documented major generational shifts in the salience and experience of religiosity, and the rising tolerance of younger cohorts boosts a common trend toward what one researcher has called moral relativism.[7] New public rituals, such as "pride" parades, appear to endorse parts of an emerging consensus.

While we could debate the exact depth and impact of moral division, its variability across time and place, and how much of a problem it is, for the purpose of my argument, I will assume two stylized facts: that the division is real and lasting, and that, thus far, Comte's religion of humanity and its functional equivalents have not succeeded as a remedy. Even without sharing Comte's or Emile Durkheim's notion of what a society might "need," it seems reasonable to look for alternatives to what Peter Berger once called a sacred canopy, alternatives that could produce a modus vivendi, a pragmatic pluralism that allows for divided communities to maintain connections. One potentially constructive approach is to start with the places where we do connect across difference, where cultural pluralism does not inhibit common practices that nurture (to adapt sociologist Grace Davie's line from another context) a form of belonging without believing. At least pragmatically, the market, or "the economy" as a societal subsystem, is such a place, both real and virtual.

In this chapter I will first show that one tradition within social theory gives us reason to think of the market as a source of virtue, of commercial society as containing shareable values that may form a durable character (leaving aside the conceptual slippage between virtue, value, and character). I then review various objections to that position, showing that other strands in social theory have generally been skeptical, either because they sought real morality outside the economic domain, as many sociologists and critics like Karl Polanyi have done, or because they regarded the economic domain itself as morally problematic—a system threatening the lifeworld, to put it in Habermasian terms. I allude to other reasons to be cautious about the merits of the market as a source of moral direction—no subsystem is likely to overcome systemic fragmentation, to use a functionalist phrase, and since its place in society is contested, it is hardly neutral ground. At the risk of contradiction, I conclude with a brief suggestion that we may be approaching an era of moral hegemony for a particular kind of progressive worldview that aims to direct, rather than take direction from, economic practi-

---

[7] Inglehart, *Cultural Evolution*; David Voas, and Stefanie Doebler, "Secularization in Europe: An Analysis of Inter-generational Religious Change," in Wil Arts and Loek Halman, "Value Contrasts and Consensus in Present-Day Europe: Painting Europe's Moral Landscapes" (Leiden: Brill, 2014), 231–50; Hermann Dülmer, "Modernization, Culture and Morality in Europe: Universalism, Contextualism or Relativism?" in Arts and Halman, *Value Contrasts and Consensus in Present-Day Europe*, 251–76.

ces. Whether this is likely to form "character" in any traditional sense seems a question worth asking.

Commercial Society and Its Values/Virtues

Among contemporary scholars, the economist and historian Deirdre McCloskey makes the most exuberant case for the moral merits of the market. The market, she says, "supports the virtues," and capitalism "nourishes lives of virtue in the non-self-interested sense, too."[8] In a capitalist economy, commercial activity fosters seven prime virtues—the classical quartet of courage, temperance, justice, and prudence, complemented by the Christian triad of faith, hope, and love.[9] In such an economy, the sober pursuit of self-interest is itself virtuous, since it demands prudence; hope and courage find expression in entrepreneurship; loyal work performance reflects temperance and faith, and so on. As a practice that fosters virtues, free exchange has an inherent ethical dimension. So does the overall system, in which the betterment of the lives of ordinary people matters: it anchors their dignity, and it is in a fundamental sense "democratic."[10] Capitalist market activity also has merit in its consequences, including the enhancement of human possibilities and the achievement of less fixedly hierarchical social relations—another way in which the market "democratizes" society. Whether from an autotelic or instrumental perspective, bourgeois culture is therefore best. Its secret ingredient—perhaps not so secret after all these centuries—is personal freedom, which boosts both modern growth *and* modern ethical improvement.[11]

Though few match her enthusiasm, McCloskey cites some classically liberal heavy hitters in support of her position. For example, Benjamin Constant praised the "commercial tendency of the age" for helping to vary the "means of individual happiness," as long as men were left "in perfect independence in all that concerns their occupations, their undertakings."[12] Economist Amartya Sen gives an even clearer endorsement: "The freedom to exchange works, or goods, or gifts does not need defensive justification in terms of their favorable but distant effects; they are part of the way human beings in society live.... We have good reasons to buy and sell, to exchange, to seek lives that can flourish on the basis of transactions."[13] So

---

[8] Deirdre N. McCloskey, *The Bourgeois Virtues: Ethics for an Age of Commerce* (Chicago: University of Chicago Press, 2006), 4.
[9] Ibid., 66–67.
[10] Deirdre N. McCloskey, *Bourgeois Equality: How Ideas, Not Capital or Institutions, Enriched the World* (Chicago: University of Chicago Press, 2016), 560 ff.
[11] McCloskey, *Bourgeois Virtues*, 38.
[12] Ibid., 61.
[13] Ibid., 29.

does theologian Michael Novak: "Commerce is the name for free, mutual, and voluntary exchange among peoples. It is the normal activity by which interdependence is realized and the common good of all served. It is an activity typically more unifying than politics, nationalism, religion, or conquest. Its nature is social, as is its function, and as are the virtues it inculcates."[14]

McCloskey's real patron saint is Adam Smith, for having connected market and virtue. In McCloskey's slightly loose rendering, Smith treated virtue as prepared sentiment—prepared by internalizing the social process of viewing situations from the point of view of others.[15] Far from leaving morality behind, Smith's moral actors enter the market with the habits of their heart intact, as they must if they are to exchange prudently and deal justly with others. Properly socialized, actors can be entrusted with perfect liberty, enabling them to better their condition as they see fit. But in contemporary readings, *The Wealth of Nations* offers much more than a paean to the pleasures and unintended benefits of self-interest. Instead, as Christopher Berry has argued, the book presents "commercial society" as a new kind of social order that pacifies manners, overturns entrenched hierarchies, expands the middle ranks, begins to equalize treatment of women, and subjects assemblies of strangers to impersonal rules.[16] In his apt words, commercial society is or has a "moralized economy" with a definite "inner coherence."[17] Others see a moral message in *The Wealth of Nations* as well: James Otteson draws from Smith a picture of the "marketplace of life," and in a book tellingly subtitled "designing the decent society," Jerry Muller cites John Pocock's description of Smith's "commercial humanism" as a "civilizing project."[18]

That project united key figures in the Scottish Enlightenment. Albert Hirschman famously argued that its main thrust was to use the pursuit of "sweet," innocuous, predictable interest to tame violent, unruly passions and to compensate for unreliable, ineffectual reason.[19] William Robertson, one of Smith's prominent contemporaries, expressed the notion of *doux commerce* most clearly: "Commerce tends to wear off those prejudices which maintain distinction and animosity between nations. It softens and polishes the manners of men. It unites them by one

---

[14] Ibid., 61.

[15] Ibid., 154.

[16] Christopher J. Berry, *The Idea of Commercial Society in the Scottish Enlightenment* (Edinburgh: Edinburgh University Press, 2013), 56, 129, 142, 145, 195.

[17] Ibid., 130–31, 195.

[18] James R. Otteson, *Adam Smith's Marketplace of Life* (Cambridge: Cambridge University Press, 2002); Jerry Z. Muller, *Adam Smith in His Time and Ours: Designing the Decent Society* (New York: Free Press, 1993), 93.

[19] Albert O. Hirschman, *The Passions and the Interests: Political Arguments for Capitalism before Its Triumph* (Princeton: Princeton University Press, 1977).

of the strongest of all ties, the desire of supplying their mutual wants. It disposes them to peace."[20]

Though he might not quite share the enthusiasm of Robertson, McCloskey, et al., Charles Taylor has taken the further step of arguing that the tradition they represent has seeped into our collective "social imaginary," the encompassing culture of modern societies.[21] What he calls the modern moral order revolves around individuals freely exchanging for mutual benefit, and that leitmotif naturally favored the economy as the sphere in which to realize that benefit. The secular age makes it possible not to believe, or to believe otherwise, but at the same time envelops us in an orthodoxy of its own; to the extent that it still prevails, it sets limits to the moral division noted at the outset.

Some Objections

McCloskey and Berry, along with many other recent interpreters of eighteenth-century Scottish scholarship, make a strong case for the market's moral merits —among the strongest in the history of modern social theory. Whether the market can quite serve to generate character or moral fervor, whether we can expect the "moralized economy" to provide moral guidance of its own, is less certain. Let me review some objections to such reliance on the market, which in effect question the orthodoxy described by Taylor, and by implication raise some questions about its potential role in character formation.

One set of objections relates to the (neo-)Scottish case itself. For example, McCloskey defines capitalism as "merely private property and free labor without central planning, regulated by the rule of law and by an ethical consensus."[22] Leaving aside how we might determine whether such a consensus actually exists—McCloskey says little about it—the formulation suggests that the consensus doing the regulating originates outside the practice of deploying property and free labor. Positing the need for a minimal consensus may be quite reasonable, but it obstructs what we could call a strong view of the moral generativity of the market. Smith himself, of course, wrote a separate book on the moral sentiments, in which economic affairs appear infrequently. Recent responses to the supposed "Adam Smith problem" of a disjunction between *The Theory of Moral Sentiments* (TMS) and *The Wealth of Nations* (WN) suggest that the moral argument and the economic analysis are quite compatible, and that the mutual social control and individual self-command of TMS nicely support the commercial society described in WN. But

---

[20] Cited in Berry, *Idea of Commercial Society*, 145.
[21] Charles Taylor, *A Secular Age* (Cambridge: Belknap Press of Harvard University Press, 2007).
[22] McCloskey, *Bourgeois Virtues*, 14.

few, if any, Smith interpreters take the further step of arguing that the system examined in WN generates a morality of its own, let alone one that can inform other sectors of society—that is, life outside the economic sphere proper. In fact, much of Smith's "economic" analysis is quite critical of the immorality fostered in actually existing commercial society, particularly in the way economic power translates into undue political advantage.

Even if the economy were more morally generative, by the terms of McCloskey's argument it is not clear how it could spill over to other sectors of society. After all, she relies on Alasdair MacIntyre's definition of virtue as "an acquired human quality the possession of which tends to enable us to achieve those goods which are internal to practices and the lack of which prevents us from achieving those goods."[23] If all virtue is practice-bound, then it is hard to see how capitalism can truly nourish "lives of virtue" outside the economic realm. Modern social theory, for example in the work of Niklas Luhmann, might sharpen the implication: if our practices unfold within different spheres or subsystems, each with its own form and code of communication, then meaningful instruction across systemic boundaries becomes problematic—and perhaps superfluous, if functionally appropriate conduct can legitimate itself.[24] In the somewhat bleak Luhmannian vision, such systemic self-legitimation needs no grounding in "ethical values"; from his standpoint, the question of pluralism and societal coherence is not well posed, still too tethered to premodern images of society. Be that as it may, I invoke Luhmann along with MacIntyre simply to illustrate two rather different challenges to the notion of market generativity.

At first blush, classical sociology might seem to support the strong view of moral market generativity. For example, Emile Durkheim argued in his early work, especially *The Division of Labor in Society*, that the division of labor itself produces a form of solidarity and, in the normal case at any rate, affirms norms pertaining to specialization and justice.[25] It also has moral effects, particularly in fostering the cultivation of individuality—which indeed becomes the object of its own "cult." In later work, especially the preface to the second edition of the *Division*, he still viewed the economy as morally productive: occupational groups were potential sources of moral commitment that also functioned effectively within a modern economy. But on balance, Durkheim sought and found the moral fiber of society elsewhere. In his famous discussion of contract, for example, he stressed not the inherently social, binding qualities of exchange as such, but rather the "noncontractual elements" in it: we keep contractual obligations because we bring a prior understanding of norms to the deal and rely on a legal-govern-

---

[23] Ibid., 64.
[24] Niklas Luhmann, *The Differentiation of Society* (New York: Columbia University Press, 1982).
[25] Emile Durkheim, *The Division of Labor in Society* (New York: Free Press, 1984).

mental system of enforcement. Much of his teaching focused on moral education, not simply as a theoretical matter but as a practical priority in communicating values to citizens of the Third Republic. True morality, Durkheim argued in his later work on religion, involved valuing society itself as sacred, as worthy of special respect—a respect generated through socially binding ritual. The ultimate virtue in Durkheim's sociological scripture, if I may put it that way, is to do one's duty in and for society. In principle, by the logic of his argument, cultivating that duty can happen in the economic sphere; we could even extend the argument to consider the value-affirming ritual dimensions of much economic behavior. But in Durkheim's own work, instilling that sense of duty, the moral side of the dualism of human nature, happens primarily outside the economic sphere proper.

Like Durkheim, Max Weber might appear to lend some support to the market generativity argument. At least for his Calvinists, methodical work had intrinsic value as a vocation: the believer was called to honor God and God's creation, and work "paid off" in a sense of security about one's salvation. In the West at large, the economic sphere carried special moral meaning as the primary arena in which to enact the ethic of "world mastery." But even in *The Protestant Ethic and the Spirit of Capitalism*, Weber's support for the argument is already somewhat tenuous, since he concludes that the spirit has fled the harsh cosmos of the modern capitalist system, which now operates on its own amoral terms.[26] In later essays, including the lectures on science and politics, he describes society as a congeries of different spheres, each with its own logic, indeed with its own "gods"—rationalization as prelude to Luhmannian differentiation. While this argument allowed in principle for a sense of vocation and moral commitment to endure even in the economic sphere, it also meant that the ethic of the market could not easily translate to the political or legal or artistic arena. We could read *Economy and Society* as an attempt to show both the embeddedness of economic activity and its historical freeing from traditional constraints, but the relative independence of *Wirtschaft* does not entail a moral impulse for the rest of society.[27] By implication, the Weberian modern actor is left to her own devices in cobbling together a form of moral character—which in Weber's own view required a kind of heroic facing up to the demands of the day. In his rendering, those demands included both intense awareness of ineluctable value differences and personal responsibility to think through their consequences. In principle, this position left open the possibility of forming character through economic activity, pursuing business as a vocation in an arena that compelled difficult choices, but it hardly assigned a prime moral impulse to the market.

---

[26] Max Weber, *The Protestant Ethic and the Spirit of Capitalism* (New York: Oxford University Press, 2011).

[27] Max Weber, *Economy and Society* (Berkeley: University of California Press, 1978).

McCloskey herself acknowledges a standard sociological objection, namely that the market is "embedded"—and, perhaps a little surprisingly after her praise of commerce and economic vibrancy, declares it the "main point" of the last book in her trilogy.[28] Sociological versions of embeddedness have taken different forms. In the once-mainstream sociology of Talcott Parsons, for example, normative orientations wormed their way into the very action of using means to reach goals, and general value orientations, properly specified in normative structures, made the economic subsystem a "moralized" economy of sorts—just as, for that matter, all Parsonsian subsystems were moralized in their own way. Sociology also has absorbed part of Karl Polanyi's strong critique of "free" markets, a bit brusquely credited and summarized by McCloskey as "trade occurs with a meaning."[29] McCloskey cites the Dutch economist Arjo Klamer to reinforce the point: markets depend on households and governments, and the "third sphere" of a cultural commons. This concession to sociological conventional wisdom undercuts the initial force of the argument that commercial society, or the overall capitalist economy, has inherent moral merits and generates its own, valuable moral direction. After tentatively distributing the virtues across the spheres, McCloskey in fact blandly concludes that, "A bourgeois life ... does involve and should involve noncommercial realms"—with markets playing their "entangled" part. Fair enough—but this does not get us very far in analytically disentangling the entanglement, or in deciding how society might achieve some moral order across the spheres. And while embeddedness imparts character to the economy, so to speak, accounts of it have little to say about the character of participants who must traverse the tangles.

As McCloskey notes repeatedly, deriding what she calls the modern "clerisy," any plea for the inherent values of commercial society cuts against the grain of a long tradition. In that tradition, her allies who "argued on individualist, capitalist or liberal premises that the market economy might benefit and transform human existence appear to be the great creative heretics and dissenters."[30] If we accept Charles Taylor's picture, that represents a puzzling paradox: intellectuals who "spoke for" the market articulated the evolving social imaginary of the culture at large, but in recent centuries they formed a minority within the clerisy. More commonly, "[i]n every phase of the Western tradition," as John Pocock put it, "there is a conception of virtue—Aristotelian, Thomist, neo-Machiavellian, or Marxian—to which the spread of exchange relations is seen as presenting a threat."[31] Taylor's orthodox social imaginary did not rise to prominence by major-

---

[28] McCloskey, *Bourgeois Equality*, 554.
[29] Ibid.
[30] John G. A. Pocock, *Virtue, Commerce, and History: Essays on Political Thought, Chiefly in the Eighteenth Century* (Cambridge: Cambridge University Press, 1985), 104.
[31] Ibid.

ity vote of critical intellectuals. In social theory, the critical tradition is well represented with Marx on exploitation, Mauss on the gift, and Polanyi on the "second movement." Their critique goes beyond suggesting that extrinsic morality must infuse economic activity with meaning and structure, as standard sociology has it; instead, in their various ways, they argue that the market economy in its modern form opposes or undermines a humanly satisfying moral life. In short, as Jürgen von Hagen phrases it in chapter 1 in this volume, they believe "markets make villains." Of course, the left version of this line of criticism has resonated far outside the academy, as in critiques of neoliberalism that attribute nefarious consequences to a "market fundamentalism" that profanes society and desecrates real values. Regardless of the substantive merits of such arguments—many of which, in my view, have failed to engage directly and effectively the claims made in the Smith-to-McCloskey line—they unmistakably show that the moral status of the economy remains thoroughly contested. It offers no neutral ground on which to cultivate character.

Concluding Reflections

A venerable tradition with roots in the Scottish Enlightenment and currently represented by Deirdre McCloskey makes a strong case for the values of commercial society and the moral merits of the market. Yet mainstream social theory and its farther-left offshoots contain a number of objections that, if they do not quite invalidate the case, nonetheless make reliance on it somewhat problematic for practical purposes. Empirical hurdles also stand in the way: researchers have found much empirical variation in the meaning of market activity to its participants—for example, people in lower-skilled occupations tend to favor material benefits over personal development in their work, and in richer societies leisure gradually takes precedence over work. In combination, theory and evidence suggest that moral division extends to the meaning of economic practice itself, making it an unlikely source of personal or societal guidance.

At the risk of self-contradiction, I end with a more speculative comment. For several decades now, a movement for "corporate social responsibility" has been sweeping across Western firms, prompting businesses to signal their moral status in various ways.[32] That movement itself deserves further attention as a prime means of "communicating values" in modern society. In rough parallel, business ethics has become a major component of the education of future leaders,[33] Emory

---

[32] Andrew Crane, et al., eds., *The Oxford Handbook of Corporate Social Responsibility* (Oxford: Oxford University Press, 2008).

[33] For example, George G. Brenkert, ed., *The Oxford Handbook of Business Ethics* (Oxford: Oxford University Press, 2009).

University's business school recently prided itself on its "ethos of ethics," in the dean's tellingly pleonastic words, and in publicity material claimed that "integrity" is not the "exception" but the "expectation." If I may interpret an accumulation of anecdotes as tentative evidence, it seems we are entering, at least in the United States, a new phase in the moralization of the economy, and as a result in the potential role of work and business in forming character and communicating values. Well-publicized incidents of recent years involved a Mozilla CEO stepping down amid controversy over contributing to a campaign to ban same-sex marriage, and a Google engineer being fired after he made comments on gender differences and technology that were treated as harassment. Various businesses have also become targets of legal challenges with a distinct moral dimension, as in the legal case of *Masterpiece Cakeshop v. Colorado Civil Rights Commission*, decided by the Supreme Court in 2018, which involved a baker who refused to decorate a cake with a positive message for a same-sex wedding. The moral expectations placed on employees also appear to be broadening, as illustrated by academic institutions requiring scholars not simply to teach well and do excellent research but also to demonstrate, as UCLA put it, their contribution to "equity, diversity and inclusion."

Of course, one could question the representativeness of the examples, the moral import of legal standards, or the relevance of academic fashion to business practice. But, extrapolating from the examples, I suggest as a working hypothesis for further research that in matters of gender, race, sexuality, and the environment, the (American) world of business is becoming a stage on which to signal progressive virtues and a vehicle for communicating progressive values. To the extent that this movement redefines the moral merits of the market, it may point to a distinct model for character formation and even a change in the social imaginary described by Taylor and others—turning the individual into a bundle of identities, subjecting voluntary exchange to norms of social and ecological justice, and replacing the primacy of mutual benefit with more collectivist conceptions of societal welfare. The precise impact of that movement remains to be examined, but one thing is already clear: we do not live in Adam Smith's moralized economy anymore.

GROWING UP IN THE MARKET
THE CHARACTER TRAITS THAT MARKETS REWARD AND PUNISH

Ginny Seung Choi and Virgil Henry Storr

While several scholars have argued that markets are moral, there is arguably something of a consensus that markets are either amoral or immoral. The amoral market view, advanced by thinkers like Philip Wicksteed and Friedrich August von Hayek, describes the market as an ethically indifferent instrument that can be used by good or bad people in pursuit of moral or immoral purposes. While the buyers and sellers in the market can behave in ways that are morally praiseworthy or blameworthy, and while their plans and purposes can be moral or immoral, goes the amoral-market view, to ascribe moral credit or blame to the market itself is inappropriate. The immoral-market view, advanced by thinkers like Aristotle, Aquinas, and Marx, describes the market as a space that transforms and corrupts us. Engaging in market activity is like playing a game that teaches us morally problematic lessons and cultivates morally problematic habits. The more we play it, the more selfish, greedy, dishonest, and disloyal we become.

In *Do Markets Corrupt Our Morals?*[1] we argued that the question of whether markets are morally neutral, moralizing, or morally corrupting is largely an empirical question, and that the evidence suggests that markets are moralizing spaces and moral teachers.[2] Markets can shape who we are. For instance, as we move about the market as customers, producers, clients, principals, colleagues, and competitors, we learn who can and cannot be trusted and reward those who

---

[1] V. H. Storr and G. S. Choi, *Do Markets Corrupt Our Morals?* (London: Palgrave Macmillan, 2019).

[2] V.H. Storr, "Why the Market? Markets as Social and Moral Spaces," *Journal of Markets and Morality* 12/2 (2009): 277–96; V.H. Storr, "The Impartial Spectator and the Moral Teachings of the Market," in *The Oxford Handbook of Freedom*, ed. D. Schmidtz and C.E. Pavel (Oxford: Oxford University Press, 2018), 456–74; R. Langrill and V.H. Storr, "The Moral Meaning of Markets," *Journal of Markets and Morality* 15/2 (2012): 347–62; G.S. Choi and V.H. Storr, "Markets as moral training grounds," in *Annual Proceedings of the Wealth and Well-Being of Nations*, vol. 9, ed. W. Palmer (Wisconsin: Beloit College Press, 2017).

are trustworthy and punish those who are untrustworthy. By interacting with our fellow market participants, we acquire firsthand knowledge about their dispositions, personalities, moral priorities, and more. We supplement our firsthand knowledge by observing how they interact with others in market settings and by accessing tools such as crowd-sourced reviews online. This knowledge about our fellow market participants, in turn, informs our decisions on whom to engage and avoid in future transactions. Since we typically prefer to do business with people who are virtuous and tend to avoid doing business with those who are immoral, the market will tend towards rewarding virtuous behavior and punishing immoral behavior.

This chapter builds on that analysis by exploring the character traits that markets teach us. Specifically, we explore whether and why market societies are more likely to perform better on measures of or proxies for selfishness/selflessness and greed/generosity, honesty/dishonesty, and loyalty/disloyalty than nonmarket societies. By market societies, we specifically have in mind the forty most market-oriented countries in the world as described and agreed by various indices measuring economic freedom, ease of commerce, and barriers to free enterprise. By nonmarket societies, we mean the other countries, whose institutional environments significantly hinder the operation of markets. On this definition, there are 150 nonmarket societies.[3] We conclude that market societies seem to do better on a measure of morality than nonmarket societies, and we suggest that this is because the market teaches us important moral lessons.

Selfishness or Selflessness? Greedy or Generous?

In *An Inquiry into the Nature and Causes of the Wealth of Nations* (henceforth *The Wealth of Nations*), Adam Smith famously wrote: "It is not from the benevolence of the butcher, the brewer, or the baker, that we expect our dinner but from their regard to their own interest. We address ourselves, not to their humanity but to their self-love, and never talk to them of our own necessities but of their advantages."[4] Often, this passage (and others in *The Wealth of Nations*) is interpreted by both economists and noneconomists as a celebration of selfishness or greed.[5] But, with this passage and others surrounding it, Smith intended to em-

---

[3]   For more information on this empirical strategy, see Storr and Choi, *Do Markets Corrupt*, Appendix.

[4]   Adam Smith, *An Inquiry into the Nature and Causes of the Wealth of Nations* [1776] (Indianapolis: Liberty Fund, 1982), 26–27.

[5]   For instance, an article in the *Harvard Business Review* cited Smith's famous passage to substantiate how "Smith claimed that free trade among the members of a society inevitably leads to an outcome that is good for the society as a whole, even though each in-

phasize the limits of benevolence as the guiding principle behind the division of labor, specialization, and, consequently, the wealth of nations. So long as people live in societies, Smith[6] explained, "man has almost constant occasion for the help of his brethren, and it is in vain for him to expect it from their benevolence only." Stated alternatively, our wants and needs exceed what we could rightly expect to receive in gifts or charity. "Nobody but a beggar," he wrote, "chooses to depend chiefly upon the benevolence of his fellow-citizens. Even a beggar does not depend upon it entirely."[7] Using the butcher, the brewer, and the baker, Smith illustrated how it is not our own self-interest but mutual cooperation that dominates the economy. The tradespeople rely on customers to remain in business, and, thus, producing good quality meat, beer, and bread for their customers is in the interest of the tradespeople. In such an environment, Smith explained, self-interest leads individuals to think in terms of what will benefit others. So self-interest plays a central role in markets and economic exchange. For instance, without some sense of self-interest, buyers will imprudently sacrifice their assets and livelihoods to purchase even small trinkets, and sellers will give away their goods for free. Without some sense of self-interest, traders would not have recognized how exporting and importing previously unavailable goods to new locations would be profitable. Without some sense of self-interest, innovative minds behind products such as Epipens, iPhones, and Xerox and behind companies such as Airbnb, Parking Panda, and Venmo would not have noticed any missing markets.

While there are surely limits to benevolence in a market setting, according to Smith, there are also limits to selfishness or an exclusive concern with one's own welfare. If selfishness is self-interest conjoined with self-centeredness, Smith here is suggesting that market settings rely on self-interest disconnected from self-centeredness. Selfishness, for Smith, cannot be the driving force in the mar-

---

dividual pursues only *his own selfish gain*": M. Buchanan, "Wealth Happens," *Harvard Business Review* (April 2002), at https://hbr.org/2002/04/wealth-happens (*emphasis added*). "Today," the article continued, "Smith's metaphor stands at the very center of Western economic thinking [i.e., free market theories of economics]." Even Kenneth Arrow, co-recipient of the 1972 Nobel Memorial Prize in Economic Science, pointed to the same passage, stating "[i]n the world that Adam Smith and the economists following him set forth, individuals acted out of [pure] self-interest": Kenneth J. Arrow, "The Division of Labor in the Economy, the Polity, and Society," in *The Return to Increasing Returns*, ed. J.M. Buchanan and Y.J. Yoon (Ann Arbor: The University of Michigan Press, 1994), 69–82, at 29. George Stigler, the recipient of the 1982 Nobel Memorial Prize in Economic Science, once described *The Wealth of Nations* as "a stupendous palace erected upon the granite of self-interest": George J. Stigler, "Smith's Travels on the Ship of State," *History of Political Economy* 3/2 (1971): 265–77, at 265.

[6] Smith, *Wealth of Nations*, 26.
[7] Ibid., 27.

ket. Indeed, the market does not teach us to be narrowly and only devoted to our own profits, welfare, and well-being without any regard for others. If the market truly taught us to be narrowly self-interested, the existing evidence should prove that people will always choose to maximize their own utility under any circumstances.

Existing literature on other-regarding preferences in experimental economics demonstrates how individuals do not always behave in narrowly selfish ways in market-like or exchange-like settings. For instance, in dictator games, which are two-person games where the dictator makes a decision on how to split a given pie between herself and a recipient, experimentalists found that dictators motivated by fairness or generosity frequently give some of the pie to the recipients. A meta-analysis of 129 papers studying dictator games published between 1992 and early 2010 showed that dictators, on average, sent 28.35 percent of the pie to the recipient.[8] Moreover, only 36.11 percent (as opposed to 100 percent) of the dictators shared nothing with their recipients, and 16.74 percent shared the pie equally with their recipients. Studies using ultimatum games report similar findings. An ultimatum (bargaining) game resembles the dictator game, but the second mover (the responder) can accept or reject the first mover's (the proposer's) proposed split, where rejection implies that both players get nothing of the initial pie. Here, the subgame perfect Nash equilibrium (SPNE) is for the proposer to offer the responder the minimum amount and for the responder to accept any nonzero amount. Unsurprisingly, experiments revealed how both proposers and responders do not behave according to this prediction. Proposers offered of an average of 40 percent of the pie, and responders tended to reject offers of 20 percent of the pie or less.[9]

As another example, experimentalists report similar results for trust games, which are two-person, sequential-move games. First, the trustor makes a decision on how much of an endowed amount she would send to the trustee. The amount she sends to the trustee is tripled by the experimenter before it is transferred to the trustee. Second, the trustee makes a decision on how much of the multiplied amount she would send back to the trustor. The amount sent by the trustor is interpreted as a measure of trust (the trustor's willingness to wager that the trustee would reciprocate her risky and costly decision), and the amount sent by the trust-

---

[8] C. Engel, "Dictator Games: A Meta Study," *Experimental Economics* 14 (2011): 583–610.

[9] See, for example, C. Camerer, *Behavioral Game Theory: Experiments in Strategic Interaction* (Princeton: Princeton University Press, 2003), 43; H. Oosterbeek, et al., "Cultural Differences in Ultimatum Game Experiments: Evidence from aMmeta-Analysis," *Experimental Economics* 7 (2004): 171–88; and W. Güth and M. Kocher, "More than Thirty Years of Ultimatum Bargaining Experiments: Motives, Variations, and a Survey of the Recent Literature," *Journal of Economic Behavior & Organization* 108 (2014): 396–409, at 398.

ee is interpreted as a measure of trustworthiness or reciprocity (the trustee's willingness to reciprocate the trustor's risky and costly decision). The SPNE is for trustors and trustees to send nothing to one another; in a noncooperative environment, trustors cannot reliably expect trustees to send any amount back to them and, as such, would send nothing to the trustees. Johnson and Mislin[10] conducted a meta-analysis of 162 replications of the trust game as developed by Berg, et al.,[11] and found that, on average, trustors sent 50 percent of the endowed amount to trustees, and trustees sent a third of the tripled amount back to the trustors.

So human beings generally do not behave in line with narrowly selfish preferences, even in economic experiments. But this, at best, speaks to human nature generally. It does not speak to (1) whether or not markets teach us to be selfish or (2) the differences between market and nonmarket societies on this margin. If the hypothesis that markets teach us to be selfish is indeed true, evidence should corroborate that those who live in market societies behave more selfishly (or behave selfishly more frequently) than those who live in nonmarket societies.

A series of experimental studies suggests that the degree to which a society is exposed to and has integrated markets positively affects society members' prosocial behavior. For example, Joseph Henrich and his coauthors administered various economic experiments, including the dictator, ultimatum, and trust games, across fifteen small-scale societies around the world. They discovered that measures of trust, trustworthiness, cooperation, and altruism increased with the degree of a society's market integration.[12] Henrich, et al.,[13] and Ensminger and Henrich[14] reported that a society's degree of exposure to markets positively correlated with fairness. Similarly, Ensminger found that market exposure could pre-

---

[10] N. Johnson and A. Mislin, "Trust Games: A Meta-Analysis," *Journal of Economic Psychology* 32 (2011): 865–89.

[11] J. Berg, J. Dickhaut, and K. McCabe, "Trust, Reciprocity and Social History," *Games and Economic Behavior* 10/1 (1995): 122–42.

[12] J. Henrich, et al., "In Search of Homo Economicus: Behavioral Experiments in 15 Small-Scale Societies," *American Economic Review* 91/2 (2001): 73–78; J. Henrich, et al., *Foundations of Human Sociality: Economics Experiments and Ethnographic Evidence from Fifteen Small Scale Societies* (Oxford: Oxford University Press, 2004); J. Henrich, et al., "'Economic Man' in Cross-Cultural Perspective: Behavior Experiments in 15 Small Scale Societies," *Behavioral and Brain Sciences* 256 (2005): 795–855; D.P. Tracer, "Market Integration, Reciprocity, and Fairness in Rural Papua New Guinea: Results From a Two-Village Ultimatum Game Experiment," in Henrich, et al., *Foundations of Human Sociality*, 232–59.

[13] J. Henrich, et al., "Markets, Religion, Community Size, and the Evolution of Fairness and Punishment," *Science* 327 (2010): 1480–4.

[14] J. Ensminger and J. Henrich, eds., *Experimenting with Social Norms: Fairness and Punishment in Cross-Cultural Perspective* (New York: Russell Sage Foundation, 2014).

dict first mover (that is, dictator and proposer) behavior in dictator and ultimatum games.[15] Henrich reported how members of the Machiguenga in the Peruvian Amazon behaved more consistently with game theoretic predictions than their US counterparts in ultimatum games.[16] Gurven found that members of villages that had less exposure to markets were more likely to contribute nothing in a public-goods game than members of villages that had more exposure to markets in the Bolivian Amazon.[17] While it is imprudent to extrapolate heavily from Henrich and Gurven, these studies are nonetheless suggestive of how markets do not seem to be teaching people to be selfish.

To the best of our knowledge, there are no cross-cultural studies and meta-analyses of economic games that explicitly investigate the effect of markets on prosocial behavior. Furthermore, many cross-country studies and meta-analyses display mixed results regarding the influence of markets on prosocial behavior.[18]

---

[15] J. Ensminger, "Market Integration and Fairness: Evidence from Ultimatum Dictator, and Public Good Experiments in East Africa," in Henrich, et al., *Foundations of Human Sociality*, 356–81.

[16] J. Henrich, "Does Culture Matter in Economic Behavior? Ultimatum Game Bargaining Among the Machiguenga of the Peruvian Amazon," *American Economic Review* 90/4 (2000): 973–79. The 2000 Index of Economic Freedom rated the United States to be mostly (economically) free with a score of 76.4 percent (out of a perfectly free score of 100 percent) and Peru to be moderately free with a score of 68.7 percent (See D. O'Driscoll, et al., *2000 Index of Economic Freedom* (Washington, DC: The Heritage Foundation, 2000). In other words, the United States was a more market-oriented society compared to Peru when the ultimatum games in Henrich ("Does Culture Matter") were administered.

[17] M. Gurven, "Does Market Exposure Affect Economic Game Behavior? The Ultimatum Game and the Public Goods Game among the Tsimane' of Bolivia," in Henrich, et al., *Foundations of Human Sociality*, 194–231.

[18] See, for example, A.E. Roth, et al., "Bargaining and Market Behavior in Jerusalem, Ljubljana, Pittsburgh, and Tokyo: An Experimental Study," *American Economic Review* 81/5 (1991): 1068–95; R. Croson and N. Buchan, "Gender and Culture: International Experimental Evidence from Trust Games," *AEA Papers and Proceedings* 89/2 (1999): 386–91; N.R. Buchan, et al., "Swift Neighbors and Persistent Strangers: A Cross-Cultural Investigation of Trust and Reciprocity in Social Exchange," *American Journal of Sociology* 108/1 (2002): 168–206; Oosterbeek, et al., "Cultural Differences in Ultimatum Game Experiments"; S.-H. Chuah, et al., "Do Cultures Clash? Evidence from Cross National Ultimatum Game Experiments," *Journal of Economic Behavior and Organization* 64/1 (2007): 35–48; Engel, "Dictator Games: A Meta Study." To be clear, these studies were not principally interested in the effect of markets (or market exposure or integration) on prosocial behavior. Instead, the authors were either investigating the cross-cultural (or cross-national) differences in particular measures of prosocial behavior (Roth, et al.; Croson and Buchan; Buchan, et al.; Chuah, et al.) or conducting meta-analyses on particular economic games (Oosterbeek, et al.; Engel). However, we could look at these studies to get

However, a few studies do hint at how societies that are more favorable to markets behave less consistently with narrowly selfish preferences than those that are less favorable to markets. For instance, Ockenfels and Weimann showed that subjects from former East Germany (a "socialist planned economy") behaved significantly more selfishly than those from former West Germany (a "market-oriented environment") after the end of the Cold War.[19] Similarly, Johnson and Mislin reported that trust games replicated in Africa consistently and significantly smaller trustor and trustee amounts compared to those replicated in North America (the United States and Canada).[20] Moreover, they reported that trustor and trustee amounts from the European replications were statistically no different from those from North American replications.

As a whole, the existing evidence seems to suggest that markets teach us to balance between selfishness and selflessness. The fact that there is mixed evidence on whether or not markets teach us to be selfish is reassuring; arguably, we would not observe mixed results had markets absolutely taught us to become selfish. Regardless of the country in which we reside or from which we originate, people do not always behave in narrowly selfish ways. Instead, market exposure and integration seem to be encouraging people to become even less selfish and be more prosocial in various ways. Furthermore, note that people do not become completely selfless with market exposure and integration. The dictators in dictator games, regardless of the society in which the games were conducted, do not give all of the available pie to the recipients; the same is true of proposers in ultimatum games and trustors in trust games.

There are, similarly, reasons to doubt the claim that markets breed greed. For instance, in a survey by US Trust, respondents reported that civic duty and the responsibility to help others were among the values that were encouraged in their families when growing up among the high-net- and ultra-high-net-worth adults in the United States.[21] The survey described how the wealthy believe they could make the greatest contributions through giving financially to nonprofit organizations (74 percent), volunteering (61 percent), and serving on a board or committee of a nonprofit organization (47 percent). It also showed that the wealthy care

---

a sense of whether market societies behave more selfishly compared to nonmarket societies. Again, we acknowledge we cannot heavily extrapolate from these studies for our purposes here.

[19] A. Ockenfels and J. Weimann, "Types and Patterns: An Experimental East-West-German Comparison of Cooperation and Solidarity," *Journal of Public Economics* 71/2 (1999): 275–87, at 276.

[20] Johnson and Mislin, "Trust Games: A Meta-Analysis."

[21] US Trust, "2016 US Trust Insights on Wealth and Worth Survey" (2016), http://doing morethatmatters.com/wp-content/uploads/2016/09/US_Trust-Wealth-and-Worth-Study-2016.pdf.

about a variety of social and environmental issues, such as empowerment of women, access to education, healthcare quality and access, and environmental production and sustainability. Fifty-eight percent of the respondents reported that they consider social and environmental impact of companies to be important factors for their investment decisions, and that they prefer investing in companies that have a positive social impact. As US Trust wrote, "finding solutions to tough problems in the world, giving back to others less financially fortunate, fueling growth in the economy—making a positive impact—is a core value among wealthy individuals and families. They look for opportunities to make a meaningful difference and do so with intent in all areas of their lives—at home, work, and in the community."[22]

Companies seem to also believe they can make a positive social impact. For example, Starbucks, along with SCS Global Services and Conservations International, developed the Coffee and Farmer Equity Practices standards to ensure that Starbucks used only sustainably grown and processed coffee. Toms Shoes donates a pair of shoes for each pair sold. Other companies have taken stances on social issues with some risk. Nike, for instance, took a stance on racial injustice and hired Colin Kaepernick for their advertisements. Proctor & Gamble's Gillette used advertisements to make a statement about toxic masculinity and female empowerment. Still more companies actively disassociate themselves from negative social incidents and entities: Dairy Queen terminated its franchise agreement with a store in Illinois after the franchise owner committed a racist act;[23] the National Basketball Association banned Donald Sterling, the former Clippers owner, for life after recordings of him making racist remarks became public;[24] and ABC canceled Roseanne Barr's successful show after she posted some racially charged Tweets.[25] Encouragingly, companies appear to have genuine social and ethical concerns.[26]

---

[22] Ibid., 37.

[23] F.S. Abderholden, "Dairy Queen Ending Franchise Agreement with Zion Store after Racial Slur Incident," *Chicago Tribune*, Jan. 7, 2017, http://www.chicagotribune.com/suburbs/lake-county-news-sun/news/ct-lns-dairy-queen-racial-slurs-zion-st-0107-20170106-story.html.

[24] C. Boren, "Clippers Owner Donald Sterling Banned for Life from NBA," *The Washington Post*, April 29, 2014, https://www.washingtonpost.com/news/early-lead/wp/2014/04/29/clippers-owner-donald-sterling-banned-for-life-from-nba/?utm_term=.9d139a71c246.

[25] J. Koblin, "After Racist Tweet, Roseanne Barr's Show Is Canceled by ABC," *New York Times*, April 29, 2018, https://www.nytimes.com/2018/05/29/business/media/roseanne-barr-offensive-tweets.html.

[26] See Storr and Choi, *Do Markets Corrupt*, 164–66, for more details.

Even more encouragingly, market societies seem more charitable than nonmarket societies. Historically, some of the wealthiest members of society have also been the greatest philanthropists, such as Andrew Carnegie, John D. Rockefeller, Bill and Melinda Gates, and Mark Zuckerberg and Priscilla Chan, suggesting that the wealthiest in (market) societies—those who should be the greediest if markets bred greed—care about the well-being of others in their society.[27] But the wealthiest are not the only charitable ones in market societies. The Charity Aid Foundation (CAF) ranks 139 countries in its World Giving Index on the basis of their generosity, measured as the proportion of respondents to a Gallup survey who reported that they had volunteered, donated money, or helped a stranger in the past month. According to the 2017 World Giving Index, the majority of the ten most-charitable countries are market societies (New Zealand, United States, Australia, Canada, Ireland, and the Netherlands) and the majority of the ten least-charitable countries are nonmarket societies (Yemen, China, Lithuania, Morocco, Georgia, Cambodia, Madagascar, Serbia, Latvia, and Mauritania).[28] People in market societies more frequently volunteer, donate, and help strangers than those in nonmarket societies, countering the prevailing belief that those in nonmarket societies are more altruistic.[29] Moreover, people in market societies donate more money (as a proportion of their GDP) and more often than nonmarket societies.[30] For example, the United States donated 1.44 percent of its GDP in 2016. Similarly, New Zealand and Canada donated 0.79 percent and 0.77 percent of their GDP, respectively. On the other hand, Mexico, China, and the Czech Republic respectively donated 0.03 percent, 0.03 percent, and 0.04 percent of their GDP in 2016. In addition, nearly half of the respondents from market societies self-reported having made a donation within the previous month, while only a quarter of the respondents from nonmarket societies reported having done so. Granted, cash donation can be a function of the wealth that people have. But if the concern that markets teach people to be greedier were well founded, members of market societies should be donating less than those of nonmarket societies.[31]

---

[27] This fact perhaps should not too surprising. In the same passage about the limits of benevolence and the beggar that we cited above in *The Wealth of Nations* (27), Adam Smith seemed to also assume that the wealthy in society would donate enough so that the beggar's basic survival is guaranteed.

[28] Charity Aid Foundation, "CAF World Giving Index 2017: A Global View of Giving Trends," https://www.cafonline.org/docs/default-source/about-us-publications/cafworldgi vingindex2017_2167a_web_210917.pdf?sfvrsn=ed1dac40_10.

[29] Storr and Choi, *Do Markets Corrupt*, 166–67.

[30] Charity Aid Foundation, "CAF World Giving Index 2017."

[31] Storr and Choi, *Do Markets Corrupt*, 166, 168. Here we take for granted that market societies are wealthier than nonmarket societies. For quantitative comparisons of wealth between market and nonmarket societies, see ibid., chapter 4. Also see "The Examined

Another way to assess whether markets teach us to be greedy may be to look at measures of materialism.[32] To the best of our knowledge, only a couple of cross-country studies examine the link between materialism and markets. Güliz and Belk concluded that affluence and Westernness do not explain differences in materialism across countries.[33] Teague, et al., confirmed that people in market societies are less likely to be materialistic than those in nonmarket societies.[34] Moreover, using data from the World Value Survey, people in market societies are less likely to perceive being rich and successful as something personally important than those in nonmarket societies (see Storr and Choi, *Do Markets Corrupt Our Morals?*, for a detailed discussion of these measures).[35] On average, 12.11 percent of respondents from market societies reported that being rich was important to them, and 29.45 percent that being successful was important, while 27.29 percent of respondents from nonmarket societies reported that being rich was important, and 67.91 percent that being successful was important. Approximately the same proportion of respondents from both market and nonmarket societies reported viewing competition to be beneficial (52.35 percent and 49.42 percent), but only about half of the respondents from market societies reported viewing competition to be harmful, compared to those from nonmarket societies (4.05 percent and 7.68 percent, respectively). If markets truly taught us to be greedy, those who live in market societies should be more preoccupied with economic gain and with getting more of it. And a person may be more materialistic if she tends to favor more (economic) competition. The existing evidence, albeit little, suggests that markets do not teach us to be greedy.

Of course, the greedy and the deceitful exist in market societies. Unfortunately, greed and deceit seem to be universal among human beings across time and space. But people in market societies do not appear to be greedier and more de-

---

Life: The OECD's Latest Measure of Well-Being," *The Economist*, May 28, 2013, for a powerful graphic examination of how the best- and least-well-off in society (measured as top and bottom 10 percent in income and education) fare across countries. In some cases, the poorest of a market society fare much better than the richest of a nonmarket society; for example, Canada's least-well-off fare better than the best-off in Italy, Israel, Russia, Portugal, Brazil, Turkey, and Mexico: https://www.economist.com/graphic-detail/2013/05/28/the-examined-life?Fsrc=scn%2Fgp%2Fwl%2Fdc%2Fbetterlifeindex.

[32] Storr and Choi, *Do Markets Corrupt*, 168–69.
[33] G. Güliz and R.W. Belk, "Cross-Cultural Differences in Materialism," *Journal of Economic Psychology*, 17/1 (1996): 55–77.
[34] M. Teague, R. Fike, and V.H. Storr, "Markets, Money and Materialism," Working Paper (2018).
[35] World Values Survey, "World Values Survey Publications," accessed March 12, 2019, http://www.worldvaluessurvey.org/WVSContents.jsp?CMSID=Publications.

ceitful than those in nonmarket societies. As a whole, markets do not seem to teach us to be greedy and instead appear to teach us to be generous.

Honesty or Dishonesty?

Bernard Mandeville's famous poem *The Grumbling Hive* is a fable that focuses on the connection between markets and morality. The Hive was a wealthy and well-governed society, and the bees who inhabited it were industrious. But cheating and deceit was pervasive throughout the Hive. For example, the lawyers colluded with each other to fuel conflicts between their clients and overcharge them. The doctors were greedy for their own fame and wealth, did not seek to improve their skills, and did not seem concerned for their patients' health. Too many priests were lazy, lustful, greedy, and prideful, and too many soldiers were cowards. The kings' ministers were often unethical and favored the wealthy. Indeed, "All Trades and Places knew some Cheat, / No Calling was without Deceit."[36] Dishonesty governed the activities and dealings of every bee in the Hive. In Mandeville's view, markets depend on our exploiting and deceiving one another for our own gains.

However, our own experiences and history suggest otherwise. Anecdotally, we do not willingly choose or return to do business with a known fraud or liar. We prefer to engage in economic exchange with those who are trustworthy and have proven themselves to be trustworthy. Real-world events corroborate our intuition. Take, for example, Bernard L. Madoff, who pleaded guilty to running Wall Street's largest financial fraud in March 2009. US prosecutors estimated the fraud to be worth $64.8 billion based on the purported amounts held by investors in about 4,800 accounts as of November 2008.[37] Madoff was skillful in managing impressions and had been described as "relaxed, poised, self-confident, reassuring, knowledgeable, humorous, and self-deprecating."[38] If honesty (or truthfulness) were not a trait that investors cared about, arguably Madoff's dishonesty would not have come as such a shock when it was exposed.

As another example, take Volkswagen. In August 2015, Volkswagen confessed that they had installed illegal software that instructed emissions controls to activate only during laboratory emissions-test settings. It took Volkswagen, which at the time owned 70 percent of the US passenger-car diesel market, more

---

[36] B. Mandeville, *The Fable of the Bees or Private Vices, Publick Benefits* [1714, 1732], with commentary by F.B. Kaye (Indianapolis: Liberty Fund, 1988), 67.

[37] M. Graybow, "Madoff Mysteries Remain as He Nears Guilty Plea," *Reuters*, March 11, 2009, https://www.reuters.com/article/us-madoff/madoff-mysteries-remain-as-he-nears-guilty-plea-idUSTRE52 A5JK20090311?pageNumber=2&virtualBrandChannel=0&sp=true.

[38] L.S. Lewis, *Con Game: Bernard Madoff and His Victims* (New York: Routledge, 2017), 187.

than a year to admit that a finding published by West Virginia University researchers in 2014 had been right.[39] The carmaker's reputation has been severely crippled since the scandal; its reputation score measured by Reputation Institute dropped from 75 in 2015 to 61.3 in 2016.[40] Bachmann, et al., documented a drastic decline in stock prices and a plummet in positive sentiments with a spike in negative sentiments towards Volkswagen expressed on Twitter following its confession.[41] With a lawsuit against Volkswagen that started on September 30, 2019, in Germany, it seems that the German carmaker is struggling to move past its blatant act of dishonesty and repair its reputation.

Several academic papers that speak to the value of honesty in the market. Consider the gift-exchange experiment by Fehr, et al.[42] The experiment compared results of two treatments: one with no punishment and one with punishment. In the first treatment, the owner first offered a contract specifying a salary amount and a desired exerted effort amount to a market of managers. A contract was formed with the first manager who accepted the owner's terms. Once a contract was formed, the manager who accepted the offer received the salary amount and supplied an effort level that did not need to match the contracted amount of effort. The manager incurred no penalty for exerting less than the contracted amount. On average, in this first treatment, the managers never met the owners' expectations regarding effort; only 26 percent of the managers delivered the contracted level of effort. Encouragingly, the delivered amount of effort grew as the salary offer and contracted amount of effort grew.

---

[39] R. Read, "Volkswagen Dieselgate Cheat Sheet: The High (And Low) Points So Far," *The Washington Post*, Nov. 13, 2015, https://www.washingtonpost.com/cars/volkswagen-dieselgate-cheat-sheet-the-high-and-low-points-so-far/2015/11/13/522e7ea0-8a53-11e5-bd91-d385b244482f_story.html; C. Atiyeh, "Everything You Need to Know about the VW Diesel-Emissions Scandal," *Car and Driver*, Dec. 4, 2019, https://www.caranddriver.com/news/a15339250/everything-you-need-to-know-about-the-vw-diesel-emissions-scandal/.

[40] A. Guttman, "Reputation of the Volkswagen Group from 2011 to 2017 (index score)," *Statista* (2018), https://www.statista.com/statistics/516426/volkswagen-reputation/.
To provide some context, the most reputable companies have an average Reputation Institute index score of 77. In 2017, the most reputable company was Rolex with a score of 80.38 and the most reputable automobile manufacturer was Rolls-Royce with a score of 77.66 (Guttman).

[41] R. Bachmann, et al., "Firms and Collective Reputation: the Volkswagen Emissions Scandal as a Case Study," Working Paper (2017).

[42] E. Fehr, S. Gächter, and G. Kirchsteiger, "Reciprocity as a Contract Enforcement Device: Experimental Evidence," *Econometrica* 65/4 (1997): 833–60. See also Akerlof on lemons: G.A. Akerlof, "The Market for 'Lemons': Quality Uncertainty and the Market Mechanism," *The Quarterly Journal of Economics* 84/3 (1970): 488–500.

The second treatment was identical to the first treatment, except for a penalty. The owners now had the chance to punish the managers based on their actual levels of exerted effort: The owner could increase or decrease her manager's payoff at a cost to herself. Owners punished those who did not meet the contracted amount of effort 68 percent of the time and rewarded those who more than satisfied the contacted amount 70 percent of the time. Admittedly, the researchers were not principally concerned with honesty. But we could understand the difference between the contracted amount of effort (expected by the owner) and the delivered amount of effort (by the manager) as dishonesty; the manager knew of the owner's expectations and deliberately failed to fulfill the promise she made with the owner. Results from this study arguably indicate that honesty is a desirable and rewardable trait in employees, even in short-lived interactions in a laboratory experiment.

This implication from this study may not be so surprising. A study by M.K. Johnson, et al.,[43] examined whether any of the Big Five personality traits could predict supervisor ratings of employees' job performance in the assisted-living support industry.[44] They found that the trait of honesty-humility significantly correlated with job performance and was uniquely the best predictor of job performance rating over the other personality traits. "A personality trait associated with social and emotional competency," they predicted, "may better predict job performance among workers in caregiving roles than high-order traits like Conscientiousness."[45] For instance, honest-humble individuals may exhibit social and emotional qualities such as empathy and forgiveness more than less honest-humble individuals. Honest-humble individuals also tend to be more cooperative in economic games and more helpful than less honest-humble individuals.[46] While the findings of Johnson, et al., from a sample of individuals from the assisted-living support industry should not be overgeneralized, they do provide a case for the importance of honesty and humility on individual and firm success among service providers.

---

[43] M.K. Johnson, R.C. Rowatt, and L. Petrini, "A New Trait on the Market: Honesty-Humility as a Unique Predictor of Job Performance Ratings," *Personality and Individual Differences* 50 (2011): 857–62.

[44] In personality research, psychologists often use five core traits (which may be conceived as stable dispositions that drive behavior) to assess personality. These traits, also known as the Big Five personality traits, are openness to experience, conscientiousness, extraversion-introversion, agreeableness, and neuroticism. See D.P. Schmitt, et al., "The Geographic Distribution of Big Five Personality Traits: Patterns and Profiles of Human Self-Description Across 56 Nations," *Journal of Cross-Cultural Psychology* 38/2 (2007): 173–212.

[45] Johnson, et al., "A New Trait on the Market," 858.

[46] See ibid. for references to appropriate studies substantiating these claims/predictions.

Additionally, J. Conrads, et al., investigated dishonest behavior among sellers in a real-world loose-candy market in Germany, where it is priced according to a pay-per-weight scheme.[47] The majority of the sellers behaved honestly despite the short-term incentive to cheat (that is, overcharge) their customers. Despite the overwhelming honesty among sellers, the researchers found that some overcharging occurred 25.61 percent of the time. Overcharging behavior, interestingly, correlated with visibility of the scale: There was hardly any overcharging among sellers whose scales were visible to the customers, but there was frequent overcharging among sellers whose scales were hidden from the customers. Unlike other products and services, such as cars and hairstylists, it is possible that the market for loose candy does not command as much customer loyalty. If so, this would suggest that sellers had even less incentive to behave honestly towards what are largely one-off interactions with customers. Despite such low incentives, sellers exhibited honest behavior in the study, suggesting that markets may encourage honest behavior.

If markets taught us to be dishonest, the existing evidence should demonstrate how people do not care about fraud, con men, and deceitful behavior. Market participants should treat honest and dishonest exchange partners equally, without discrimination, and should always choose to trade with those who makes the best offers. Yet real-market participants do not behave as such. People, even long-time patrons, abandon cheats and deceitful companies when they are caught committing fraudulent behavior. Furthermore, market participants care about honesty. Supervisors reward honest behavior and punish dishonest behavior by their supervisees. But perhaps most importantly, people who engage in frequent market activity tend to be honest, even when they are not being strictly monitored. Instead, evidence suggests that markets teach us to be honest.

Loyalty or Disloyalty? Trust or Distrust?

Jean-Jacques Rousseau constantly worried about the immoralizing effects of markets and reasoned that members of commercial societies are necessarily greedy and deceitful. In *Discourse on Inequality,* Rousseau discussed how human beings ("savage man") are inherently neither greedy nor deceitful but instead are both incapable of virtue and vice in this primitive state.[48] However, as societies grew, what Rousseau called political or moral inequalities (as opposed to natural or physical inequalities arising from differences in age and health) were introduced

---

[47] J. Conrads, F. Ebeling, and S. Lotz, "(Dis-)honesty: Measuring Overcharging in a Real-World Market," *Journal of Behavioral and Experimental Economics* 57 (2015): 98–102.

[48] J.J. Rousseau, *A Discourse on Inequality* [1754], translated by M. Cranston (New York: Penguin Random House, 1984), 104.

and fostered.[49] As societies grew and division of labor became necessary, according to Rousseau, people were no longer "free and independent" but instead became "diminished ... into subjection ... to [their] fellow men, men of whom he has become the slave, in a sense, even in becoming their master; for if he is rich he needs their services; if he is poor he needs their aid; and even a middling condition does not enable him to do without them."[50] Because people rely on one another to survive in a commercial society, people can succeed only through (continual) persuasion of others: persuading other people to employ them or to work for them, and persuading others to purchase goods they have for sale or to sell the goods they want. This never-ending persuasion of others "makes him devious and artful with some, imperious and hard towards others, and compels him to treat badly the people he needs if he cannot make them fear him and does not judge it in his interest to be of service to them."[51] If Rousseau is right, humans develop the capacity for virtue and a tendency towards vices as societies grow and the market expands. The connections between individuals in a modern commercial society are unlikely to be characterized by trust and loyalty.

In neoclassical economics, loyalty (or commitment) plays no role in market exchange. It is expected that market participants will switch trading partners when they can grow their profit (even at a negligible amount) with a new trading partner. In fact, it is said that an individual is being irrational or that there must be some unseen, miscalculated, or illicit benefit to the individual when she decides to continue trading with a more expensive trading partner. Thus, traits such as loyalty, trust, and trustworthiness cannot exist in a truly competitive market and do not have any roles in neoclassical economics.

Yet firms definitely desire loyal customers. For instance, many corporations employ customer-retention marketing strategies to keep repeat customers. One of these strategies is the customer-loyalty program through which customers are recompensed for their patronage. For instance, Starbucks has a reward program by which patrons earn and exchange accumulated stars for free drinks and foods. Department stores like Bloomingdale's, grocery stores like Safeway, and national movie theater chains such as AMC Theatres have similar loyalty programs that transform accumulated points into awards, store credit, or discounts. Many other retailers also offer service guarantees and complaint-management programs.

On the customer side, loyalty cuts down on the cognitive costs of finding suitable products and services. On the firm side, loyalty generates profit. For example, Reichheld and Sasser found that a 5 percent increase in customer retention translated into a 25-to-125 percent increase in profits in nine service industry

---

[49] Ibid., 77.
[50] Ibid., 119.
[51] Ibid.

groups.[52] Bowen and Shoemaker investigated a sample of American Express Platinum card members who took at least six overnight business trips per year and stayed in luxury hotel chains such as the Ritz Carlton and Four Seasons.[53] Compared to nonloyal customers, loyal customers were less likely to ask about prices when making a reservation and more frequently self-reported that they purchased other hotel services (such as laundry and restaurant emails) at hotels to which they felt loyalty compared to those to which they felt less loyalty. Furthermore, the study found that loyal customers were more likely to tell management about a potential problem and to advertise to an average of twelve people the hotels to which they felt loyalty. According to an estimate by the Ritz-Carlton, a loyal customer was valued at more than one hundred thousand dollars in the 1990s.[54] Needless to say, there seems to be a financial case for customer retention.

One way of investigating interpersonal commitment or loyalty is by looking at community generally and social capital in particular. Loosely defined, social capital refers to those "informal networks of (non-contractual) relations that exist between people in society, and to the beliefs and norms—like trust and reciprocity—to which those informal relations give rise and which govern the character of the networks in question."[55] Social capital, like economic and human capital, can be used to achieve economic goals. For instance, numerous studies have explored the use of social connections in obtaining information about jobs.[56] Social links can explain why market participants repeatedly exchange with the same trading partners despite the fact that they are not achieving maximum utility or profit by remaining in the same partnerships. Furthermore, social connections can substitute for missing or expensive legal structures and help overcome unforeseen contingencies and incomplete contracts. In this environment, loyalty could be viewed as an attribute of a successful social relationship.

---

[52] F. Reichheld and W.E. Sasser Jr, "Zero Defections: Quality Comes to Services," *Harvard Business Review* 68 (1990): 105–11.

[53] J. Bowen and S. Shoemaker, "The Antecedents and Consequences of Customer Loyalty," *Cornell Hotel Restaurant and Administration Quarterly* 39/1 (1998): 12–25.

[54] P. Kotler, J.T. Bowen, and J.C. Makens, *Marketing for Hospitality and Tourism* (Englewood Cliffs, NJ: Prentice Hall, 1996), 346.

[55] P. Lewis and E. Chamlee-Wright, "Social Embeddedness, Social Capital and the Market Process: An Introduction to the Special Issue on Austrian Economics, Economic Sociology and Social Capital," *Review of Austrian Economics* 21 (2008): 107–18.

[56] C.A. Myer and G.P. Shultz, *The Dynamics of a Labor Market: A Study of the Impact of Employment Changes on Labor Mobility, Job Satisfactions, and Company and Union Policies* (Upper Saddle River, NJ: Prentice-Hall, 1951); M. Granovetter, *Getting a Job: A Study of Contacts and Career*, 2nd ed. (Chicago: University of Chicago Press, 1995); M. Pellizzari, "Do Friends and Relatives Really Help in Getting a Good Job?" *Industrial and Labour Relations Review* 63 (2010): 494–510.

If it were indeed true that markets cultivated disloyalty, and that market values were likely to spill over into nonmarket spaces, we should expect to see stronger communities and more social capital in nonmarket societies compared to market societies. Fortunately, however, the growth of markets does not appear to have led to a decline in community. First, there are numerous studies that corroborate how meaningful social relationships can emerge from market relationships. For instance, competitors have developed friendships (and even sister-like bonds) with one another;[57] principal-client and seller-buyer relationships have developed into deep friendships;[58] and coworkers developed strong bonds based on their common experiences and circumstances.[59] Because our market activities bring us into contact with people across ethnicities, nationalities, and other social identities whom we might not otherwise encounter, the market enables dissimilar individuals to peacefully reconcile their plans and thus creates favorable conditions for friendships.

Second, some measures suggest that people in market societies have more social capital than those in nonmarket societies. For instance, in the 2019 World Value Survey, a larger proportion of the respondents from market societies reported being active members of organizations and associations compared to those in nonmarket societies. While about the same proportion of respondents claimed to be active members of religious organizations in both market and nonmarket societies (15.66 percent and 17.51 percent, respectively), the larger proportion of respondents who claimed to be active members of sports and recreational organizations was almost two and a half times larger in market societies than in

---

[57] E. Chamlee-Wright, *The Cultural Foundations of Economic Development: Urban Female Entrepreneurship in Ghana* (New York: Routledge, 1997); P. Ingram and P.W. Roberts, "Friendships among Competitors in the Sydney Hotel Industry," *American Journal of Sociology* 106/2 (2000): 387–423.

[58] L.L. Price and E.J. Arnould, "Commercial Friendships: Service Provider-Client Relationships in Context," *Journal of Marketing* 63/4 (1999): 38–56; K. Butcher, B. Sparks, and F. O'Callaghan, "On the Nature of Customer-Employee Relationships," *Marketing Intelligence & Planning* 20/5 (2002): 297–306; D.L. Haytko, "Firm-to-Firm and Interpersonal Relationships: Perspectives from Advertising Agency Account Managers," *Journal of Academy of Marketing Science* 32 (2004): 312–28.

[59] See, for example, P. Zavella, "'Abnormal Intimacy': The Varying Work Networks of Chicana Cannery Workers," *Feminist Studies* 11/3 (1985): 541–57; K. Bridge and L.A. Baxter, "Blended Relationships: Friends as Work Associates," *Western Journal of Communication* 56/3 (1992): 200–25; M. Argyle and M. Henderson, *The Anatomy of Relationships: And the Rules and Skills Needed to Manage Them Successfully* (London: Penguin, 1985); R. Hodson, "Group Relations at Work: Solidarity, Conflict, and Relations With Management," *Work and Occupations* 24 (1997): 426–52.

nonmarket societies (20.8 percent and 8.4 percent, respectively).[60] As one of the indicators of the annually released Prosperity Index, the Legatum Institute evaluates social cohesion and engagement, community and family networks, social norms, political participation, and institutional trust. According to the 2011 Prosperity Index, people in market societies have significantly stronger social capital than those living in nonmarket societies (scores of 58.58 and 47.44. respectively).[61]

There is also suggestive experimental evidence of market exchanges shaping whom people trust and thus building the foundation for long-term relationships between market participants. Kollock investigated how patterns of exchange may be influenced by uncertainty and operationalized uncertainty by manipulating the amount of information revealed to buyers regarding the product quality.[62] In the treatment, buyers were not told about the product quality until after they had completed their trade with a seller. Kollock reported that, compared to those in the full-information treatment, subjects in the information asymmetry treatment showed more commitment to their exchange partners and were more likely to remain with their trusted exchange partners even when they received better price offers from other potential partners. Moreover, he found that subjects in the information asymmetry treatment tended to rate the trustworthiness of their most-frequent exchange partners to be greater than that of their least-frequent exchange partner. Brown, et al., also experimentally showed that owners preferred to form long-term relationships based on trust and gift exchange with their managers, rather than to form contracts to align incentives when contracts were incomplete.[63] In their experiment, long-term relationships dominated the market for managers.

Similarly, we showed that positive social relationships based on trust and trustworthiness can emerge in market settings.[64] In our experiment, subjects first played a market game followed by the trust game. Our market permitted participants to defect on price agreements. More specifically, the market participant who initiated an agreement got to decide whether she would like to execute or defect on the trade; by deciding to defect on the agreement, the initiator effectively stole all the cash and the goods, leaving nothing for the agreement recipient. We

---

[60] Storr and Choi, *Do Markets Corrupt*, 111.
[61] Legatum Institute, *The 2011 Legatum Prosperity Index: An Inquiry into Global Wealth and Wellbeing* (London: Legatum Institute, 2010); see also Storr and Choi, *Do Markets Corrupt*, 111–12.
[62] P. Kollock, "The Emergence of Exchange Structures: An Experimental Study of Uncertainty, Commitment, and Trust," *American Journal of Sociology* 100/2 (1994): 313–45.
[63] M. Brown, A. Falk, and E. Fehr, "Relational Contracts and the Nature of Market Interactions," *Econometrica* 72/3 (2004): 747–80.
[64] Storr and Choi, *Do Markets Corrupt*, 2005–12.

found that trading partners between whom more than half of the agreements were executed (that is, who shared positive relationships) tended to show more trust and trustworthiness towards one another (that is, tended to send each other greater amounts as trustors and trustees in the trust game) than those trading partners between whom fewer than half of the agreements were executed (that is, shared negative relationships). Furthermore, on average, only the trustees in positive relationships were fully repaying the trust they were shown by the trustors in the trust game. Jointly with Kollock, these results suggest that loyal partnerships based on trust and trustworthiness can and do emerge in market settings.

Again, if the market taught us to be disloyal, social networks should deteriorate as relational traits such as loyalty lose their value with the expansion of the market and increased participation in the market. However, several studies corroborate how meaningful social relationships can emerge from market relationships. Moreover, people in market societies seem to have more social capital than those in nonmarket societies. And, perhaps most convincingly, we have meaningful social relationships despite the encroachment of markets into all aspects of our daily lives and have some friendships (or friendship-like relationships) with our colleagues. Evidently, markets do not teach people to be disloyal towards one another; in fact, markets seem to teach people to be loyal instead.

Conclusion

In *The Way We Live*, Anthony Trollope chronicles a series of events instigated by the arrival of Augustus Melmotte, a financier, in the City of London.[65] From early on, Melmotte is portrayed as an unpleasant fellow. Of his appearance, the narrator says that Melmotte looked, "on the whole[,] unpleasant," "untrustworthy," and "as though he were purse-proud and a bully" (17). Of his reputation, the narrator describes how

> people said that Mr. Melmotte had a reputation throughout Europe as a gigantic swindler—as one who in the dishonest and successful pursuit of wealth had stopped at nothing. People said of him that he had framed and carried out long premeditated and deeply-laid schemes for the ruin of those who had trusted him, that he had swallowed up the property of all who had come in contact with him, that he was fed with the blood of widows and children (38).

But Melmotte is an immensely wealthy man, who "no doubt had had enormous dealings in other countries" (19), a "merchant prince" (45) whose parties are at-

---

[65] A. Trollope, *The Way We Live Now* [1875] (Overland Park: Digireads.com Publishing, 2011).

tended by "a Royal Prince, a Cabinet Member, and the very cream of duchesses" (17). In fact, he is so wealthy that the socioeconomic elite of London put up with his unpleasant habits. For example, Lord Alfred Grendall does not correct Melmotte's breach of etiquette, despite his almost violent distaste for Melmotte's habit of calling him by his first name and not his title (20). Indeed, "in the City Mr. Melmotte's name was worth any money—though his character was perhaps worth but little" (19).

Over the course of the novel, Melmotte commits a series of morally questionable acts. While Sir Felix Canbury does not approach Melmotte's daughter with innocent intent, Melmotte still rejects him as a suitor for his daughter solely on the basis that he is a penniless aristocrat. Instead, Melmotte tries to arrange a marriage between his daughter and Lord Nidderdale, who has superior family connections to Sir Felix. Furthermore, Melmotte devises and leads financial schemes. For instance, "Pickering [the family estate owned by a Mr. Longstaffe] had been purchased and the title-deeds made over to Mr. Melmotte; but the £80,000 had not been paid" (236). Melmotte sells shares in a railway that stretches from Salt Lake City, USA, to Veracruz, Mexico, and may never get built. Indeed, the narrator explains how, with Melmotte, "[g]reat purchases were made and great transactions apparently completed without the signing even of a cheque" (236). Towards the end of the novel, Melmotte even forges financial documents in his attempt to save his dying reputation and credibility. He ultimately poisons himself at the end of novel, unable to handle the mounting stress resulting from suspicions surrounding his financial schemes and forgeries and from his tattered political reputation.

For some, characters like Melmotte are the archetype of a market participant. They demonstrate that the traits and values that make us successful in the market are completely disconnected from those that make us moral and likeable human beings. In fact, these characters suggest that participating in the market teaches us to be immoral, despicable human beings. Yet, markets in the real world—the ones in which we participate daily—are not saturated with Melmottes. Our daily experience little resembles the stereotypes of stock exchange trading floors, where interactions consist of chaotic shouting and hand signals between cutthroat, profit-maximizing traders. Our daily experience more resembles the farmers' market, interactions filled with pleasantries, warmth, and generosity. Every day, many of us joke with our colleagues, clients, and business partners and converse with them about our personal lives. In reality, the market is a moral and social space.[66]

This chapter has attempted to evaluate whether markets teach us selfishness or selflessness; greed or generosity; honesty or dishonesty; and loyalty or disloyalty. We have evaluated some quantitative evidence (though primarily experi-

---

[66] Storr, "Why the Market?"; and Storr and Choi, *Do Markets Corrupt Our Morals?*

mental) to assess which traits markets teach us. Markets, we conclude, teach us to balance between selfishness and selflessness, honesty, generosity, and loyalty. Granted, none of the evidence we present here should be interpreted as a claim that markets are not capable of harm. Of course, there are greedy, disloyal, immoral individuals who inhabit market societies and who actively participate in market activities. Such bad individuals are everywhere and inhabit any community, regardless of its friendliness toward markets. But if markets truly systematically favored and rewarded the wealthy, the greedy, the frauds, and the heartless, there would be genuine concerns about the free reign of markets in our society and genuine reasons to restrict the free operation of markets. Fortunately, this concern seems to be moot. At worst, it appears that markets to not promote misbehavior any more than alternative economic systems do.

How Market Society Affects Character

Jason Brennan

Critics of economically liberal market societies often claim that while market societies and trade tend to enrich us, this comes at the expense of our character. They assert that markets in general, or specific markets in certain taboo goods and services, corrupt us in various ways, rendering us more selfish and callous. In contrast, early Marxists (and even a few contemporaries) claim that, were we raised in a radically different economic environment, we would be more altruistic, generous, and fair. Such critics advance what Peter Jaworski and I call the "Corruption Objection" to markets.[1] According to the Corruption Objection, markets cause us to develop defective preferences or character traits. The market, in this view, is not simply a value-neutral mechanism for exchange, but rather an institution with built-in norms and values. Money, critics say, has a profane, utilitarian, and hedonistic meaning, so putting a price on something tends to induce people to think in selfish or instrumentalist terms and turns their attention away from higher values. Over time, markets make us worse people, or so the objection goes.

In this paper, I argue that the Corruption Objection generally has the facts backwards. On the contrary, the empirical evidence generally shows that markets tend to have an ameliorative effect on our character, though in some specific contexts introducing markets can reduce trust or lead to more selfish behaviors.

Do Markets Make Us Selfish?

Many economists extol markets for their tendency to economize on moral virtue; they say a good feature of market societies is that they induce generally selfish people to serve one another. In a properly functioning competitive market, the only way I can promote my own interest is to provide goods and services that oth-

---

[1] Jason Brennan and Peter Jaworski, *Markets without Limits* (New York: Routledge Press, 2016).

ers want at a price they are willing to pay. Thus, the logic goes, trade induces self-interested people to work for others. Markets induce social cohesion and cooperation without needing high levels of good will or generosity.

Marxist philosopher G. A. Cohen claims that the major problem with socialism is that people are not good enough to make it work properly. Insofar as socialism requires some degree of central planning or government control over economic production, it creates a high degree of power. Unfortunately, in the real world, bad people like Pol Pot or Stalin capture this power for ignoble ends, rather than using it to serve the common good. Socialism asks people to work together for the common good without any special reward, but in the real world, people are not sufficiently motivated by public spirit to do their part. So, Cohen says, socialism fails, but the failing reflects flaws in human nature. Capitalist systems do not try to straighten the crooked timber of humanity, and thus they function better. But capitalism relies upon vice—upon greed and selfishness.

Cohen claims that markets do not simply induce selfish motives to serve publicly beneficial ends, but instead they lead to "hypertrophy" of greed and selfishness.[2] Even when we work to benefit others, we are "essentially indifferent" to others' welfare.[3] Markets cause us to regard everyone else as either customers or competitors. We care about them only insofar as they can help us or get in our way, but we do not care about them for their own sake. Cohen says:

> The immediate motive to productive activity in a market society is ... typically some mixture of greed and fear .... [T]he motives of greed and fear are what the market brings to prominence, and that includes greed on behalf of, and fear for the safety of, one's family. Even when one's concerns are thus wider than those of one's mere self, the market posture is greedy and fearful in that one's opposite-number marketeers are predominantly seen as possible sources of enrichment, and as threats to one's success. These are horrible ways of seeing other people.[4]

Markets, he claims, do not merely repurpose our greed and fear for good ends but actually exacerbate our greed and fear. Thus, he claims, they corrupt us.

These are strong accusations, but accusations alone will not do. Cohen himself never—as far as I can find in his voluminous writings—cites any empirical work confirming this view that markets make us more selfish. He takes it as a given, as something so obvious it requires no citations. To my surprise, though, the critics of markets who do cite empirical evidence usually rely on two highly ambiguous and problematic studies. They then tend to ignore the more rigorous and robust recent studies that disconfirm their views.

---

[2] G.A. Cohen, *Why Not Socialism?* (Princeton: Princeton University Press, 2009), 58.
[3] Ibid., 50.
[4] Ibid., 39–40.

The Haifa Day Care Case

Back in the 1970 s, day care facilities in Haifa, Israel, faced a problem in which too many parents picked up their children late. Some economists decided to use this problem to study how financial penalties would affect parents' behavior. They ran an experiment with the parents as subjects.

For the first four weeks of the study, there was no financial penalty for late pickups. In the fifth week, the economists introduced a small fine—less than ten dollars in today's money after adjusting for inflation. To their surprise, when this small penalty was introduced, the number of late pickups increased—in fact, it more than doubled.[5] When the penalty fee was increased to a more substantial amount, the parents then started complying with the rules more, and late pickups eventually dropped to near zero.

At first glance, these results appear to contract what naïve microeconomics would predict. As the price of late pickups rises upward from zero dollars, the demand for picking up kids late should steadily decrease. But instead, demand first rises as the price rises above zero, then falls. What gives?

Michael Sandel and Debra Satz view this case as evidence that certain markets have a corrupting effect on our character.[6] In their interpretation, by introducing a small fine, the Israeli day care transformed how parents thought of late pickups. It transformed what was seen as a significant moral transgression into just another financial transaction. Before the penalty was introduced, parents viewed themselves as having a closer than an arm's-length relationship with the day-care workers. They felt guilt for harming the workers by picking up their kids late. But when a small fee was introduced, they no longer felt guilt; they instead felt that late pickups were just a service to be purchased at will. So, in effect, the smaller monetary price actually changed the full price (money + emotional guilt) the parents were paying. It was only when the monetary price became sufficiently high that parents started picking up their kids on time again, but now solely out of a concern for their own interest. Introducing a market made parents care less about the welfare of day-care workers.

Or so they say. The evidence is rather ambiguous. The reason it's ambiguous is that money means something. The price we attach to a good signals something, not just about the kind of good the thing is, but about the value of the good.

As an illustration, suppose my neighbor doesn't clean up after his dog. When I complain to my neighbor, he starts bagging the dog poop, but after a week or so, he reverts back to leaving it on the sidewalk. Finally, after years of complaining,

---

[5] Steven D. Levitt and Stephen J. Dubner, *Freakonomics* (New York: William Morrow, 2008): 15-16.
[6] Michael Sandel, *What Money Can't Buy* (New York: Farrar, Straus, and Giroux, 2012), 64-65; Debra Satz, *Why Some Things Should Not be For Sale: The Moral Limits of Markets* (New York: Oxford University Press, 2010), 193-94.

I induce a sympathetic tort judge to issue a court order, which says that whenever my neighbor fails to clean his dog's poop off my front lawn, he must pay me 10 cents.

In this case, I'd expect my neighbor would end up cleaning less, not more. The reason is that a price of ten cents communicates information about the relative harm of leaving his dog's poop out. He might react by saying, "Wow, when you complained before, I thought I was really harming by not cleaning up. But apparently all it takes for you to feel whole is to get a measly dime. I don't understand why you were complaining so much. Apparently, leaving the dog poop on your lawn barely affects you, which is why you only want ten cents for it."

The same issue applies to the Haifa case. Maybe introducing a monetary fine caused parents to stop caring about the day-care workers' welfare. Alternatively, maybe the *small fine* inadvertently signaled to the parents that they had been mistaken to believe that picking up their kids really hurt the facility. If all it takes is a small fee to make the day care whole, then picking up kids late was never a big deal. They were mistaken for believing that it was ever all that harmful. The problem is that the Haifa case doesn't distinguish between these two interpretations. Critics of market society should be wary of hanging their argument on this case, though they all do.

THE SWISS WASTE-FACILITY CASE

Elizabeth Anderson offers an argument similar to Sandel's. She claims that market prices can induce people to switch from public-spirited to selfish motivations. To demonstrate that, she cites a study based on a survey the Swiss government administered, which asked residents whether they would be willing to have a waste facility installed near them. Although no compensation was offered, many citizens responded that they would be willing.

Economists thought it would be interesting to see how much more willing the residents would be if a financial incentive were involved. They sent another survey, this time saying the government was considering offering citizens a payment for accepting the facility. The results were surprising: when the possibility of being paid was suggested, fewer, not more, residents were willing to have the facility constructed near them.

Anderson claims that this is evidence of the corrupting effects of markets. She claims that the original survey, which didn't offer money, induced Swiss citizens to think of themselves as citizens in a common venture working toward the common good. The survey respondents asked themselves what kind of sacrifices they should be willing to accept as citizens, recognizing that the waste has to go somewhere. But, she says, when offered money, the citizens instead saw their property as an entitlement. They no longer were worried about solving the waste problem for which they were partly responsible, and instead selfishly wanted the waste to go elsewhere. They would accept the waste facility only in exchange for hefty compensation.[7] Anderson has offered us a plausible interpretation of this study. But there are other, equally plausible, interpretations that do not support her argument.

For one, these surveys are mere hypotheticals. Asking people how they would behave in hypothetical situations frequently fails to tell us how they would in fact behave when actually placed in that situation. Few people claim they would shock an unconscious subject when placed in the Milgram experiment, but nearly all real subjects do. We know that survey respondents generally exhibit social desirability bias; that is, they respond to anonymous surveys in ways that make them look nicer and more virtuous than they actually are. In both of the Swiss surveys, citizens knew nothing was at stake; they were not actually agreeing to have a waste facility installed near them. We need to know how many people would *really* volunteer to have a waste facility put in their neighborhood. The supposed altruism in the original survey wasn't altruism at all.

Further, Anderson (like Sandel and Satz above) misses the deeper point that prices convey information. When the government offers to pay you for accepting a waste facility, the very fact that it offers to pay conveys *new* information. It conveys that the waste facility will impose a significant hardship on you, a hardship so severe that the government will *impromptu* offer you compensation. You can reasonably interpret this as evidence that hardship will be even more severe than the government indicates, and you would reasonably be wary of accepting the facility. On the other hand, if the government offers you no compensation, it thereby signals that the facility will not impose any significant hardship. Different prices signal different levels of anticipated hardship.

As an analogy, consider that my deputy dean sometimes asks faculty to take on various service assignments for the university or my business school. Some of these come with no compensation. Some come with financial compensation. Some come with a course release—if you accept the assignment, you teach one less class that year. When she makes these offers, faculty rightly infer something about the difficulty of the assignments. An uncompensated service assignment must take few hours; a service assignment that includes a course release must take hundreds. Given that my dean (and my government) seem to want to undercompensate people, I might well be more wary of accepting the assignment with higher compensation than an assignment with none.

The Swiss experiment is ambiguous between interpretations. In Anderson's interpretation, introducing a monetary offer makes people more selfish and thus lowers their (apparent/hypothetical) willingness to accept the facility. By another plausible interpretation, offering money signals that the facility is likely to cause

---

[7] Elizabeth Anderson, "Beyond Homo Economicus: New Developments in Theories of Social Norms," *Philosophy and Public Affairs* 29 (2000): 170–200, at 197.

citizens significant harm, so the citizens are less willing to accept it. The first interpretation suggests that money corrupts character; the second does not.

Microeconomic Evidence

The two cases above are highly ambiguous and do not quite demonstrate that markets corrupt. They may instead simply demonstrate that attaching a price to something communicates information about its relative harm or badness, so that people change their behavior accordingly. In the Swiss study, nothing was actually at stake, so we must be cautious in assuming people really would accept a waste facility for free.

Evidence from Economic Games

Fortunately, there is a larger body of evidence in experimental economics examining effects of markets on people's behavior. Economists often have subjects play specially designed games with each other in which large sums of money—sometimes the equivalent of a month's pay—are at stake. In experimental economics games, all subjects know the rules and are required to demonstrate an understanding of what is at stake. Further, the games are played between strangers who do not see or interact with each other outside the game, so they have no external incentive to play the games any particular way.

The Trust Game tests whether players are trusting and trustworthy. The first player receives, say, ten dollars. She may then give as much as she wants to the second player. Every dollar she gives will be multiplied by three; if she gives the second player ten dollars, he'll in fact receive thirty dollars. The second player can then give as much as he wants back to the first or keep for himself. If the first player is completely trusting and the second trustworthy, she will give him everything and he'll send her back fifteen dollars. If she doesn't trust him, she'll send him nothing; if he's not trustworthy, he'll keep whatever he gets and won't reward her trust.

The Dictator Game tests unconditional generosity. Two players are picked at random. One is randomly assigned to be the dictator, the other randomly assigned to be the subject. The dictator is given a lump of cash and told she may share as much as she pleases with the subject. If the dictator is completely selfish, she will keep all the money for herself. The more she gives to the subject, the more generous she is.

In the Ultimatum Game, the proposer is given a lump sum of money. The proposer must then propose splitting the money with a second player called the respondent. If the respondent accepts the split, both players receive the proposer's proposed payoff. If the respondent rejects the split, both players get nothing. This game tests whether the proposer will give money to the respondent out of a sense of fairness, and further whether the respondent will incur a financial loss on herself to punish what she regards as unfair behavior from the proposer.

In the Prisoners' Dilemma, two players are each given the option to cooperate or defect. The payoffs are designed as follows: both players are better off if they both cooperate rather than both defect. Mutual cooperation beats mutual defection. However, both have an incentive to defect, because regardless of what the other player does, each of them receives a higher personal payoff if they defect than if they cooperate. This game tests trust and cooperativeness.

A number of economists have played these games all around the world, looking to determine what factors induce or undermine trust, trustworthiness, cooperativeness, fairness, and so on. In a response to an essay by Michael Sandel, Herbert Gintis chastises Sandel for ignoring this massive literature, and then summarize these studies:

> Movements for religious and lifestyle tolerance, gender equality, and democracy have flourished and triumphed in societies governed by market exchange, and nowhere else. My colleagues and I found dramatic evidence of this positive relationship between markets and morality in our study of fairness in simple societies—hunter-gatherers, horticulturalists, nomadic herders, and small-scale sedentary farmers—in Africa, Latin America, and Asia. Twelve professional anthropologists and economists visited these societies and played standard ultimatum, public goods, and trust games with the locals. As in advanced industrial societies, members of all of these societies exhibited a considerable degree of moral motivation and a willingness to sacrifice monetary gain to achieve fairness and reciprocity, even in anonymous one-shot situations. More interesting for our purposes, we measured the degree of market exposure and cooperation in production for each society, and we found that the ones that regularly engage in market exchange with larger surrounding groups have more pronounced fairness motivations. The notion that the market economy makes people greedy, selfish, and amoral is simply fallacious."[8]

As it turns out, empirically, the strongest *cultural* predictor that participants will play fairly with strangers is how market-oriented their society is.

Joseph Henrich and his colleagues summarize their work as follow: "group-level differences in economic organization and the degree of market integration explain a substantial portion of the behavioral variation across societies: *the higher the degree of market integration and the higher the payoffs to cooperation, the greater the level of cooperation in experimental games.*"[9] Selfishness abounds in nonmarket societies. *Homo economicus* exists, but surprisingly, not in market societies. In general, people from market-based economies seem to have adopted a

---

[8] http://www.bostonreview.net/gintis-giving-economists-their-due.
[9] J. Henrich, et al., "In Search of Homo Economicus: Behavioral Experiments in 15 Small-Scale Societies," *The American Economic Review* 91/2 (2001): 73-78.

tendency to empathize with strangers and exhibit a stronger sense of fairness than people from nonmarket societies.

In one major study, Patrick Francois and Tanguy van Ypersele, found that the more competitive a market is, the more trust, rather than less, people have toward one another.[10] This might surprise noneconomists, who think the phrase "competitive market" describes a dog-eat-dog cutthroat world of pure selfishness. Perhaps it won't surprise economists, though, who understand instead that highly competitive markets are an institutional framework that requires people to work for the ends of others and that eliminates anyone's ability to exert undue influence or push for an unfair bargain. In competitive markets, everyone is a price-taker rather than a price-maker. Most laypeople have no idea how prices emerge, or why, from an economic standpoint, competitive markets are more desirable than noncompetitive ones. Nevertheless, they have internalized the norm that competitive markets make others trustworthy, while monopsonistic or monopolistic models make them less trustworthy.

Relatedly, Paul Zak and Stephen Knack have shown that market societies also tend to be high-trust societies, while nonmarket societies tend to be low-trust societies.[11] One of the major questions about any society is whether its inhabitants exhibit generalized social trust. Generalized social trust means that people expect strangers—including waiters, auto mechanics, lawyers, or others with whom they do business—to do their part, to keep their word, fulfill their contracts on time, be honest in their representations, and so on. It turns out that different societies have different levels of generalized social trust. New Zealand and Denmark have more generalized trust than the United States or Germany, which in turn have much more generalized trust than Russia or Afghanistan. However, in general, there is a strong positive correlation between how market-oriented an economy is and the level of generalized social trust. This appears to be causal, not merely a correlation, because as countries become more economically liberal, they tend also to develop higher levels of trust.

Omar Al-Ubaydli, Daniel Houser, and colleagues have shown that "priming" people with words related to markets and trade makes them *more* (not less!) trusting, trustworthy, and fair in experiments.[12] Many philosophers have argued, on the contrary, that introducing a market mindset, or reminding people about the concepts of money and profit, would somehow cause them to switch modes of

---

[10] P. Francois and T. Van Ypersele, "Doux Commerces: Does Market Competition Cause Trust?," CEPR Discussion Paper No. DP7368 (2009).

[11] Paul Zak and Stephen Knack, "Trust and Growth," *Economic Journal* 111 (2001): 295–321.

[12] Al-Ubayli, et al., "The Causal Effect of Market Priming on Trust: An Experimental Investigation Using Randomized Control," *PLoS One* 8/3 (2013): e55968. doi: 10.1371/journal.pone.0055968.

thinking, moving from prosocial attitudes toward more selfish behaviors. On the contrary, Al-Ubaydli and his colleagues have run a wide range of experimental economics games in which people have opportunities to exhibit various moral dispositions. They find that experimental groups who are made to think about market-oriented concepts behave *better* and in a more prosocial way than control groups who are not so primed. That is, when we get people into the market mindset, they become *nicer*.

Mitchell Hoffman and John Morgan found, contrary to everyone's expectations, that "adult populations deliberately selected from two cutthroat internet industries—domain trading and adult entertainment (pornography)" are "more prosocial than [undergraduate] students: they are more altruistic, trusting, trustworthy, and lying averse."[13]

One reason why critics of markets expect markets to corrupt us is that, in their view, money has a kind of negative or degenerate social meaning. As Terence Mitchell and Amy Mickel summarize, "In the conventional [that is, contemporary Western] economic perspective, money is viewed as a utilitarian commodity that is ordinary, mundane, impersonal, and neutral. It is profane, with only quantitative meanings."[14] Note that Mitchell and Mickel do not mean to endorse this view of money. Rather, their point is that contemporary Westerners have imbued money with this kind of socially constructed meaning. However, ample sociological and anthropological work shows that this meaning is not universally shared. Some non-Western cultures, and Western culture itself at various times, did not ascribe this kind of profane meaning to money.[15]

Regardless, given that Westerners have in fact today imbued money with such meanings, this may mean that market exchanges or putting a price on something may change how people think of it, perhaps causing them to shift from thinking in terms of higher or intrinsic goods and instead to focus on instrumental goods and personal satisfaction. Or so critics claim.

---

[13] Mitchell Hoffman and John Morgan, "Who's Naughty? Who's Nice? Experiments on Whether Pro-Social Workers Are Selected out of Cutthroat Business Environments," *Journal of Economic Behavior & Organization* 109 (2015): 173-87.

[14] Terence R. Mitchell and Amy E Mickel, "The Meaning of Money: An Individual-Difference Perspective," *Academy of Management Review* 24 (1999): 568-78.

[15] Viviana Zelizer, "The Price and Value of Children: The Case of Children's Insurance," *American Journal of Sociology* 86 (1981): 1036-56.; Viviana Zelizer, "The Social Meaning of Money: 'Special Moneys,'" *American Journal of Sociology* 95 (1989): 342-77; Viviana Zelizer, "The Creation of Domestic Currencies," *American Economic Review Papers and Proceedings* 84, (May 1994), 138-42; Viviana Zelizer, "The Many Enchantments of Money," in *Sociological Visions*, ed. Kai Erickson (New York: Rowman and Littlefield 1997), 138-48.

A recent study by Gabriele Camera and his colleagues finds more ambiguous results than that. The BBC reported that the study discovered that "money can reduce trust in groups."[16] But that's a misleading interpretation of the study. Camera and his colleagues played a series of experimental games in which people could choose to cooperate or not, and could choose to be generous or selfish when cooperating.[17] They found that introducing money into small groups made players more selfish and less cooperative—as the BBC reported. But they *also* found that introducing money into large groups made them less selfish and more cooperative. Perhaps the negative half of this experiment is not so surprising—in our culture, introducing money into small-scale, personal interactions signals estrangement. If you introduce money into a small-scale relationship, you signal a lack of trust and an intention to have a more instrumental relationship. Yet in large-scale communities and among strangers, introducing money enables trust. It's a sign of cooperativeness.

At any rate, even these results may depend on the contingent meaning Westerners attach to money. In societies where money does not signal *profane, utilitarian, impersonal*, and so on, presumably introducing money within more intimate relationships would not lead to less prosocial behavior. Yet even within Western societies, despite money's somewhat negative social meaning, introducing money into relationships between strangers enhances rather than undermines trust.

Radin on the Supposedly Corrupting Effects of Economic Rhetoric

Numerous critics of markets claim markets corrupt us because putting a price on something transforms the kind of value that thing has. As we saw above, though, such critics frequently rely on a priori arguments or highly ambiguous empirical studies to defend this claim.

For instance, Margaret Jane Radin argues that markets corrupt us, but one of her main strategies for trying to demonstrate this is to point to the *words* that economists use in their theories. For instance, at a public talk at the University of Colorado, she argued that markets in adoption rights would corrupt parents' character.[18] For evidence, she did not cite empirical work on how such markets affect people's actual behaviors or attitudes. Rather, she pulled out some work by Gary Becker describing parents as having a demand curve for children; Becker further stated that as the price of children grew higher, the quantity of children demanded would diminish. Radin complained at length that the language of eco-

---

[16] http://www.bbc.co.uk/news/science-environment-23623157.
[17] Gabriele Camera, Marco Casari, and Maria Bigoni, "Money and Trust among Strangers,"*Proceedings of the National Academy of Sciences* 110 (2013): 14889-93.
[18] Margaret Jane Radin, "The Moral Limits of Free Markets," public lecture, University of Colorado, April 4, 2016.

nomics—which she calls "market rhetoric"—is dehumanizing. Thus, she concludes, markets corrupt us.

Frankly, her argument is silly. One reason it's silly is that it misunderstands what Becker says. A demand curve for a good does not mean that the good in question has no intrinsic value. I think my own life has intrinsic value, but as the price of saving my life rises, my willingness and ability to pay to save it falls. Second, Becker is providing a model for how to describe human behavior from a third-person standpoint. He is not providing an account of the internal dialogue or attitudes actual people use. In the same way, a physicist asked to explain how people catch balls would explain that there are physics equations which explain the path of the ball, and that people skilled at catching balls track the physics equations. But that doesn't mean ball catchers actually think in terms of the equations—in fact, they don't. They instead use a heuristic that happens to track the underlying physics. Accordingly, someone like Radin might complain that describing human behavior with physics equations is dehumanizing, but no one would think that physicists describing people playing catch somehow causes those people to think of themselves as mere machines.

Most people are entirely ignorant of basic economics and do not think in terms of supply and demand curves. Thus, at worst, Radin's complaint could be that perhaps studying economics makes people more selfish or nasty or tends to corrupt them in various ways. She offers no evidence to that effect. But in the end, what she calls "market rhetoric" is not the actual rhetoric or modes of thought people use on the market, but instead the terminology and models a small number of professional economists use to explain human behavior. A priori, we should no more expect this to be corrupting than the terminology physicists, biologists, or other scientists use when describing human behavior.

BLOOD MARKETS: CROWDING OUT AND LOW QUALITY

Closely related to the selfishness objection is the claim that markets crowd out virtue. The idea is that people would generally be willing to do good things for free, but once markets are introduced, they switch from public-spirited giving to self-interested behavior. They are willing to do good things only for money. Worse, says the Crowding-Out Objection, sometimes paying people to do that thing means *less* of it gets done.

For instance, Radin offers a version of the crowding-out objections, which she calls the domino theory. She claims that if we allow people to buy and sell certain things, this will crowd out the altruistic donation of that thing. Therefore, we should ban such sales. She summarizes her view as follows: "The domino theory implicitly makes two claims: First, as a normative claim, that it is important for a nonmarket regime to exist; and second, as an empirical premise, that a nonmarket regime cannot coexist with a market regime."[19]

Before reviewing the empirical evidence, we should ask whether it's a good objection a priori. To illustrate, imagine that in the absence of payment, roughly ten thousand people are willing to volunteer to teach college classes full time in the United States. Once being a professor comes with full salary and benefits, though, it's easy to find over 750,000 people willing to provide that service. However, now only 100 people would be willing to teach for free; 9,900 of the original 10,000 volunteers now hold out for cash. In that case, should we bemoan that paying professors increases the supply of professors but decreases the supply of potential volunteers? That's not obvious to me.

Richard Titmuss argued in *The Gift Relationship* that paying for blood donations would sometimes result in fewer willing donors, and would, at other times, result in worse quality blood. Titmuss argued that compensating for blood donations would replace altruistic motives with selfish financial ones, and that people would no longer be engaged in a gift relationship but would, instead, be involved in a simple financial transaction, an exchange of commodities. He argued that under such conditions, unless the price of blood were very high, few people would donate. Further, he claimed that financial incentives would lead the wrong kind of people—alcoholics, bums, the sickly poor—to sell blood, and so lead to lower-quality blood supplies on average. Healthy, affluent people might give blood, but they wouldn't be willing to sell blood for the low market price—they see that as beneath them. On the other hand, homeless people and others who tend to be sick might be willing to take that price.

The evidence suggests Titmuss is wrong. Researchers Nicola Lacetera, Mario Macis, and Robert Slonim have done a series of scientific experiments on what affects blood donations. They find, contrary to Titmuss, that economic incentives such as gift cards do in fact increase blood donations and do not affect the quality of the blood received.[20] They complain that the World Health Organization has for forty years advised against paying for blood, but the WHO, like Titmuss, was using data from uncontrolled experiments and nonscientific surveys. Titmuss's complaint is based on bad data, they claim.

Cécile Fabre notes that blood selling is legal in the United States but illegal in England. Despite that, she notes, more or less the same percentage of Americans and English donate blood (and they donate with the same regularity), although some Americans also sell blood.[21] In a comprehensive study, sociologist Kieran Healy found that what determines the quality and quantity of blood given is *not*

---

[19] Margaret Jane Radin, "Justice and the Market Domain," *Nomos* 31 (1989): 165–97, at 173.
[20] N. Lacetera, M. Macis, and R. Slonim, "Economic rewards to motivate blood donations," *Science* 340 (2013): 927–28.
[21] Cécile Fabre, *Whose Body is it Anyway?* (New York: Oxford University Press, 2006).

whether blood is bought or sold, but a wide range of other factors in how blood is produced.

More recently, William English and Peter Jaworski gained access to a massive data set on nearly every paid plasma clinic in the United States. The data showed not merely where the clinics are located but how much paid blood was collected in any given month over a period more than a decade. Using these data, they were able to prove not only that paid plasma leads to an overall higher supply of blood but that for most plasma sellers, altruistic concerns remain a significant reason why they supply blood. They found that, pace Titmuss, the blood came from higher, not lower, quality "sources." But most intriguing of all, they found that when a paid-plasma clinic enters an area and advertises for paid plasma, in both the short and long term this induces more people to *donate* blood for *free* at the Red Cross and elsewhere. Paid plasma not only increases the supply of blood overall but actually increases the supply of *donated* blood.[22] At least in the case of blood markets, the evidence strongly suggests that markets do not crowd out altruistic motives.

What about in general? Here, major meta-analyses have arrived at contradictory conclusions. Judy Cameron conducted two separate meta-analyses on the so-called overjustification effect, with a different coauthor for each. (The overjustification effect occurs when introducing an external motivation reduces or eliminates a person's internal motivation. For instance, imagine that offering a child a cash reward for practicing violin causes her to stop valuing violin for its own sake.) One study analyzed ninety-six experimental studies that compared subjects who received an extrinsic reward to those who received no reward.[23] The other study assessed a quarter century of research on the overjustification effect. The result for the former meta-analysis was that, "overall, reward does not decrease intrinsic motivation." A small negative effect was obtained only when "expected tangible rewards are given to individuals simply for doing a task." In the case of the latter meta-analysis, the conclusion was that the crowding-out effect of extrinsic rewards, like money, on intrinsic interest and creativity was only observable "under highly restricted, easily avoidable conditions."[24] They also concluded that getting a positive effect on generalized creativity from extrinsic rewards is "easily attainable using procedures derived from behavior theory."

---

[22] Peter Jaworski and William English, "Paid Plasma Has Not Decreased Unpaid Blood Donations," working paper, 2009.

[23] Judy Cameron and W. David Pierce, "Reinforcement, Reward, and Intrinsic Motivation: A Meta-Analysis," *Review of Educational Research* 64 (1994): 363–423.

[24] Robert Eisenberger and Judy Cameron. "Detrimental Effects of Reward: Reality or Myth?," *American Psychologist* 51 (1996): 1154–66.

That said, other researchers have challenged these results.²⁵ At the very least, though, we do not have strong evidence for the kind of crowding-out that critics of markets often cite.

TOLERANCE AND MARKETS

Most people think markets make us more selfish and less trustworthy. However, as we just saw, the available empirical evidence speaks against this. In fact, markets make us more trusting and trustworthy, and more cooperative.

Might markets have other ennobling effects? François-Marie Voltaire wrote in 1733:

> Go into the London Stock Exchange—a more respectable place than many a court—and you will see representatives of all nations gathered there for the service of mankind. There the Jew, the Mohammedan, and the Christian deal with each other as if they were of the same religion, and give the name of infidel only to those who go bankrupt. There the Presbyterian trusts the Anabaptist, and the Anglican accepts the Quaker's promise. On leaving these peaceful and free assemblies, some go to the synagogue, others go to drink … others go to their church to wait for the inspiration of God, their hats on their heads, and all are content.²⁶

Here, Voltaire asserts that markets make us *less* rather than more inclined to discriminate against one another.

More recently, economist Gary Becker argued that the market has a tendency to reduce unjust discrimination—in particular, the more competitive the market is, the more it will tend to eliminate racial and other forms of discrimination.²⁷ He asks us to suppose that people have a "taste for discrimination"—they prefer to hire white workers instead of equally high-quality black workers. This will tend to reduce blacks' wages. However, this discrimination gives firms willing to hire blacks an advantage. Black labor becomes a comparative bargain—by hypothesis, it is equally productive but at lower prices. Less-discriminatory firms can hire blacks at a lower rate, sell their products for less (because the labor costs are lower), and make higher profits. The more *other* people discriminate against blacks, the more a business owner would benefit from hiring them. The market thus *punishes* taste discrimination; it makes discrimination come at the expense of profitability.

---

[25] E. L. Deci, R. Koestner, and R.M. Ryan, "A Meta-Analytic Review of Experiments Examining the Effects of Extrinsic Rewards on Intrinsic Motivation," *Psychological Bulletin* 125 (1999): 627–68.

[26] Voltaire, *Letters on England* (Lexington, KY: Seven Treasures Publications, 2008), letter 6.

[27] Gary Becker, *The Economics of Discrimination* (Chicago: University of Chicago Press, 1957).

South Africa provides a good example of Becker's theory in action. In the early 1900 s, despite threats of violence and legal sanctions, white mine owners fired nearly all of their highly paid white workers in order to hire lower-paid blacks. The South African government had to pass the apartheid laws to stop them from hiring blacks.[28] As Becker's theory predicts, to sustain discrimination in competitive labor markets often requires government intervention.

The economist Jennifer Roback notes that the economics of the streetcar business weighed heavily against providing separate compartments. Jim Crow (the set of laws in the American South requiring segregated seating and bathroom facilities) was expensive. White businesspeople who owned train, streetcar, or lunch counter businesses may have been racist, but Jim Crow rules made them *pay* for their racism. Train companies lost money by having to run extra train cars. Lunch counters lost money by having to supply twice as many bathrooms. Absent laws forcing them to segregate whites and blacks, many businesses owners were unwilling to do so. If you read old newspaper editorials from the Southern states under Jim Crow, you'll frequently find editors complaining about how greedy businessmen just chase the dollar and are unwilling to uphold the moral ideal of segregation.[29] Southern states thus intervened to *require* private companies to mistreat blacks. The laws were there because many businesses did not discriminate until forced to do so.

Roback adds that the Southern states had a wide range of laws designed to stop blacks from competing for work. Enticement laws forbade white farm owners from trying to hire black farmworkers away from other farmers during the planting or harvesting season. Black farmworkers who tried to leave their jobs for higher-paying jobs could be thrown in jail. Vagrancy laws required blacks to be employed at all times. Any unemployed black man was considered a vagrant and could be put on a chain gang. Thus, blacks could not search for better employment; they had to stick with whatever job they had. Emigrant-agent laws forbade white recruiters from enticing laborers to leave their current cities or states to take jobs elsewhere. These and other laws and regulations were created in order to *stop* the market from helping blacks.

Markets give people an economic incentive to overlook their differences and instead work together. And empirical studies show that once people work together, they tend to *stop caring* about those differences. It's not merely that people put up with those whom they hate in order to make a buck; rather, they tend to stop hating their trade partners. This is why market societies are also usually the most

---

[28] Linda Gorman, "Discrimination," *The Concise Encyclopedia of Economics* (2013), online edition, http://www.econlib.org/library/Enc1/Discrimination.html.

[29] Jennifer Roback, "The Political Economy of Segregation: The Case of Segregated Streetcars," *Journal of Economic History* 56 (1986): 893–917.

tolerant societies.[30] Competitive market pressures and the desire for profit push people to see past racial or religious divides. This explains Voltaire's observation that at the London Stock Exchange, people of all races and creeds came together to do business.[31]

Evidence from Macro Data

Experimental economics generally finds that people from market societies are more trusting, trustworthy, fair, and cooperative than people from traditional, socialist, or otherwise nonmarket societies. What about other more macro-level indicators?

The Charity Aids Foundation World Giving Index measures how likely people in different countries are to give money to charity, to help strangers, and volunteer.[32] Fig. 1 below illustrates the positive relationship between how market-oriented a society is (as measured by the Fraser Institute's Index of Economic Freedom) and how "giving" it is.

Another way to test the hypothesis that markets are corrupting is to see whether there is a relationship between how market-oriented a society is and how much political corruption there is. As figure 2 below shows, contrary to what the Selfishness Argument predicts, there is a robust *positive* correlation between a country's degree of economic freedom (as measured in by the Fraser Institute's economic freedom ratings) and its lack of corruption (as measured by Transparency International's Corruption Perceptions Index[33]). A closer look at the data also reveals that the most marketized societies tend also to be significantly *above* the trend line.

A closely related argument holds that markets corrupt societies as a whole, not necessarily by corrupting individual virtue but by increasing the degree of economic inequality, which in turn leads to greater class division and mutual animosity. But the relationship between how capitalist a society is and how unequal it is complex. As Simon Kuznets demonstrated years ago, when societies first start to experience economic growth (usually as a result of market liberalization), they tend to become more unequal, but then they hit a turning point and move

---

[30] E.g., see Niclas Berggren and Therese Nilsson, "Does Economic Freedom Foster Tolerance?," *Kyklos* 66 (2013): 177–207; Saumitra Jha, "Trade, Institutions, and Ethnic Tolerance: Evidence from South Asia," *American Political Science Review* 107 (2013): 806–32.

[31] Jha, "Trade, Institutions, and Ethnic Tolerance."

[32] See the Charity Aids Foundation, *World Giving Index* 2013, https://www.cafonline.org/PDF/WorldGivingIndex2013_1374AWEB.pdf.

[33] Transparency International, *Corruption Perceptions Index 2012*, http://cpi.transparency.org/cpi2012/results.

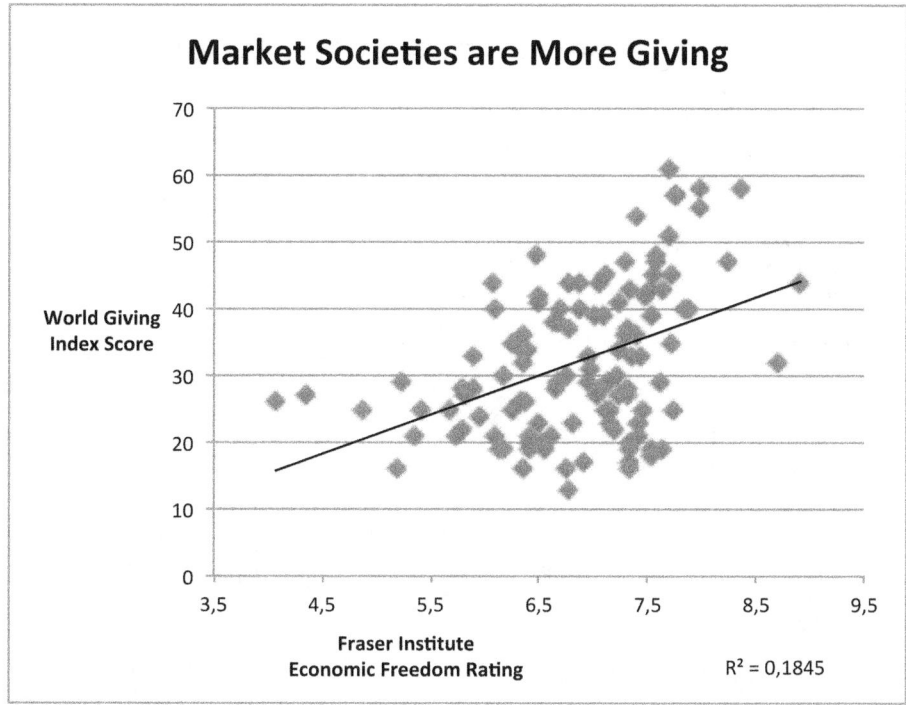

Fig. 1. Markets and Generosity

back toward more equality (even before government-base redistribution). In figure 3, I plot the Fraser Institute's 2014 economic freedom ratings against the World Bank's most recently available (that is, closest to 2014) GINI coefficient rating. Contrary to what critics of markets may expect, the relationship between markets and inequality in recent decades is slightly negative.

Political theorist Benjamin Barber often complained that markets would erode citizens' civic virtue. To argue for this, he relied not on empirical evidence but instead on an a priori philosophical argument. He asserted that markets induce people to think of freedom as an ability to fulfill their personal desires rather than freedom as collective autonomous control over rules of society.[34] He offers no surveys or data showing that markets actually change anyone's attitudes about freedom, so readers have no reason to believe him. Regardless, contrary to what Barber would expect, in fact there is a slight positive relationship, in modern democracies, between how capitalist a country is and how much its citizens participate in politics.[35]

---

[34] Benjamin Barber, *Consumed* (New York: W. W. Norton and Company, 2008), 131–32.
[35] Brennan and Jaworski, *Markets without Limits*, 140–41.

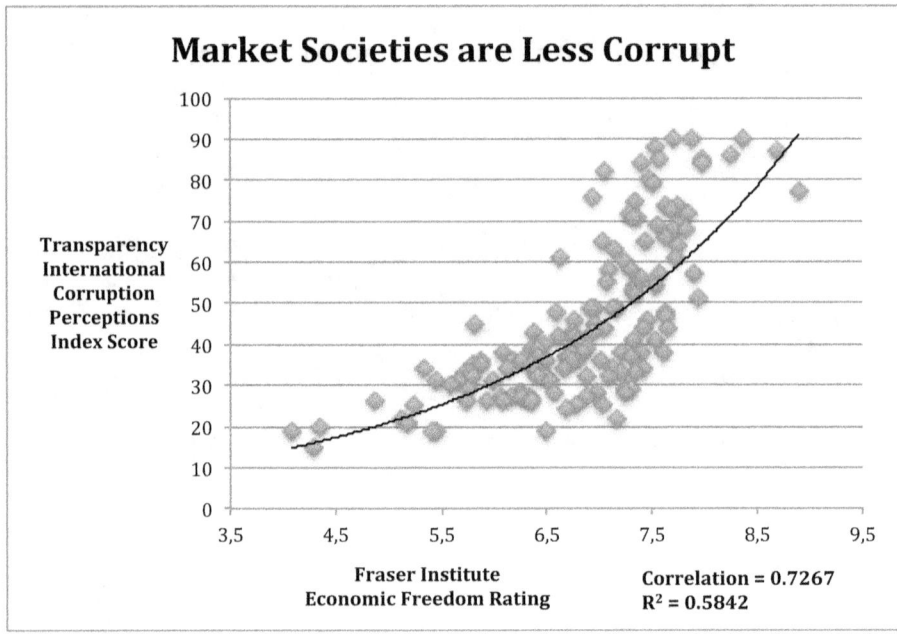

Fig. 2. Economic Freedom vs. Corruption

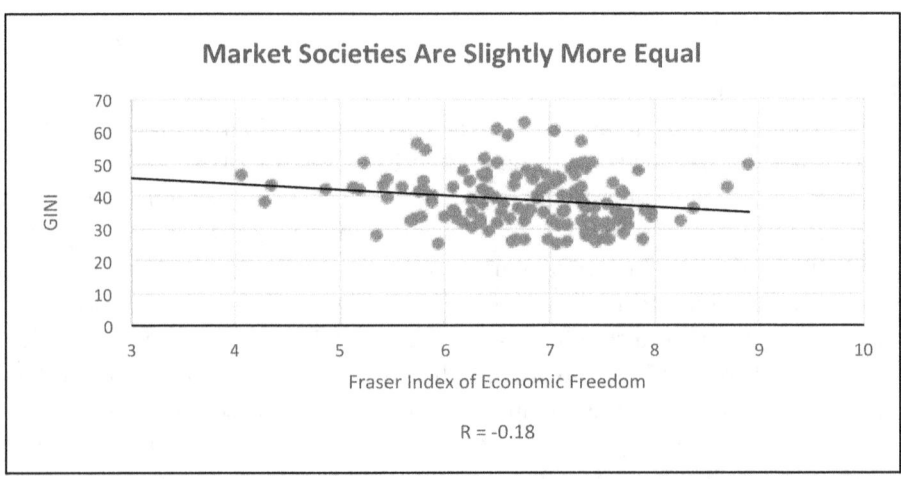

Fig. 3. GINI Coefficient and Capitalism

None of the studies or correlations mentioned here are definitive on their own. I wouldn't expect a market skeptic to look at figure 1 and conclude, "Well, that settles it. Markets make nice." My point here is to shift the burden of proof. Critics of markets often rely on philosophical or armchair arguments; it seems obvious to them that markets must corrupt our character. They claim that market relations are inherently about promoting one's self-interest, and then conclude that markets must induce greater selfishness. Such a priori argumentation won't do; we instead need to test what market exposure and participation actually do to people.

Why Philosophers Assume Markets Corrupt

Many philosophers and laypeople tend to assume that markets have a corrosive effect on our character. As I've explained above, empirical work generally finds instead that it has an ameliorative effect, though there are special cases where introducing money or offering payment can have negative effects on people's motivations or attitudes. Nevertheless, philosophers tend to continue to worry that markets must somehow corrupt us.

My suspicion is that they will not find the empirical studies convincing because they think monetary prices are inherently incompatible with thinking of things as having intrinsic value. Elizabeth Anderson, Margaret Jane Radin, Benjamin Barber, Michael Sandel, and others hold that to put a price on something means that the thing has only instrumental value, that its value consists in its ability to satisfy our desires, and that it must be fungible without loss with anything else of the same price. After all, if the US government says a human life is worth $7.5 million in its expected utility calculations, isn't the government thereby expressing that human life has the same kind of value that money does, and, worse, that one human life has the same value as 7.5 million Ritter candy bars? The answer is no—this represents a major misunderstanding of the meaning of prices and of utility theory in economics. Economists do not say that all things have only one kind of value, called utility, which is simply a function of desire satisfaction.

Rather, consider Rational Randy. Randy has a utility function, which is simply a ranking of all possible states of affairs from best to worse. Ties are permitted —if Randy is indifferent between A and B, then A and B occupy the same spot on his utility function. All of this is compatible with things having intrinsic value. I think my spouse and my dog have intrinsic value, but I would choose to save my spouse over my dog.

To say that Randy has a utility function is *not* to say that Randy thinks all values reduce to one *common denominator* called "utility." For Randy, there may indeed be a plurality of different kinds of values and modes of valuing. "Utility" in the economist's sense isn't the *fundamental value all things have.* Rather, it's just a way that economists *represent* Randy's preference rankings.

Most critics of markets accept that Randy can have an *ordinal* utility function, which ranks states of affairs from better to worse. After all, moral theorists try to construct what is in effect a moral utility function. Their worry is that putting it into a *cardinal* utility function with prices somehow is incompatible with things having intrinsic value. Isn't saying that everything has value equal *overall* to some monetary price just saying that everything's value *just is* its monetary price?

Again, the answer is no. In the 1940 s, Jonathan von Neumann and Osker Morgenstern showed that if you accept a few basic axioms about how rational people respond to *lotteries* and deal with *risk* (for example, that rational people prefer better prizes to worse prizes and better odds to worse odds), then one can mathematically translate any ordinal utility function into a cardinal utility function. That is, given A) Randy's ranking of all possible states of the world and B) Randy's rational way of choosing among lotteries, we generate C) a new utility function, in which all values can be expressed on a cardinal, numerical scale.[36] If we suppose that Randy also values money in the same way, we'll then be able to express this scale in monetary terms. It turns out that *every* possible set of trade-offs a rational agent might have—regardless of whether that agent is selfish or altruistic, amoral, immoral, or moral, a value monist or a pluralist, a Kantian or a utilitarian—can be expressed on a continuous, numerical utility scale in monetary terms. Again, that's not to say that the only thing that the agent really values is *utility,* money, or self-satisfaction, but just to say that we can correctly represent the agent's values on this one scale. All of this is compatible with holding that some things have more than instrumental value, or that not everything is fungible with money, or that there is a plurality of values. Economists can and do accept all of that.

---

[36] John Von Neumann and Oskar Morgenstern, *Theory of Games and Economic Behavior* (Princeton: Princeton University Press, 1944).

Understanding the Economic Impacts on Virtue and the Pursuit of Good

Paul Oslington

Among the various impacts of spheres on virtue and the pursuit of goods, none is more powerful than the impact of economics. Economists might object that markets are morally neutral. However, the impact of markets on virtue is widely recognized, although the exact channels and directions of the impact are debated.[1] No less an authority than Adam Smith expressed his concerns about the deleterious effects of the division of labor in the emerging market economy of eighteenth-century Britain.[2] The work of Bruni and Sugden is significant because it engages the recent virtue-ethical critique of market society directly.[3] They argue that the market is a practice, in the language of contemporary virtue ethics, and generates virtues such as "universality, enterprise and alertness, respect for the tastes of one's trading partners, trust and trustworthiness, acceptance of competition, self-help, non-rivalry, and stoicism about reward" (143). They see markets as having positive effects on virtue and the pursuit of goods.

As well as effects through participating in markets, there are also influences on virtue and the pursuit of goods through economic thinking, which is the lens through which we view markets. Contemporary mainstream economic theory is a well-developed and powerful set of analytical tools, built around a rational-choice theory of action where individuals maximize with given preferences and resources, and a preference-satisfaction view of human welfare. It is an approach closely associated, historically and conceptually, with utilitarian moral philoso-

---

[1] See, for instance, Albert O. Hirschman, "Rival Interpretations of Market Society: Civilizing, Destructive, or Feeble?," *Journal of Economic Literature* 20/4 (1982): 1463–84; and Jason Brennan, "Do Markets Corrupt?," in *Economics and the Virtues: Building a New Moral Foundation*, ed. J. A. Baker and M. D. White (New York: Oxford University Press, 2016).

[2] Adam Smith, *An Inquiry into the Nature and Causes of the Wealth of Nations* [1776], ed. R.H. Campbell, A.S. Skinner, and W.B. Todd (Oxford: Oxford University Press, 1976).

[3] Luigino S. Bruni and Robert Sugden, "Reclaiming Virtue Ethics for Economics," *Journal of Economic Perspectives* 27/4 (2013): 141–64.

phy. Among philosophers and theologians, this approach has been heavily criticized as unhealthily individualistic, too narrow in its account of human motivation, leaving no place for character or the virtues, and neglecting questions of ultimate purpose, among other criticisms. If even some of the criticisms of economists' approach is well founded, then the economists' approach is limited for considering the impact of markets on character formation, ethical education, and the communication of values.

The Rise of Economics

The rise of the market economy is indisputable. Markets of course existed long before their great expansion in eighteenth-century Britain—what many economic historians call the industrial revolution, what Adam Smith called the rise of commercial society, and what Marx called the rise of capitalism. Markets were important in medieval Europe and even in biblical times.[4]

The rise of economic thought to a central place in our culture is related to the rise of the market economy, although their relationship is complicated. Marx explained the rise of economics, or what he called "vulgar political economy," as the rise of an ideological superstructure to justify capitalism. He claimed that the exploitative and unstable nature of capitalism was laid bare by his own "scientific" political economy. Waterman connects the rise of economics with the decline of the cultural influence of theology.[5] He argues that economics replaced Christian theology as the authoritative discourse from the middle of the nineteenth century in Britain. Economics has similar theoretical structures and functions to theology, but better fits the new environment of the market economy than theology. This is part of the larger history of the separation of economics from Christian theology in Britain, America, and other regions.[6]

The rise of economics is documented in figure 1, which shows the use of the relevant terms in English-language books digitized by Google (using the Google N-gram tool outlined by J.B. Michel, et al.).[7] The term "political economy" gradu-

---

[4] Paul Oslington, "Economics and Biblical Studies," in *Oxford Bibliographies*, ed. C. Matthews (New York: Oxford University Press, 2015), http://www.oxfordbibliographies.com/.

[5] A. M. C. Waterman, *Revolution, Economics, and Religion: Christian Political Economy 1798-1833* (Cambridge: Cambridge University Press, 1991).

[6] Paul Oslington, "A Natural Law Framework for Economists Understanding Impacts on Virtue and the Pursuit of Goods." Paper Presented at University of Heidelberg Consultation on Economics and Theology, October 2018.

[7] J. B. Michel, et al., "Quantitative Analysis of Culture Using Millions of Digitized Books," *Science* 331(6014) (2011): 176-82.

ally grows in use through the nineteenth century, is superseded in the twentieth century by the term "economics," whose use accelerates in the early years of the twentieth century and continues to grow at a modest rate. Discussion of that construct of economic thinking, "the economy," takes off soon after the acceleration of the use of "economics." Figure 2 compares these economic terms with theology, showing that economics overtakes theology early in the twentieth century and continues well above it thereafter.

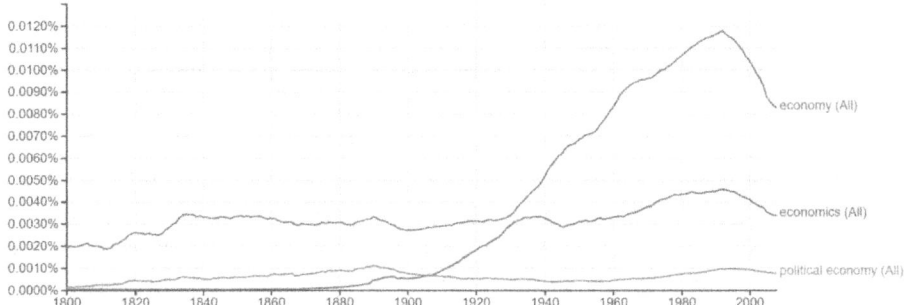

Fig. 1. Economics and Economy

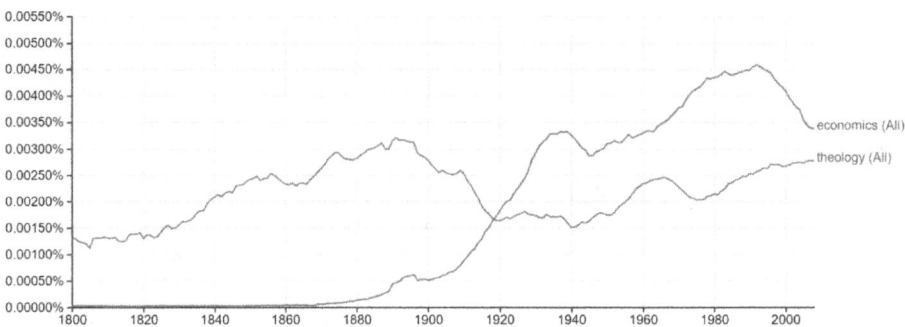

Fig. 2. Theology and Economics

What is the significance of this rise of the cultural importance of economics? Earlier discussions of the goods we should pursue as individuals and a society have been sidelined by economists' focus on what was regarded earlier regarded as instrumental to the goods we pursue—the generation of wealth. Mary Hirschfeld expresses this well: the "elevated status of economic concerns in modern culture" is understandable because in a

> liberal pluralistic culture ... the inability to achieve a shared understanding of the higher goods a society might pursue leads naturally to the thought that we should collectively work to ensure that the means for pursuing private understandings of the

higher good are broadly and abundantly available yet it is problematic because once the public square is shaped around the shared goal of achieving prosperity, the instrumental character of prosperity becomes obscured. We forget to ask what our material wealth is for and often end up sacrificing more important human goods for the sake of greater income.[8]

The Impact of Economics Is Mediated by Language and Models

In this chapter I am focusing on economic theory, which is the lens through which the market economy has been viewed since the rise of economics. Contemporary mainstream economics operates as a lens in several ways.

In contemporary society economists' powerful concept of rationality as maximization on given individual preferences pushes aside other accounts of rationality.[9] Note that this conception of rationality as maximization goes beyond many contemporary economists' more minimalist view of rationality as transitivity, reflexivity, and completeness of the ordering of choices (Shaun Hargreaves-Heap has surveyed economists' accounts of rationality).[10] Most economists see rationality as a tool for explaining and predicting, without any normative claims, and this position can be defended logically.[11] It cannot, however, be defended sociologically. When a discipline successfully explains and predicts phenomena, its methods and concepts inevitably acquire prestige and normative force. Other methods and concepts are pushed aside, and the discipline shapes the thinking of wider society about how things should be done.[12]

The teaching of economics (and its offshoot, business management) forms increasing an proportion of university students. In my own country, Australia, more than 40 percent of undergraduate students are studying for economics or business degrees, and even beyond this sphere, economics exerts an influence. Economists often claim that their discipline is a positive science and that they are merely teaching students a neutral set of tools. However, there is much evidence

---

[8] Mary L. Hirschfeld, *Aquinas and the Market: Toward a Humane Economy* (Cambridge, MA: Harvard University Press, 2018), 2.
[9] Gary S. Becker, "Nobel Lecture: The Economic Way of Looking at Human Behaviour," *American Economic Review* 101/3 (1993): 385–409.
[10] Shaun Hargreaves-Heap, *Rationality in Economics* (Oxford: Basil Blackwell, 1989).
[11] For instance, John Broome, "Is Rationality Normative?," *Disputatio* 11 (2008): 153–71.
[12] Arjo Klamer, "A Pragmatic View on Values in Economics," *Journal of Economic Methodology* 10/2: (2003): 191–212; Idem, *Speaking of Economics: How to Get in the Conversation* (New York: Routledge, 2007); Idem, *Doing the Right Thing: A Value Based Economy* (London: Ubiquity Press, 2017).

for the influence of economic teaching on behavior. The research of Frank, Gilovich, and Regan, for instance, found that studying economics made people less trusting, cooperative, and generous.[13]

In public policy, economic thinking is arguably even more powerful than in general society. Economic ways of thinking and criteria of evaluation dominate spheres such as health and education. It is difficult to conceive new public policy initiatives without some economic justification. Cost-benefit analysis is ubiquitous in these and other public-policy spheres.

Both in teaching and in public policy discussion, it is often the rhetoric around theory rather than economic theory itself that communicates messages such as maximization being the appropriate or even sole mode of rationality, the supreme value of efficiency, wealth as an end, and so forth. The economic theorists who plead that they are just theorists and not communicating any such messages should read Deirdre McCloskey's work on the rhetoric of some of the classic papers of economics.[14] The teachers who plead that they are just conveying a neutral set of theoretical tools to their students should read Colander and Klamer on the formation of economists, particularly at the graduate level. It is not a matter of the intentions of theorists or teachers, but of disciplinary cultures.[15]

Alternative Frameworks for Understanding Economic Impacts on Virtue and the Pursuit of Goods

There are alternative frameworks for considering the impact of the market on character formation, ethical education, and the communication of values. Many of these alternative frameworks do not throw away the powerful analytic tools of contemporary economics. In this chapter, I concentrate on natural-law approaches, which I believe are the most robust alternative to the approach of mainstream economics. But first it is worth briefly reviewing some of the other alternatives.

Augmented Rational-Choice Approaches
Some economists have responded to the criticisms of the neglect of virtue by augmenting mainstream rational-choice models. An example is the work of Menzies

---

[13] Robert H. Frank, T. Gilovich, and D. Regan, "Does Studying Economics Inhibit Cooperation?," *Journal of Economic Perspectives* 7/2 (1993): 159–71.

[14] Deirdre N. McColskey, *The Rhetoric of Economics* 2nd ed. (Madison: University of Wisconsin Press, 1998).

[15] David Colander and Arjo Klamer, *The Making of an Economist, Redux* (Princeton: Princeton University Press, 2007). This updates their earlier 1990 book, *The Making of an Economist*.

and Hay,[16] which connects with the recent literature on the economics of identity. Akerlof and Kranton, for instance, replace the standard maximization problem of the individual with maximization of what they call a "mixed motive valuation function," which values both the individual's own consumption and generosity to neighbors.[17]

This mixed-motive valuation function is $V = \theta^\alpha n^\alpha (s + n')^{1-\alpha}$, where n denotes income given to neighbors, s own consumption, n' income received from neighbors, α the share of income given to others, and θ^α identity indexed by giving to others, with $\theta \geq 1$. With this augmented value function, Akerlof and Kranton show that generosity can be advantageous for the individual, and they derive an optimal level of the generosity parameter α. Such augmentations allow virtue into the analysis only in the very limited sense of virtue as giving away resources to others.

Another example, which probes the motivational questions more deeply, is the work of Geoffrey Brennan and his coauthors.[18] The idea of Brennan and Hamlin, borrowing from the English economist Denis Robertson, is that virtue is essential to the functioning of society and scarce, and therefore should be economized by the institutions of society. Virtue here is synonymous with acting in the public interest. They are particularly interested in the question whether virtue-economizing institutions undermine virtue.

In their model, agents choose a disposition, either to be a virtuous agent, V, who values both income y and the public interest Z, so that $U_i = f[y_i, Z]$; or to be an egoistic agent, E, for whom $U_i = f[y_i]$. This disposition is unobservable. Furthermore, there are two sectors, a market sector, M, and politics, P. Individuals with disposition V employed in sector P promote the public good, while individuals with disposition E employed in sector P promote their own interests. The two types of individual act identically in sector M employment. Pursuing the public interest has a reward of value z for a V agent in the P sector, and b is the additional income extracted by an E agent employed in the P sector. Wages y^p and y^m in the sectors are fixed. E agents may be attracted to the P sector, but there is an imperfect screening mechanism that restrains their entry into that sector.

Brennan and Hamlin explore equilibria in the model under various values of b, z, y^p, and y^m and the screening efficiency parameter έ, most interesting of which

---

[16] Gordon Menzies and Donald Hay, "Self and Neighbours: Towards a Christian Anthropology in Economics," *Economic Record* 88 (June 2012): 137–48.

[17] George Akerlof and Rachel Kranton, *Identity Economics* (Princeton: Princeton University Press, 2010), 142.

[18] Geoffrey Brennan and Alan Hamlin, "Economizing on Virtue," *Constitutional Political Economy* 6/1 (1995): 35–56; Michael Baurmann and Geoffrey Brennan, "On Virtue Economics," in *Economics and the Virtues: Building a New Moral Foundation*, ed. J. A. Baker and M. D. White (New York: OUP, 2016), 119–40.

is where b > z, screening is inefficient, and $y^p > y^m$. Here the screening mechanism supports agents choosing the virtuous disposition (globally at least—the comparative statics are more complex), which they interpret as a case of institutional arrangements promoting rather than undermining virtue, and in a sense economizing on virtue. As they emphasize, though, other equilibria in the model and variations of the model can generate the opposite result. This is an interesting exercise in relation to their question whether institutional arrangements support or undermine virtue, but the definition of virtue as acting in the public interest means it does not help very much in addressing the issues of this paper. Like the analysis by Menzies and Hay, it leaves the underlying logic of individual maximization of arbitrary preferences intact. Ends and virtues in the Aristotelian sense are not addressed.

Kantian Approaches

One way of moving outside the framework of contemporary mainstream economics, heavily influenced as it is by utilitarianism, is to connect with Kantian deontological approaches to action and evaluation. Martin Hollis brought Hume and Kant into dialogue with economists' approach to rationality and evaluation,[19] and Mark D. White offers a more recent, more developed engagement with Kant.[20] Kieran Sharpe discusses planning and suggests that Kant offers a way of resolving analytical dilemmas of planning.[21]

None of this work, though, has so far led to formal modelling. It is interesting that both Sharpe and White emphasize the closeness of their work to Aristotelian natural-law approaches.

The Capability Approach

Perhaps the most influential writing outside the utilitarian framework has been Amartya Sen's capability approach.[22] It has been particularly influential in development studies.[23] The capability approach considers well-being to consist in freedom and functionings, where a functioning is a way of being and acting that people have reason to value. Freedom in this approach is valued both in itself and as a

---

[19] Martin Hollis, *The Cunning of Reason* (Cambridge: Cambridge University Press, 1987).
[20] Mark D. White, *Kantian Ethics and Economics: Autonomy, Dignity, and Character* (Stanford, CA: Stanford University Press, 2011).
[21] Kieran Sharpe, "Plans, Commitments and Practical Norms of Reason," *International Journal of Social Economics* 30/7–8 (2003): 893–905.
[22] Amartya Sen, *On Ethics and Economics* (Oxford: Blackwell, 1987); Idem, *Development as Freedom* (Oxford: Oxford University Press, 1999); Amartya Sen and Martha C. Nussbaum, eds., *The Quality of Life* (Oxford: Clarendon Press, 1993).
[23] Sabina Alkire, *Valuing Freedoms: Sen's Capability Approach and Poverty Reduction* (New York: Oxford University Press, 2002).

means of achieving valuable functionings. Sen is reluctant to provide a list of functionings—especially a list valid for all times and places—flowing from his emphasis on reasoning and discussion to determine what functionings are valuable. He does insist that functionings are incommensurable, though in practice the measurement of well-being requires some index of functionings.

Sen's approach has obvious connections with an Aristotelian natural-law approach, as Sen himself discusses, acknowledging the influence of his sometime collaborator Martha Nussbaum in bringing these out. Nussbaum is more willing than Sen to ground the capability approach in human nature and to provide a list of valuable functionings. A fuller comparison of Sen's capability approach with Aristotle is provided by Ricardo Crespo.[24]

Sen's capability approach has been operationalized in Stiglitz, Sen, and Fitoussi's work on well-being measurement for the French government,[25] in Sen's involvement with the UNDP Human Development Reports, and in multidimensional poverty indices such as those constructed by Sabina Alkire and James Foster.[26] The approach here is to construct a matrix of individuals' functionings, and then, if we are interested in poverty or deprivation, we can set thresholds for various functionings and derive deprivation matrices and indices of deprivation.

Aristotelian/Thomistic Natural-Law Approaches

In my view, the most robust alternative to economists' current approach is Aristotelian/Thomistic natural-law theory. This approach rejects the consequentialism of which the economists' maximization approach is a special case, and its moral realism contrasts with the subjectivism of the economic approach. Natural law can bring virtue and purpose into play in a way that economists' current approaches and the various other alternatives cannot. In his survey of natural-law theory, Mark Murphy takes Thomas Aquinas to be the paradigmatic natural-law theorist, for whom natural law is an expression of divine providence, known to all and binding on all.[27] This approach is distinguished from others by its moral re-

---

[24] Ricardo F. Crespo, "On Sen and Aristotle," IAE Business School–Austral University Working Paper, 2010; Idem, *A Reassessment of Aristotle's Economic Thought* London, Routledge, 2013.

[25] Joseph E. Stiglitz, Amartya Sen, and J. P. Fitoussi, *Report of the Commission of the Measurement of Economic Performance and Social Progress* (Paris, 2009), at www.stiglitz-sen-fitoussi.fr.

[26] Sabina Alkire, "The Capability Approach and Well-Being Measurement for Public Policy," in *Oxford Handbook on Well-Being and Public Policy*, ed. M. Adler and M. Fleurbaey (Oxford: Oxford University Press, 2016).

[27] Mark C Murphy, "The Natural Law Tradition in Ethics," *Stanford Encyclopedia of Philosophy* (2009).

alism and its fundamental principles, which state that good is to be done and evil avoided, and that human action responds rationally to the good.

There is a vast literature on Aristotelian/Thomistic natural-law theories of action and ethics. This approach says that action both is and should be oriented towards the fundamental goods of human life. These goods are natural, in that they comport both with human nature and the nature of the world. In religious versions of natural law, the claim is that fundamental human goods comport with creation, which expresses the will of God. In all versions, acting in pursuit of goods is the pathway to human flourishing—which is a broader concept than the notion of experienced happiness that is a popular topic of the moment among economists, even broader than life satisfaction, which is the focus in the international happiness surveys. Virtues in an Aristotelian/Thomistic framework are acquired dispositions which assist humans in pursuing goods—they are not ends in themselves. Wealth in this framework is necessary for the achievement of some goods, but treating wealth as an end in itself would be a major error.

Natural-law theory and virtue ethics have experienced revival in recent years, after their eclipse in the eighteenth and nineteenth centuries by the utilitarianism of Jeremy Bentham and the Mills, James and John Stuart.[28] Aristotle as much as Thomas Aquinas has been the reference point for this revival, represented by theorists such as Elizabeth Anscombe, Philippa Foot, Martha Nussbaum, Jean Porter, Julia Annas, and, most of all, Alasdair MacIntyre.[29] The revival is not just a Roman Catholic phenomenon and includes a renewal of interest in Protestant natural-law thinkers such as John Calvin, Hugo Grotius, and Samuel von Pufendorf (for instance by Stephen Grabill and David Van Drunen).[30] Even Pentecostals such as Shane Clifton have shared in this revival.[31]

---

[28] Alessandro Passerin D'Entrèves, *Natural Law: An Introduction to Legal Philosophy*, 2nd ed. (London: Hutchinson, 1970).

[29] Philippa Foot, "Virtues and Vices," in *Virtues and Vices and Other Essays in Moral Philosophy* (Oxford: Blackwell, 1978); Martha C. Nussbaum, *The Fragility of Goodness: Luck and Ethics in Greek Tragedy and Philosophy* (Cambridge: Cambridge University Press, 1986); Jean Porter, *The Recovery of Virtue: The Relevance of Aquinas for Christian Ethics* (Louisville, KY: Westminster John Knox Press, 1990); Idem, *Nature as Reason: A Thomistic Theory of the Natural Law* (Grand Rapids: Eerdmans, 2004); Julia Annas, *The Morality of Happiness* (New York: Oxford University Press, 1995); Alasdair MacIntyre, *After Virtue—A Study in Moral Theory* (London: Duckworth, 1981); Idem, *Whose Justice? Which Rationality?* (London: Duckworth, 1988); Idem, *Three Rival Versions of Moral Enquiry: Encyclopaedia, Genealogy, and Tradition* (South Bend, IN: University of Notre Dame Press, 1990); Idem, *Ethics in the Conflicts of Modernity: An Essay on Desire, Practical Reasoning, and Narrative* (Cambridge: Cambridge University Press, 2016).

[30] Stephen Grabill, *Rediscovering the Natural Law in Reformed Theological Ethics* (Grand Rapids, MI: Wm. B. Eerdmans, 2006); David Van Drunen, *Natural Law and the Two King-*

A recent development has been the new natural-law theory that arose in the 1980 s as an attempt—led by Germain Grisez, John Finnis, Robert George, and others—to renew Catholic moral theology.[32] It is sometimes portrayed as a new reading of Thomas Aquinas,[33] although new natural-law theorists explicitly depart from Thomas on many points.[34] New natural-law claims to be an integrated theory of action and well-being that is superior to available alternatives, in particular avoiding the common criticism of natural-law theories that "ought" cannot be derived from "is." It does this by making the derivation of the goods of human life (such as knowledge, excellence in work and play, friendship, peace, consistency) an empirical matter, and then action to achieve these goods a matter of practical reason. Importantly, the goods cannot be reduced to a single index to permit maximization, and actions cannot be derived theoretically from the goods. Most of the proponents of new natural law, though Catholic philosophers and moral theologians, claim that the theory operates independently of divine revelation. As Rufus Black laments, Grisez's vigorous defense of papal teaching on sexuality has distracted many commentators from the deeper issues of the coherence and value of the theory.[35]

---

doms: *A Study in the Development of Reformed Social Thought* (Grand Rapids, MI: Eerdmans, 2010).

[31] Shane Clifton, *Crippled Grace: Disability, Virtue Ethics, and the Good Life* (Waco, TX: Baylor University Press, 2018).

[32] Key texts include Germain Grisez, Joseph Boyle ,and John Finnis, "Practical Principles, Moral Truth, and Ultimate Ends," *American Journal of Jurisprudence* 32 (1987): 99–151; John Finnis, *Natural Law and Natural Rights* (Oxford: Clarendon Press, 1980); Germain Grisez, "Natural Law, God, Religion, and Human Fulfillment," *American Journal of Jurisprudence* 46 (2001): 3–36; Germain Grisez, "The True Ultimate End of Human Beings: The Kingdom, Not God Alone," *Theological Studies* 69/1 (2008): 38–61.

Surveys and evaluations include Rufus Black, *Christian Moral Realism: Natural Law, Narrative, Virtue, and the Gospel* (Oxford: Oxford University Press, 2000); Rufus Black and Nigel Biggar (2000), *The Revival of Natural Law: Philosophical, Theological and Ethical Responses to the Finnis-Grisez School* (Aldershot: Ashgate, 2000); Robert P. George, *In Defense of Natural Law* (New York: Oxford University Press, 1999); John Finnis, "Natural Law: The Classical Tradition," in *Oxford Handbook of Jurisprudence and Philosophy of Law*, ed. J. Coleman and S. Shapiro (Oxford: Oxford University Press, 2002); and Murphy, "The Natural Law Tradition in Ethics," *Stanford Encyclopedia of Philosophy*.

[33] John Finnis, (*Aquinas: Moral, Political, and Legal Theory* (Oxford: Oxford University Press, 1998); Germain Grisez, "Natural Law, God, Religion, and Human Fulfillment," *American Journal of Jurisprudence* 46 (2001): 3–36.

[34] Michael Pakaluk, "Is the New Natural Law Thomistic?," *National Catholic Bioethics Quarterly* (2013): 57–67.

[35] Black, *Christian Moral Realism*.

Some scholars note significant tension between the Aristotelian/Thomistic approach and much of the contemporary virtue-ethics literature (for instance Nussbaum, Buckle, and Sanford),[36] and I will concentrate on natural-law approaches flowing from Aristotle and Thomas Aquinas in the following survey of economists' engagement with natural law.

Natural Law and Economics

Given the amount of writing on economic questions, and the historical importance of natural-law approaches to ethics, it would be surprising if the two had not interacted. There is a substantial literature on Aristotle's reflections about price, value, and exchange in the *Nicomachean Ethics* and *Politics*,[37] and historians of economics have tended to be more interested in Aristotle's positions on theoretical questions taken up by later economists than in the potential of Aristotle's natural-law approach to frame thinking about economic matters. The situation is similar in the literature of history of economics regarding Thomas Aquinas and other mediaeval scholastic authors.[38]

Recent years have brought a great deal of interest in the influence of Protestant natural-law thinkers, especially Samuel von Pufendorf, Adam Smith,[39] and

---

[36] Martha C. Nussbaum, "Virtue Ethics: A Misleading Category?," *The Journal of Ethics* 3/3 (1999): 163–201; Stephen Buckle, "Aristotle's Republic, or Why Aristotle's Ethics Is Not Virtue Ethics," *Philosophy* 77 (2002): 565–95; Jonathan J. Sanford, *Before Virtue: Assessing Contemporary Virtue Ethics* (Washington, DC: Catholic University of America Press, 2015).

[37] For instance, Joseph A. Schumpeter, *A History of Economic Analysis* (Oxford: Oxford University Press, 1954); Joseph J. Spengler, *Origins of Economic Thought and Justice* (London: Feffer and Simons, 1980); Todd S. Lowry, *The Archaeology of Economic Ideas* (Durham, NC: Duke University Press, 1987); Scott Meikle, *Aristotle's Economic Thought* (Oxford: Clarendon Press, 1995); Dotan Leshem, "The Ancient Art of Economics," *European Journal of the History Economic Thought* 21/2 (2014): 201–29.

[38] For instance, Jacob Viner, *Religious Thought and Economic Society*, ed. J. Melitz and D. Winch (Durham NC: Duke University Press, 1978); Marjorie Grice-Hutchinson, *Early Economic Thought in Spain 1177–1740* (London: Allen & Unwin, 1978); Odd Langholm, *Economics in the Medieval Schools: Wealth, Exchange, Value, Money, and Usury According to the Paris Theological Tradition, 1200–1350* (Leiden: Brill, 1992); Odd Langholm, *The Legacy of Scholasticism in Economic Thought* (Cambridge: Cambridge University Press, 1998).

[39] Knud Haakonssen, *The Science of a Legislator: The Natural Jurisprudence of David Hume and Adam Smith* (Cambridge: Cambridge University Press, 1981); Idem, *Natural Law and Moral Philosophy from Grotius to the Scottish Enlightenment* (Cambridge: Cambridge University Press, 1995); Samuel Gregg, "Commercial Order and the Scottish Enlightenment:

the Aristotelian elements in Smith.[40] John Haldane finds Smith deficient as a natural-law thinker.[41] Smith is definitely not a utilitarian; although he sometimes comments on the utility of various policies, he never offers utility as the justification of action, and it is impossible to find anything like a modern theory of rational choice in his writings.[42] It was Smith's early nineteenth-century British followers who adopted utilitarianism as the default moral philosophy of economists, and later nineteenth-century British economists and twentieth-century American economists developed the theory of rational choice as maximization based on preferences.

Natural law has now fallen away almost completely from contemporary mainstream economic discussion. Among the small number of economists who have any awareness of natural-law theory it would be hard to find many who would dissent from Jeremy Bentham's famous assessment of natural law as "nonsense on stilts."

Not surprisingly, it is Roman Catholic economists who have maintained an interest in natural-law thinking, with Thomas Aquinas their usual point of reference. Heinrich Pesch's massive survey of the history of economic thinking takes a natural-law perspective.[43] Similarly, the nineteenth- and early twentieth-century Catholic economists discussed by Teixeira and Almodovar mostly work within a natural-law framework.[44] Natural law has been the framework for papal commen-

---

The Christian Context," in *Christian Theology and Market Ethics*, ed. I. R. Harper and S. Gregg (Northampton, MA: Edward Elgar, 2008).

[40] Gloria Vivenza, *Adam Smith and the Classics: The Classical Heritage in Adam Smith's Thought* (Oxford: Oxford University Press, 2001); Idem, "Adam Smith and Aristotle," in *Elgar Companion to Adam Smith*, ed. J. Young (Cheltenham: Edward Elgar, 2009); Ryan Patrick Hanley, *Adam Smith and the Character of Virtue* (Cambridge: Cambridge University Press, 2009).

[41] John Haldane, "Adam Smith, Theology and Natural Law Ethics," in *Adam Smith as Theologian*, ed. P. Oslington (London: Routledge, 2011), 24–32.

[42] Jeffrey T. Young, *Economics as a Moral Science: The Political Economy of Adam Smith*. (Cheltenham, UK: Edward Elgar, 1997).

[43] Heinrich Pesch, *Lehrbuch Der Nationalokonomie: Teaching Guide to Economics* 5 vols. (Lewiston, NY: Edwin Mellen Press, 2003 [original German 1905]).

[44] Pedro Teixeira and Antonio Almodovar, "Catholic Economic Thought," in *New Palgrave Dictionary of Economics*, ed. S. Durlaf and L. Blume, 2nd ed. (London: Palgrave Macmillan, 2008); Antonio Almodovar and Pedro Teixeira, "Is There a Catholic Economic Thought? Some Answers from the Past," in *Humanism and Religion in the History of Economic Thought*, ed. D. Parisi and S. Solari (Milan: Franco Angeli, 2010).

tary on economics matters from Leo XIII's encyclical *Rerum Novarum* in 1891 to Benedict XVI's *Caritas in Veritate*.[45]

A small number of Roman Catholic economists in the twentieth century took up the challenge of the papal encyclicals to develop economic theory within this framework—to be able to take papal teaching on economic matters further. An early example was the work of Maurice Potron, using what later became known as input-output models to determine the compatibility of profitable firms and living wages in a market economy.[46] Another was the work of Bernard Dempsey on what he called the functional economy.[47] The most impressive economics developed recently within this framework has been Bernard Lonergan's dynamic macroeconomic models, built in the 1940 s to diagnose economic fluctuations and provide guidance in alleviating the suffering they cause. His work is set explicitly within the Thomistic natural-law framework, but the mathematical modeling draws on his extensive reading in classical economics and the business cycle theories of Schumpeter and Hayek.[48]

Outside Roman Catholic circles, Deirdre McCloskey has for many years been a strong advocate of virtue ethics among economists, for instance in her reading of Adam Smith and in the first volume of her three-volume theological defense of capitalism.[49] She picks up Adam Smith's account of virtue in *The Theory of Moral Sentiments*[50] and connects it with the twentieth-century revival of virtue ethics. However, she often writes as if virtue was an end in itself rather than contributing to higher goods in the Aristotelian sense, making her vulnerable to the critique of

---

[45] See, for instance, Albino Barrera, *Modern Catholic Social Documents and Political Economy* (Washington, DC: Georgetown University Press, 2001); A. M. C. Waterman, "The Intellectual Context of Rerum Novarum," *Review of Social Economy* 49/4 (1991): 465-82; A.M.C. Waterman, "Rerum Novarum and Economic Thought," *Faith & Economics* 67 (2016): 29-56; Paul Oslington, "Popes and Markets " *Policy* 26/4 (2011): 31-5.

[46] M. Potron, C. Bidard, and G. Erreygers, *The Analysis of Linear Economic Systems: Father Maurice Potron's Pioneering Works* (London: Routledge, 2010).

[47] Bernard W. Dempsey, *The Functional Economy* (Englewood Cliffs, NJ: Prentice Hall, 1958).

[48] See Bernard Lonergan, "An Essay on Circulation Analysis," in *Macroeconomic Dynamics: An Essay in Circulation Analysis*, ed. F. Lawrence, P. Byrne, and C. Hefling (Toronto: University of Toronto Press, 1999; original manuscript 1944); Neil Ormerod, et al., "The Development of Catholic Social Teaching on Economics: Bernard Lonergan and Benedict XVI," *Theological Studies* 73 (2012): 391-421.

[49] Deirdre McCloskey, "Adam Smith, the Last of the Former Virtue Ethicists," *History of Political Economy* 40/1 (2008): 43-71; McCloskey, *The Bourgeois Virtues: Ethics for an Age of Commerce* (Chicago: University of Chicago Press, 2006).

[50] Adam Smith, *The Theory of Moral Sentiments* [1759/1790], ed. D.D Raphael and A. Macfie (Oxford: Oxford University Press, 1975).

Nussbaum, Buckle, and others for separating analysis of virtue from its larger Aristotelian/Thomistic framework.

Irene Van Staveren describes Aristotle's theory of virtue ethics and argues that it offers a superior account of economic rationality, picking up dimensions like commitment, emotion, and deliberation that the standard economists' account neglects.[51] As she writes:

> Somewhere along the route of modernisation economics has lost its connection to the most basic characteristics of human behavior. It has come to disregard human motives, emotions, evaluation and the different forms of interaction through which human actors in economic life provide for themselves and for others. With this neglect the discipline not only lost much of its charm but also became less persuasive.[52]

However, her focus on alternative "values" is an unwise move that detracts from the Aristotelian account of action and well-being that she discusses. This focus on values rather than ultimate ends is clear in her summary statement: "In the foregoing chapters I have argued that the core values operating in economic life—freedom, justice and care—are commitments that are intrinsically valuable, incommensurable and to an important degree economic, as well as social, cultural and political."[53] The values focus is also clear in her conclusion: "If the preceding argument amounts to anything, values prove to be at the core of any economic analysis…. [V]alues do matter in the economy."[54]

Arjo Klamer, who was Van Staveren's doctoral supervisor, makes many similar points with less explicit reference to Aristotle.[55] His focus on values is similar to Van Staveren's, and similarly problematic from an Aristotelian point of view. "I propose to define economics as the discipline that studies the realization of values by people, organizations and nations."[56] He recognizes, along with Van Staveren, that commodities are instrumental and values meaningful only in the context of ultimate ends. As he writes, "to realize values we need to procure goods, the most important of which are shared."[57] There is some ambiguity here between economists' concept of goods as commodities and the richer Aristotelian conception of ultimate goods. He writes that goods are what we arrive at by asking repeatedly

---

[51] Irene Van Staveren, *Values of Economics: An Aristotelian Perspective* (London: Routledge, 2001).
[52] Ibid., x.
[53] Ibid., 108.
[54] Ibid., 202.
[55] Klamer, *Doing the Right Thing*.
[56] Ibid., xiv.
[57] Ibid., 75.

what things are for,[58] and that what he calls "transcendental goods" have a special place over personal, social, and societal goods. His explorations have a strongly Aristotelian flavor, though he references diverse sources.

Christian Becker's essay "Aristotelian Virtue Ethics and Economic Rationality" is another description and recommendation of Aristotelian ethics for economists.[59] He observes that "There is no distinct theory or substantial research explicitly addressing the role of virtues for economic decisions and actions within mainstream economics. I will argue that this is not an accidental neglect but reflects a systematic inability of economics to address virtues grounded in the methodological foundation of standard economic theory" (18). He asks, "How do economic actions and spheres contribute to the overall set of virtues and ultimately to an overarching conception of the good?" (4). He discusses perceptively the different views of rationality in Aristotle and contemporary mainstream economics and argues that "the crucial link between virtues and economic actions or spheres is rationality, and that integrative approaches to the relationship between virtues and economic activity need to be based on a substantial understanding of the role of rationality for both" (11). Moreover, virtues are formed in markets as well as personal and small-scale social-political spheres.

> Aristotelian virtue ethics considers a broader societal sphere—a broader community—as crucial for the determination and development of individual virtues. A limited system, such as the oikos or a modern company, is by itself not a sufficient community for determining and developing virtues, because such limited systems lack sufficient internal free and independent reflection and consultation and have a narrow focus on specific internal (business) purposes rather than on an overarching (societal) good. In Aristotle, the crucial broader community for virtue development is the polis, although the context that is relevant for the modern economy and economic actor is certainly no longer the small polis Aristotle had in mind. However, one may ask if there are any modern equivalents to the polis, modern societal spheres in which economic spheres are embedded and which are the ultimate reference points for human excellence. This seems to be more difficult to determine with regard to today's complex and global economy. Also, the relationship between economic spheres and broader societal contexts can be expected to be more complex than the oikos–polis relation in Aristotle's thought. (25)

Becker somewhat strangely invokes Herbert Simon as a supporter of an Aristotelian view of practical rationality (20). Even more puzzling, as the essay pro-

---

[58] Ibid., 118.
[59] Christian U. Becker, "Aristotelian Virtue Ethics and Economic Rationality," in *Economics and the Virtues: Building a New Moral Foundation*, ed. J. A. Baker and M. D. White (New York: Oxford University Press, 2016).

ceeds, is Becker's turn to sustainability as the way of incorporating the Aristotelian view into economics.

American think-tank economist John Mueller has written a nonacademic book which sets out a "neoscholastic" or "A-A-A" (Aristotle-Augustine-Aquinas) vision of a new economics.[60] He develops this vision through a contrast with classical and neoclassical economics, and identifies the neglect of distribution as the major shortcoming of classical and neoclassical economics. To remedy this neglect, he develops a distribution function incorporating gifts to those we love, crimes to those we hate, and exchanges with others. Another shortcoming he identifies in classical and neoclassical economics is a lack of attention to the internal structure of families. Much of his book is taken up with how his alternative vision might play out in American family and political life. I found much of the description of the work of historical figures difficult to reconcile with their actual writings in context, and Mueller's identification of the distinctives of neoscholastic or "A-A-A" economics bizarre. The work is probably best seen as a political tract which attempts to gain credibility from using the names of past natural-law thinkers.

Albino Barrera has, for many years, been offering a Thomistic natural-law account of economic life.[61] He has dealt with issues of justice, economic complicity, and compulsion where a Thomistic account is quite different from contemporary mainstream economics. His work is of high quality and grounded in the relevant texts. He makes no attempt to develop a Thomistic economic model.

Andrew Yuengert, though a conservative Roman Catholic economist like Barrera, draws on Aristotle rather than Thomas Aquinas.[62] At times he has suggested that an alternative Aristotelian economic model might be possible, but in his recent work he has expressed the view that the Aristotelian natural-law approach cannot be formalized. He clearly sets out the reasons for this view in a recent ar-

---

[60] John D. Mueller, *Redeeming Economics: Rediscovering the Missing Element* (Wilmington, DE: ISI Books, 2010).

[61] Barrera, "Economic Life, Rights, and Obligations: Perspectives from Theological Teleology," *Forum for Social Economics* 29/1 (1999): 63–74; Idem, *Economic Compulsion and Christian Ethics* (Cambridge: Cambridge University Press, 2004); Idem, *Market Complicity and Christian Ethics* (Cambridge: Cambridge University Press, 2011).

[62] Andrew M. Yuengert, "Why Did the Economist Cross the Road? The Hierarchical Logic of Ethical and Economic Reasoning," *Economics and Philosophy* 18 (2002): 329–49; Idem, *Approximating Prudence: Aristotelian Practical Wisdom and Economics Models of Choice* (New York: Palgrave Macmillan, 2012); Idem, "The Space between Choice and Our Models of It: Practical Wisdom and Normative Economics," in Baker and White, eds., *Economics and the Virtues*; Idem, "Varieties of Virtue in Economics," presentation at Eudaimonia Institute Conference on Culture, Religion, and Eudaimonia, Wake Forest University, 2019.

ticle: "[F]our aspects of the decision-making environment—its contingency, the nature of objectives, the need for virtues, and the personal nature of action—make it impossible to treat the objectives of action and the choice set as if they were unproblematically given, as if the only decision skill needed were calculus."[63] He goes on: "These aspects of the decision environment and the virtues that decision-making requires in this environment together explain the unformulability of practical wisdom.... Neither the contingent environment nor the aspects of practical wisdom that are fitted to that environment can be captured in an economic optimization model."[64] Yuengert now advocates utilizing mainstream economic theory with an Aristotelian appreciation of the limits of mainstream theory.

Mary Hirschfeld, another American Roman Catholic economist, has engaged more deeply with the theology of Thomas Aquinas than any other economist. Aquinas's account of happiness is the focus of her contrast between what she calls a "theological economics" and contemporary mainstream economics.[65] While Aquinas and economists agree that desire is infinite, for Aquinas "infinite desire can only be satiated when we rest in the infinite good that is God" and "human happiness as perfection rather than as the satisfaction of desires" (24). As she later explains, economists extend desire quantitatively to infinity, while for Aquinas it is the quality and ordering of desires that perfect them, achieving happiness.

The depth of Hirschfeld's treatment of the issues is shown in the discussion of the alternative metaphysic that underlies the different accounts of happiness. She takes us through Aquinas's account of human nature, distinct from other animals. The distinctiveness lies in human purposiveness, which is the ability "to discern qualitatively distinct finite goods in the light of the universal good and make judgements regarding which of these finite goods we will pursue" (75), so that "all properly human acts are also moral acts" (78). She associates (in my view questionably) the economists' rational-choice model with our lower animal natures, somewhat akin to the way other Christian economists (equally questionably) associate the rational-choice model with fallen human nature. The other important point is that for Aquinas, "human action is ordered to one final end." It has to be a definite end, so the economists' approach of incremental progression to something better with the ultimate end unclear, does not cut it for Aquinas.

After discussing human nature, she takes the reader even more deeply into metaphysics with the argument that the analogical relationship between God and the world is in tension with the univocality of the economists account. In her Thomistic vision our happiness comes from participation in divine being. It is a vision of "goodness, which in God is simple and uniform, in creatures is manifold and

---

[63] Yuengert, "The Space between Choice and Our Models," 169.
[64] Ibid., 170.
[65] Mary L. Hirschfeld, *Aquinas and the Market: Toward a Humane Economy.* (Cambridge, MA: Harvard University Press, 2018).

divided; and hence the whole universe together participates in the divine goodness more perfectly, and represents it better than any single creature whatever" (92). This is a richer vision than the economists' vision of divinized individuals.

Within this metaphysical framework, she argues that virtue is the center of human happiness in this life. Virtues are "good habits" that "help us reach the full potential of our nature," (102) and she discusses the classic list faith, hope, charity, prudence, justice, fortitude, and temperance (105–06). Prudence has a special place as the controlling virtue, though she emphasizes that Aquinas's conception of prudence is quite different from the economists' rational choice under constraints. Here the author covers ground familiar to readers of the modern virtue-ethics movement translated for economists by writers such as Irene Van Staveren, Arjo Klamer, and Deirdre McCloskey.

There are, however, a number of issues with Hirschfeld's account of the role of the virtues in the moral life. Are virtues to be pursued for their own sake, or are they instrumental in the achievement of the goods? Hirschfeld strongly takes the first view, but this is in tension both with other readings of Aquinas and with most of the Aristotelian literature on the relationship between virtues and goods. What is the relationship between the goods of this life and those of the next? Or in other words, how does the future hope affect moral life in this world? Hirschfeld takes this in a particular analogical way, but others connect the two more concretely. Finally, and perhaps of most direct interest for economists, is the question of whether this approach to human action, virtues, and goods can be modeled mathematically. She suggests that Aquinas's approach can't, following Andrew Yuengert's similar conclusion about the impossibility of mathematically modeling Aristotle's approach.

For Hirschfeld there is a hierarchy of goods, with natural wealth ordered and instrumental to happiness, and artificial wealth (such as money) ordered in turn to natural wealth. In this framework, the trouble with money is that it tempts us to infinite expansion, disconnected from its ordering to natural wealth, and in turn to the higher-order goods which generate happiness. Or in the author's words, "Money is a quantitative abstraction that does not respect qualitative distinctions" (150). She then goes through concrete examples of how misunderstanding money, disconnecting it from natural wealth and the higher order goods, is behind some of the damaging financial excesses of recent times. The overall message is that "The Thomistic framework has room to accommodate many of the best insights on offer from economics. That said, the Thomistic framework also identifies the limitations of economic analysis" (196).

An unexplored version of natural law for economists is the new natural-law theory developed by philosophers John Finnis, Germain Grisez, and others.[66] It

---

[66] John Finnis, *Natural Law and Natural Rights(* Oxford: Clarendon Press, 1980); Germain Grisez, Joseph Boyle, and John Finnis, "Practical Principles, Moral Truth, and Ultimate

has the great advantage for economists that it is expressed in the tight, logical style of analytical philosophy and so amenable to mathematization. It also deals explicitly with the Humean critique that natural law derives "is" from "ought." Finnis and Grisez argue that the establishment of the ultimate goods is an empirical matter, with the normative element entering in when practical reason guides action towards those ends. It is an approach that resonates with the professional culture of contemporary economics.

Contemporary natural-law theorists are not terribly friendly towards economics. For instance, Finnis,[67] who is particularly concerned with the economic approach to law developed by the American legal theorist and judge Ricard Posner, acknowledges that economics is useful in a limited domain, but he asserts that it is inadequate as a comprehensive theory of choice. Economic theory of choice cannot take the place of practical reason in weighing goods in the context of action and is dangerous when it claims to do so. He claims, for instance, that when applied to euthanasia, the economic methods and concepts lead to devaluing persons and neglecting unfair side effects of action.

Can a Natural-Law Approach to Action be Formally Modelled?

I have experimented with a mathematical formulation of the new natural-law theory where action is oriented to seven fundamental goods that Finnis and Grisez identify.[68] Virtue is treated as a kind of moral capital, which actions may augment or reduce, and which then contributes to the attainment of the goods. Unlike the economists' maximization model, this formulation does not yield a determinate outcome, although actions which contribute less to each of the goods than another action can be eliminated. Moral judgments need to be made on the basis of impacts of action on the goods, and the model is a tool to assist the agent's practical reasoning rather than to determine the uniquely rational action.

This formal model is still a work in progress, but contrary to Yuengert and Hirschfeld, I believe that it is possible to mathematically model an Aristoteli-

---

Ends," *American Journal of Jurisprudence* 32 (1987): 99–151; Germain Grisez, "Natural Law, God, Religion, and Human Fulfillment," *American Journal of Jurisprudence* 46 (2001): 3–36; Idem, "The True Ultimate End of Human Beings: The Kingdom, Not God Alone." *Theological Studies* 69/1 (2008): 38–61.

[67] John Finnis, "Economics, Justice, and the Value of Life," in *Economics and the Dependent Elderly: Autonomy, Justice, and Quality of Care*, ed. Luke Gormally (Cambridge: Cambridge University Press, 1992).

[68] Oslington, "A Natural Law Framework for Economists," presentation at University of Heidelberg, 2018.

an/Thomistic approach to action, virtue, and the good. There are inevitable losses in translation to mathematics. However, without formal mathematical models, it is difficult to see this approach having an impact on the economics profession and being used in economic analysis and public policy. Krugman makes this argument,[69] which is exemplified by the models of Menzies and Hay and of Brennan and Pettit discussed earlier.[70] Critique and verbal exposition are not useful for professional economists.

Conclusion

The argument of this paper is that economists' language and theoretical modeling of actions matter for impacts on virtue and the pursuit of goods. If the approach of contemporary mainstream economics is limited or unhelpful in relation to virtue and the pursuit of goods, then we need to explore alternative ways of framing action and judging well-being. I reviewed several alternative approaches, the most viable of which is the natural-law approach. This approach to human action offers a broader conception of rationality than maximization and combines what economists would see as positive and normative elements. An open question remains whether this approach can be translated into a tractable mathematical model. I believe a natural-law reframing of economics has the potential to change the economic conversation, without throwing away most of the powerful analytical tools of contemporary mainstream economics.

---

[69] Paul Krugman, "Two Cheers for Formalism" *Economic Journal* 108/451 (1998): 1829–36.
[70] Geoffrey Brennan and Philipp Pettit, *The Economy of Esteem: An Essay on Civil Society* (Oxford: Oxford University Press, 2004).

Part Two:
Biblical and Historical Impulses

Law, Economy, and Charity
Formations in Torah and Talmud

Michael J. Broyde

The aim of this chapter is to present a single case study, albeit a core moral one, that provides a religious and legal example of ethical orientation and character formation in late modern Jewish societies. Using the duty to give charity as that case, the chapter explores the aspects of moral development found in the laws of charity and the ways they have been shaped by social and cultural norms. The chapter reveals that Jewish Law took the simple role of charity—to provide for the poor—and, as the Western world and Jewish community evolved, shaped the laws regarding charity to contribute to the general ethical and educational formation of the community as a whole. Charitygiving became a legal category useful in shaping "the common good" and not only supporting the poor. What we see is the adaptation of a biblical tool—driven in premodern times by agricultural norms and tithing, with its related charitable idea of feeding the hungry—into a modern tool to help form the nucleus of modern Jewish society and its many institutions.

The chapter intentionally does not discuss charity in Israel today and confines itself to the community in the Diaspora. It does so for three reasons. First, Israel is a nation in economic transition to the First World, with basic modes of government-provided social services less clearly established than in Western Europe and North America. Second, one could advocate the idea that a Jewish state should adhere to a more insular, uniquely Jewish communal model of charity, more deeply confusing the distinction between the Jewish community and the general community in Israel than in England, France, or the United States. Third, the role of a society's dominant community towards the underprivileged creates a more robust moral obligation in a society that is Jewish-dominant than in a society where Jews are a distinct minority. For all of these reasons, charity in Israel today deserves to be the subject of a different study.

Introduction

There is no doubt of a biblical obligation to give charity; however, basic Jewish Law issues are in dispute.[1] This chapter will show that there is disagreement over such fundamental questions as who may receive charity, how much money each person should give, what the nature of charitable duty is, and whether charity money should be spent on educational concerns rather than support of the poor. The conclusion of all of this is that the very parameters of "charity" in Western nations have changed during the last centuries as the government—and not the religious community—provides for the basic social welfare—food, shelter, and education—for all citizens.

Even more generally, the Talmudic and medieval issues relating to giving charity are a balance between abstract Jewish Law ideals and a concrete social and economic reality. Like many other areas of Jewish Law, certain aspects of charity law are designed to teach us a religious and ethical value, rather than be implemented routinely. An example is the concept of *dey machsoro* (as the needs were), suggesting that a poor person ought to be theoretically supported at a level that reflects his loss of dignity and not based on some objective formulation.[2] Former millionaires who become impoverished ought to be supported at their preimpoverishment level in some idealized model.[3] In the real world, this practice could not routinely be done, and Jewish law notes that no individual is generally called upon to support another in such a fashion.[4] Indeed, the consensus of authorities is that it is improper to distribute one charitable gift to a single person *dey machsoro*, but instead one should give smaller amounts to many people who are in actual desperate need.[5] As an authoritative work in this area notes, "One should not give

---

[1] Shulchan Aruch, Yoreh Deah 247:1.

[2] This idea is actually based on the rabbinical exegesis of Deuteronomy 15:8, which states: כִּי־פָתֹחַ תִּפְתַּח אֶת־יָדְךָ לוֹ וְהַעֲבֵט תַּעֲבִיטֶנּוּ דֵּי מַחְסֹרוֹ אֲשֶׁר יֶחְסַר לוֹ: "But you shall open your hand to him and lend him sufficient for his needs, whatever it may be." The English term "sufficient for his needs" is a translation of the Hebrew term *dey machsoro*.

[3] Another example of this is the concept that found objects, even after they were abandoned, should be held in escrow unused until Elijah arrives. On an ethical level, Jewish law mandates that a found object is not owned by the finder—but on a practical level, once it is clear that its original owner can never reclaim the object, the finder functions as if it is his. See Michael J. Broyde and Michael Hecht, "The Return of Lost Property According to Jewish and Common Law: A Comparison," *Journal of Law and Religion* 12 (1996): 225-254.

[4] Shulchan Aruch, Yoreh Deah 250:1, and Rama ad loc.

[5] Taz, Yoreh Deah 250:1, and Shach, Yoreh Deah 250:1; but see Bach, Yoreh Deah 250.

all of one's charity to a single person."[6] Indeed, there always was a fear that if the fallen wealthy were supported at a high level, there would be little incentive not to fall.

This tension between the ideals of charity, on one hand, to give as much as one can to as many in need to raise them to as high a level as possible and, on the other hand, the reality that money is limited and incentives are needed to elicit work and avoid dependence, is a central theme of Jewish law's approach to charity. This chapter explores that balance in light of the social, economic, political, and religious reality of modern Western life.

The remainder of this chapter is divided into six sections. The first explores the basic purpose of charity and notes the grand dispute about whether its fundamental purpose is to support the poor or communal institutions or both. The second section explores the fundamental dispute between Maimonides and others about whether charity should support education and study by scholars in addition to providing for the indigent. The third section explores the way many modern Jewish law authorities have responded to the rise of government-funded social services and the concomitant higher taxes in the context of duty to give charity. The fourth section examines the use of charity funds for unusual situations and the parameters of such uses according to Jewish Law. The fifth section touches on how much each person needs to give. The conclusion argues that what started as a basic construct of charity law within Jewish Law has evolved in modern times to reflect societal shift in charitable methods over time.

Two Visions of Charity: For the Poor or for the Community?

Even a cursory examination of charity law in Maimonides's code of Jewish Law (Mishneh Torah) would strongly suggest that that great sage limited charity as a duty only to support of the poor.[7] Maimonides makes not a single mention of any way to fulfill the duty of charitable giving other than by gifts or loans to the poor.[8]

---

[6] Yaakov Yishayahu Blau, Sefer Tzedakah u-Mishpat 3:5 (Jerusalem: Beit Meir Press, 5740 [1979/80]).

[7] Maimonides, Law of Gifts to the Poor 7:1; Book of Commandments, Positive Commandment 195.

[8] This chapter does not discuss the theoretical matter of how the community ought to act were it to have the power to coerce payments for communal matters. See R. Moshe Feinstein, Iggrot Moshe, Choshen Mishpat 1:41, who defends the early compromise of half per capita and half wealth-based tax. Cf. Beit Yosef, Orach Chaim 53 in the name of R. Hai Gaon and Aaron Levine, *Free Enterprise and Jewish Law* (New York: KTAV and Yeshiva

This approach to charity is also the view of many others, and is based on the fact that nowhere in the Babylonian Talmud is the idea of charity ever applied other than to aid the poor.

Rabbi Joseph Kolon (known by his Hebrew acronym Maharik[9]) formulates the counterview and maintains that charity ought to be used—first and foremost—for building communal resources, such as a synagogue or study hall. Maharik writes simply, "It is better to give charity money to a synagogue." Rabbi Joseph Karo, the author of the classical 1563 law code, the Shulchan Aruch, in his subcommentary titled Beit Yosef,[10] expands on the view of the Maharik as follows:

> [The Maharik] wrote (Shoresh 128, vol. 3, part 4) that from the writings of R. Simeon b. Tzemach Duran (Tashbetz Katan 536), which cites the view of Rabbi Samuel of Bonburg based on Y. Peah (8:8) one can demonstrate that building a synagogue is more important than giving [ordinary] charity, for the Talmud states that Rav saw [alt. offered rebuke] for building a fancy entrance to the synagogue ... [and stated]: Were there no individuals studying Torah or sick people sustaining themselves from the refuse pile? To this he applied the verse, "Israel forgot its maker and built sanctuaries" (Hosea 8:14)—from here R. Samuel derived that it is preferable to give charity to young men to study Torah or to the ill and impoverished than to give to the synagogue. From the Yerushalmi saying "sick individuals sustaining themselves from the refuse pile" and likewise R. Samuel stating, "ill and impoverished" and not simply "the poor," this implies that were such individuals not ill but simply poor, it would be preferable to give [the charity funds] to a synagogue.[11]

This view is cited in the Shulchan Aruch,[12] a vital code of law still used in modern Judaism.

Others insist that this license to spend charity on other than poor people includes the building of other communal institutions such as hospitals. Indeed, one recent writer posits that from charity funds, "It is obligatory for members of a city to purchase all communal needs: to build a synagogue, purchase a Torah scroll and other books that people can study from, hire a rabbi as a Jewish Law authority,

---

University Press, 1980), 152; as well as Rama, Choshen Mishpat 163:3 and Chatam Sofer, Choshen Mishpat 159 (who presents a sophisticated and complex formula).

[9] Rabbi Joseph ben Samuel Kolon [Cologne] (ca. 1420-80), Italian authority and author of numerous responsa. This one is found in Responsa 128.

[10] Beit Yosef, Yoreh Deah 249[16].

[11] It is worth noting that our text of Y.Peah 8:8, as well as the parallel passage in Y.Shekalim 5:4, does not include the words "or sick people sustaining themselves from the refuse pile."

[12] Yoreh Deah 249:6.

and a cantor; so, too, one can pay tuition for those children whose parents cannot pay tuition and to build a ritual bath."[13]

Of course, as Rabbi Yeheil Epstein notes in his classic Jewish Law code of the late 1800 s, titled the *Aruch ha-Shulchan*,[14] there is a difference between lavish construction of an extra synagogue—the one we do not worship in, as the joke goes—and the genuine needs of the community. But it is clear that many contemporary Jewish Law authorities rule that communal needs may be paid from charity funds.

Certainly, there are still dissenting voices to this approach. The great eighteenth-century sage Rabbi Elijah of Vilna (Gra)[15] rejects the view that charity can ever be spent other than to aid the poor, as do others.[16] However, as many note,[17] there is an explicit passage in the Jerusalem Talmud that sides with the broader view.[18] By the beginning of the twentieth century,[19] Jewish Law conversations surrounding the question are focused on whether it is more important to build a hospital or a synagogue, or a synagogue in Israel rather than one in the Diaspora.[20] Charity to the poor becomes secondary. Of course, one could limit this—as Rabbi Epstein proposes—and insist on the supremacy of giving charity to the poor when their actual lives are at stake; but when charity merely is of benefit to the poor, then the building of a synagogue assumes priority.[21]

Thus, we have three models of the duty to give charity in Jewish Law:
1. Charity is exclusively for the benefit of poor individuals.
2. Charity's highest priority is the building of communal institutions.
3. Charity's highest priority is saving the lives of those in danger. Its next-highest priority is the building of communal institutions. The third-highest virtue is benefiting the poor.

---

[13] Rabbi Yacov Yashaya Blau, *Tzedakah u-Mishpat* 3:28.
[14] Yoreh Deah 249:18–20.
[15] Yoreh Deah 249:20.
[16] See Yikrei Lev, Yoreh Deah 5, who appears to reject Maharik. Indeed, the view of Tosafot appears to agree with Rambam that charity to the poor is more important than synagogue construction; Tosafot, Bava Batra 9a, s.v. *she-ne'emar*.
[17] See Rabbi Yeheil Mikhel Epstein Aruch ha-Shulchan, Yoreh Deah 249:18–19.
[18] Y.Peah 8:8. Undoubtedly, the resolution of this matter relates to the more general subject of the status of the Talmud Yerushalmi within normative halacha, which is the subject of an observation of mine titled "The Yerushalmi as a Source of Halacha," at https://www.torahmusings.com/2011/05/the-yerushalmi-as-a-source-of-halacha/.
[19] See, for example, Sedai Chemed Kelalim 2:44.
[20] Chatam Sofer, Orach Chaim 203; Maharsham 4:147.
[21] Aruch ha-Shulchan, Yoreh Deah 149:20.

This dispute is a central one. If the purpose of charity and the exclusive beneficiaries of charity are the poor, then many of the complex questions of this chapter disappear, and the solution is simple. However, if charity funds may be used for general communal projects—even when poor people need charity, or only when the lives of the poor are not in actual danger—then a much greater variety of projects are eligible for charitable funding.[22]

SHOULD CHARITY FUNDS BE ALLOCATED TO THOSE WHO COULD WORK BUT STUDY INSTEAD?

The second important issue is the use of charity funds to support ongoing Jewish study. Three views are found. The first view is that of Maimonides, who—consistent with his insistence that charity only be used to benefit poor people—insists that a Torah scholar may not choose a life of poverty so that he may study Torah and accept charity. Maimonides's harsh words indicate that he is all too familiar with the practice. He states:

> 10. Anyone who decides to occupy himself with Torah and not work but obtain his livelihood from charity desecrates God's name, denigrates the Torah, extinguishes the light of the faith, brings evil upon himself, and excludes himself from life in the world to come, for it is forbidden to benefit from Torah matters in this world. The Sages stated: Anyone who benefits from Torah matters excludes himself from life in the world to come. They also commanded and stated: Do not make them a crown to magnify oneself, nor an ax to chop with. They further commanded and stated: Love work and hate the rabbinate. And any Torah that is not accompanied by work will be nullified in the end and lead to sin, and ultimately such a person will come to steal from others.
>
> 11. It is a great virtue for one to earn one's livelihood from one's own handiwork, and a positive quality of the early pious ones. By doing so, one merits all the glory and goodness in this world and the world to come, as scripture states, "When you eat the labor of your hands, happy shall you be, and it shall be well with you." "Happy shall you be"—in this world—"and it shall be well with you"—in the world to come, which is completely good.[23]

In this model, any scholar who accepts charity when he can work has forfeited the moral and ethical value of his contributions. This is true even if he really is poor because he studies all day. Maimonides maintains that such a Torah scholar

---

[22] For an example of this, see Rabbi Moshe Weinberger, *Jewish Outreach* (New York: KTAV and NY Assn. of Jewish Outreach Professionals, 1990), chapter 9, "Is a Contribution to a Kiruv [Outreach] Organization Charity?"

[23] Maimonides, Laws of Torah Study 3:10–11.

should get a job and not accept charity rather than continuing to learn while accepting charity.

Even Rabbi Karo could not accept the words of Maimonides, and in his commentary Kessef Mishneh he takes pains to refute them, even as he acknowledges that they are grounded in numerous Talmudic sources. So, too, Rabbi Shimon ben Tzemach Duranstates:

> After we have explained all of the above, we must consider the view of Maimonides on this matter.... It seems that he overstepped his bounds and cast all the scholars and rabbis of his time and those who preceded him as being in error. And because he spoke in anger he came to err and to call them mad. "The Prophet is a fool; the man of the spirit is mad" [Hos. 9:7]. Just because it was his [Maimonides's] good luck to be close to royalty and honored in his generation, and—owing to his medical and scientific knowledge—he was not required to accept fees from the communities he served, what are the rabbis and sages who have not reached this level to do? Shall they die of starvation or demean their honor or remove the yoke of Torah from their necks? That is not the intent of the Torah, the commandments or the Talmud.[24]

This view, which the great Spanish Jewish Law authority of the 1300 s Rabbi Asher ben Yechiel[25] endorses as well, albeit with much less enthusiasm, reflects a reality. It is well-nigh impossible to support serious scholarship and leadership while mandating that such leadership also work independently. If Maimonides could do it, it was because he was exceptional. Still, the ideal is that Torah scholars should earn a living if they can, by working.

Of course, as Rabbi Asher goes on to say, if one has no other choice, then one may take charity.[26] This is the view that Rabbi Moshe Isserless (Rama)[27] arrives at

---

[24] Tashbetz 1:147.

[25] Responsa of Rosh 15:10.

[26] Although this chapter is not focused on comparative religion, it is worth noting here the contrast between Catholic priests and Jewish rabbis in this area. The basic model of the Jewish tradition was—and still is—of rabbis leading lives that are "regular" but simply "more holy." This is quite in contrast to the Catholic model of priests having unique rules of conduct. Two excellent examples of this are priestly celibacy and priestly poverty, neither of which is part of the Jewish tradition. The Jewish tradition, while it ponders rabbinic celibacy and recognizes the religious plausibility of it (see Shulchan Aruch Even Haezer 1:4), rejects that model as normative, and it is never practiced in fact. The same is true for the poverty model, as this chapter shows. There is no tradition of rabbis being supported by charity unless it is desperately needed.

[27] Yoreh Deah 246:6.

as well, albeit with a great deal of hesitation, as does the *Aruch ha-Shulchan*.[28] Rabbi Epstein states:

> 41. Our master Rabbi Isserless wrote, "The custom in all Jewish communities was for the rabbi of the city to receive income and sustenance from the city's inhabitants so that he not need to occupy himself publicly with work, and the Torah be thereby denigrated in the eyes of the populace." This is true specifically with regard to a needy scholar, but a wealthy person is forbidden to do so. Some are more lenient and allow a scholar and his students to accept contributions from donors in order to strengthen the hands of those who study Torah, for by doing so they are able to involve themselves in Torah with ease. Nonetheless, one who is able to sufficiently support himself through his own handiwork and study Torah, this is the nature of the pious and a gift from God—but it is not the nature of all people, for it is impossible for every person to involve oneself in Torah and become wise while at the same time supporting oneself. All of the above which is permissible is limited to instances when a person receives his fare from the community or a set allocation, but one may not accept gifts from people. When the Talmud states, "anyone who gives a gift to a sage is considered as if he has offered first fruits," this is with regard to small gifts, for the general practice is to bring small gifts to important people, even if they be unlettered.
>
> 42. Moreover, one of the great latter-day authorities has written: "We have seen that the practice of all Jewish scholars is to accept support from the community. I say that one who is a master of the academy and disseminates Jewish Law to the public and cannot leave his own home except for the purpose of a mitzvah, it is a sin for such a person not to accept funding from others, even if he knows a particular trade or discipline that he can toil in and make money in order to support his household, for the love of Torah will surely be denigrated. However, if one already had sufficient resources to support oneself and earn interest on the funds, in a manner which does not involve neglecting Torah study at all, then one should not benefit from public funds but rather consume the labors of his own hands, and whatever he does receive from the public he should spend on the expenses of teaching Torah."

This view reflects an unfortunate reality that Rabbi Epstein sadly acknowledges. Charity needs to be collected to pay for Jewish law study, so that people can be learned scholars; otherwise they will work, and we will have a community with fewer scholars.

A third view presents such charity as the ideal. In this view, it is more important to spend one's charity funds to support Torah scholars than to support poor people. As the contemporary Jewish law authority Rabbi Jacob Isiah Blau states, in *Charity and Justice (Tzedakah u-Mishpat):* "Charity to strengthen the study of Jew-

---

[28] Yoreh Deah 246:38–42.

ish Law is superior to charity for the poor."[29] The basic explanation for this view is logical at some level. If building a synagogue is a greater form of charity than supporting the poor, the building of a study hall—whose holiness is greater than that of a synagogue[30]—is an even greater form of charity. Supporting people to use the study hall must then be a still greater religious obligation.

Thus, we have now encountered our second fundamental dispute about charity. Are charity funds to be spent to support study or not? Three views are again presented:
- Maimonides maintains that charity funds may never support Torah study.
- Many maintain that if the times require it, such funds should be spent to support study, but it is better that they not be.
- Some maintain that it is the ideal to spend such funds to support Torah study.

The essence here can be distilled. Maimonides's formulation of the charitable obligation is structured and clear: charity is exclusively for the poor. It may not be spent for communal needs or to support Jewish law study. Others disagree and rule that charity may or should be spent for communal needs.

The Modern Social Welfare System, Taxes, and Governmental "Charity"

The classical medieval Jewish Law was clear: a Jew should never take charity from a non-Jew.[31] If one must take charity from a Gentile, because the powerful Gentile would be angry otherwise, then one should take that charity and secretly give the money to poor Gentiles.[32] If one will get into trouble by doing even that, then one may grudgingly accept the charity.[33] While the exact reason for this rule is in some dispute, the consensus remains that the taking of charity from a Gentile is a sign of moral failure, and it is a desecration of God's name for Jews to be seen as moral failures.

Notwithstanding this clear recitation of the law, most Jewish law authorities aver that "modern times are different." Governmental welfare, the argument goes, is not charity. As Rabbi Blau puts it:

---

[29] *Tzedakah u-Mishpat* 3:26. He adds that such is not true when the poor might actually perish.
[30] Shulchan Aruch, Orach Chaim 90:18.
[31] Shulchan Aruch, Yoreh Deah 254:1.
[32] Ibid, 254:2.
[33] Rama ad loc.

> In our times, Jews live among the nations [in the Diaspora], and if, according to the secular laws, the poor are entitled to accept government support (social welfare and the like), it seems that it is permissible for a Jew to accept it, according to the reasons mentioned above. And also because Jews, too, live in the state, and they, too, pay taxes, and this support comes from tax revenues, it is not considered taking charity from Gentiles.[34]

The claim is that Jews, as members in good standing of modern society, are entitled to participate in the social welfare system as per the law. The basic rationale of desecration of God's name through wholesale Jewish poverty is dismissed, as governmental welfare is an entitlement. Still, one could argue with this rationale and insist that Jews being comfortable participants in the social welfare safety net still is a desecration of God's name, even in a just democracy, since taking charity is still a sign of moral failure.[35] But as far as research suggests, this view has yet to be put forward by a Jewish law authority in the last half century.

The same observation can be made with regard to what is income for Jewish law purposes. Rabbi Feinstein's observation[36] that money one pays as taxation on income does not count as income from which one needs to give charity, is the only logical result in the construct of our modern community. The contrary view—considered by Rabbi Eliezer Waldenberg[37]—is that money one pays in taxes counts as a form of charity. This view has considerable support,[38] but in high-tax nations such as England, France, Germany, Canada, and the United States, this approach would reduce the obligations of charity to zero and be untenable as a matter of normative ethical practice. Who could imagine a Jewish society without charity?

Not surprisingly, these voices within Jewish law recognize that since very little charity is needed to fend off starvation in Western nations—where the government provides, more or less, nearly all the social services needed to function on a basic level—charity should be directed elsewhere. Where should the charitable giving be directed? One should invest in the form of charity that is better than alleviating the plight of the poor (whose lives are not in danger)—that is, one should give to institutions that increase Jewish Law study.

---

[34] Tzedakah u-Mishpat, ch. 1, end of n. 68.
[35] Welfare still comes with the social stigma of failure and poverty. This might be different for other governmental awards, such as education benefits.
[36] Igrot Moshe, Yoreh Deah 1:143.
[37] Tzitz Eliezer 9:1:5.
[38] See Taz, Yoreh Deah 249:1. For a defense of the Tzitz Eliezer's position as proper normative halacha, see Yitzchak Yaakov Weiss, Minchat Yitzchak 5:34(9).

It is difficult to find a contemporary work in English dealing with charity that does not make this point in one way or another.[39] Essentially, as the Jewish community has been relieved of the great burden of autonomy—to feed, clothe, cure, and shelter the impoverished solely through the means of the Jewish community—charity can now be used for a different purpose: study of Jewish law, worship in synagogues, and supporting institutions that facilitate these goals.

What supports much of this conclusion, both in this section and the previous one, is the acceptance of the idea that studying and facilitating the study of Jewish Law is a core precept in the Jewish tradition. As recounted directly by the first Mishnah in the first chapter of the section of agricultural laws—which were all gifts to the poor or the priests:

אֵלּוּ דְבָרִים שֶׁאֵין לָהֶם שִׁעוּר: הַפֵּאָה, וְהַבִּכּוּרִים, וְהָרְאָיוֹן, וּגְמִילוּת חֲסָדִים, וְתַלְמוּד תּוֹרָה.....וְתַלְמוּד תּוֹרָה כְּנֶגֶד כֻּלָּם.

> These are the things that can be done without upper measure: The corner charity of the fields (to the poor), the first fruits given at the Temple, the appearance [at the Temple in Jerusalem on pilgrimage festivals], acts of kindness, and the study of the Torah.... But the study of Torah is equal to them [maybe correctly translated as: greater than them] all.

Deeply rooted in the central aspects of the Jewish tradition is that studying Jewish Law, engaging in acts of kindness, and observing ritual law are all of approximately equal value and should all be done consistently. As Chaim Saiman shows in his recent work,[40] the theoretical study of Jewish Law—divorced from its practice—has been a hallmark of the Jewish tradition for nearly two thousand years. In this model, it is not at all surprising that Torah study as a religious duty can serve as a substitute for charity when basic needs of the poor are provided by the government.

Indeed, the data—at least for North American Jews and likely all Jews in Western Europe as well—support three basic ideas: Jews give charity at heightened levels as compared to others; those who identify with the traditional Jewish law community support scholars of Torah study as appropriate recipients of charity; and charitable giving is or becomes a central focus of manifesting one's religious identity, which is possible only if the government provides the basic social services which are not aspects of Jewish identity but of basic human necessity.[41] Indeed,

---

[39] For example, see Moshe Goldberger, *Priorities in Tzedaka: Higher Forms of Giving* (New York: Judaica Press, 2007), 66-74.

[40] Chaim N. Saiman, *Halakha: The Rabbinic Idea of Law* (Princeton: Princeton University Press, 2018).

[41] See, for example, Hanna Shaul Bar Nissim "American Jews and Charitable giving: An enduring tradition," at https://theconversation.com/american-jews-and-charitable-giving-

the numbers are not small: "Total American giving to Jewish causes in the United States and Israel amounted to $5.5 billion to $6 billion in 2015."[42] However, if people are actually endangered by a lack of resources, charity to the poor becomes the central obligation.

Unusual Balances of Charity Law

The previous sections have discussed balancing aid to the poor with the needs of the community. This section emphasizes one important limitation in that balance: the obligation to give the highest priority to situations that actually save lives. The classical codes[43] are clear that in situations where the spending of charity money actually and directly saves lives, that action has the highest priority, and one may divert money from general charity matters or law study to preventing the loss of life. This is the clear lesson of the rabbinic understanding of the duty to redeem captives whose lives are endangered. The critical priority the Talmud and codes give to this obligation reflects the fact that this situation entails not only charity but also fulfillment of the obligation "not to stand idly by while one's neighbor's blood is shed."[44] Where life is in danger, little else takes higher priority.

Still, this application of charity has some limitations, in that a community need not sell its assets to raise money to save lives.[45] However, the suggestion of a lone scholar[46] that the support of scholars even takes priority over saving lives is nearly universally rejected under the rationale that "nothing ought to stand in the way of saving lives."[47] Why does a community not have to actually sell its own assets to save lives? The two great Jewish law commentators Rabbi Shabtai Hacohen (*Shach*)[48] and Rabbi David Halevi Segal (*Taz*)[49] both seem to in-

---

an-enduring-tradition-87993. Note that the undergirded data for these claims are derived from the general study of the Jewish community found in the well-regarded Pew Charitable Trust findings published in October 2013 as "A Portrait of Jewish Americans" found at "https://www.pewresearch.org/wp-content/uploads/sites/7/2013/10/jewish-american-full-report-for-web.pdf.

[42] See https://www.timesofisrael.com/mega-donors-are-taking-over-jewish-philanthropy-study-says/. For more general figures, see https://nonprofitssource.com/online-giving-statistics/.

[43] See Shulchan Aruch Yoreh Deah 252:1.

[44] Lev. 19:16; as well as several other commandments. See Hil. Matnot Aniyim 8:10; Shulchan Aruch, Yoreh Deah 252:2.

[45] Shulchan Aruch, Yoreh Deah 252:1.

[46] Rabbi Joshua Falk Cohen Deresha Commenting on Tur, Yoreh Deah 252.

[47] Taz, Yoreh Deah 252:2; Tzedakah u-Mishpat 3:27, note 83; Shevut Yaakov 2:84.

[48] Yoreh Deah 252:1.

timate that giving up assets that one cannot otherwise replace and that are no longer charity funds but communal assets, is simply not covered by the rules of charity.[50] Once a poor person or a communal institution actually receives charitable money, it is no longer charitable funds and then cannot be diverted.[51] The same is true when the donor has expressly limited his donation to a particular cause. In such a case, the beneficiaries of that cause take possession at the time of the pledge and cannot be deprived of their ownership except by dint of "consent of the community."[52]

How Much Charity Should a Person Give?

Jewish law seems clear that the exact amount of charity that a person must give is not fixed and established. At the minimum, one must give at least one-third of a small biblical coin (a shekel) each year (less than ten dollars), and one who gives less than that amount has not fulfilled his formal technical duty.[53] In the close-to-ideal world—one in which many individuals have enormous amounts of wealth and the inclination to give such wealth away—Jewish law is also clear that a person may give away as large a sum of money as the poor need.[54] Shulchan Aruch goes on to state the general formulation for how much a person should actually give in the real world: "If one cannot afford to give to all the poor as much as they need, one can give up to 20 percent of one's possessions, and that is the ideal; 10 percent is the average way to fulfill this mitzvah, and less than that is considered miserly."[55]

---

[49] Yoreh Deah 252:1.

[50] Why such conduct is not obligatory under the rule of *lo taamod al dam reiecha* is beyond the scope of this chapter.

[51] Taz, Yoreh Deah 256:4; Shach, Yoreh Deah 252:2. But see Bach, Yoreh Deah 252.

[52] Rama, Yoreh Deah 252:1.

[53] Shulchan Aruch, Yoreh Deah 249:2

[54] See the formulation in Shulchan Aruch, Yoreh Deah 249:1, which makes it clear that the 20 percent limitation does not apply in such a case. See also Rabbi Ezra Batzri, Dinei Mamonot, vol. 4, 218 (chapter 3:1 of tzedakah). Rabbi Blau notes (Tzedakah u-Mishpat ch. 1, n.8) that there are some who disagree with this formulation and think that the rabbis capped charity at 20 percent. This approach is fraught with some difficulty, as he indicates. See Igrot Moshe, Yoreh Deah 1:143 (final paragraph).

[55] Shulchan Aruch, Yoreh Deah 249:1. On whether 10 percent is a Torah obligation, a rabbinic obligation, or merely a recorded proper practice, see Maharshag, Yoreh Deah 36; Maharit 1:127; Ahavat Chesed 19:4; and Minchat Yitzchak 5:34.

However, even this construct is tempered by the comments of the Rama,[56] who writes:

> Providing for one's own livelihood takes priority over all others, and one is not obligated to give charity until one's own livelihood is secured. After that, one should give priority to the livelihood of one's parents if they are poor, and they take priority over the livelihood of one's children. After that, one's children, and they take priority over one's siblings, who take priority over other relatives. Relatives take priority over one's neighbors, who take priority over the residents of one's own city, who in turn take priority over residents of another city. The same priorities apply to the redemption of captives.

As one reads Isserless's words, one could well imagine that a reasonable person might never, in fact, give charity to anyone outside one's near family.

The great Rabbi Epstein (in *Aruch Hashulchan*)[57] notes the problem and asserts:

> Thus, it seems clear to me that what Rabbi Saadia Gaon wrote, that one's own livelihood having priority is limited to an individual who earns only sparing bread and scant water. That is why he elicited proof from the Zarephathite widow, for in that case lives were indeed hanging in the balance as there was a famine throughout the land, as described in I Kings (17:8–24). In such a case, if one has any bread or water left, one's parents take priority, then one's children, etc. However, it is obvious that a person who earns a prosperous living like an important householder; who eats bread, meat, and other cooked items as befits him; and clothes and cloaks himself appropriately is obligated to disburse 10 or 20 percent of his income as charity. A greater portion of the charity should be given to one's relatives and the residents of one's own city, but a small portion must be given to nonrelatives and the poor of other cities, for otherwise the inhabitants of an impoverished city would die of starvation, God forbid. Rather, it is certainly as I have outlined. This formulation must be correct, otherwise there would be no limit on one saying that one's own livelihood takes priority, and everyone would claim that they need all of their income for their livelihood—for there is no limit to expenses, as we know. Rather, it must be as I have presented, that this rule applies only to one who has but a small amount of food to sustain his own life and the lives of his wife and young sons and daughters.

This is exactly the problem in the world of giving: almost no one ever really feels that he or she has enough income to give away, and everyone senses that there are still more things that he or she *really, really, really* needs. Further, there can creep in an equivocation and self-serving conclusion that the poor are hardly really

---

[56] Yoreh Deah 251:3.
[57] Yoreh Deah 251:5.

poor. Measuring when a person has "enough," so that he ought to give away more is extremely difficult. As Rabbi Blau notes—and this is from a man who has spent his life clarifying many narrow details of Jewish law in his numerous volumes[58]— "The measure of suitable livelihood is unclear to me."[59]

It is also true that there is little discussion in the modern Jewish tradition of how poor a person must be to receive charity. Since governments provide basic needs now in all Western societies, one could flip this discussion and argue that almost no one should receive charity due to poverty, as basic needs are all provided for. Curiously, this would imply that it is better to support the study of Jewish Law and its scholars than the poor, "since the poor are not really needy anymore." Yet it is clear that there remain institutions that profess need and individuals whose needs are not provided for even under any of the current elaborate welfare systems.

Conclusion

First, the general structure of the entire Jewish community in the modern Western world is unique. Identification and support of Jewish causes is voluntary. No Jewish community has the power to tax, and no community has a functioning court that can compel the giving of charity. Because of this, if we wish to have communal institutions, they must be funded by voluntary contributions. Therefore, it is the normative practice within the community to reject the view of Maimonides that limits charity to poor people and instead to accept the view that all public needs are charities. Thus, everyone funds Jewish institutions with charity funds.

Second, the Jewish community can function this way, in fact, because the governments of nearly all Western nations (England, France, Germany, the United States, and Canada) are just and honest governments which provide for the basic needs of all of their citizens. These nations provide for the social and economic necessities for the poor on a consistent basis. This allows the Jewish community to allocate its funds less to the poor and more to institutions that support the study and observance of Jewish Law. This posture would be untenable if the poor were starving.

---

[58] On such complex topics as all of Choshen Mishpat, Ribit, Eruvin, etc.

[59] Tzedakah u-Mishpat, ch. 1, n. 15. For one example of how to compute one's income and tzedakah obligations, see Rabbi Dovid Bendory, "Computing Maaser—How Much *Tzedakah* do I Owe?" (online at http://rabbi.bendory.com/docs/maaser.php). (It is far from obvious to me that the detailed calculations found in this article can be explained with reference to normative halacha, even as the general principles presented seem to be correct.)

Third, our society is a relatively opulent one, with a great deal of pressure placed on individuals to be materialistic. To put this another way, a thousand years ago, society sensed that "God loves the poor,"[60] and those Jewish and Christian communities ennobled poverty, allowing the poor to look down on the wealthy. Our Western society—and certainly our American and European Jewish society—has not accepted this message, and it does not think that we can raise committed Jews in a religious community with that message and at a standard of living significantly lower than that of our neighbors.

Fourth, since Jewish Law accepts that the needs of the community in a general sense are to be considered charity, and since we lack any firm communal hierarchy for determining and prioritizing communal need, there are no clear guidelines establishing which communal institutions ought to be funded once the public charities that feed and clothe the poor are funded. It is difficult say with any certainty whether investing in medical research or funding a rabbinical seminary should have a higher or lower priority. Each donor decides. Unquestionably, it is better that they donate to one cause or the other rather than spend the same money on themselves.

Fifth, the concentric circles of charity found in the classical codes (self, family, city members, Israel, strangers) is of no basic importance, as it is clear that they are limited to funding the desperately poor and are of no relevance to the question whether a person should give money to United Synagogue of the UK, Yeshiva University, the ACLU, or a political party, none of which directly feed the poor.

Sixth, charity has become such a source of competition for scarce resources exactly for the reasons noted in the above five paragraphs. Since there are no firm Jewish law guidelines, each person uses his own judgment; once the needs of the poor who are profoundly hungry or others whose lives are at stake are taken care of, there are few guidelines left in Jewish law that compel giving of a specific type. This discretion encourages donations and should ideally make for a more charitable community (I hope).[61]

---

[60] See Bava Batra 10a. (See also James 2:5; and Luke 6:20–21, from which James's question actually derives.)

[61] In the course of the review of this chapter, one of the reviewers asked, "There is an interesting point about competition in charity. How does that competition work in practice? Is it allowable for community institutions to ask for contributions?" As I reflected on it, I found this a fascinating question from a different sociological point. Within the Jewish community, it should come as no surprise that there is a fierce competition to receive charity—overt and aggressive solicitation of charity and very comfortable and robust asking for money. There is little or no gentle tithing as is found in some churches. Indeed, when I was a synagogue rabbi, one of the tasks I regularly had was to write letters of endorsement to charities, so as to inform congregants that this charity was worthwhile.

In sum: charity is a totally different religious construct in the modern Western world than it was three centuries ago in Eastern Europe. Governments in Western Europe and North America have relieved the Jewish community of the basic burden of caring for the ill and the desperately poor and have made the redemption of captives a rarity in this world. This has allowed for a blossoming of giving to various communal needs designed to further the Jewish community by building social, religious, and Torah institutions that serve our community. I hope we can rise to the challenge of building wisely.

A nonletter from me was also a statement to my community. Since charity was not tithing and was not grounded in the synagogue at all, it should come as no surprise that there were aggressive institutional selection pressures and considerable competition.

OLD TESTAMENT PRINCIPLES OF ECONOMIC ETHICS

Jürgen von Hagen

Human lives everywhere and at all times are impregnated with economic relationships. Human beings live together, work together, and share economic resources. It is, therefore, not surprising that the Bible contains many passages relating to economic issues and principles of economic ethics. An exhaustive survey and discussion of biblical economic ethics would go far beyond the scope of this chapter. Instead, I wish to point out two foundational principles of Old Testament economic ethics—namely, stewardship and charity—and how they relate to four basic economic issues—work, property, exchange, and solidarity. I begin with an outline of the economic order of creation and then turn to the teaching of Old Testament Law with regard to these issues. I will conclude with a few remarks about markets.

IN THE BEGINNING: THE ECONOMIC ORDER OF CREATION

In the beginning, God created the world and entrusted it to humankind with a charge, namely, to "be fruitful and multiply, to fill the earth and subdue it," and to "have dominion over the fish of the sea, over the birds of the air, and over every living thing that moves on the earth" (Gen. 1:26, 28; Ps. 8:5-6).[1] God gave the same command to be fruitful and multiply to all animals, implying that he wants a world filled with a diversity of species of all kinds. By assigning all plants yielding seed as food to animals, God explicitly gave animals the right of subsistence, and human beings are to share with them what nature makes available.

According to the creation account, God made humans stewards over creation and trustees over the earth. Having dominion does not mean that humankind can do as they please. As God's steward, humanity is accountable to the Creator. John Calvin wrote: "All earthly blessings ... have been given to us [humans] by the kindness of God and appointed for our use under the condition of being regarded as trusts, of which one day we must give an account. We must, therefore, administer

---

[1] I use the New King James translation here and in the following.

them as if we constantly heard the words sounding in our ears: 'Give an account of your stewardship.'"[2]

God qualified the command to subdue the earth with the command to "tend and keep" it (Gen. 2:15). The Hebrew word עָבַד, which is here translated "to tend," generally means to work or labor. The God of the Bible is God at work,[3] and since human beings are created in God's image, work is part of human nature from creation. The Vulgate translates Job 5:7 as "Man [in the sense of humankind] was made to work as the bird to fly," a dictum also attributed to Martin Luther.[4] As John Calvin put it: "Men were created to employ themselves in some work, not to lie down in inactivity and idleness…. Wherefore, nothing is more contrary to the order of nature, than to consume life in eating, drinking, and sleeping, while in the meantime we propose nothing to ourselves to do."[5] For Calvin, work is the opposite of idleness and inactivity. It goes far beyond paid employment and includes all creative activities leading to "harmony and communion between humans."[6] Miroslav Volf offers this definition: "Work is honest, purposeful, and methodologically specified social activity whose primary goal is the creation of products or states of affairs that can satisfy the needs of working individuals or their co-creatures, or (if primarily an end in itself) activity that is necessary in order for individuals to satisfy their needs apart from the need for the activity itself."[7] Stated in the imperative plural, the divine command to "fill the earth and subdue it" addresses Adam and Eve as a community. They and their offspring are to do this cooperatively. From creation, human work is a social process that creates, maintains, and shapes social relationships.[8]

---

[2] John Calvin, *Institutes of the Christian Religion*, trans. Henry Beveridge (Grand Rapids, MI: Wm. B. Eerdmans Publishing Company, 1989) Book III, X.5, 34.

[3] David J. Jensen, *Responsive Labor: A Theology of Work* (Louisville, KY: Westminster John Knox Press, 2006); Friedrich Kiss, "Die menschliche Arbeit als Thema der Theologie," in *Mitarbeiter der Schöpfung: Bibel und Arbeitswelt*, ed. Luise Schottroff and Willy Schottroff (Munich: Chr. Kaiser, 1983), 20.

[4] "Homo ad laborem nascitur et avis ad volatum." Kuratorium Singer der Schweizerischen Akademie der Geistes- und Sozialwissenschaften (ed.), *Thesaurus proverbiorum medii aevi = Lexikon der Sprichwörter des romanisch-germanischen Mittelalters* (Berlin/New York: De Gruyter Kuratorium Singer, 1999), 200.

[5] John Calvin, *Commentary on the Book of Genesis*, vol. 1 (Grand Rapids, MI: Christian Classics Ethereal Library, n.d.), 77.

[6] Caroline Bauer, "The Necessity to Work, According to John Calvin's Duty of Stewardship," *European Journal of the History of Economic Thought* 24/4 (2017): 689–707, at 696.

[7] Miroslav Volf, *Work in the Spirit: Toward a Theology of Work* (Oxford: Oxford University Press, 1991), 10–11.

[8] See Wolfhart Pannenberg, *Was ist der Mensch? Die Anthropologie der Gegenwart im Lichte der Theologie*, 2nd ed. (Göttingen: Vandenhoek & Ruprecht, 1964), 77.

As God's stewards, human beings find fulfillment in and glorify God by their work.[9] God makes his creative power visible through their work and cooperates with them in it. Martin Luther wrote that work is "God's mask behind which he hides himself and rules everything magnificently in the world."[10] According to John Calvin, God said to humankind: "Come to possess [creation].... Only apply to serve me and let me do: because I shall work such kind that the one who strives to follow me will not lose his efforts, he will not work of one useless labor, I shall make the whole fruit."[11] In this cooperation, human beings realize their own inability to accomplish anything without the Lord's blessing (Ps. 127:1). At the same time, God blesses them by blessing their work (Ps. 90:17). Martin Luther wrote: "It is our role to do hard work, but we must know that our labor does not suffice. We are to till the ground, to sow, and if it ripens, to harvest; nevertheless we are to confess and say: 'Unless the Lord had given it, all our work would have been in vain, dear Lord, it is your gift.'"[12]

The command to "fill the earth" indicates that God is pleased with the expansion of the human race to the point that it makes full use of the earth's ability to provide sufficient food for every human being. Humanity's task is to protect the earth against destruction and to increase its fertility, to make the fullest use of it and to share its resources among all people, those living and those yet to be borne.[13] In Calvin's words:

> [W]e possess the things which God has committed to our hands, on the condition, that being content with a frugal and moderate use of them, we should take care of what shall remain. Let him who possesses a field, so partake of its yearly fruits, that he may not suffer the ground to be injured by his negligence; but let him endeavor to hand it down to posterity as he received it, or even better cultivated. Let him so feed on its fruits that he neither dissipates it by luxury, nor permits it to be marred or ruined by neglect. Moreover, that this economy, and this diligence, with respect to those good things which God has given us to enjoy, may flourish among us; let everyone regard himself as the steward of God in all things which he possesses.[14]

---

[9] David S. Lim, "The Doctrine of Creation and Some Implications for Modern Economics," *Transformation: An International Journal of Holistic Mission Studies* 7 (April–June 1990): 31.

[10] Martin Luther, *Werke Kritische Gesamtausgabe*, vol. 15 (Weimar, 1883), 373; Volf (note 7), 99.

[11] John Calvin, "Second Sermon on Deuteronomy 1:3-8," quoted in Bauer (note 6), 696.

[12] Martin Luther, "Sermon on Matthew 6:24-34," in *Die Werke Luthers in Auswahl*, vol. 8, ed. Kurt Aland (Göttingen/Zürich: UTB Vandenhoek, 1991), 361.

[13] Christopher J. H. Wright, *God's People in God's Land: Family, Land, and Property in the Old Testament* (Grand Rapids, MI: Wm. B. Eerdmans Publishing Company, 1990), 115.

[14] Calvin (no date), 77.

Calvin's understanding of human stewardship calls for increasing human flourishing and, therefore, economic growth, not as an end in itself but to achieve a better life for all people.[15] Adam and Eve were not supposed to use the abundance of creation for themselves alone. They were called to use time, effort, and resources to raise the next generation.

The common understanding of the command to be fruitful is to procreate. In the present context, however, it is worth pointing out a broader meaning of fruitfulness in the Bible. The Hebrew root word, פָּרָה, refers to a tree bearing edible fruit hanging from its branches. Its distinctive feature is to make what it produces available to other created beings for food that any passerby, human or animal, can freely pick. Metaphorically, being fruitful can be understood as producing things for the benefit of others. In biblical wisdom literature, fruitfulness is the essence of living a life in righteousness (e. g., Ps. 1:3).[16] In this wider sense, fruitfulness can take many forms. The command to be fruitful is a command to exercise charity generously, an attribute which, as God's stewards, human beings are to share with their creator.

The commandments to work, be fruitful, and multiply are the three fundamental constituents of the economic order in the Garden of Eden. They express what it means for human beings to be stewards of God. Coming from creation, they remain in full force after the Fall.

Stewardship and Charity in the Torah Economy

At the heart of the Torah is the account of how God liberated the people of Israel from the oppressive and cruel slavery in Egypt and gave them the Land of Canaan to live in. On the way there, God gave Israel the Law, spelling out the principles of living in righteous relationships with God and among themselves. Not surprisingly, many parts of the Law relate to economic issues. M. Douglas Meeks speaks about the Torah as political economy and argues that the Torah economy is defined by the protection of the poor and the weak members of society.[17] But this definition is too narrow. While charity remains a foundational principle of economic ethics under the Torah, so does stewardship. I will illustrate this by considering work, property, exchange, and acts of solidarity.

---

[15] Bauer (note 7), 698.
[16] Leland Ryken, et al., eds., *Dictionary of Biblical Imagery* (Downers Grove, IL: Intervarsity Press, 1998), 310.
[17] M. Douglas Meeks, *God the Economist: The Doctrine of God and Political Economy* (Minneapolis: Fortress Press, 1989), 84.

WORK

It is a common misperception that the necessity to work is a punishment for sin. True, while work in paradise was "pleasant, and full of delight, entirely exempt from all trouble and weariness,"[18] after the Fall humans must work with difficulty and in the sweat of their faces (Gen. 3:17–18). Nature no longer cooperates with them. And yet, humankind is not condemned to work in vain; the divine verdict that "in the sweat of your face you *shall eat bread*" (Gen. 3:19) contains promise that work will yield sufficient food to feed them. It is certainly not, as Meeks claims, a condemnation to never finding fulfillment in one's work.[19]

In this, the Old Testament is radically different from ancient Greek mythology. The Greek poet Hesiod spoke of a golden age in which men and women were free from work. The need to work hard was one of the plagues by which Zeus punished humankind for obtaining fire through Prometheus.[20] Sisyphus, the man who wanted to be equal to the gods, was condemned to eternal, senseless hard labor. In contrast, according to the Old Testament, it is part of God's mercy to condemn humankind, who wanted to be like Him, to the very activity which makes human beings similar to God, namely, to be creative in their work. From a biblical perspective, work cannot be reduced to a mere toil necessary to feed oneself.[21]

Biblical Law stipulates that human work should be continuous work. John Murray points out the error of reading the Fourth Commandment only as the ordinance of a day of rest. It says more than that: "Six days you shall labor and do all your work." Work and rest are to be on a regular cycle.[22] As God did all his work in six days, humans must do all that is required of them in the appointed time. The book of Proverbs abounds with warnings that idleness leads to moral degeneration and takes away God-given freedom and dignity. It points out the adverse consequences of not working: poverty, shame, loss of freedom and the fruit of one's work, craving for unfulfilled desires, painful coveting of what others have, and self-deception about one's abilities.[23] The Fourth Commandment also excludes carelessness with regard to the duties of one's work,[24] and the book of Proverbs calls for diligence and warns against slothfulness (Prov. 21:5, 24:30 ff.).

---

[18] Calvin (no date), 77.

[19] Meeks, 128.

[20] Hesiod, "Works and Days," II.90–105, in Hugh G. Evelyn-White, *The Homeric Hymns, and Homerica*, Electronic Classic Series (Philadelphia: University of Pennsylvania Press, 1914), 40 ff.

[21] Herbert Schlossberg, *Idols for Destruction: The Conflict of Christian Faith and American Culture* (Wheaton, IL: Crossway, 1994), 16.

[22] John Murray, *Principles of Conduct: Aspects of Biblical Ethics* (Grand Rapids, MI: Wm. B. Eerdmans Publishing Co., 1957), 83.

[23] Prov. 6:6, 10:5, 12:24, 27, 13:4, 18:9, 19:15, 24, 20:4, 13, 21:25, 26:15, 16.

[24] Murray, 85.

Biblical Law does not declare work to be an end in itself. It remains the expression of stewardship. This is very clear from the fact that the social laws of Deuteronomy tie human work closely to the law of charity: God promises to bless a person's work if he or she treats the poor and weak members of society well.[25] One may become wealthy as a result of his or her work and God's blessing, but the purpose of wealth is not one's own luxury. It is the exercise of charity for those who are less privileged.[26]

Since God rested on the seventh day of creation, the Law commands humankind to rest on the Sabbath. The Sabbath limits the time that men and women are to devote to work and frees up time for other purposes. Biblical Law does not tell how one should use this free time. But not observing the Sabbath dishonors God, since breaking from work reminds humans of their complete dependence on God for their well-being.[27]

Work is a social phenomenon. According to Thorstein Veblen, "no individual has fallen into industrial isolation so as to produce any one article by his own independent effort alone. Even where there is no mechanical cooperation, men are always guided by the experience of others."[28] This view accords well with the biblical account of the emergence of specialized professions in Genesis 4. Kegler notes that the Old Testament uses a much differentiated vocabulary to describe activities such as metal working, indicating that the degree of specialization and division of labor was quite high in ancient Israel.[29] Economists regard specialization and the division of labor as the roots of the increase in the productivity of labor, a point noted also by the Old Testament's judgment that humanity is unrestrained in its achievements by coordinated division of labor.[30]

---

[25] Frank Crüsemann, "'...damit er dich segne in allem Tun deiner Hand...' (Dtn 14,29). Die Produktionsverhältnisse der späten Königszeit, dargestellt am Ostrakon von Mesad Hashavjahu, und die Sozialgesetzgebung des Deuteronomiums," in Schottroff and Schottroff, *Mitarbeiter der Schöpfung*, 88; see Deut. 12:7, 12:18, 14:29, 15:10, 15:18, 16:15, 23:21, 24:19.

[26] John Calvin, "Predigt über Deuteronomium 15:11–15 vom 30.10.1555 (Nr. 95)," in *Predigten über das Deuteronomium und den 1. Timotheusbrief (1555/1556)—A Selection*, Calvin Studienausgabe, vol. 7, ed. Eberhard Busch, et al. (Neukirchen-Vluyn: Neukirchener Verlag, 2009), 69 ff.

[27] Jensen (note 3), 23.

[28] Thorstein Veblen, "The Beginning of Ownership," *American Journal of Sociology* 4 (1898–99): 352–65, at 353.

[29] Jürgen Kegler, "Arbeitsorganisation und Arbeitskampfformen im Alten Testament," in Schottroff and Schottroff, *Mitarbeiter der Schöpfung*, 51–71.

[30] Adam Smith, *An Inquiry into the Nature and Causes of the Wealth of Nations*, 5th ed. (London: Methuen and Co., 1904), book 1, chapt. 1, online at econlib.org; Genesis 11:6.

Such a division of labor within society, in which different members specialize in the production of different things, requires the coordination of their activities to ensure that together they produce what they need as a society. Furthermore, it necessarily leads to the question of how the final products are distributed in society. If different people specialize in the production of different goods, and the range of goods each one produces is narrower than the range of goods he or she wishes to consume, producers must exchange their products to enable everyone to consume products of all kinds. Such exchange presupposes property rights over the goods produced.

PRIVATE PROPERTY

In accordance with the principle of stewardship, the Old Testament presents a hierarchical order of property: God, the Creator, is the ultimate owner of the world. "Indeed heaven and the highest heavens belong to the Lord your God, also the earth with all that is in it" (Deut. 10:14). He alone has the full right of disposal over all things, including the right to destroy what he has created.[31] Human ownership of anything is derived from and subordinated to God's ownership of it.[32] Two kinds of property receive special treatment in the Old Testament, ownership of human beings and ownership of land.

Slavery, that is, the private ownership of human beings, was a common economic institution in the ancient world. Slaves had no freedom and could be bought and sold at their owners' will.[33] In the *Gorgias*, Plato speaks about slaves as beings "who are of no earthly use except for their bodily strength," and in the Roman Empire, slaves were regarded as "a kind of tool that can talk."[34] The liberation from slavery in Egypt was the foundational event of the relationship between the people of Israel and their God. The book of Leviticus interprets this liberation as God assuming ownership of the Israelites: they are now his own, and an Israelite must not be enslaved by another (Lev. 25:39–46). Israelites impoverished by excessive debt could sell themselves into slavery, but only for periods of up to six years. Furthermore, the Old Testament regulated slavery in order maintain the slaves' human dignity. Slaves in Israel were regarded as part of their owners' households. They were circumcised, took part in the religious festivals and rit-

---

[31] Wright (note 13), 116f.
[32] Rousas John Rushdoony, *The Institutes of Biblical Law* (Nutley, NJ: The Craig Press, 1973), 451.
[33] Roland de Vaux, *Les Institutions de l'Ancien Testament* (Paris: Editions du CERF, 1958), 80.
[34] S. Todd Lowry, *The Archeology of Economic Ideas: The Classical Greek Tradition* (Durham, NC: Duke University Press Lowry, 1987), 106; and De Vaux, 80.

uals, had a right and a duty to enjoy the Sabbath, and a right to be compensated for injuries and mutilation inflicted on them by their masters.[35]

The granting of ownership of the land of Canaan is at the core of God's covenant with the people of Israel. The land is a conditional gift: the people will be allowed to dwell in it if they live by the Law. They will lose it and go back into slavery if they obstinately refuse to obey.[36] This conforms with the principle of stewardship. God is the ultimate owner of the land, and God's people are accountable to him for how they live in it.

God's primary ownership of the land finds its concrete expression in his claim on the firstborn of all animals and the first fruit of all plants as sacrifices (Exod. 34:12; Deut. 15:19, 26:2). Leviticus 25:23 says, "The land shall not be sold for ever: for the land is mine; for you are strangers and sojourners with me." God's ownership of the land is also reflected in the Sabbath Year regulations for the land and the imposition of various levies on its product.[37] These levies were to be used for sacrifice; for meals shared by the families and with their servants and strangers; for the Levites (to support those working for the Lord's sanctuary); and for the strangers, the orphans, and the widows. Landowners were obliged to leave some of the crop of their fields and vineyards to be harvested by the poor, who could feed themselves and provide themselves with other necessities of life, such as clothing, in this way. These regulations emphasize the dignity of work and the principle of self-responsibility as a basis for caring for the poor. Begging is connected with laziness in the Old Testament (Prov. 20:4), and the poor ought not to practice it.

Adam and Eve knew of no private ownership in the Garden of Eden. They had everything in common. Private property came into existence only after sin had corrupted human relationships. The Old Testament never actually institutes private property. The Torah simply takes it as given and protects it. Since all private property is a blessing and a gift from God, robbing a person is an intrusion into his relationship with God: it deprives the victim of the full enjoyment of the blessings God has bestowed on him, and he might lose his standing within the community of the people of God.[38] The prophets, therefore, condemned theft as a major sin. According to Psalm 50:16-18, theft, like adultery, is irreconcilable with the covenant between God and his people.[39] This connection of theft to a breach of the covenantal relationship between God and his people indicates that the Old Testament does not regard property rights as inherently sacrosanct; their violation is

---

[35] Gen. 17:12-13; Deut. 12:12, 18; Exod. 20:10, 23:12; Deut. 16:11; Exod. 21:26-27.
[36] Lev. 26:31 ff., Deut. 28:63 ff., Ezek. 33:25.
[37] Exod. 23:10-11; see also Lev. 25:2 ff; Lev. 27:30-3; Deut. 12:5-19.
[38] Wright (note 13), 136, Rushdoony (note 32), 453 f.
[39] Hos. 4:2, 7:1; Isa. 1:23; Jer. 7:9-10.

punished because it damages the covenantal relationship.[40] The Law against theft comes with the commandment of restitution, the amount of which depends on the extent of the damage done.

Calvin writes in his treatment of the Eighth Commandment:

> Since charity is the end of the law, we must seek the definition of theft from thence. This, then, is the rule of charity, that every one's rights should be safely preserved, and that none should do to another what he would not have done to himself.... We must bear in mind also that an affirmative precept, as it is called, is connected with the prohibition; because, even if we abstain from all wrongdoing, we do not therefore satisfy God, who has laid mankind under mutual obligation to each other, that they may seek to benefit, care for, and succor their neighbors.[41]

The proper understanding of the Eighth Commandment is that it prohibits all manner of treating others dishonestly or unfairly in economic matters. Luther made the same point in his commentary on the same commandment in the Greater Catechism. Calvin adds that Old Testament Law demands treating with care any property that a person might have lost and returning it to the owner.[42]

Private property flows from the principle of stewardship. St. Thomas Aquinas taught that it provides greater incentives than common ownership does for a person to take care of the means of production available in an economy and to use them productively.[43] Society as a whole is better off when every individual strives to increase his possessions, because he exerts greater effort to do so when they belong to him privately than when they are common property.[44]

According to the Old Testament, private property has the purpose of fostering human welfare. "Everyone his own fig tree and everyone his own vineyard" is the epitome of well-being (Mic. 4:4, Zach. 3:10). "A man and his house" and "a man and his inheritance" succinctly express the economic ideal of early Israel

---

[40] Wright (note 13), 140 f. Lev. 6:2 ff. calls dishonest behavior with regard to another person's property a "trespass against the Lord."

[41] John Calvin, *Harmony of the Law*, volume 3 (Grand Rapids, MI: Christian Classics Ethereal Library, n.d), 138, online at http://www.ccel.org/ccel/calvin/calcom05.

[42] John Calvin, "Predigt über Deuteronomium 22:1-4 am 2.1.1556 (Nr. 125)," in Busch, et al., (note 26), 130 f.

[43] Odd Langholm, *Economics in the Medieval Schools: Wealth, Exchange, Value, Money, and Usury according to the Paris Theological Tradition 1200-1350* (Leiden: E.J. Brill, 1992), 213 ff.

[44] "It is a good thing that each one shall enlarge his possessions more, applying himself to them more carefully as being his own." Cited from Langholm, ibid., 215.

(Mic. 2:2b).⁴⁵ Yet the Old Testament also warns of the dangers of materialism, that is, the tendency to seek one's security and happiness in the wealth of material things (Deut. 8:17-18, Ps. 52:7, 12).

Collective property is the exception in the Old Testament, and there is no state property.⁴⁶ Thus, the family and the individual have preeminence over the state in matters related to property and are protected from the power of the state. When the people of Israel demanded a king, the prophet Samuel warned them that kings would confiscate their best property (1 Sam. 8:11 ff.). First and Second Kings show that his warning was all too justified. With the kings came the confiscation of lands and goods, excessive taxation, and the emergence of a rich class oppressing the poor. Later, it fell to the prophets to preach against the rich oppressing the poor and economically vulnerable people in Israel and to warn of God's punishment.⁴⁷

The use of things privately owned can cause damage to other persons and their property. Foreseeing this, Old Testament Law contains rules of liability. Owners must assure that no harm is caused to others by their property. If an accident occurs and they have not taken proper precautions, they are liable and must make restitution. If the accident causes human fatalities, they are punished further (Exod. 21:33-34). A person whose property causes damage because he was negligent must make restitution (Exod. 22:5-6). There is a gradation in the kind and extent of restitution which seems to depend on the degree of diligence that one can reasonably expect.⁴⁸

Diligence, however, is expected not only from owners. The case of a goring ox is an interesting one. An ox which has inflicted a fatal wound on a man or a woman must be killed, and its meat must not be eaten. Beyond that, there is no further penalty to the owner. If, however, the owner knew that the ox was aggressive, he is guilty of the victim's death and either must be stoned to death or must redeem his life by paying whatever price is demanded from him (Exod. 21:28-32). A similar rule holds if one ox kills another (Exod. 21:35-36; Deut. 22:8).⁴⁹ In both cases, knowledge that the ox was aggressive plays a critical role. Here, Old Testament Law requires diligence from both sides. Dealing with an ox is dangerous, and everyone involved with it should know that and should either take proper care or

---

[45] John A. Dearman, *Property Rights in the Eighth-Century Prophets: The Conflict and its Background* (Atlanta, GA: Scholars Press, 1988), 12.

[46] One exception is the common land outside the city, where the inhabitants of the city farmed and kept their herds; cf. Num. 35:3, Josh. 21:13 ff., 2 Chron.31:19. Ezek. 48:15, 18 f.

[47] E. g., Amos 2:6-8; 4:1; 5:10-12; Isa. 5:8; Jer. 22:13; Mal. 3:5; Mic. 2:1-2.

[48] David L. Baker, *Tight Fists or Open Hands? Wealth and Poverty in Old Testament Law* (Grand Rapids, MI: Wm. B. Eerdmans Publishing Company, 2009), 60.

[49] Ibid., 54-56.

share part of the liability. If the liability always fell on the owner of the goring ox, there would be little reason to be careful when using another person's property. Animal owners would be reluctant to lend their animals to others, with the consequence of reducing the potential borrower's farming productivity and welfare. But if the ox is known to be aggressive, its owner has a greater responsibility to prevent damage. Here again, we see a balance between the owner's responsibility to avoid harm and society's interest in increasing economic efficiency.

EXCHANGE AND TRADE

As explained in chapter 1 of this volume, trade creates opportunities for welfare gains that buyers and sellers share. But trade also creates opportunities for fraud, the more so when people buy and sell less frequently—that is, when markets are smaller and competition less. Old Testament Law puts fraudulent trade in direct connection with theft (Lev. 19:11-13, 6:2-7). Trust and honesty in exchange and trade are thus rooted in the greater principles of stewardship and charity. They are not merely instrumental to facilitating efficient economic transactions. The use of false measures and weights in trade is seen in the same context, and the book of Deuteronomy warns that it might lead to being expelled from the Land of Canaan (Lev. 19:36; Deut. 25:13-15). Indeed, the prophet Isaiah (1:22) lamented the spreading of dishonest business as an example of the moral decay of Judah which ultimately led to its destruction. Leviticus 25:14 commands sellers and buyers to deal honestly and fairly with one another. This requirement prohibits selling goods of quality worse than promised and underpaying for good quality.[50]

Employment relations are treated in the same way. According to Leviticus 19:13 and Deuteronomy 24:14-15, not paying a person what has been agreed to and holding back wages are acts of stealing. The prophets Jeremiah (22:13) and Malachi (3:5) warned of divine retribution against the practice of not paying workers their wages fully and in time.

SOLIDARITY

"Charity is the end of the Law," and it is owed to all people, rich and poor. In addition to this general principle, Old Testament Law demands special acts of solidarity with the poor and the weak members of society, widows, orphans, and strangers. These demands do not flow primarily from the principle of charity. If they did, caring for the poor would merely be a matter of maintaining social order, and the extent to which such care is practiced would be a matter of subjective

---

[50] John Calvin, "Predigt über Deuteronomium 5:19 vom 3.7.1555 (Nr. 39)," in Busch, et al. (note 26), 55. The incentive for buyers to understate the quality of what is sold is recognized in Proverbs 20:14: "'Bad, bad,' says the buyer. But when he goes his way, he boasts."

sympathy with them.[51] Instead, the Law's demands for solidarity flow primarily from the principle of stewardship. John Calvin taught that those who are economically well off are called to be "stewards of God's charity"....

> If [God] gives a man more than he needs for his livelihood, He makes him a representative of His own person and says: 'It is my nature to do good, for all benefactions come from Me.' Accordingly, all rich who have something with which they can do good, are certainly God's officers. They exercise what is His nature, namely, to help their neighbors to live.[52]

This rooting of the demands for solidarity in the principle of stewardship can be seen in the many instances in which the Old Testament justifies them by reminding God's people of the fact that they were weak, poor slaves in Egypt, and that God fought for them and liberated them from their misery (Deut. 24:22). Divine charity rather than subjective sympathy, then, is the standard of solidarity according to the Law.

Acts of solidarity include freely giving the poor what they need (Deut. 15:7-8). But the concepts of almsgiving and begging are noticeably absent from the Old Testament. When the Law commands those who have enough to open their hands wide to the poor, the context suggests that what it means is not to give alms but rather to lend to the poor what they need, with the implication that they will return what they owe later on (Deut. 15:8, 11). Is there any chance that they might be able to do that? The Law calls on landowners not to glean their fields and not to harvest their trees and vineyards to the maximum possible, but to leave parts of them unharvested as an opportunity for the poor and weak to earn their own livelihood by their own work (Deut. 24:19-21). This would give them a possibility to return what they borrowed.[53] It is in this context of lending to the poor that the prohibition to charge interest applies. In the regions surrounding Israel, interest rates could be very high, and having to pay interest could become a source of perpetual impoverishment. Credit was commonly secured by pledges, but the Law restricts pledges to ensure that they not cause borrowers to lose their dignity or their livelihood (Deut. 24:6 ff.).

In a similar vein, an Israelite man or woman could be sold into slavery to solve a problem of excessive debt, but such slavery was limited to six years, and the

---

[51] Meeks (note 17), 84.
[52] John Calvin, "Predigt über Deuteronomium 24:19-22 vom 11.2.1556 (Nr. 141)," in Busch, et al. (note 26), 185.
[53] Sydney Homer and Richard Sylla, *A History of Interest Rates*, 4th ed. (Hoboken, NJ: John Wiley & Sons, 2005), report real interest rates of 30 percent and more in ancient Assyria and Babylonia.

slave master was commanded to supply the slave generously with products of his own farm when he or she was let go (Deut. 15:12 ff.).

Old Testament law does not prescribe the leveling of differences in wealth. It states explicitly that there will always be poor people in Israel (Deut. 15:11). Both the rich and the poor are thus called to recognize and accept their God-given economic situations. The rich in particular should use their wealth not only for themselves but as an opportunity to better the condition of the poor. According to John Calvin, a rich person should spend his wealth "so that the profit returns to all his household."[54] Wealth accumulation for its own sake is thus ruled out. Significantly, in addressing the rich about the obligation to care for the poor, Deuteronomy 15:11 speaks of *"your poor,"* thus indicating a special relationship between the two. As God cares particularly about the poor and hears them when they cry out against oppression and injustice, so the rich as God's steward must use their economic means to care for the poor.[55]

Apart from these regulations of individual relationships between rich and poor persons, Old Testament Law also creates social institutions designed to care for the poor. The large sacrificial meals prescribed for the religious festivals of Passover, Booths, and Tabernacles were to be shared among the families gathering together and the poor and the sojourners in Israel. Furthermore, Deuteronomy 26:28 ff. commands a special tithe to be collected in Israel every third year. The proceeds were to be put into storehouses of the cities and to serve as provisions for the poor, the strangers, and the Levites.

CONCLUSIONS: MARKETS

Old Testament principles of economic ethics touch on important aspects of the human character and its formation. They are valid regardless of the particular economic system prevailing at any time, whether a subsistence, feudal, centrally planned, or capitalist market economy. Indeed, the concept of markets is remarkably absent from the Old Testament. The King James Version of the Bible uses the Hebrew word מַעֲרָב (market, merchandise) a mere eight times and exclusively in the book of Ezekiel, and uses the word עִזָּבוֹן (commerce, market) only seven times, again only in Ezekiel.

Nevertheless, it would be wrong to say that the Old Testament has no views on economic systems. The stories surrounding the Law give some hints. The economies of ancient Mesopotamia and Egypt were built along river valleys. This economic base seems to have contributed to the emergence of central administrations to assure the efficient operation of large systems of irrigation. These econo-

---

[54] Cited after Bauer (note 6), 700.
[55] John Calvin, in Busch, et al. (note 26), 72 f.

mies were able to produce large surpluses and wealth but concentrated them in the hands of strong bureaucracies. Abraham left this environment for the land of Canaan, a hill country with many small rivers and creeks facilitating decentralized and diversified agricultural activity.

The story of Joseph points in the same direction. Joseph advised the Egyptian Pharaoh to build a system of store houses. As Pharaoh's manager, Joseph collected the harvests from all Egypt and stored them there. When the famine hit Egypt, Joseph used the grain stored to feed the Egyptians, but in the process disowned them of their land and made Pharaoh the largest landowner, in fact, the only landowner apart from the priests. Joseph saved his family, but the people of Israel were later enslaved in Egypt.

There is a lesson here that governments in centrally planned economies take the most valuable assets (land) from their own subjects and pay them with what originally was their own, namely, their harvest, and that they have a tendency to enslave people. The book of First Kings informs us that the reign of King Solomon in Jerusalem brought with it a strong centralization of the Israelite economy managed in the interest of the royal palace. As a result, the people were taxed heavily and subject to forced labor. Solomon gradually became involved with the pagan practices of his foreign wives. The parallel developments of economic centralization and the king's apostasy shed a negative light Solomon's economic administration.

Economic Conditions Impacting Luke's Concept of Economic Solidarity

Kaja Wieczorek

The shepherds in Calpurnius Siculus's *Eclogues* sit happily singing under a plane tree. They praise the new divine Roman emperor Nero, attributing godlike qualities to him and stating that he has brought fertility, prosperity, and peace to the whole empire. "As soon as the earth felt his divine influence, crops began to come in richer abundance, where furrows erstwhile disappointed hope; at length the beans scarce rattle in their well-filled pods: no harvest is choked with the spread of the barren tare, or whitens with unproductive oats."[1] Calpurnius Siculus leaves no doubt that, under Nero's reign, agriculture has developed into a paradisiacal idyll of nature: sheep have full udders, flowers no longer need care, seed sprouts by itself, vegetables and fruits of the earth thrive more abundantly than ever, and human labor seems almost superfluous.[2] The Golden Age has begun in all its fertility and glory.

After decades of civil wars and famines, Augustus was able to herald a period of lasting peace and political stability in 27 BCE. As a result, he was worshiped as the sacred savior of the world, and his reign was regarded as the return of the utopia of the ancient Golden Age. From that time on, great political visions and hopes for a new age, woven into harmless shepherd songs and an idyllic, solemnly joyful atmosphere, developed into a Roman "brand label" that generally served as an instrument of propaganda for Roman emperors.[3] The description of his reign as an idyll of nature, with agricultural fertility bringing improved economic welfare and universal freedom, was a central motif of honoring the emperor. Images in monuments and reliefs of the imperial age present the harmonic and symbiotic existence of animals and nature in all its abundance. Whether the political efforts

---

[1] Calpurnius Siculus, "Bucolica," Eclogue IV, ll. 115–16, in *Minor Latin Poets*, vol. 1, trans. John Wight Duff and Arnold M. Duff, Loeb Classical Library 284 (Cambridge, MA: Harvard University Press, 1934).

[2] Ibid., ll. 102–16.

[3] Stefan Schreiber, *Weihnachtspolitik. Lukas 1–2 und das Goldene Zeitalter*, Novum Testamentum et Orbis Antiquus 82 (Göttingen: Vandenhoeck & Ruprecht, 2009), 28, 35–45.

of the emperors were successful or not seemed to be of secondary importance. The imagery of a permanent state of happiness represented a counterworld to the existing conditions and pushed itself to the fore, masking the realities.[4]

How does Luke react to this kind of Roman propaganda? Luke 2:1 mentions the census of Augustus and his universal power over the whole world (πᾶσαν τὴν οἰκομένην), alluding to the image of the emperor as the ruler of the earth. The birth of Jesus is set on the stage of world history. Suddenly, the focus shifts from the emperor to the crib and declares the infant—not the emperor—to be the main character of the story. By using the motif of the newborn divine child, by which not the emperor is meant, Luke shows Jesus's superiority and indicates that Augustus and his proconsul play only a small role in the great plan of salvation by Jesus Christ.[5]

Stefan Schreiber and Michael Wolter have shown that typical Christmas motifs such as the divine child, the shepherds, and the crib seem to be allusions to the bucolic texts and images of the Golden Age propaganda and should, therefore, be interpreted in political terms.[6] In Luke's narrative of Jesus's birth, every episode in Luke 1–2 contains virtually lyrical passages.[7] Their form and content not only imitate the mode of expression of the Old Testament psalms but also display essential stylistic elements and topoi of the Golden Age, such as freedom, justice, a new reign, liberation, and salvation.[8] Plenty of words in Luke 1–2 have a Jewish connotation and are also typical for Roman propaganda. For example, Κύριος (lord) and σωτήρ (savior) were political terms: σωτήρ was specifically used for Augustus or Vespasian.[9] Κύριος was used more generally for Roman emperors (see, for example, Luke 2:11). Furthermore, εὐαγγελία (good news) was a technical term for a new emperor's birthday and accession to power. Correspondingly, Luke announces the births of John the Baptist and Jesus with εὐαγγελίζομαι (see Luke 1:19; 2:10). Luke also uses the typical elements of a Hellenistic vita of a

---

[4] Paul Zanker, *Augustus und die Macht der Bilder*, 5th ed. (Munich: Beck, 2009), 177–88, 284–90.

[5] Schreiber, *Weihnachtspolitik*, 63 f., 69 f.

[6] Cf. Schreiber, *Weihnachtspolitik*. Cf. Michael Wolter, "Die Hirten in der Weihnachtsgeschichte (Lk 2,8-20)," in *Religionsgeschichte des Neuen Testaments. Festschrift für Klaus Berger zum 60. Geburtstag*, ed. Axel von Dobbeler (Tübingen: Francke, 2000), 501–17.

[7] See the announcements of both the birth of John the Baptist and the birth of Jesus (Luke 1:13-17; 1:30-33); See Magnificat (Luke 1:46-55), Benedictus (Luke 1:68-79), Song of the Angels (Luke 2:14), Nunc Dimittis (Luke 2:29-32).

[8] Compare to the following part Schreiber, *Weihnachtspolitik*, 16 f., 66, 69 f., 91.

[9] See, e.g., Josephus, Bellum Judaicum, 7,71. In the synoptic gospels the term σωτήρ is used only in Luke 1–2. Therefore, Brown recognizes here "the format of an imperial proclamation": Raymond E. Brown, *The Birth of the Messiah: A Commentary on the Infancy Narratives in the Gospels of Matthew and Luke*, 2nd ed. (New York: Garden City, 1993), 424.

prominent sovereign. Last but not least, even the motif of the virgin birth was very popular in Roman propaganda.[10] Luke is not copying or alluding to a text of a specific poet but imitates a particular mode of expression very common in his time, developing a political theology in a narrative form and, through this narrative, criticizing the ideology of the Golden Age of the Roman Empire by putting Jesus in the emperor's place.

Most interesting for our topic is the observation that, while using central motifs, terms, and stylistic devices of Roman propaganda of the Golden Age, Luke's narrative lacks the motif of agricultural fertility. Luke uses the shepherd motif in 2:8–20, but in a more subtle way and without glorifying an idyllic nature.[11] In his version, shepherds do not sing while skipping across lush meadows. Considering the actual socioeconomic situation at the end of the first century, when Luke wrote, the absence of this motif is not coincidental. I argue that, rather than promising a carefree bucolic country life, Luke confronts the reader with difficult socioeconomic realities, rejecting the Roman propaganda of the Golden Age. I propose to understand the birth story as a starting point for Luke's socioeconomic critique, which motivated Luke to develop social models that need to be understood as alternatives to the imperial ideology.

This chapter focuses on Luke's implicit criticism of the economic conditions in the Roman Empire and his attempt to develop alternative concepts of economic solidarity. I presume that Luke questions the Roman notion of salvation as bringing economic welfare to everyone. According to his teaching, salvation is not to be expected from the policies of the Roman Empire but from the kingdom of God, which is announced in the birth of Jesus Christ. At the end of the first century, when Luke' gospel was written, the Parousia still had not occurred, and the kingdom of God certainly had not yet sprung forth in all its glory throughout the world. I want to show how Luke deals with the resulting disappointment. On one hand, the gospel in particular confronts the reader with a heavy socioeconomic critique and dismantles the utopia of a Golden Age by showing all the grievances of the present socioeconomic reality. Nevertheless, the gospel is not a blind social revolutionary text. It shows full well how the life of Jesus ended: Jesus was crucified, and the Roman Empire was not dispossessed. Luke does not expect a political downfall or a revolution, and never promises a paradise on earth. The kingdom of God is not like a human kingdom, and Luke is aware of the fact that, for an indefinite period, it won't arrive in full (see Luke 17:20 ff.; 19:11; 9:2; Acts 1:6–8).

On the other hand, Luke's writing does not lack a utopian spirit. The fact that the kingdom of God has not yet become a full reality does not mean that it is not the ideal fulfillment of all beliefs. For this reason, it is important for Luke to create a successful community structure of solidarity allowing Christians in the present

---

[10] See, e.g., the divine procreation of Augustus. Cf. Suet. Aug. 94,4 f.

[11] Wolter, "Hirten," 514–16.

state already to live an alternative to the economic and hierarchal structures of the Roman Empire.

In order to understand Luke's concept of solidarity as a social alternative, it is first necessary to give a short overview of the socioeconomic conditions of the Roman Empire at the end of the first century. Then, I will show how Luke reacts to these conditions by referring to the Parable of the Rich Farmer (Luke 12:16-34) and the Parable of the Prudent Steward (Luke 16:1-13).

The Socioeconomic Situation in the First Century

Despite the great boom in handicrafts and trade, which was mainly a result of the beneficial conditions created by the Pax Romana for the urbanization and development of the provinces, the Roman Empire was still an agrarian economy at the end of the first century. The only significant change in the economic structure of the early imperial period compared to the republic was its extension across the entire empire.[12] Land ownership continued to be regarded as the lowest-risk investment, which is why profits made in the commercial sector often were invested in land. In addition, many handicrafts were used for agriculture, and most trade consisted of agricultural products. Municipal craftsmen and traders were in the minority. Most of the members of the lower social strata worked in agriculture. Consequently, economic power at the time was vested in the owners of the large estates (*latifundia*), who belonged to one of the three aristocratic ranks.[13] The *latifundia* system, which had already developed slowly over the last centuries of the Roman Republic, increasingly spread to the provinces. By the end of the first century, large estates were common in all parts of the empire. Some of them, especially those owned by senators, covered entire parts of provinces. The small-holding family farms, which had initially come into existence in the provinces, could not compete with (and were displaced in large numbers by) the gigantic slave economy.[14] Pliny the Elder was one of the first to predict the destruction of the Italian economy by the increasing concentration of land in the *latifundia*, and he saw a similar development in the provinces. For example, he reported in the middle of the first century that the estates of six large landowners comprised half of the province of Africa.[15] Throughout the empire, the ownership of land was very

---

[12] Géza Alföldy, *Römische Sozialgeschichte*, Wissenschaftliche Paperbacks 8 (Wiesbaden: Steiner, 1975), 84-86.

[13] Ibid., 86f.

[14] Kuno Füssel, "Politische Ökonomie des römischen Imperiums," in *"...So lernen die Völker des Erdkreises Gerechtigkeit," Ein Arbeitsbuch zu Bibel und Ökonomie*, ed. Kuno Füssel and Franz Segbers (Lucerne/Salzburg: Edition Exodus, 1995), 36-59.

[15] Pliny, Natural history 18, 35.

unevenly distributed. This can be inferred from the so-called Tabula Alimentaria of Veleia from the area near Beneventum in Italy, which shows that 65 percent of the landowners possessed land of a value of 100,000 sesterces, seven percent possessed estates of a value of 500,000 sesterces, and only three percent had estates of values exceeding one million sesterces.[16]

Towards the end of the first century, the small-tenant system, under which large landowners divided up their estates and leased them to small farmers, became predominant. High rents often drove the small tenants into strong economic dependence on the landowners and often into a state of ever-increasing indebtedness.[17] Philo tells us that the rural population suffered terribly under the burden of taxes. Whenever a small tenant tried to flee, his family members were brutally abused.[18]

The social order of the Roman Empire from the reign of Augustus to the middle of the second century essentially corresponded to the social stratification that had developed in the late republic. In contrast to the republic, however, the emperor stood at the top of the social pyramid as the sole princep. The three aristocratic classes (ordines)—senators, equestrians (knights), and decurions (local politicians)—made up practically the entire political and economic elite. Including wives and children, the aristocracy constituted less than one percent of the total population of the empire.[19]

The senators were the most influential. The wealth of the senatorial families, especially their agricultural assets, was significant. All senators were large landowners possessing property in Italy as well as in the provinces. For example, the assets of the younger Pliny consisted largely of estates in northern Italy and Umbria.[20] Although his total assets are estimated to have been about 20 million sesterces, this made him nowhere near the richest senators. Gnaeus Cornelius Lentulus, one of the wealthiest senators, whose fortune was documented at the beginning of the imperial era, was valued at 400 million sesterces.[21] There was a pronounced social hierarchy among the senatorial ranks, a result of individual senators' different official positions and of official careers. Only a small number of selected individuals filled the most important offices.[22] In contrast to the republic, the boundaries between the senatorial and equestrian ranks were no longer fluid.

---

[16] Alföldy, *Römische Sozialgeschichte*, 95.
[17] Füssel, "Politische Ökonomie," 41–45.
[18] Philo, De spec. leg. 3,159 ff.
[19] Alföldy, *Römische Sozialgeschichte*, 130.
[20] Pliny, Epistles 3,19,8.
[21] Seneca, De benef. 2,27.
[22] Alföldy, *Römische Sozialgeschichte*, 106 f.

Augustus had arranged for the sons of senators to be automatically admitted to the senate by birth right, while equestrians had to apply for senatorial office.[23]

There were considerably more equestrians than senators. Their total number under Augustus is estimated at twenty thousand, and it grew steadily during the first two centuries as a result of provincial growth. Admission to the equestrian rank was not a birthright. Instead, an individual could work his way up the ranks to become part of it. An equestrian's economic situation could vary greatly depending on his professional activity and origin. Most equestrians, however, owed their social rank mainly to their wealth. In comparison to the senators, equestrians were also more interested in the nonagricultural economic sector. Among them were many wholesalers, bankers, and tax collectors, such as Cornelius Senecio, about whom Seneca reports that he took every opportunity of earning a living.[24] Nevertheless, land ownership was also their main source of income.[25]

A similar situation existed for the decurions, who formed an independent body of one hundred men in each city. This body included the magistrates and council members and thus formed the local and provincial aristocracy. Membership in this group was not hereditary either, but any rich citizen who held a municipal magistracy and was called upon for council membership was admitted. In fact, however, it was not uncommon for members of a family to belong to the decurions of a city for generations, since the sons of decurions inherited their fathers' properties.[26]

In order to belong to the influential top of the society, one had to have wealth, power, and prestige as well as be a member of one of the three leading aristocratic ranks. But there were also some rich people who did not belong to any of the three aristocratic ranks. These were freed slaves. Although they had a lot of economic power, with very few exceptions they did not hold political offices. They formed a very influential entrepreneurial class in trade, banking, and artisanal production. However, the stigma of their slave origins prevented them from breaking through social barriers and being admitted to the aristocratic ranks.[27] This is clearly shown by some provisions of the emperors: Tiberius forbade accepting sons of freedmen into the equestrian order.[28] Claudius permitted admission of the sons of freedmen to the senate only if Roman equestrians had previously adopted them. Nero, in contrast, strictly forbade this loophole.[29] Tacitus reports that in distinguished circles, even the most powerful freedmen were still looked down on as

---

[23] Suetonius, Aug. 38,2.
[24] Seneca, Epistles 101,1 f.
[25] Alföldy, *Römische Sozialgeschichte*, 108–10.
[26] Ibid., 112 f.
[27] Ibid., 116.
[28] Pliny, Natural history 33,32.
[29] Suetonius, Cl. 24,1; Nero 15,2.

slaves.³⁰ While power and wealth automatically followed from belonging to the aristocratic ranks, the reverse did not apply. In this way, the hierarchy of the social order was more or less maintained.³¹

In addition to the rich freed slaves, another group is to be mentioned which, due to its slightly more elevated social situation, also belonged to the higher social strata, although not to the aristocracy: the so-called retainers, who were direct assistants of the aristocracy. The retainers included, for example, noncommissioned officers, slaves, employees of magistrates such as scribes and lictors, priests, or even stewards of large estates.³² Most of these stewards were free, but in the first century slaves were also used for this task and were allowed to build their own fortune as well as to have a family; they thus had a special status.³³ Slaves belonging to the retainer group had a quite comfortable life and fulfilled important functions.³⁴

The small but extremely powerful elite was confronted by a large range of lower social strata. Everywhere in the empire, however, the rural poor were the poorest and most oppressed members of society. Contrary to what one might expect, the large number of enslaved workers on the *latifundia* were not the most miserable people. Because they represented an economic value for their masters, they were regularly fed. The many destitute small farmers who had to work hard to feed their families fared much worse.³⁵ In Egypt and Judea, their situation was particularly dire.

The Greek language distinguishes between two forms of poverty: πένης and πτωχός. Πένης describes an existence just above the subsistence level, or someone who had to work very hard for a living. The majority of the lower classes in the Roman Empire fell under this category. They were traders, free smallholders, craftspeople, soldiers, and small tenants. To be distinguished from this class are the pauperized people (πτωχός), who mostly lived below the subsistence level. These included day laborers, indebted small tenants, slaves who were not retainers, beggars, bandits, people with disabilities, lepers, shepherds, and widows.³⁶

Between the rich and the poor existed an almost unbridgeable gap, which was maintained by an extremely hierarchical elite. Political offices were awarded only according to reputation, rank, and wealth. The rich could become even richer at a rapid pace. For example, Tacitus reports that Seneca generated 300 million ses-

---

[30] Tacitus, Ann. 14,39.
[31] Alföldy, *Römische Sozialgeschichte*, 98 f.
[32] Vincenzo Petracca, *Gott oder das Geld. Die Besitzethik des Lukas* (Tübingen/Basel: Francke, 2003), 17–19.
[33] Pliny, Ep. 9,20,2.
[34] Alföldy, *Römische Sozialgeschichte*, 126, 128.
[35] Ibid., 128–30.
[36] Petracca, *Gott oder das Geld*, 18 f.

terces under Nero within four years.³⁷ In contrast, with few exceptions, it was practically unthinkable for the lower strata to advance to the upper ones. There was no real middle class. Only between one and five percent of the population could to enjoy "lush meadows." For the majority of the population in the Roman Empire, country life was anything but carefree, and the propaganda of the Golden Age was nothing more than a distant dream. Taking this into consideration makes the bucolic propaganda of a carefree and idyllic country life look cynical. In the following, I will discuss how Luke reacts to this reality.

LUKE'S CRITICISM OF THE SYSTEM OF LATIFUNDIA (LUKE 12:16–34)

In Luke 18:28-30, the disciples are promised not only eternal life in the future but also—and this is found only in Luke's gospel—"to receive many times more in these present times." It is very clear that Luke is not thinking about material wealth and property here, since Peter says in Luke 18:28 that they left their possessions (τὰ ἴδια), or at least the thought of owning things, behind them.³⁸ What is Luke thinking about?

The parable of the rich farmer in Luke 12:16-21 offers a first answer to this question. It deals with the situation of large estates in the Roman Empire and is, therefore, of sociopolitical importance for Luke's approach. That Luke is speaking about a large landowner is evident from the fact that the farmer is very rich (Luke 12:16) and has several barns at his disposal (Luke 12:18). But even these seem too small for him after a good harvest, which is why he wants to tear them down and replace them with larger ones. He apparently intends to store the grain for trade, since one can hardly assume that such a large amount of grain was intended for personal consumption alone. It is possible that the parable alludes to many large landowners' strategy of trying to push up the prices by holding back their stocks for a while and thus artificially reducing the general supply on the market. In times of grain shortage, prices sometimes rose enormously.³⁹ The Roman state

---

[37] Tacitus, Ann. 13,42.

[38] This might be an allusion to the supposed communal ownership of goods of the early Christian community in Acts 4:32, where nobody called anything his or her own (ἴδιον). By picking up on Hellenistic social utopian ideals, Luke presents the communal ownership of goods as the model of the early Christian community in the past, but he never presents it as the model of the present or the future. I therefore suggest an understanding of the communal ownership of goods as one possibility among many different alternative models of living in solidarity that Luke presents in Luke-Acts.

[39] See, for example, Franz Segbers, "'Ich will größere Scheunen bauen (Lk 12,18)'. Genug durch Gerechtigkeit und die Sorge um Gerechtigkeit," in Füssel and Segbers, "...So lernen

therefore had to intervene again and again to regulate the supply.⁴⁰ Philostratus mentions a revolt at the end of the first century in the Pamphylian city of Aspendos because some large landowners withheld grain.⁴¹ Dio Chrysostom describes how he, together with the large landowners, was almost killed by a mob in Prusa, because they were suspected of having driven up grain prices.⁴²

Luke condemns the profiteering by a few at the expense of many and calls for economic responsibility. He is concerned not only with the conversion of individual rich people but also with systemic change in economic practice. The landowner thinks of only his own well-being, showing no social responsibility in his plans for the future. His boundless selfishness is expressed linguistically by the many possessive pronouns he uses: καρπούς μου (v.17, *my* fruits/harvests), μου τὰς ἀποθήκας (v.18, *my* barns), πάντα τὸν σῖτον καὶ τὰ ἀγαθά μου (v.18, all *my* grain and *my* goods), τῇ ψυχῇ μου (v.19, *my* soul). From his point of view, everything belongs to him alone. But what if the goods do not belong to human beings at all, but were given by God to be used in solidarity? By suddenly taking the landowner's soul away, God demonstrates that the grain and even his soul do not belong to the landowner at all.⁴³ This is expressed by the rhetorical question in Luke 12:20, "Who will get what you have prepared for yourself?" That is, how do you benefit from all this wealth if you suddenly die? For whom and for what did you actually live? How pointless is a precaution that does not mind others? The point is: "This is how it will be with whoever stores things up for themselves but is not rich toward God (12:21)." To be rich toward God, according to Luke, means to live in solidarity and in harmony with one's environment. In order to clarify exactly this, the parable is placed right before the Q-text (Luke 12:22–32).

This Q-text seems to present an "economy" that opposes the profiteering demonstrated by the rich landowner. The ravens do not build barns, they do not sow or harvest, and yet they are fed. Likewise, the lilies and the grass grow and thrive without taking special precautions. All needs are satisfied, because God knows about them (Luke 12:30). One therefore should not worry constantly about one's own well-being, but rather trust in God's goodness and seek the kingdom of God (Luke 12:31).⁴⁴ A life according to the standards of the kingdom of God, in contrast

---

die Völker des Erdkreises Gerechtigkeit," 106–09. Or Luise Schrottroff and Wolfgang Stegemann, *Jesus von Nazareth. Hoffnung der Armen* (Stuttgart/Berlin/Cologne/Mainz: Kohlhammer, 1978), 126.

[40] Moses I. Finley, *Die antike Wirtschaft*, 3rd ed. (Munich: Deutscher Taschenbuch Verlag, 1993), 209.
[41] Philostratus, Apoll. 1,15.
[42] Dion Chrysostom, Disc. 46,7 ff.
[43] René Krüger, *Dios o el Mamón. Análisis semiótico del proyecto económico y relacional de Evangelio de Lucas* (Buenos Aires: Lumen, 2009), 254 f.
[44] Segbers, "'Ich will größere Scheunen bauen (Lk 12,18),'" 105, 112–14.

to the Golden Age, does not promise economic wealth or paradisiacal conditions. Rather, it stands for an emotional distance from property, more modest economic conditions, and a striving for solidarity. Luke sums this up in verses 33 ff., which probably also originate from Q: one should part with possessions, give alms, and not be profiteering, so that the wallets do not wear out. In this way one secures for oneself an eternal place in the kingdom of God. The transience of wealth and possessions is thus contrasted with the eternity of the kingdom of God (Luke 12:33–34).

> Consequently, to live in the spirit of the kingdom of God in one's heart does not mean only to wait for the arrival of the eschaton. Instead, it implies a reorientation of one's present life in matters of social values, an emotional distance from wealth and property and from a definition of happiness in purely material terms. In the promise of Luke 18:28 ff., the disciples are not guaranteed material compensation. Instead, compensation in this world consists of participation in a community marked by solidarity, in a life in conformity with one's neighbors and the environment. The question then is to what extent, according to Luke, this solidarity can be realized in a community of Christians. The following Parable of the Prudent Steward offers a good example of a concept of solidarity that perfectly clarifies that the belief in the kingdom of God represents an alternative reality that is not just spiritual but also possible as a socially lived experience.

A Socioeconomic Reading of the Parable of the Prudent Steward (Luke 16:1–13)

This parable is again about the situation of the large landholdings (*latifundia*). It is introduced with the words that "some rich man" (ἄνθρωπός τις ἦν πλούσιος) dismisses his steward (οἰκονόμος) because he is said to have squandered his money (Luke 16:1–2). The rich man represents a large landowner. Landowners often employed stewards who managed their estates in the provinces. Authorized stewards enjoyed great autonomy, but they were obliged to operate in the interest of their masters. For this steward, his dismissal is a financial and social catastrophe.[45] Now that he has nothing more to lose, he forges a plan to save him from his precarious situation. His last administrative act is to relieve his master's indebted tenants of large parts of their debts (Luke 16:5–7).[46] Doing so, he hopes

---

[45] The fact that he was dismissed makes it clear that he was not a slave but a contractor (Luke 16:2, 4).

[46] The subjunctive aorist μετασταθῶ in Luke 16:4b proves that the temporal sentence speaks of an action that is still outstanding in the future. This does indeed speak for the fact that his administrative authority at the time of termination has not yet completely expired, at least to the extent that the final statement of account is still outstanding (see

to be able to win friends among them, who will take him into their homes when he himself will be in need (Luke 16:4). Luke here adopts the principle of *do ut des* (Latin: I give so that you may give), which is typical of the Roman Hellenistic world. It was regarded as a fundamental principle of social behavior, but at the same time, it emphasizes the selfishness of the procedure.[47] The steward uses his economic powers strategically. He neither acts selflessly nor gives away his own money. He plays his part cunningly both to improve the situation of the farmers and to take precautions for himself. For this utilitarian approach, he is praised as clever even by his former master, the landowner, which may irritate the readers (Luke 16:8).

The point of the parable is verbalized in Jesus's commentary in Luke 16:9: "Make friends for yourselves by means of the mammon of unrighteousness." Luke does not condemn money itself, but the way it is used. Mammon is a metaphor for all the unfair structures inherently connected to money and possessions in the Roman Empire: the dispossession of small landowners in favor of the *latifundia*, the enrichment of the superrich at the expense of the lower strata of society, and the hierarchal structure of society in general. Finally, Luke also criticizes the role of religious representatives who miss the point and do not take care of the needs of the people.[48] In the Gospel of Luke, possession embodies a whole system of injustices. In a wise saying of Q (Luke 16:13/Matt. 6:24), this is expressed at the end of the parable, contrasting mammon, an idol, with God (Luke 16:13).[49]

The parable calls on the reader to interfere in this process, to take action in accordance with the virtues of the kingdom of God through small but meaningful acts such as the steward's cancellation of debts. In this interpretation, "making friends by means of mammon" does not mean giving to charity. This would not make sense here, because in this story the steward does not give his own money to

---

Luke 16:2). However, this does not mean that his termination is still negotiable. It is merely a statement that the administrator still seems to have access to all business records until his final settlement is paid. Cf. Michael Wolter, *Das Lukasevangelium*, Handbuch zum Neuen Testament 5 (Tübingen: Mohr Siebeck, 2008), 547.

[47] Petracca, *Gott oder das Geld*, 173f. This reciprocal principle is illustrated by a wordplay with δέχομαι, which means both "to take somebody in" in the sense of "to receive" somebody as a guest and "to take" in the sense of "to pick up a document": "so that they take me in" (ἵνα....δέξωνταί με, Luke 16:4) versus "take your debt notes" (and don't worry about them anymore) (δέξαι σου τὰ γράμματα, Luke 16:6–7). Cf. ibid., 164, footnote 11.

[48] Cf., for example, Luke 15:1–2, 7, where the Pharisees disapprove of Jesus sharing a table with tax collectors and sinners.

[49] Dieter Pauly: "'Ihr könnt nicht beiden dienen, Gott und dem Mammon' (Lk 16,13). Die Wiederherstellung einer gerechten Ökonomie und die Bekehrung eines Managers," in Füssel and Segbers, *"...So lernen die Völker des Erdkreises Gerechtigkeit,"* 199f.

the tenants. By canceling the debts, he spends the money of his master, the great landowner, and intentionally harms him. The message of the story is rather that the steward, in his economic position as steward, is part of the *latifundia* system and thereby participates in the "mammon of unrighteousness," but then he interferes with the system by using his economic authority in favor of the tenants.[50]

Verse 9 finally puts the entire parable into an eschatological light. The correct use of mammon becomes a test for the kingdom of God (Luke 16:9-12). Good deeds in this world that correct the system will be followed by heavenly rewards. There will be a time when the entire system of mammon will break down, and "when it *(mammon)* shall fail, they may receive you into the eternal tabernacles" (Luke 16:9). The finite system of unjust mammon is thus again contrasted with the infinite kingdom of God. When this might happen is not clear to Luke. Humans should not try to predict when this day will come (see Luke 17:20-21 or Acts 1:6-8), but instead be responsible by acting wisely and in solidarity with others in the present. The steward is compensated not only in the future by the eschatological promise but also in the present time by being able to count on the help of the tenant farmers when he finds himself in need. In my opinion, this is exactly what Luke 18:28 ff. has in mind: "to receive many times more in these present times" does not imply receiving wealth or goods for the individual. Instead it refers to joining a community characterized by solidarity and living in keeping with your social environment.

One question widely discussed in research is why, of all people, the master, whom the steward deliberately harmed, praises him for his bold actions in Luke 16:8a. Some exegetes identify Jesus with the master (Κύριος), claiming that Jesus's commentary on the parable can be found in verse 8a.[51] I propose that the irony of the parable is precisely the confusing twist that the master is impressed by the steward's clever dealings. This compliment turns upside down the social division between the large landowner on one hand and the tenants on the other. The steward, who still belongs to the system of *latifundia*, suddenly has broken the normal order, at least for a moment, with magnificent consequences for the tenants. In this kind of anarchistic instant, one sees a flash of the kingdom of God entering into the present, so that static categories and established structures lose their meaning.

---

[50] Ibid., 200.

[51] See, for example, Adolf Jülicher, *Die Gleichnisreden Jesu, zwei Teile in einem Band*, 2nd ed. (Darmstadt: Wissenschaftliche Buchgesellschaft, 1976), 503. Giambrone presumes, that the story world of the parable is intertwined with the narrative of Jesus and his disciples. Consequently, the word Κύριος lets the outer story merge with the inner story and the master of the parable with Jesus. Cf. Anthony Giambrone, *Sacramental Charity, Creditor, Christology, and the Economy of Salvation in Luke's Gospel*, Wissenschaftliche Untersuchungen zum Neuen Testament 2, 439 (Tübingen: Mohr Siebeck, 2017), 250 f.

But why is the steward in verse 8a still described as "unjust" (οἰκονόμος τῆς ἀδικίας)? Of course, his debt remission could be construed as fraud, or even theft. Jesus's comment starting in verse 8b, however, regards the debt remission as a good deed and as the correct way of dealing with unjust mammon, which cannot be comfortably aligned with any religious purity requirements. Therefore, verse 8b reads: "The children of this age are wiser in dealing with their kind than the children of light" (ὅτι οἱ υἱοὶ τοῦ αἰῶνος τούτου φρονιμώτεροι ὑπὲρ τοὺς υἱοὺς τοῦ φωτὸς εἰς τὴν γενεὰν τὴν ἑαυτῶν εἰσιν). This statement is to be seen as an ironic sideswipe at the Pharisees, who very intently seem to have listened to the parable that Jesus actually addressed to his disciples (Luke 16:14-15). They see themselves as immaculate "children of light" and disapprove of Jesus sharing a table with tax collectors and sinners (Luke 15:1-2, 7).[52] As a collector of the debts of his master, the steward is to be regarded as a tax collector. The fact that the Pharisees are being confronted with the image of a tax collector as a system breaker who comes closer to the kingdom of God than they do provocatively turns the existing socioreligious situation upside down. The parable does not, by any means, aim at characterizing the steward as a fraud, but rather shows the extent to which the existing conditions are already trapped in the power of mammon, and that the system requires uprooting. Consequently, it is not the steward himself who is unjust, but his general function as steward, being an extended arm of the economic system of the *latifundia*.[53]

This story thus demonstrates that it is possible to interfere in the system and change things by using economic knowledge and power in favor of the needy.[54] The steward's debt relief illustrates a tiny shift, a minimal difference from the normal order, which from the outside looks unsustainable at first. The system of *latifundia* has not been abolished, and the tenants have not been completely liberated from their precarious situation. However, at a microlevel, human encounters happened that previously had been prevented by different social positions. Steward and tenants interact with one another, laying the foundation for a principle of solidarity that goes beyond hierarchies and leads to mutual support. Therefore, the message is that real shifts, things that really make a difference, can arise from small encounters.

The parable can be seen as an example that motivates the reader to search for his or her own way of being more involved in solidarity. Using a narrative, Luke teaches that the kingdom of God appears in the present—or breaks through—when

---

[52] Giambrone, *Sacramental Charity*, 255 f. In contrast to Giambrone, Bovon assumes that the disciples are the "sons of light." Cf. François Bovon, *Das Evangelium nach Lukas. Lk 15,1-19,27* (Neukirchen-Vluyn: Neukirchner, 2001), 79.

[53] See also Krüger, *Dios o el Mamón*, 341. Similarly, Pauly, "Bekehrung eines Managers," 193.

[54] Pauly, "Bekehrung eines Managers," 200.

humans attempt to act and shape their world in solidarity, without claiming that the specific actions of the parable are the one and only way of living.

Conclusion

What is the main difference between the Roman utopia of the Golden Age and the hope for the kingdom of God as Luke presents it? The term "utopia" derives from the ancient Greek οὐ- (not) and τόπος- (location), meaning "no location." It thus describes a fictive societal community that is not yet realized or no longer exists, usually in the sense of a positive fiction, in contrast to the term "dystopia." This positive fiction poses an inherent criticism of the current society. From this perspective, one could label Luke a utopian. He clearly has a vision of a better society. The kingdom of god is not fulfilled yet, but—like a utopia—it encourages alternative ways of living together. Alternatively, "utopian" images reflect and criticize the actual socioeconomic situation; they suggest that at least fragments of alternative ways can already be lived in the present. Luke appeals to the reader to search for such alternatives.

In our common language, we use the term "utopia" mostly as a synonym for a fictitious plan or a vision of a new society that is not realizable, a wonderful dream that is never meant to come true. But most utopias actually claim to be realizable at some time. This has led and still leads to attempts to live utopian alternatives in the here and now, at least in a fragmentary way. The Roman propaganda of the Golden Age goes one step further by proclaiming that the utopia has already been fulfilled in the present. In contrast to the Romans, Luke never promises a paradise on earth and wants the reader to realize various possibilities for experiencing fragments of the kingdom of God. In different acts of solidarity, the kingdom of God flashes into the present, but it is never fully represented in any of these actions or models and should not be identified with a secular authority or secular system.

Luke's proclamation of the kingdom of God thus differs from the Roman Golden Age or any utopia in the understanding that Christians are responsible for trying to make this world one of greater solidarity. At the same time, they should not expect to achieve this by their own efforts alone. The belief in the kingdom of God is always grounded in the hope that, in the end, God Himself will act, and that there is no human system in the world that can replace this need.

Christian-Apocalyptic Protest from the First-Century 90s as a Reaction to Economic Conditions

Peter Lampe

In the previous chapter, Kaja Wieczorek has shown how Luke's New Testament writings criticized the Roman Empire's economic conditions as well as its ideology of the Golden Age and developed alternative models of economic solidarity. The biblical book of Revelation, written at the end of the first century,[1] took a less diplomatic and less constructive stance, protesting and not really developing alternatives—except that God would, in the near future, overturn the present power system and make room for a thousand-year-long reign of Christ and his followers on earth (Rev. 20:1–6).[2] Expecting an impending eschaton, the author did not pay much attention to improving life under the present political-economic system. Upholding the Christian identity even when under attack, resisting attack patiently and passively, and being ready to suffer were the author's instructions for the present time (Rev. 2:10, 25; 3:3, 8; 14:13; 20:4; 6:9; 22:11). Thus, instead of

---

[1] For the dating, see note 8, below.

[2] In this sense, and only in this sense, the author can be called a revolutionary. Yet his ethos was nonviolent, with the monopoly on legitimate violence being in God's hands. Thus, a nonviolent ethos correlated with a violent image of the divine. God's violent intervention in the near future released humans from having to use violence themselves. For this and the nonviolent ethos of Christian writings such as Revelation, see P. Lampe, "Die Apokalyptiker—ihre Situation und ihr Handeln," in *Eschatologie und Friedenshandeln: Exegetische Beiträge zur Frage christlicher Friedensverantwortung*, Stuttgarter Bibelstudien 101, ed. U. Luz, J. Kegler, P. Lampe, and P. Hoffmann (Stuttgart: Katholisches Bibelwerk, 1982), 59–114; regarding Revelation, 95–98; online at http://www.ub.uni-heidelberg.de/archiv/25279; DOI: http://doi.org/10.11588/heidok.00025279; P. Lampe, "La littérature apocalyptique: un Dieu violent et un ethos orienté vers la violence?," in *Dieu est-il violent? La violence dans les représentations de Dieu*, ed. M. Arnold and J.-M. Prieur (Strasbourg: Presses Universitaires, 2005), 31–48; P. Lampe, *Ad ecclesiae unitatem: Eine exegetisch-theologische und sozialpsychologische Paulusstudie* (Bern: Universität Bern, 1989), 253–81, online at https://digi.ub.uni-heidelberg.de/diglit/lampe1989; DOI: 10.11588/diglit.48669.

trying to make the present world better, the author preferred its apocalyptic negation.

Yet Revelation is an outcry against the contemporary political and economic systems as the author perceived them. Preserved in the Christian canon, the book is a rare piece of underground literature from the provincial lower social strata of the Roman Empire,[3] raising harsh political and economic protest in encrypted language that shows satirical features. It is worth zooming in on some of the texts in this document.

A white and a red horse race across the country (Rev. 6:2–4), their riders carrying a bow and a sword, probably symbolizing troops of the Parthian war and the first-century (BCE) civil war or the wars of succession in the year 68/69 CE. Behind them, hunger rides on a black horse with a scale in his hand (Rev. 6:5–6), representing high food prices caused by a shortage that plagued the province of Asia Minor in the early 90s: "A quart of wheat for a denarius, and three quarts of barley for a denarius, and do not harm the oil and wine!" (Rev. 6:6). An edict by the Emperor Domitian from the years 90–92 CE, which intended to increase grain production but also ordered the destruction of half of the vineyards of Asia Minor,[4] and a decree by L. Antistius Rusticus[5] show that, at least in the year 92/93 CE, a famine affected Asia Minor. The hunger horse is followed by a pale nag, representing death (Rev. 6:7–8).

Notwithstanding war and food shortages in the provinces, people in Rome lived the high life (Rev. 18:12 f,16; 17:4). By juxtaposing chapters 6 and 17–18, Revelation emphasizes the contrast between the provinces and the capital

---

[3] The author most probably was an early Christian ascetic itinerant prophet in Asia Minor, who moved around in the region of the seven cities in western Asia Minor addressed in Rev. 2–3. With his visions and oracles, he wanted to belong to the Christian prophets mentioned in Rev. 22:6, 9, 16; 11:18; 16:6; 18:20, 24; 19:10; 10:7 (cf. 22:7, 10, 18 f; 1:9–20). For rigorous and ascetic ethics, propagated as an ideal by the author, see 14:4 f; 2:14, 20–22; 3:15. For Christian itinerant prophets and teachers, see, e. g., Didache 13; 15:1 f.; 11:8, 5 f.; 2 John 10 f.; 2 Cor. 11:4; Acts 11:27 f.; 21:10; 18:24–27; 8:4 f, 25 f.; 11:19–21; 15:32 f.; 13:1–3; 1 Cor. 9:14; finally, the people behind the Q-source, and Eusebius, *H.E.* 3.39.4 regarding the first half of the second century in Asia Minor, http://www.ub.uni-heidelberg.de/archiv/25279; DOI: http://doi.org/10.11588/heidok.00025279.

[4] B. Levick, "Domitian and the Provinces," *Latomus* 41 (1988): 50–73, at 68. The edict stipulated, among other things, that in Asia Minor half of the vineyards had to be destroyed, possibly to protect the Italian vintners by keeping prices up. The exhortation not to harm the wine in Rev. 6:6 may refer to this stipulation.

[5] AE 1925, 126; Robert K. Sherk, *The Roman Empire: Augustus to Hadrian* (Cambridge: Cambridge University Press, 1988), 149 f. The famine in Antioch/Pisidia seems to have been caused by a harsh winter.

city.⁶ Chapter 17 caricatures Rome satirically as a prostitute who intoxicated the entire Mediterranean world and their rulers, all having become dependent on her:

> I will show you the judgment of the great prostitute [Rome] who is seated on many waters [dominating the Mediterranean world and its shores], with whom the kings of the earth [client kings such as the Herodians in Palestine, for example] have committed sexual immorality, and with the wine of whose sexual immorality the dwellers on earth have become drunk.
>
> I saw a woman [Rome] sitting on a scarlet beast [the institution of imperial rule, having produced seven emperors until the reign of Domitian, in which the author writes] that was full of blasphemous names, and it had seven heads [Augustus 31 BCE-14 CE, Tiberius 14-37 CE, Caligula 37-41 CE, Claudius 41-54 CE, Nero 54-68 CE, Vespasian 69-79 CE, his son Titus 79-81 CE, and again Nero who, redivivus, returned⁷ as Domitian in 81-96 CE, thus seven emperors instead of eight; see 17:10-11, below]⁸ and ten horns [the client kings; see Rev. 17:12, below].
>
> The woman was arrayed in purple and scarlet, and adorned with gold and jewels and pearls, holding in her hand a golden cup full of abominations and the impurities of her sexual immorality. And on her forehead was written a name of mystery: Babylon the great [cf. Rev. 14:8], mother of prostitutes and of earth's abominations. And I saw the woman, drunk with the blood of the saints, the blood of the martyrs of Jesus.

---

⁶ The pagan *Sibilline Oracle* (3.350-55), written before the battle of Actium (31 BCE), similarly highlights Rome's economic exploitation of the Asian province and prophesies that Asia will wreak revenge on Rome: "However much wealth Rome received from tribute-bearing Asia, Asia will receive three times that much again from Rome and will repay her deadly arrogance to her. Whatever number from Asia served the house of Italians, twenty times that number of Italians will be serfs in Asia, in poverty, and they will be liable to pay ten-thousandfold. O luxurious golden offspring of Latium, Rome, virgin, often drunken with your weddings with many suitors, as a slave will you be wed, without decorum." The latter motifs parallel Rev. 17, where Rome is portrayed as a prostitute sleeping with many rulers in the Mediterranean world and making the provinces drunk (see also Rev. 18:3). The theme of repaying in the Sibilline Oracle is echoed in Rev. 18:6: "Pay her [Rome] back as she herself has paid back others, and repay her double for her deeds; mix a double portion for her in the cup she mixed."

⁷ For the popular belief that Nero as redivivus returned to life in several men, such as Terentius Maximus and others, see, e.g., Tacitus, *Hist.* 2.8; Suetonius, *Nero* 57; Cassius Dio 66.19.3; *Oracula Sibillina* 5.360-69; 8.139-59 and 8.68-72. Revelation 13:3-18 most probably claims that Domitian was the *Nero redivivus:* Nero's deadly wound healed (Rev. 13:3, 12, 14), he is present in Domitian, who is criticized harshly in chapter 13.

⁸ This is still the most plausible identification of the seven "heads" or emperors, with Domitian (and not later emperors, such as Hadrian) being contemporary to the apocalyptic writer and thus the main target of Revelation's criticism. This essay thus upholds the traditional dating of Revelation in the first half of the 90 s CE.

> The seven heads are seven hills on which the woman is seated; they are also seven kings [*basileis*, which also was the Greek title of the emperors], five of whom have fallen [Augustus, Tiberius, Caligula, Claudius, and Nero], one is [Vespasian, during whose era the apocalyptic author *pretends* to write], the other has not yet come [Titus], and when he does come he must remain only a little while [from 79 to 81 CE]. As for the beast [Nero] that was [54–68 CE] and is not [during Vespasian's reign], it is an eighth [Domitian] but it belongs to the seven [as *Nero redivivus*], and it goes to destruction.
>
> And the ten horns that you saw are ten kings who have not yet received royal power [at the time of Vespasian's reign], but they are to receive authority as kings for one hour [in the wars of the end times], together with the beast. These are of one mind, and they hand over their power and authority to the beast. They will make war on the Lamb [Christ], and the Lamb will conquer them, for he is Lord of lords and King of kings, and those with him are called and chosen and faithful.
>
> And the angel said to me, the waters that you saw, where the prostitute is seated, are peoples and multitudes and nations and languages. And the ten horns that you saw, they and the beast will hate the prostitute. They will make her desolate and naked, and devour her flesh and burn her up with fire…. The woman that you saw is the great city that has dominion over the kings of the earth.

This political protest by a provincial author, who raised his voice from a Christian underground using encrypted language understood only by insiders, draws a satirical caricature of the colonial power Rome and her emperors by depicting them as a harlot riding on a multiheaded beast. It was an outcry against colonialism and against Rome's rule in general, under which some Christians had suffered persecution (Rev. 2:13; 16:6; 17:6; 18:24).[9] Chapter 13:1–10 also proclaims political protest, using the same satirical caricature as well as adding a protest against the imperial cult:

> And I saw a beast rising out of the sea … , with ten horns and seven heads, with ten diadems on its horns and blasphemous names on its heads. And the beast that I saw was like a leopard; its feet were like a bear's, and its mouth was like a lion's mouth. And to it the dragon [Satan, who is identified with Zeus in 2:13, enthroned in the Zeus temple of, e. g., Pergamon] gave his power and his throne and great authority. One of its heads [Nero] seemed to have a mortal wound [Nero's suicide with a dagger; Sueton, *Nero* 49], but its mortal wound was healed [in Domitian as Nero redivivus], and the whole earth marveled as they followed the beast.

---

[9] The author has a case in Pergamon in mind (2:13) and possibly the Neronian persecution of Christians in the city of Rome in the year 64 CE (Tacitus, *Ann.* 15.44). Larger persecutions especially targeting the Christians are not documented under Domitian but were feared to be imminent by the apocalyptic author.

And they worshiped the dragon, for he had given his authority to the beast, and they worshiped the beast [in the imperial cult], saying, "Who is like the beast, and who can fight against it?" And the beast was given a mouth uttering haughty and blasphemous words, and it was allowed to exercise authority for forty-two [more] months [until the eschaton; cf. 11:2; 12:6; Daniel 12:11].... It was allowed to make war on the saints and to conquer them [cf. note 9]. And it was given authority over every tribe and people and language and nation, and all who dwell on earth will worship it, everyone whose name has not been written before the foundation of the world in the book of life of the Lamb who was slain.

The priesthood of the imperial cult of Domitian (Rev. 13:14)–"making the earth and its inhabitants worship the first beast whose mortal wound was healed" (13:12) and "telling them to make an image for the beast that was wounded by the sword and yet lived" (13:14)–is satirically depicted as a second beast in Revelation 13:11–18. However, besides protesting against the political superpower Rome, the imperial rule, and the imperial cult, the apocalyptic prophet also targeted *economic deficiencies*, and did so with more aggressive language than Luke. As shown above, the apocalyptic author was aware of the economic imbalance between the capital city and the provinces and castigated high prices and famine because of the food shortages in the Asia Minor provinces. Moreover, in Revelation 13:15–17, he addressed the economic disadvantages Christians incurred by refusing to partake in the imperial cult or in public life in general:

It [emperor's image] might cause those who would not worship the image of the beast to be slain [a few Christians had already been killed; see 2:13; 6:9–11; 12:11; 20:4]. It [the second beast, that is, the priesthood of the imperial cult] also causes all, both small and great, both rich and poor, both free and slave, to be marked on the right hand or the forehead, so that no one can buy or sell unless he has the mark, that is, the name of the beast or the number of its name.[10]

These remarks imply that Christians not venerating the emperor suffered from disadvantages when trying to be active market participants as traders or craftspeople (when "buying or selling"). They were stigmatized as outsiders, even suspected of "hating other humans" (*odium humanum generis*, Tacitus, *Ann.* 15.44.4 and Luke 6:22–23), thus not trusted, which was fatal for trade. Conversely, not only Christian businesspeople suffered but also other market participants, since

---

[10] If the *charagma* (imprinted mark) of the emperor, with which all people of the empire are marked, is not to be understood as purely symbolic, it possibly alludes to the Roman coins that usually showed the embossed face of the emperor. Whoever refused to use these coins had problems selling and buying. Cf. A. Y. Collins, *Crisis and Catharsis: The Power of the Apocalypse* (Philadelphia: Westminster, 1984), 126.

many Christians refused to buy meat that had been offered at pagan temples (Rev. 2:14, 20). According to Pliny, *Epist.* 10.96.10 (from the beginning of the second decade of the second century CE), many Christians refused not only to swear by the emperor's name and to participate in public festivals but also to go to the meat markets to buy meat slaughtered at pagan temples. Pliny observed that the meat markets suffered (*rarissimus emptor inveniebatur*) because of the sheer number of Christians in his province of Pontus-Bythinia, in northern Asia Minor. In addition, Pliny observed that the pagan temples, usually not just religious but also economic institutions, suffered from dwindling attendance. Christians, when sufficiently numerous, impeded normal functioning of the market economy. To a significant extent, their hands were bound by their religion.

The apocalyptic prophet's loudest economic protest can be heard in chapter 18: Merchants from all over the known world importing precious goods to Rome, shipowners and "all captains and seafaring people, sailors and all whose trade is on the sea" (18:17) have grown rich from luxurious living in the capital city (18:3, 11, 14–15, 17, 19, 22), while people starve in the province (6:6). Rome's merchants are princes on earth (18:23). "All who have ships at sea grow rich by her wealth" (18:19). But all of her glory (18:16 f.) will turn into torment, the prophet's oracle predicts:

> She glorified herself and lived in luxury, so give her a like measure of torment and mourning, since in her heart she says, I sit as a queen, I am no widow, and mourning I shall never see (18:7).... And the kings of the earth, who committed sexual immorality and lived in luxury with her, will weep and wail over her when they see the smoke of her burning (18:9).

The protest is especially powerful in 18:11–13:

> The merchants of the earth weep and mourn for her, since no one buys their cargo anymore, cargo of gold, silver, jewels, pearls, fine linen, purple cloth, silk, scarlet cloth, all kinds of scented wood, all kinds of articles of ivory, all kinds of articles of costly wood, bronze, iron, and marble, cinnamon, spice, incense, myrrh, frankincense, wine, oil, fine flour, wheat, cattle and sheep, horses and chariots, and slaves, that is, human souls!

The text shows how much merchants were dependent on shipments into the capital city. The list of their luxury goods escalates, with living creatures (cattle, sheep, horses) being featured at the end, and human slaves, being nothing but material goods, representing the climax. This is the only outcry against slavery in the New Testament. All other New Testament writers did not question the institution of slavery. They sometimes tried to make the lives of slaves easier (for example, Philem.; Eph. 6:9). However, the apostle Paul even discouraged slaves from striving for freedom because, in his view, the eschaton was imminent, and therefore any changes of a Christian's legal and social status did not make sense to him.[11] The author of Revelation, however, who also propagated a near-end eschatology, seemed to sense the scandal of slavery and protested against it. Thus, the eschatology of an imminent end of the world did not necessarily have to lead to an acceptance of the institution of slavery.

Revelation's economic protest was broad-brush and lacked sophistication. Before the readers' eyes, it drew caricatures of the powerful and extravagant Rome, the imperial rule, imperial cult, and the Rome-centered trade of luxurious goods. The satirical character of this protest has not been acknowledged sufficiently.

Yet another first-century satire, a pagan novel, contains a similar text castigating Rome's luxurious life. In Petronius's *Satyrica*, one of the protagonists, the artistically and financially rather unsuccessful poet Eumolpus, recites his lengthy, moralizing poem about Rome's civil war between Caesar and Pompeius. The poem also presents an oracle, a *vaticinium ex eventu* or prediction of an event. Eumolpus calls his concoction "prophecies of a frenzied seer" (*furentis animi vaticinatio*), decorated with "allusions," "divine interpositions," and "mythology" (*Sat.* 118.6). In places, Eumolpus's protest sounds similar to that of Revelation. It starts with Rome's greed and lavish life, nurtured by colonialistic expansion, the plundering of other regions, and the importing of their lush goods to Rome:

(*Sat.* 119) The conquering Roman now held the whole world, sea, and land.... The waters were stirred and troubled by his loaded ships; if there were any hidden bay beyond, or any land that promised a yield of yellow gold, that place was Rome's enemy, fate stood ready for the sorrows of war, and *the quest for wealth* went on.... Bright colors dug from earth [mining] rivaled the purple [purple dye murex]; here the African curses Rome, here the Chinaman plunders his marvelous silks, and the Arabian hordes have stripped their own fields bare.... Tables of citron wood are dug out of the soil of Africa and set up, the spots on them resembling gold, which is cheaper than they, their polish reflecting hordes of slaves and purple clothes, to lure the senses.... The wrasse is brought alive to table in seawater from Sicily, and the oysters torn from the banks of the Lucrine lake make a dinner famous, in order to renew men's hunger by their extravagance. All the birds are now gone from the waters of Phasis; the shore is quiet; only the empty air breathes on the lonely boughs.... The house of senators is corrupt, their support hangs on a price. The freedom and virtue of the old men has decayed, ... their dignity was stained by money and trodden in the dust.... Moreover, filthy usury and the handling of money had caught the common people in a double

---

[11] 1 Cor. 7:17–24. Only unless the slave's master decides to manumit, the slave should embrace freedom (7:21b). In view of the imminent eschaton, for Paul, the legal and social status in the world was an *adiaphoron*. If Christians resisted manumission offered to them, or if they actively strove for manumission, they would show that the worldly status was *not* an *adiaphoron* for them.

whirlpool, and destroyed them.... The youth of Rome contemns its own strength, and groans under the wealth its own hands have heaped up. See, everywhere they squander their spoils, and the mad use of wealth brings their destruction. They have buildings of gold and thrones raised to the stars, they drive out the waters with their piers, the sea springs forth amid the fields: rebellious man turns creation's order upside down.

Fortuna, being upset by what she sees and ready to punish the Romans, predicts the devastation of the civil war, just as the apocalyptic seer in Revelation 17–18 foretells a destruction of Rome in the near future:

(*Sat.* 121) If I may foretell the truth without fear; for the anger that rises in my heart is stern.... I hate all the gifts I have made to towering Rome, and I am angry at my own blessings. The god that raised up those high palaces shall destroy them too. It will be my delight also to burn the men and feed my lust with blood.

Omens undergird Fortuna's prediction:

(*Sat.* 122) Straightway the slaughter of men and the destruction to come were made plain by omens from on high. For Titan [the sun] was disfigured and dabbled in blood, and veiled his face in darkness: you thought that even then he gazed on civil strife. In another quarter Cynthia [the moon] darkened her full face, and denied her light to the crime. The mountaintops slid down, and the peaks broke in thunder, the wandering streams were dying and no more ranged abroad between their familiar banks. The sky is loud with the clash of arms, the trumpet shakes to the stars and rouses the War God, and at once Aetna is the prey of unaccustomed fires, and casts her lightnings high into the air.

Finally, the civil war between Caesar and Pompeius is about to be unleashed:

(*Sat.* 123) Battle, blood, slaughter, fire, and the whole picture of war flits before their eyes. Their hearts shake in confusion, and are fearfully divided between two counsels. One man chooses flight by land, another trusts rather to the water, and the open sea now safer than his own country. Some prefer to attempt a fight and turn Fate's decree to account. As deep as a man's fear is, so far he flies. In the turmoil the people themselves, a woeful sight, are led swiftly out of the deserted city [Rome], where their stricken heart drives them. Rome is glad to flee, her true sons are cowed by war, and at a rumor's breath leave their houses to mourn. One holds his children with a shaking hand, one hides his household gods in his bosom and, weeping, leaves his door and calls down death on the unseen enemy.... (*Sat.* 124) And among them Madness, like a steed loosed when the reins snap, flings up her bloody head and shields her face, scarred by a thousand wounds, with a bloodstained helm.... The trumpets shook, and Discord with disheveled hair raised her Stygian head to the upper sky. Blood had dried on her face, tears ran from her bruised eyes, her teeth were mailed with a scurf of rust, her tongue was dripping with foulness, and her face beset with snakes, her clothes were torn before her tortured breasts, and she waved a red torch in her quivering hand.

"Eumolpus poured out these lines with immense fluency" (*ingenti volubilitate verborum effudisset, Sat.* 124), the novel continues. Tongue in cheek, Petronius put this poem in the mouth of his Eumolpus figure. The (self-)criticism of Rome's sissified and luxurious lifestyle at the expense of conquered countries seems a genuine concern of the moralizing Eumolpus, but the poem's wordiness, dramatic pathos, and hyperbole at the same time render it ludicrous. The senator Petronius is a satirist, not a moralist, not calling for change. He himself is an expert in questions of taste and luxurious living (Tacitus, *Ann.* 16.18), making fun of Eumolpus and his moralistic indignation. His satire merely wants to entertain and please his readers' artistic tastes.

By contrast, Revelation's political and economic criticism was deadly serious and had a moralizing touch. The caricature-like images of two beasts, a harlot, and weeping merchants were satirical, but drenched in bitterness. They were outcries, genuine accusations. The author expected God to abolish the economic and political conditions that he castigated. The satirical elements thus are to be found on different levels in the two texts.

In conclusion, in a rare piece of underground literature from the provinces, the author of Revelation was sensitive to economic injustice and deficiencies, including slavery. He had the courage to harshly criticize and protest, albeit in an encrypted way to be understood only by insiders. Yet his protest vented his own and his Christian readers' frustration and anger.

Contrary to Luke, Revelation did not offer much in terms of alternatives. The author did not suggest explicitly what should be done to create a better world, because the world he lived in was doomed to perish in the near future. This expectation was the apocalyptic author's solution to all problems, preventing him from envisioning significant socioeconomic changes in the present age. Yet, the author de facto lived an alternative, which came somewhat close to Luke's vision of a communal life in solidarity. As an itinerant prophetic preacher, the author of Revelation ignored the hierarchical tendencies and church offices in the local Christian congregations that had emerged in his time.[12] He did not mention church offices—except for charismatic "prophets" as well as "presbyters" in heaven (Rev. 4:4, 10; 5:8), not on earth. For the Christians, he seemed to have an egalitarian botherhood/sisterhood in mind, in which all were "priests" and jointly

---

[12] Cf., e.g., Ignatius, *Eph.* 4.1; *Magn.* 3.1; 2.1; Polykarp; the Pastoral Letters (e.g., Tit. 1:5); Acts 20:17, 28; 14:23; 1 Pet. 5; Eph. 4:11; 2:20; 3:5, et al.

partook of Christ's reign (ἱερεῖς, ἀδελφός, συγκοινωνός, σύνδουλος).[13] However, he did not spell out any specific economic consequences of this ecclesiological model. Only once, in 2:19, did he praise *diakonia* as a virtue. This was scanty compared with Luke's utopian visions of economic solidarity in Acts 2:44–46 and 4:32–5:11, for example.[14] One of the reasons for this difference again was the eschatology. Revelation's near-end eschatology did not motivate its author to develop models for the present time. Luke, on the other hand, did not count on an imminent eschaton when laying the ground for ethics, reckoning that the "end" could come in a distant future that left room to design alternative forms of social and economic life in the present.

---

[13] Rev. 1:6, 9; 19:10; 22:9; 6:11; 12:10; cf. 2:20; 7:3; 19:2, 5; 22:3; 3:21; 20:6; 21:7. See further Lampe, "Die Apokalyptiker" (note 2, above), 102–04.

[14] For these and their background in socio-utopian pagan texts, see, e.g., P. Lampe, *Athen und Jerusalem: Antike Bildung in frühchristlich-lukanischen Erzählungen* (Vorlesungsreihe uni auditorium: Alte Geschichte; München: Komplett-Media, 2010), 11–14.

COMMERCE, FINANCE, AND MORALITY IN THE THOUGHT OF EARLY MODERN CATHOLIC SCHOLASTICS

Samuel Gregg

INTRODUCTION

Recent decades have brought increasing attention to the contributions made to the development of modern economics by Catholic theologians and canonists writing in the early modern period: that is, after the late Middle Ages (c. 1500) until the outbreak of the French Revolution (1789).[1] In his *History of Economic Analysis*, Joseph Schumpeter drew attention to the work of Jesuit and Dominican scholars during this period who helped to identify and clarify key economic concepts. These concepts range from the distinction between value in use and value in exchange to the idea of comparative advantage, the multiple functions of money, the concept of scarcity, how prices are formed, economic utility, the character of opportunity-cost, the origins and nature of capital, and the form and role of interest. Schumpeter's conclusion was that "the economics of the doctors absorbed all the phenomena of nascent capitalism and ... served ... as a basis for the analytic work of their successors, not excluding A. Smith."[2]

It is important to recognize that these individuals did not write as economists. Nor would they have ever thought of themselves in such terms. They primarily wrote either as moral theologians (and thus as individuals concerned about whether or not people's free choices conformed to the demands of the Gospel and natural law)[3] or as canonists (and thus as lawyers interested in determining if the

---

[1] This chapter draws on Samuel Gregg, *The Commercial Society: Opportunities and Challenges in a Global Age* (Lanham, MD: Lexington Books, 2007); and Samuel Gregg, *For God and Profit: How Banking and Finance Can Serve the Common Good* (New York: Herder and Herder, 2016).

[2] Joseph A. Schumpeter, *History of Economic Analysis* (New York: Oxford University Press, 1954), 94.

[3] The emphasis on "free choices" as opposed to simply "choices" reflects the Catholic tradition's view that people are often the master and source of their own actions, which is captured in Thomas Aquinas's distinction between an "act of a human being" (such as

same choices conformed to the law, ordinances, and regulations decreed by church authorities).

This was a world in which canon law had direct implications for life in Catholic countries. Canon law, for example, treated monopoly profits as ill-gotten profits.[4] Similarly, moral theologians such as Antonio of Florence and Bernadine of Sienna argued against the formation of any temporary or permanent cartels in any industry for the purpose of securing higher prices and larger profits, not least because this hurt the poor.[5] Early modern Catholic theologians such as Leonardus Lessius, SJ, were especially critical of monopolies established by legal grants from rulers and portrayed them as sins against justice and charity.[6]

The assumption underlying the workings of Catholic moral theology and the canon law of the Catholic Church was (and is) that people's free choices for moral good or moral evil could affect their salvation. Violation of the moral absolutes underscored by the Catholic Church from the very beginning could render one's faith "dead," thereby putting at risk their salvation. At the same time, pursuing the good life, especially through trying to integrate the theological virtues (faith, love, and hope) and the cardinal virtues (prudence, courage, justice, and temperance) into one's life, also mattered because they were (and are) viewed as central to answering the call to holiness that the church taught (and still teaches) is the vocation of every Christian.

It was during the early modern period that increasing numbers of people in both Protestant and Catholic Europe began to spend more and more time in the world of commerce. As feudalism broke down, Catholic moralists and canonists began to consider how people could conform to the demands of morality and justice in rapidly changing and new economic conditions.

The purpose of this chapter is to outline how the inquiries of these moralists and canonists led to more positive moral assessments of commercial and financial activity. In other words, reflection on how to do good and avoid evil in the economy facilitated greater understanding of economic activity by Catholic thinkers, which in turn helped shape their assessment of people's choices in areas ranging from banking to trade.

---

spontaneous reactions) from a "human act" (*actio hominus*), which involves a person freely choosing X rather than Y. See Thomas Aquinas, *Summa Theologiae* (London: Blackfriars, 1963; hereafter ST), I-II, q.1 a. Ic.

[4] *Corpus iuris canonici*, Decr. II, c. xiv, qu.4, c.9. http://digital.library.ucla.edu/canonlaw/.

[5] See Raymond de Roover, *Money, Banking and Credit in Medieval Bruges: Italian Merchant Bankers, Lombards and Money Changers: A Study in the Origins of Banking* (Cambridge, MA: Medieval Academy of America, 1942), 80.

[6] See Leonardus Lessius, *De iustitia et iure caeterisque virtutibus cardinalibus*, 4 vols. (Paris, 1606), vol. 2, cap. 21, dub. 20.

A New Economic World

The religious wars which shook Europe in the wake of the Protestant Reformation produced considerable economic devastation throughout what had been Christendom. At the same time, many of the ideas and institutions associated with the spread of commerce began to acquire a more mature form between approximately 1500 and 1800. The dominant economic framework of Catholic Western Europe through this period is what Adam Smith would retrospectively call "the mercantile system." Focused primarily on enriching a nation through trade surpluses by encouraging exports and restricting imports, mercantilism invariably involved a close relationship between trading companies (such as the Dutch East Indies Company or the Hudson Bay Company) and the governments of emerging nation-states in the early modern period. Governments acted to protect merchants from foreign competition through devices such as tariffs, monopolies, and quotas. Trade by sea, and thus potential competition from abroad, was especially restricted under mercantile arrangements. Established merchants who benefited from these arrangements typically returned the government's favors by acquiescing in the raising of taxes and the paying of customs dues that provided funding for, among other things, wars undertaken by the state to make territorial acquisitions through conquest and establishing colonies around the globe.

While mercantilism became the dominant mode of economic life as absolutist governments began to establish a grip over much of Protestant and Catholic Europe, previously unimaginable commercial possibilities also emerged. Adam Smith once described the first European contact with the Americas and the discovery of a passage to the East Indies via the Cape of Good Hope as two of the most important events recorded in human history. In terms of their significance for the expansion of commerce throughout the world, Smith did not exaggerate. The gradual conquest and settlement of the New World by Spanish and Portuguese adventurers, the establishment of French colonies in North America, and the Portuguese and French expansion into Africa, India, and Southeast Asia transformed Catholic Europe's economic life. International trade expanded at an unprecedented rate. As Spanish colonies were established in the Americas, they became the source of a growing demand for basic and luxury products made in Castile and Aragon.[7]

It is important to recall here that mercantilism did not seek to suppress trade per se. Rather, the mercantile system went hand in hand with efforts by governments to control and direct trade. It thus fit well with colonization, especially in those instances of colonialism associated with Catholic powers such as France,

---

[7] See *Economic Thought in Spain: Selected Essays of Marjorie Grice-Hutchinson*, eds. Laurence S. Moss and Christopher Ryan, trans. Christopher K. Ryan and Marjorie Grice-Hutchinson (Aldershot: E. Elgar, 1993).

Spain, and Portugal. One consequence of these developments was the rise and expansion of the commercial classes. Cities like Seville—the destination of the treasure fleets from America—grew in size as they attracted merchants and traders from the rest of Europe. Skills such as accounting and estimating monetary worth became highly valued. The center for merchant activity in Europe began to shift towards Spanish merchant families, many of which were of foreign origin, having first established themselves in north Italy and the Low Countries before gravitating towards Spanish markets.

Another major development occurring during this period concerns the expansion of the financial sector as a major economic force throughout Europe. The background to this was what the medieval historian Robert Lopez has called a Commercial Revolution. As Lopez describes it, "Catholic Europe moved from stagnation at the lowest level to a social and economic mobility full of dangers but open to hope" towards the end of the tenth century.[8] The vicious circle of low production, small consumption, and population decline that had followed the slow-motion implosion of the Roman Empire was broken by what another medievalist calls a "spectacular transformation" in Western economic life.[9] Population growth and technological innovations led to more intensive farming. This produced more products, industry, trade, and, most importantly, surplus capital—capital that could be mobilized for investment and could help move society beyond subsistence economies. One of the most important features of the Commercial Revolution was a remarkable growth in the available amount of capital in the form of equity and debt, the trading of money and credit, and the demand for commercial loans.[10]

These and other changes did not simply amount to a type of protocapitalism. It was, as Randall Collins writes, "a version of the developed characteristics of capitalism itself."[11] The growth of commerce, urban living, and business went hand in hand with the spread of commercial mindsets, values, and priorities throughout Europe.[12]

A crucial element driving many of these developments was the refinement of several financial tools that gradually assumed legal and economic form. A good

---

[8] Robert S. Lopez, *The Commercial Revolution of the Middle Ages 950–1350* (Cambridge: Cambridge University Press, 1976), 31.

[9] See Diana Wood, *Medieval Economic Thought* (Cambridge: Cambridge University Press, 2002), 5.

[10] Ibid., 79.

[11] Randall Collins, *Weberian Sociological Theory* (Cambridge: Cambridge University Press, 1986), 47.

[12] See Rodger Charles, SJ, *Christian Social Witness and Teaching: The Catholic Tradition from Genesis to Centesimus Annus*, vol. 1, *From Biblical Times to the Late Nineteenth Century* (Leominster: Gracewing, 1998), 129.

illustration is the proliferation of legal instruments such as partnership contracts. These instruments reduced costs and smoothed the process of exchange. By the thirteenth century, single-entry bookkeeping had emerged—a critical tool by which people were able to assess more accurately the true costs of a given economic venture. As trade expanded, Italian merchants developed double-entry bookkeeping to distinguish cash receipts from cash payments. This practice helped formalize the rule that there should never be a debit without a corresponding credit.[13] Important accounting concepts such as the depreciation of goods and the distinction between revenue and capital did not take long to emerge.[14]

Banks sold letters of credit and bills of exchange to traveling merchants, pilgrims, and clergy that could be redeemed by a named beneficiary or the issuer. These instruments were also used as conduits for life annuities, mutual funds, and share-ownership of limited-liability corporations.[15] Much of this business was transacted through personal relationships, with credit operations being mediated through private contracts between lenders and borrowers.[16] To expedite the efficiency of these transactions, Italian banking families established clearinghouse operations and transfer banks in Europe's important commercial centers.[17] They subsequently opened branches throughout Europe in cities such as Barcelona, Avignon, Bruges, Geneva, Lyons, London, Hamburg, and Antwerp.[18] These private banks, in what has been called a growing "international republic of money,"[19] did more than just pay interest on deposits. They also used such deposits as a basis for furnishing interest-bearing loans to those parts of Europe that lacked capital. Some loans were given out by banks for long-term purposes to businesses and governments. Like modern businessmen, many merchants took out short-term loans to cover cash-flow gaps or fund particular short-term projects.[20]

It is not an exaggeration to say that all of these changes amounted to the emergence of the world's first relatively sophisticated money and capital markets. Such was the pace of growth that money markets and banking more generally

---

[13] Roover, *Business, Banking, and Economic Thought*, 120.
[14] See Edwin S. Hunt and James M. Murray, *A History of Business in Medieval Europe, 1200–1500* (Cambridge: Cambridge University Press, 1999), 62–63.
[15] See Thomas Divine, SJ, *Interest: An Historical and Analytical Study in Economics and Modern Ethics* (Milwaukee, WI: Marquette University Press, 1959), 40.
[16] See Henri Pirenne, *Economic and Social History of Medieval Europe* (New York: Harcourt Brace, 1937), 139.
[17] See Roover, *Business, Banking, and Economic Thought*, 184.
[18] See Charles Kindleberger, *A Financial History of Western Europe* (London: Routledge, 1984), 43.
[19] See Aldo de Maddalena and Herman Kellenbenz, eds., *La repubblica internazuonale del denaro tra XVe XVII secolo* (Bologna: Il Mulino 1986).
[20] See Hunt and Murray, *History of Business*, 71.

escaped the dominance of Italians relatively quickly. By the early seventeenth century, Italian bankers were complaining to the Grand Duke of Florence that they were no longer "the masters of the money of other countries."[21]

The Schoolmen and Commerce

In texts authored by what are often called early modern (or "late") Catholic scholastics, writing from the beginning of the sixteenth century until as late as the mid-eighteenth century, we find awareness that there was something new and energetic about this expansion of commerce.

Writing in the late sixteenth century, the lay jurist Bartolomé de Albornóz described commercial activity as

> the nerve of human life that sustains the universe. By means of buying and selling, the world is united, joining distant lands and nations, people of different languages, laws, and ways of life. If it were not for these contracts, some would lack the goods that others have in abundance, and they would not be able to share the goods that they have in excess with those countries where they are scarce.[22]

Looking at the commercial life of Seville, Tómas de Mercado, OP, saw a society in which a "banker traffics with a whole world and embraces more than the Atlantic, though sometimes he loses his grip and it all comes tumbling down."[23]

The effects of the growing commercialization and "financialization" of Spain and many other European Catholic states throughout the sixteenth century and into the seventeenth century were not limited to the social and political realm. The increase in the volume of credit transactions in Catholic Europe only reminded people of the traditional prohibition of usury. Many merchants and traders, anxious about their salvation, turned to their confessors for guidance.

Confronted with this and other moral questions in their consciences and the confessional, many priests looked in turn to those theologians and canon lawyers who were charged with the responsibility of providing guidance on such subjects. In his discussion of moneychanging, for example, Mercado informs his reader that he wants to help confessors "who, abstracted as they are from the world, cannot understand the ways of these entangled dealings."[24]

---

[21] See Armando Sapori, "La registrazione del libri di commercio in Toscana nell'anno 1605," *Rivista del diretto commercial e del diretto generale delle obbligazionale* 29 (1931): 9–10.
[22] Bartolomé de Albornóz, *Arte de los Contratos* (Valencia 1573), VII, 29.
[23] Tómas de Mercado, OP, *Suma de tratos y contratos*, ed. R. Sierra Bravo (Madrid: IEP, [1571] 1975), no. 15.
[24] Ibid.

The response of many early modern canonists and theologians was to reflect on the wisdom of medieval scholars and thinkers of antiquity and apply their insights to the new situation enveloping European life. This produced an unprecedented number of lengthy treatises on the moral dimension of economic life. Some of the most detailed descriptions of sixteenth-century commercial life are contained in these writings. Written by early modern scholastics such as Mercado, Francisco de Vitoria, OP, and Domingo de Soto, OP, these works sought to determine which of the new commercial practices conformed to the demands of morality.

The inquiries of early modern scholastics consequently embraced activities and practices as varied as taxation, coinage, foreign exchange, credit, prices, and interest. They also analyzed the workings of the banking business of their time and showed how the fluctuations in foreign exchange were related to changes in the purchasing power of different currencies. One unforeseen result of these reflections was the theoretical conceptualization of important aspects of commercial life. These include the subjective theory of value, the identification of all the determining factors of price, a simple version of the quantity theory of money, and new insights into how coinage debasement facilitated inflation.[25]

Some of these early modern scholastics regarded commercial activity as morally indifferent.[26] Others, however, ascribed positive moral characteristics to trade and commerce. The economic historian Henry Robertson records that Jesuits like Francisco Suarez and Luis de Molina were unashamed promoters of the social benefits of enterprise, financial speculation, and the expansion of trade.[27] De Soto even portrayed commercial activity as evidence of civilizational development:

> Humankind progresses from imperfection to perfection. For this reason, in the beginning barter was sufficient as man was rude and ignorant and had few necessities. But afterward, with the development of a more educated, civilized, and distinguished life, the need to create new forms of trade arose. Among them the most respectable is commerce, despite the fact that human avarice can pervert anything.[28]

---

[25] This summary is drawn from Murray Rothbard's summary of the late scholastics in *Economic Thought before Adam Smith*, Vol. 1: *An Austrian Perspective on the History of Economic Thought* (Aldershot: Edward Elgar, 1995), 97–136.

[26] See Alejandro Chafuen, *Faith and Liberty: The Economic Thought of the Late Scholastics* (Lanham, MD: Lexington Books, 2003).

[27] See Henry Robertson, *Aspects of the Rise of Economic Individualism: A Criticism of Max Weber and His School* (Clifton, NJ: A.M. Kelly, 1973).

[28] Domingo de Soto, OP, *De Iustitia de Iure* (Madrid: Inst. de Estudio Politicos, 1968), VI, q.2, a.2.

This positive view of commerce was prefigured by Thomas Aquinas. Though influenced by Aristotle, Aquinas rejected "the Philosopher's" view that those involved in commerce would become obsessed with their own riches and unconcerned with the common good.[29] Instead, Aquinas held that it was possible for people to engage in commerce with correct intentions, such as the desire to help the needy or take care of one's family.[30] He certainly warned against greed. Yet Aquinas also believed that those involved in commerce, including the use and management of capital, were capable of doing great things.

Reading Aquinas's reflections on the nature of the virtue of magnificence is especially revealing. He defines magnificence as the virtue of "that which is great in the use of money."[31] It is not so much, he specifies, about making gifts or charity. Nor, Aquinas adds, does the person who embraces this virtue "intend principally to be lavish towards himself."[32] Rather, he says, magnificence concerns "some great work which has to be produced" with (1) a view to the good that goes beyond the immediate gain, (2) which cannot be done "without expenditure or outlay" of great sums of money, and (3) which requires the use of reason to ensure minimal risk of great loss. Moreover, magnificence for Aquinas also concerns "expenditure in reference to *hope*, by attaining to the difficulty, not simply, as magnanimity does, but in a determinate matter, namely expenditure."[33]

It is important to note that Aquinas is not focused here upon questions of property or wealth per see. Likewise, *magnificentia*, as understood by Aquinas, is not so much about who owns the wealth. As Aquinas specifies, the poor man can also choose to do great things.[34] Rather, *magnificentia* is about the one who *deploys* great sums to help realize a "great work." That encompasses an extraordinary spectrum of figures, who range from the banker lending others capital to the entrepreneurs and businesses that seek to use the wealth given to them in the form of a loan to start and grow an enterprise. This is very different from Aristotle's view that moneylending encouraged people "to make gain in improper ways"[35] but also discouraged the virtues of liberality and generosity towards others, especially the poor.

Observe, moreover, how Aquinas links the act of magnificence to one of the three great theological virtues: the act of hope. This is especially relevant to com-

---

[29] This account follows that in John Finnis, *Aquinas: Moral, Political, and Legal Theory* (Oxford: Oxford University Press, 1998), 200–10.
[30] See ST, II-II, q. 77, a.4c.
[31] ST, II-II, q.134, a.3.
[32] Ibid., q.134, a.1.
[33] Ibid., q.134, a.4. Emphasis added.
[34] See ibid., q.134, a.3.
[35] Aristotle, *The Nicomachean Ethics* (further rev. ed.), ed. Hugh Tredennick, trans. J. A. K. Thomson (London: Penguin Books, 2003), Book 4, 1, no. 44.

merce, trade, and finance, for without hope—the expectation of, and firm confidence in, positive outcomes, even in conditions of uncertainty—the entire world of business would slowly crumble from within.

Morality, Capital, and Finance

Early modern Catholic scholastics developed some aspects of the medieval scholastic engagement with commerce more than others. De Soto repeated Aquinas's criticisms of common ownership but also stressed that common ownership tended to corrode the virtue of liberality, not least because "those who own nothing cannot be liberal."[36]

The focus of early modern Catholic scholastics in the realm of economics, however, was squarely on the related subjects of capital, money, and interest. Towards the end of the medieval period, the Catholic Church had arrived at a relatively settled position on these topics. It maintained that one could not charge interest on a fungible good—the *mutuum*[37] (from *meum tuum:* mine becomes thine)—because it implied a transfer of ownership of a *res fungibilis:* that is, something measurable in quantity and quality which was consumed in use and thus couldn't be used creatively. Hence, if borrowed, a *mutuum* could be restored only in the *exact* kind and quantity. Given what was understood to be money's sterile nature, it was impermissible to charge interest on money loans.

The medieval period, however, saw increasing recognition that money was not always sterile: that in the conditions of a productive economy which produced surplus wealth, money acquired the quality of capital: something that, by nature, could be used creatively to generate more wealth. This opened up the possibility of distinguishing between (1) consumption loans and (2) loans of capital in the context of economic growth rather than subsistence economies. This insight was crucial to Aquinas's treatment of the topic. He identified two titles external to a loan itself that justified a return to the lender that exceeded the principal. John Finnis summarizes Aquinas's titles in the following way:

(1) *Share of profits in joint enterprises.* If I "lend" my money to a merchant or craftsman on the basis that we are in partnership [*societas*] ... so that I am to share in any overall losses or profits, my entitlement to my dividend of the profits (as well as to the return of my capital *if its value has not been lost by the joint enterprise*) is just and appropriate. (2) *Recompense or indemnity* [*interesse*] *for losses.* In making any loan I can levy a charge on the borrower in order to compensate me for whatever expenses I have out-

---

[36] De Soto, *De Iustitia et Iure*, bk.4, q.3, fol. 105–06.
[37] See Rudolf Sohm, *The Institutes: A Textbook of the History and System of Roman Private Law* (Oxford: Clarendon Press, 1892), 372–73.

laid or losses I have incurred by making the loan. And the terms of a loan can include a fee or charge which is payable if you fail to repay the principal on time, and is sufficient to compensate me for the losses I am liable to incur if the principal is not repaid on time.[38]

The most striking feature of Aquinas's two titles for justly recovering something beyond the principal is its compatibility with the development of a market in loans of money at a market rate of interest. How so? Finnis explains this in the following way:

With the development of a genuine investment market, in which stocks and shares (i. e., association in the risks of productive and other commercial enterprise) are traded alongside bonds (transferable money loans), it becomes possible to identify a rate of interest on bonds and other loans which compensates lenders for what they are reasonably presumed to have lost by making the loan rather than investing their money, for profit, in shares. Indeed, an efficient market will tend to identify this indemnifying rate of interest automatically.[39]

Many medieval scholastics saw that a forgone gain could be an actual loss when you are living in an economy in which opportunities for gain are part of everyday life. Schumpeter points out that this meant two things: First, merchants themselves who hold money for business purposes, evaluating this money with reference to expected gain, were considered justified in charging interest both on outright loans and in cases of deferred payment for commodities. Second, if the opportunity for gain contingent on the possession of money is quite general, or, in other words, if there is a money market, then everyone, even if not in business himself, may accept the interest determined by the market mechanism.[40]

Thus, while maintaining that a *mutuum* excluded the possibility of charging interest on the basis of an *intrinsic* title to the loan itself, many medieval Catholic scholastics thought it was possible to justify interest on grounds not adherent to the contract itself. They subsequently identified four *extrinsic* titles:

(1) First, there was the payment of a penalty if money was not repaid in time. This was known as a *poena conventionalis:* the difference between what had been due and what was paid. Such a fine was the "interest." Once this was accepted, it became accepted practice to write into contracts penalty clauses against such delays.

---

[38] Finnis, *Aquinas*, 205. A good discussion of *interesse* versus usury may be found in Victor Brants, *L'économie politique au Moyen-Age* (New York: Franklin, 1970), 145–56.
[39] Finnis, *Aquinas*, 205.
[40] Schumpeter, *History of Economic Analysis*, 103–04.

(2) It was possible that a lender could suffer real damages because of the borrower's failure to return the capital on the schedule determined by the contract. Hence, the lender could claim what was called a *damnum emergens* (actual monetary loss incurred). Significantly, this title had been accepted as legitimate by medieval figures preceding Aquinas, such as his master, St. Albertus Magnus.[41]

(3) A lender could claim for the loss of a possible profit (*lucrum cessans*), if he missed the opportunity of making a profit as a result of lending to others. Over time, this would become virtually synonymous with *interesse*.[42]

(4) There was a legitimate payment that the lender could charge for the risk of losing his capital (*periculum sortis*).[43]

In these cases, it remained wrong to charge interest on a loan by virtue of the very making of the loan. This prohibition, however, was compatible with maintaining that moneylenders could fairly charge for other factors. These included risk of nonpayment, probable inflation, taxes, the costs incurred in making and administering a loan, and the forgoing of other legitimate uses to which the money could have been put. Hence, it was with little difficulty that the last ecumenical council in the West before the Reformation, the Fifth Lateran Council (1512–17), could define usury as "nothing else than gain or profit drawn from the use of a thing that is by its nature sterile, a profit acquired *without labor, costs, or risk.*"[44] Not only did these words imply that money was not always sterile or a fungible consumable; they also underscored the insight that risk, labor, and costs provided a basis for receiving back more than the principal.

Early Modern Catholic Scholastics, Contracts, and Speculation

What did early modern Catholic scholastic thinkers add to this understanding? In the first place, they continued arguing among themselves about the scope of the titles. Could interest be justified only on the grounds of extrinsic titles? Or might it be possible to charge on an intrinsic title? For practical purposes, these amounted to the same thing. In terms of the development of finance, however, what matters is that these intellectual explorations, as Diana Wood notes, "sanctioned many of the monetary considerations that underlie modern economies."[45]

---

[41] See Divine, *Interest*, 54.
[42] Ibid., 55.
[43] John Gilchrist, *The Church and Economic Activity in the Middle Ages* (New York: Macmillan, 1969), 69.
[44] Ibid., 115. Emphasis added.
[45] Wood, *Medieval Economic Thought*, 207.

One effect of these intellectual developments was to help shift the epicenter of economic life away from a focus on natural resources and agriculture to an economy in which capital and finance played a central role. The new attitudes about money also steered liquid capital away from consumption loans and towards economically productive enterprises. John T. Noonan, for instance, contends that "it is probable that the scholastic theory may have encouraged bankers to participate as risk-sharers in commercial ventures."[46]

The debate about usury also yielded a number of devices that helped spur the ever-growing sophistication of the economy's financial sector. Especially significant in this connection was the manner in which the usury discussion before and after the Reformation facilitated the use of a financial device known as the "triple contract." This arrangement amounted to a combined package of insurance, a partnership, and a sales contract. The first contract was an investment contract and partnership for a specified period of time in a particular venture in which it was assumed that the investment would yield a specified profit. A London merchant would thus invest two thousand pounds for one year in a given enterprise on the assumption that it would produce a 10 percent profit of two hundred pounds in that period, but no more than that.

The second contract was an insurance contract on the amount of the principal of the investment. The investor would pay the premium from the profits of the investment contract. The premium of the policy on the example cited above would thus be 5 percent of the investment, or one hundred pounds. The third contract was for a specified return on the investment that was paid to the investor out of the profits from the investment contract. In other words, the future uncertain (high) gain was traded for a more certain (lower) gain.

An example of the workings of a triple contract would be as follows. The creation of a company may cost 5,000 pounds. The business owner needs to borrow 2,500 pounds from an investor, who invests the needed 2,500 pounds in the business on the premise that the business will produce a profit of 500 pounds a year, of which the investor will be entitled to a maximum of 250 pounds. This provision is the first contract. Whether the investor receives his 250 pounds from the company depends on the commercial success of the business.

The second contract involves the same investor taking out insurance on his investment. The annual premium which he must pay for the policy might be 5 percent of his investment (125 pounds). The investor must pay this premium to the insurer, regardless of whether the business makes a profit.

The third contract is between the investor and the owner of the business in a private capacity (rather than the business itself) and specifies that the investor will receive a guaranteed minimal payment from the company owner. This en-

---

[46] John T. Noonan Jr., *The Scholastic Analysis of Usury* (Cambridge, MA: Harvard University Press, 1957), 173.

sures a regular income that, strictly speaking, is not dependent on the success of the business. The investor may negotiate a 150-pound annual payment from the company owner in the event that the business makes less than a 500-pound annual profit. In this way, the investor locks in an annual payment from the company owner that comes into effect when profits from the business are less than expected. In return, the investor may agree that he will receive no more than 250 pounds from the company in the event that the company's profit exceeds 500 pounds per year.

As a financial device, triple contracts allowed their participants to hedge their risk in the face of uncertainty over time and still realize a profit. It amounted to selling an uncertain future gain for a certain lesser gain (that being a guarantee of a fixed return based a percentage rate). It also allowed contracted partners to create a contract of insurance for the principal investment in return for an assignment of the future probable gain from the partnership.[47]

The increasing use of triple contracts introduced greater stability into business partnerships. Nor did it take long for canny investors looking to further diversify risk to realize that one way to do so was to make the three contracts with different persons. In practical terms, the transactions involved in the triple contract were distinguished from those of a loan only by the designation for a business purpose of the funds conveyed by the triple contract. Those justifying the contract invoked the extrinsic title of *lucrum cessans*, arguing that it was always present in such arrangements.

The triple contract's morality did not go undisputed. Some early modern Catholic theologians argued that it constituted covert usury. Others, however, defended it, the most notable being Johannes Eck (1486–1543). A lecturer in Augsburg, Eck lived in a city full of financial houses, not least among which was the Fugger family, who were, by this point, the papacy's bankers.[48] Examining criticisms of the triple contract, Eck held that it was not usury. Thomas Divine, SJ, summarizes Eck's underlying logic as follows: "Since, (1) it is lawful to make a profit from an enterprise involving risk and (2) the larger the risk the larger would be the profit allowed, therefore (3) it should be lawful for a man to contract for a low rate of interest on his capital in return for the security of the capital involved."[49]

Eck was astute enough to direct his most complete defenses of this position to merchants, clergy, and one of Europe's most important centers of learning, the University of Bologna, where he presented his views before an audience of some of Europe's leading theologians and canonists. Here Eck insisted that the industry

---

[47] See Noonan, *Scholastic Analysis*, 209.
[48] See J. Strieder, *Jacob Fugger: The Rich Banker and Merchant of Augsburg, 1459–1526*, trans. M. Hartsough (New York: Adelphi, 1931).
[49] Divine, *Interest*, 58.

associated with money was productive. Hence, the investor who "gives the commodity of his capital" (the use of the word "capital" shows how far the idea of capital had become part of the everyday language of the early sixteenth century) was owed his share.[50]

Eck's defense of the triple contract was important for four reasons. First, the very fact that Eck defended the contract underscored just how open one of the most orthodox of Catholic theologians was to financial innovations. Second, Eck's expositions amounted to the most public explanation of the triple contract's workings not just to theologians but also to men of commerce. This served to reassure them of the morality of what many of them were doing daily. Third, Eck's prestige as one of Catholic orthodoxy's most prominent defenders in the wake of the Reformation helped his arguments gain wide acceptance throughout the Catholic world. So, too, did the fourth effect: that in analyzing Eck's analysis of the triple contract, the enormously influential Dominican Cardinal, Thomas Cajetan, concluded that the triple contract was preferable to outright usury.[51]

Like all debates concerning usury, discussion of the triple contract continued for decades. The most dynamic of post-Reformation religious orders—the Jesuits—took a particular interest in the subject. In his *De iustitia et iure*, for example, Leonardus Lessius, SJ, engaged in a cost-benefit analysis of the triple contract and outlined the economic case for investment of private wealth in safe commercial-credit contracts for the sake of making profit.

By helping bankers and investors manage risk, the triple contract played a significant role in the growth of important money markets in cities such as Lyons, Antwerp, and Amsterdam. These facilitated an increased availability of credit for businesses working across national boundaries as well as large loans for governments strapped for cash.

The growth of money markets led to individuals and banks speculating on money itself. Indeed, the very fact that exchange rates fluctuated meant that it was impossible for a moneychanger to make a riskless profit.[52] Part of the early Catholic contribution to these developments was the realization that money itself was not a fixed measure of the value of other goods. In his *Comentario resolutoio de usuras*, written as an appendix to a penitential manual on moral theology, Martín de Azpilcueta articulated what amounted to one of the first quantity theories of money. The scholastics understood very well that the quantity of money circulat-

---

[50] See Noonan, *Scholastic Analysis*, 210.
[51] See Thomae De Vio Caietani, *De societate negotiatoria*, in *Scripta philosophica; De nominum analogia; De conceptu entis*, ed. Paul Zammit (Rome: apud Institutum "Angelicum," 1934), no. 432.
[52] See Wood, *Medieval Economic Thought*, 198.

ing in an economy affected the average of prices, or the price level.[53] Azpilcueta observed that the influx of precious metals from South America into Europe from the early sixteenth century onwards was a major cause of price increases.[54] This insight was further developed, historians of economic thought point out, by theologians associated with the School of Salamanca.[55] Some commentators estimate that these importations tripled the price level between 1500 and 1600 in Spain and Spain's dominions in Western Europe.[56]

According to Azpilcueta, the value of money was not fixed, because it varied according to the supply (that is, quantity) available. "All merchandise," he stated, "becomes dearer when it is in great demand and short supply, and money, in so far as it may be sold, bartered, or exchanged by some other form of contract, is merchandise, and therefore also becomes dearer when it is in great demand and short supply."[57] Hence, Azpilcueta wrote, "Money is worth more where and when it is scarce than where and when it is abundant.... And it may be concluded that money is more valuable in one country than another, and more valuable at one time than at another."[58]

This meant that there was no objection, in principle, to speculation on money. As Molina pointed out, significant legitimate profit could be realized if an exchange dealer was clever enough to "conjecture the place and time, in which money will be worth much more [in the sense of an increase of value and purchasing power], because of the lack of it and the necessity for it of the merchants and others."[59] What separated speculators from usurers, in Molina's view, was that speculators could not be certain of a profit. If usury involved risk-free, certain gain on a loan, then the *uncertain* character of speculation with regard to exchange dealings rendered speculation legitimate in the eyes of scholastic thinkers.[60] The justification for speculative profit thus lay in the *risk* undertaken by the speculator.

---

[53] See, for instance, Luis de Molina, SJ, *De Iustitia et Iure*, Vol. 2, *Coloniae Allobrogum*, 1759 (originally published Cuenca, 1593/1597), Tract II, dispn., 348.
[54] See Martín de Azpilcueta, "Commentary on the Resolution of Money" (1556), trans. Jeannine Emery, *Journal of Markets & Morality* 7/1 (2004): 240.
[55] See, for instance, Marjorie Grice-Hutchinson, *The School of Salamanca: Readings in Spanish Monetary Theory, 1544-1605* (Oxford: Clarendon Press, 1952).
[56] See E.F. Gay, *American Treasure and the Price Revolution in Spain, 1501-1650* (Cambridge, MA: Harvard University Press, 1934).
[57] See Azpilcueta, "Commentary on the Resolution of Money," 171.
[58] Ibid.
[59] Molina, *De Iustitia et Iure*, II, 408.3.
[60] See Roover, *Business, Banking, and Economic Thought*, 356; and Noonan, *Scholastic Analysis*, 175-92, 311-39.

Moreover, such speculation was understood by these theologians to be a form of *work*. Though it was not manual labor, speculation was no different from that of the mental work undertaken by, for instance, investors. Molina also saw this form of speculation as serving the real economy, inasmuch as it helped direct money and capital to those places and persons in the economy where it is needed but not yet present.

Conclusion

These ideas of the Catholic moralists and theologians did not amount to a Christian justification of every single activity associated with speculation or finance in general. In his seventeenth-century treatise on business, *Il Negotiante*, the Italian merchant and protoeconomist Giovanni Domenico Peri singled out as reprehensible those bankers who tried to manipulate exchange rates in order to create artificial rigidities in the money market. Peri also described the practice of spreading rumors in order to speculate on prices as a species of fraud.[61] In this connection, he invoked and echoed high church authorities. Sixty years earlier, Pope Pius V had formally condemned such practices.[62] The sins listed there, however, are not derived from speculation itself. Rather, they involve other moral errors such as deceit and lying.

This distinction matters, because it underscores that early modern Catholic scholastics provided moral legitimacy to financial activities ranging from capital loans to speculation that had hitherto been viewed in terms of moral neutrality or outright condemnation as unworthy of any Christian. No longer was virtuous work regarded as limited mainly to manual labor, agriculture, law, or politics.

With commerce and the business of capital increasingly destigmatized and no longer understood as sunk in the evil of usury, the way was open for Catholics to regard these segments of economic activity as areas in which people could live morally responsible and flourishing lives. The need to address moral challenges, it turned out, had facilitated deeper knowledge of economic concepts and economic activity, which in turn had helped increase both understanding of the potential for economies to grow and for people to embrace the virtues in the context of a new economic world.

---

[61] Giovanni Domenico Peri, *Il Negotiante* (Venice 1638), Part III, cap. Xx, 74–75.
[62] See Raymond de Roover, *Gresham on Foreign Exchange: An Essay on Early English Mercantilism* (Cambridge, MA: Harvard University Press, 1949), 164.

OIKOS AND *OIKONOMIKA*
THE EARLY MODERN FAMILY AS A MATRIX OF MODERN ECONOMICS

John Witte Jr.

INTRODUCTION

In this chapter, I focus on the social interaction between the spheres of economics and the family in shaping moral character. The marital household (the *oikos*) and the discipline of economics (*oikonomika*) have long been interlinked in Western societies, and both have depended on each other in providing tangible and intangible goods of various sorts. The marital household has long been a vital economic unit of its own—especially households with attendant shops, services, and servants which depend on and contribute to stable markets and currencies. It has also long been a vital source of education, apprenticing, and vocational training central to the success of economic, political, and religious life. The household has long provided essential security and provision for parents, children, and other kin, for caring and sharing, nutrition and nursing, welfare and poor relief when household members became impoverished, injured, incapacitated, sick, elderly, or otherwise dependent—even if these tasks are now shared more fully with other social institutions and professions and by the modern welfare state. Moreover, the formation of a new marital family is often a critical time of property and financial exchange between two families in a prior generation, and it provides a fundamental conduit for transmitting property to the next generation through gift, trust, inheritance, and more.

Much has been written about the corrosive impact of modern economics and attendant industrialization and bureaucratization on the marital family. Marx and Engels early issued dire warnings. "Modern industry, in overturning the economic foundation on which was based the traditional family has unloosened all traditional family ties," Marx wrote in 1867.[1] By 1884, Engels reported that "by the

---

[1] This chapter is drawn in part from John Witte Jr., *Church, State, and Family: Reconciling Traditional Teachings and Modern Liberties* (Cambridge: Cambridge University Press, 2019), ch. 4. I am grateful to Dr. Justin Latterell for his excellent help with this chapter. Karl Marx, *Capital*, ed. Frederick Engels (New York: Modern Library, 1906), 489.

action of modern industry, all family ties among the proletariat are torn asunder, and their children transformed into simple articles of commerce and instruments of labor."[2] A generation later, Max Weber warned about the corrosive impact of "technical rationality" on the family and society more generally. By technical rationality, he meant the drive to bring more and more of life under the control of means-ends procedures that most effectively and efficiently accomplish short-term benefits and material satisfactions. The logic of technical rationality holds that efficiency is always the best means to the end of satisfying human desire, and that human desire is satisfied most efficiently by always having more. The logic of technical rationality, Weber predicted, would eventually become an "iron cage" that trapped modern societies into a relentless and insatiable pursuit of property, power, and prestige. And it would gradually reduce persons to mere "cogs in the machine" of progress, whose means and ends were no longer within their control.[3]

Technical rationality, in this sense, is a prominent feature of the modern state —not only in its capitalist forms, as Weber showed, but also in its socialist forms, as Jürgen Habermas later made clear.[4] Free-market capitalism, especially in the form of neoliberal economic systems of private enterprise, is a textbook case of a technical rational system of supply and demand, cost and benefit being applied to the production and delivery of goods, services, and experiences. Bureaucratic rationality, in the form of modern welfare policies or harder kinds of Marxist-Leninist communism, is also a form of modernization. These two kinds of modernization have technical rationality in common: the belief that the efficient use of powerful technical means in the form of either market procedures or government bureaucracies can increase our individual and collective satisfactions.[5]

The spread of technical rationality has tended to shift time-tested patterns of mutual dependency within the household, extended family, and local civil society to increased dependency on and influence by the market and the state. It has tended to shift the calculus of self-worth, and the measures and methods of aspiration and achievement, from these local standards and sources to national and interna-

---

[2] Karl Marx and Friedrich Engels, *The Communist Manifesto*, ed. Samuel H. Beer (Wheeling, IL: Harlan Davidson, 1955), 28; Friedrich Engels, *The Origin of the Family, Private Property, and the State* (New York: Pathfinder, 1972). See Scott Yenor, *Family Politics: The Idea of Marriage in Modern Political Thought* (Waco, TX: Baylor University Press, 2011), 137-58.

[3] Max Weber, *The Protestant Ethic and the Spirit of Capitalism* (New York: Scribner, 1958), 181-83.

[4] Ibid., 181; Jürgen Habermas, *The Theory of Communicative Rationality*, Vol. 2: *Lifeworld and System: A Critique of Functionalist Reason* (Boston: Beacon Press, 1987), 333.

[5] Don Browning, *Marriage and Modernization: How Globalization Threatens Marriage and What to Do about It* (Grand Rapids, MI: Eerdmans, 2003).

tional standards that trade principally in the hard currency of property, power, and prestige. And it has tended to strain the deeper, more enduring, and more personalized interactions of daily life in the household and local civil society. Whenever technical reason spreads, and life comes under its rules of efficiency and productivity and its definitions of satisfaction and happiness, the organic, spontaneous, and conversational aspects of daily life, found most poignantly in the family, tend to get deemphasized and disrupted. This story has been told often, including recently by Don Browning,[6] William Goode,[7] and Harvey Cox.[8]

In this chapter, I explore the flip side of this story, namely, the constructive role of the early modern Protestant family in shaping the values of modern economics. One of the hallmarks of early modern Protestantism was its view of the family as a "little commonwealth"—the most primal school of justice and mercy, morality and virtue, education and welfare in a godly republic. Martin Luther called the marital household the "mother of all earthly laws"; John Calvin called it "the first covenant of a covenant community"; Anglican divines called it "the seminary of the republic."[9] All of these metaphors were designed to underscore the early modern Protestant belief that a stable and well-functioning marital household was an essential foundation of a well-ordered church, state, society, and economy. The early modern Protestant family was structured and schooled to cultivate the critical habits of discipline and organization in the economic and moral lives of its members. Its moral codes, communicated in hundreds of sermons and household manuals, set out in detail the moral and religious rules, rights, and responsibilities of household members to each other and to their neighbors in different stages of life. It is here, in the elementary ethics and experiences of the Protestant household, that so many of the basic norms and habits of modern economic life were slowly instilled and cultivated in the moral character of each new generation.

This thesis supplements and partly corrects Max Weber's famous thesis about the Protestant spirit of capitalism. It was not just the mystical spirit of capitalism in Protestantism, as Weber posited, or the ironic convergence of new Protestant teachings on vocation, predestination, and asceticism that helped to ground and guide early modern economics. It was also the direct role that the Protestant household played as an important site of economic activity and an incubator of market morality.

---

[6] Ibid.

[7] William Goode, *World Changes in Divorce Patterns* (New Haven, CT: Yale University Press, 1994).

[8] Harvey Cox, *The Market as God* (Cambridge, MA: Harvard University Press, 2016).

[9] See detailed references in John Witte Jr., *From Sacrament to Contract: Marriage, Religion, and Law in the Western Tradition*, 2nd ed. (Louisville, KY: Westminster John Knox Press, 2012).

Max Weber and the Protestant Spirit of Capitalism

It is worth reminding ourselves of Weber's central thesis. He observed that the most highly developed (or "rationalized") economies in his day correlated with regions and cultures in which Protestant reform movements had developed most fully and forcefully; and that, within those contexts, the "business leaders and owners of capital, and even more the higher technically and commercially trained personnel of modern enterprises" were "overwhelmingly Protestant."[10] This seemed paradoxical since the "spirit" of modern capitalism—often characterized by unrepentant utilitarianism and relentless acquisitiveness—seemed to contradict traditional Christian values and virtues that Protestants so strongly emphasized. Yet to Weber, the correlation between Protestantism and capitalism was no coincidence. It was precisely the ideas, anxieties, and institutional forms of Protestantism that had helped drive and direct the emergence of the modern capitalist order and the displacement of traditional feudal economies and church-dominated monopolies that prevailed over medieval Catholic life.

Three Protestant teachings were particularly important, said Weber. First, Martin Luther's conception of the Christian vocation (*Beruf*) leveled the professional and spiritual hierarchies of his day and catalyzed greater participation by all in hard work, professionalized labor, and a market economy. Medieval Catholics regarded the clergy as superior to the laity in virtue and spiritual attainment; the lowliest parson was thought to be closer to God than the highest emperor. Luther, by contrast, insisted that priests and monks were no more virtuous or nearer to God than solders or maidservants. All were equally slaves to sin, and equally dependent upon divine grace for salvation. And all were equally entitled and equipped to pursue the Christian vocation that best suited their talents and stations in life. Christians were not called to leave their secular callings for a cloistered life of self-sanctifying religious asceticism and discipline. They were faithfully and dutifully to serve God and neighbor in the ordinary vocations, firm in the knowledge that the work of the butcher, housewife, or soldier was just as spiritual and conducive to salvation as that of the bishop, abbot, or priest. The same devotion and discipline that a cleric directed to spiritual and ecclesiastical ends could be devoted to secular and material ends, with equal assurance of salvation by grace through faith. The broad effect of this teaching, Weber concluded, "as compared to the Catholic attitude" of the Middle Ages, was that "the moral emphasis on and the religious sanction of, organized worldly labor in a calling was mightily increased."[11]

Second, Weber argued, John Calvin's doctrine of predestination engendered religious anxieties that fueled the development of an intense and systematic work

---

[10] Weber, *The Protestant Ethic*, 35.
[11] Ibid., 83.

ethic among subsequent generations of believers. Lacking the sacramental means of grace that provided Catholics with a reassuring certitude of salvation, Calvinists were anxious to know whether they were among those whom God had elected for eternal salvation, rather than eternal damnation. Over time, Weber argued, Calvinists came to view diligent and productive labor and success in one's vocation as, on one hand, a nonnegotiable religious duty and, on the other hand, a reliable indicator of one's election. The "systematic self-control" and discipline that Calvinists consequently applied to their lives and work thus served "as the technical means, not of purchasing salvation, but of getting rid of the fear of damnation." "The God of Calvinism demanded of his believers not single good works, but a life of good works combined into a unified system [and] subjected to a consistent method for conduct as a whole."[12] Soteriological anxieties, then, fostered a form of economic asceticism and organization that impacted broader economic structures.

Third, it was this progressively systematic rationalization of life and work, Weber contended, that drove Protestant societies away from late-medieval feudalism dominated by church monopolies and clergy-dominated guilds toward the highly rationalized and competitive capitalistic economies of Protestant lands in Western Europe and North America. Protestant individuals and communities, spurred by a sense of vocation and a burning need to prove their state of grace, adopted a feverish and systematic work ethic that subsequently transformed the economic ethos and institutions around them. Even those who did not share the Protestant faith and zeal were forced to embrace the same ethic in order to compete. The institutional dynamics of Protestant sects in the American colonies further catalyzed this process by enforcing strict moral standards for membership and participation in sacramental rites, which allowed, in turn, for fuller participation in the economic life of the community.[13] Feudal traditions and small-scale guilds gave way to the breakneck pace of modern factories and finance. Even as its religious underpinnings and trappings faded from view, the Protestant ethic and the institutions it created remained in place as the basic socioeconomic framework into which all were now born. Ironically, where early Protestant reformers sought to elevate the work of ordinary people, emerging economies made the so-called Protestant work ethic all but compulsory. The burgeoning "spirit of capitalism"—ultimately a denatured and perverted caricature of earlier forms of Protestant asceticism—was hollow and mundane: "The Puritan wanted to work in a calling," Weber concluded, whereas now "we are forced to do so."

---

[12] Ibid., 115–17.
[13] See Max Weber, "The Protestant Sects and the Spirit of Capitalism," in *From Max Weber: Essays in Sociology*, ed. H.H. Geerth and C. Wright Mills (New York: Oxford University Press, 1946), 302–22.

For when asceticism was carried out of monastic cells into everyday life, and began to dominate worldly morality, it did its part in building the tremendous cosmos of the modern economic order. This order is now bound to the technical and economic conditions of machine production which today determine the lives of all the individuals who are born into this mechanism, not only those directly concerned with economic acquisition, with irresistible force. Perhaps it will so determine them until the last ton of fossilized coal is burnt. In Baxter's view the care for external goods should only lie on the shoulders of the "saint like a light cloak, which can be thrown aside at any moment." But fate decreed that the cloak should become an iron cage.[14]

The Baxter whom Weber mentions in this famous "iron cage" passage is Richard Baxter (1615-91), a distinguished English Puritan theologian who penned exhaustive practical guides for faithful living. If Baxter thought that care for external goods should rest but lightly on the shoulders of God's predestined believers, his writings suggest that Christians' responsibility to order their daily lives, especially their households, constituted a much weightier responsibility. Baxter is a prime example of the rationalizing and systematizing impulses that Weber attributes to Protestantism generally, and especially to seventeenth-century Calvinism. Yet the title of the 504-page volume in which Baxter discusses most thoroughly the Christian's economic life offers an important clue about the real locus and focus of early Protestants' economic reform efforts. Baxter's volume was titled *Christian Economics (or, Family Duties)*,[15] showing his straightforward equivalence of Christian economics and Christian family life.

Baxter's treatise is only one of scores of extant Protestant household manuals and family directories from the sixteenth to eighteenth centuries.[16] These understudied texts show that, insofar as Protestants did help to shape the spirit and institutions of early modern capitalism, they did so first of all by rationalizing the household (the *oikos*) and teaching its members the meanings and measures of vocation, discipline, and hard work. Indeed, the birth of capitalism rested not only on the reorganization of guilds and church monopolies into highly rationalized factories and competitive markets of supply and demand, but also and more ba-

---

[14] Weber, *The Protestant Ethic*, 181-82.

[15] This was one volume in Baxter's much-read set of publications titled *A Christian Directory: or, A Summ of Practical Theologie, and Cases of Conscience: Directing Christians, How to Use their Knowledge and Faith; How to Improve all Helps and Means, and to Perform all Duties; How to Overcome Temptations, and to Escape or Mortifie Every Sin*, 2nd ed., 4 parts in 5 vols. (London 1678).

[16] On household manuals, which also had earlier Catholic and later liberal forms, see John Witte Jr. and Heather M. Good, "The Duties of Love: The Vocation of the Child in the Household Manual Tradition," in *The Vocation of the Child*, ed. Patrick M. Brennan (Grand Rapids, MI: Eerdmans, 2008), 266-94.

sically on the radical rationalization of the home—an institution that many Protestants viewed as sociologically, politically, and theologically prior to all other social institutions, including the economy. Household manuals taught the Christian faithful how to manage the interlacing rights and responsibilities of husbands and wives, parents and children, and masters and servants. They offered guidelines for everything from table manners to clothing, diet, work habits, worship, and prayer. They instructed parents how to instill virtues and combat vices in their children and exhorted children to heed the word (or suffer the rod) of their elders and to tend to them in old age. And they exhorted household members to develop mutual habits of order and discipline that allowed everyone to produce good work in their unique Christian vocations, knowing that hard work was a reflection and affirmation of divine favor.

These household manuals both confirm and qualify some of Weber's key insights into the relationship of markets, morality, and character formation. Weber's and later Weberian accounts of economic rationalization were focused on the public economy—the productive activities and attitudes of tradesmen and merchants, buyers and sellers, and others who made, exchanged, sold, and purchased goods and services in the marketplace. Early modern Protestants who engaged in such activities may well have been guided, to varying degrees, by the religious motives and beliefs that Weber highlighted, including the idea of the Christian vocation and the good works and moral discipline that it fostered. Yet early modern Protestant conceptions of vocation were, emphatically, not limited to a person's public work or career. Fatherhood, motherhood, and childhood were regarded as important vocations for early Protestants no less than the vocations of blacksmiths or bakers, bankers or barristers. Moreover, a great deal of economic activity in early modern Europe and North America occurred within the household, which often included servants, apprentices, and students along with blood relatives, and which provided a great deal of the nurture, education, social welfare, and moral discipline historically furnished by the medieval Catholic Church and later provided by the modern welfare state. The norms and habits each household member learned in this carefully structured domestic sphere formed an important part of their preparation for public economic life. And the rationalization of the early modern Protestant household was an important step in the gradual rationalization of early modern economies in the later institutionally differentiated societies on both sides of the Atlantic.

ILLUSTRATIONS FROM THE PROTESTANT HOUSEHOLD MANUALS

Let me take four Protestant household manualists as illustrations: Heinrich Bullinger, Robert Cleaver, William Perkins, and then Baxter again. All four of these writers built their manuals on biblical, classical, patristic, and humanist learning.

All wrote in highly accessible terms for all pious persons to understand either by reading or hearing their instruction. All were highly influential writers throughout Great Britain, the European Continent, and later North America; their works were reprinted often, and in multiple languages.

Heinrich Bullinger (1504–75)

A good example of an early Protestant household manual comes from the pen of Zurich Reformer Heinrich Bullinger, whose work on the family bridged the Lutheran, Calvinist, and Anglican worlds. Bullinger's *The Golde Boke of Christen Matrimonye* (1540), written in German but translated into English by the famous Bible translator Miles Coverdale,[17] set out a covenantal model of marriage and family life at the foundation of the covenant community of church, state, and workplace. "Wedlock," he wrote, "is a covenant, a coupling or yoking together" of one man and one woman "by the good consent of the both." "Holy wedlock was ordained of God himself in Paradise." It is thus an "honorable and holy" estate, enjoyed by the "holiest, and most virtuous, the wisest and most noble men" in the Bible, and commended to all persons today—clerical and lay, young and old, single and widowed, rich and poor. For Bullinger, the single adult man or woman living outside a marital household was an aberration.[18]

God created marriage so that a man and a woman "may live together honestly and friendly the one with the other, that they may avoid uncleanness, that they may bring up children in the fear of God, that the one may help and comfort the other." Bullinger followed conventional Protestant arguments regarding the marital purposes of protection from lust and procreation of children, arguing that marriage is God's "remedy and medicine unto our feeble and weak flesh" and that children are "the greatest treasure" of a marriage. But he placed special emphasis on marital love and friendship, returning to this theme several times. "The love ... in marriage ought to be (next unto God) above all loves," with couples rendering to each other "the most excellent and unpainful service, diligence and earnest labor, ... one doing for another, one longing, depending, helping and forbearing another, suffering, also like joy and like pain one with another." The marital household was the principal social welfare institution for adults, the nerve center for kinship networks that were of vital importance to human flourishing. He spelled out the mutual duties of husband and wife in detail.[19]

---

[17] Heinrich Bullinger, *Der christlich Eestand* (Zurich, 1540), translated as *The Christen State of Matrimonye* (London, 1541) (STC 4045) and then as *The Golde Boke of Christen Matrimonye* (London, 1542) (STC 1723) under Thomas Becon's pseudonym, Theodore Basille.

[18] Bullinger, *The Golde Boke*, folios i.b–ii, iii, v, xxi.b, xxiii, xxxvi.b, lxxvii.b–lxxviii.

[19] Ibid., folios iii.b–iiii; iv–v.b; xix; xxi.b; xxii–xxiiii; xxxvi.b–xxxviii; Heinrich Bullinger, *Decades of Henry Bullinger: The First and Second Decades*, ed. Thomas Harding (Cambridge: Cambridge University Press, 1849), 397–98.

Marital couples blessed with children could find ample instruction in Bullinger's *Golde Boke* on the parental duties of breast-feeding, nurture, protection, discipline, education, and dress of children, and, later, their courtship and contracting of marriage with a suitable partner. Bullinger's comments on discipline and training were typical of the sixteenth-century household manuals. He encouraged parents from the start to engage their children with "godly, honest, grave and fruitful" instruction and example. Parents should teach their children by word and example all the cardinal virtues, lead them in memorizing and reciting the Ten Commandments, Apostle's Creed, and other apt texts from the gospels and epistles. They should teach their children to "spend all the time in virtuous uses and never be idle," nor steal, fight, gossip, or harm others or themselves. When children did stray, parents should "correct them duly and discretely for their faults, so that they stand in great fear and awe of them, and if words will not reclaim them, then take the rod or whip of correction discretely used. For the rod of correction ministers wisdom."[20]

Bullinger also encouraged parents to instill industriousness in their children, by helping each child "learn that science or handicraft ... whereunto the child is naturally inclined and unto that occupation let him be put to." It was not good enough just to teach children literacy and numbers, said Bullinger, or set them up in their own home and marriage in due course, important as all those steps were. A child also needed the preparation, encouragement, and means to thrive in his or her own vocation. Parents who fail to provide and emphasize proper education and vocational training, are, in fact, "ungodly destroyers of themselves, their children, and of all commonwealths and congregations" who need well-trained leaders and members to function, conversant not only with "God's Law, Prophets, and Gospel" but also the methods and means to succeed in their occupations. "What is the cause of all this dissension, cruel persecution, tyranny, evil laws making unjust acts, false religion, wicked ordinances and ungodly decrees and institutions, but only the blind ignorance of unlearned rulers" and undereducated citizens unable to fend properly for themselves or stand up for each other when buffeted by tyrants or ill served by incompetent officials.[21]

Bullinger connected this new understanding of vocations to broader economic reforms, calling for a system of universal education and vocational training to replace the medieval system of church-based education for principal service in the church's bureaucracy. "In times past, when men saw so many spiritual promotions unto rich bishoprics, benefices, deaneries, abbeys, priories, chancellorships, etc., then they did set fast their children to schools to make them popish priests, idly to live by other men's sweat." But with the Reformation, this clerical exploitation of the laity is over, Bullinger argued. Now "the common labor, god-

---

[20] Bullinger, *The Golde Boke*, folio lxxii.b.
[21] Ibid., folio lxxii.b.

liness, and the public profit of all commonwealths and congregations depend upon" all citizens and subjects being trained in proper schools in all manner of vocations, including but going well beyond work within the church. "Now, therefore, O ye Christian parents: seeing that your youth is now by the favor of God endowed with so good wits and inclined unto good letters, let not the graces and gifts of God be offered you in vain, but exercise them" in such a way that your children can "come to be profitable unto the commonwealth, whereunto they be born." Indeed, train them at home and let them be further trained by teachers and masters in "all just and true occupations justly exercised and used," knowing that "God's blessing maketh them to prosper" if they remain "true doers and laborers in their calling."[22]

Thomas Becon, Thomas Cranmer's chaplain, published an edition of Bullinger's tract in 1542, and it was regularly reprinted and used thereafter. Becon added his own long foreword to the 1542 edition, in which he extolled the marital household not only for the spiritual good of the couple and their children, but also for the civil good of the commonwealth and church. With a properly functioning marital household, Becon wrote with ample bombast,

> many noble treasures chance unto us, virtue is maintained, vice is eschewed, houses are replenished, cities are inhabited, the ground is tilled, sciences are practiced, kingdoms flourish, amity is preserved, the public weal is defended, natural succession remaineth, good arts are taught, honest order is kept, Christendom is enlarged, God's word promoted, and the glory of God highly advanced and set further.

Indeed, on the strength and stability of "this household's common weal" hangs the security and success of the whole commonwealth of England.[23]

Robert Cleaver (c. 1561–1613)

This emphasis on the public utility and values of the private marital household was a central theme in Robert Cleaver's hefty tome on *A Godly Form of Householde Gouernment* (1598). Cleaver was a Puritan preacher in Oxfordshire who wrote popular tracts on the Ten Commandments, Sabbath Day observance, and other aspects of Christian piety. In *A Godly Form of Householde Gouernment*, Cleaver worked hard to systematize and rationalize domestic life, expanding on the themes illustrated by Bullinger. "All government of a family must be directed to two principal ends," Cleaver wrote: "First Christian holiness, and secondly the things of this life." "Religion must be stirring in Christian families, and that good

---

[22] Ibid., folios lxxiii–lxxiii.b.
[23] Ibid., Aiiii.

government looketh to bring godly behavior into families, as well as thrift and good husbandry."[24]

The paterfamilias must play the leading role in the good government of the family, Cleaver believed. As a husband, he must "live with his wife discreetly." He must "cherish and nourish" her as Christ loves and supports his church. He must work with her "in all due benevolence, honestly, soberly, and chastely." And he must "govern her in all duties, that properly concern the state of marriage, in knowledge, in wisdom, judgment, and justice." A husband must not be "bitter, fierce, and cruel" to his wife and must "never beat her," even if he, as her head, must reproach and admonish her. Instead, "as a man of knowledge," he must "edify her, both by a good example, and also, by good instructions." As a father, the married man must lead his household in private devotions, daily prayer, catechization, and Bible reading. He must ensure that children and servants are faithful in public worship and Sabbath observance. He must be vigilant in offering his children instruction and admonition with wisdom, and punishment and rebuke with patience.[25]

If husbands were to govern the household, the duty of the married woman was to be "faithful and loving" to her husband, "wise and prudent" to her family. She must "reverence her husband" and "submit herself unto him," as the Bible enjoins. She must dress and deport herself and her children in accordance with the family's means and station in life. She must avoid sloth and not keep idle, lazy, or untoward company. She must be thrifty, just, charitable, and prudent in her choice of friends. She must keep order and help maintain "the exercise of religion within the household." She must tend especially to the care of her daughters and maidens, teaching them and exemplifying for them the norms and habits of Christian womanhood.[26]

Husband and wife also have mutual duties to each other and to their children. They "must love one another with a pure heart fervently." They must be faithful to each other, constantly "bending their wits, and all their endeavors, to the help each of other, and to the common good of the family." They must pray together, "admonish one another," and serve as "mutual helps to each other in matters concerning their own salvation, and the service of God." Together, they must "instruct and bring up their children even from their cradle, in the fear and nurture of the Lord, ... in shame fastness, hatred of vice, and love of all virtue." Such dispositions

---

[24] Robert Cleaver, *A Godly Form of Householde Gouernment* (London 1598), 6-7. See further John Dod and Robert Cleaver, *A Plaine and Familiar Exposition of the Ten Commandments, with a Methodicall Short Catechisme, Containing Briefly all the Principall Grounds of Christian Religion* (London, 1604) (STC 6968), 181.

[25] Ibid., 24, 226-228; Cleaver, *A Godly Form of Householde Gouernment*, 92, 114, 159 ff., 202 ff.

[26] Ibid., 52-91, 203-222; Dod and Cleaver, *Plaine and Familiar Exposition*, 221-22.

were to be carried out of the home and into the extended economic sphere. As children mature, parents must "bring them up in some profitable and lawful calling, by which they may live honestly and Christianly, and not be fruitless burdens of the earth ... or commonwealth." They must also "provide for the disposing of them in marriage," counseling them in their courtship and consenting to their marriage when they come of age and have chosen wisely among available prospects for marriage. In response to this, "the duties of the natural child" are very simple: "reverence, obedience, and thankfulness"—exemplified notably in seeking the parents' consent to the child's own marriage, and in caring for the parents when they become elderly or disabled.[27]

In many households, the man and woman are also the masters and mistresses of servants and apprentices, who work and sometimes live within the home or are a daily part of the family business. Cleaver saw the master-servant relationship as a natural and necessary extension of the parent-child relationship. Masters and mistresses must teach their servants diligence and discipline and keep them from idleness and sloth. They must bring up their servants "in honesty, and in comely manners, and in all virtues." They must "instruct their servants and apprentices in the knowledge of their occupations and trades, even as parents would teach their own children, without all guile, fraud, delaying, or concealing." And they must discipline them with "such discretion, pity, and desire of their amendment, as loving parents use to deal with their own dear children." They must maintain order, courtesy, respect, diligence, and peace among children and servants, and work "to banish sin and corrupt religion out of their dwellings."[28]

The household was to be not only an incubator of Christian morality but also a model of a good Christian business, said Cleaver. In taking on servants and apprentices, for example, the master must be as sure of "their honest, godly conversation and how they have profited in the knowledge of God" as he is of their skills and strengths and how they have excelled in their craft or profited in their work. For the two are "closely tied": "such servants that take in hand the Lord will much better prosper and give success unto him than otherwise." Once he hired his servants, the master thus was obliged to tend to his servants' souls as much as their bodies. Indeed, he was called to discharge the threefold office of Christ at home and in business: "rule like a King, teach like a Prophet, and pray like a Priest to show how a godly man should behave himself" at home and at work. Alongside this spiritual leadership, the master must set rules and create conditions of labor that provided servants with adequate food and shelter, rewarded hard work, paid

---

[27] Cleaver, *Householde Gouernment*, 188-91, 243 ff.; Dod and Cleaver, *Plaine and Familiar Exposition*, 174-222.

[28] For this section on masters and servants, see the expanded edition, *A Godlie Forme of Hovsehold Government: For the Ordering of Private Families According to the Direction of God's Word* (London, 1600), 363-83.

fair wages, maintained reasonable hours, and granted weekly Sabbath rest to all. He must strike a balance between lawful acquisition and proper accumulation of wealth, on one hand, and "profligacy" and "niggardliness" on the other hand. He must promote collaboration among the workers and throw himself into the work "so that their necessary affairs and business are dispatched well." Servants, laborers, and apprentices, in turn, must "cheerfully and willingly from their hearts perform the labors and works" they are assigned. Calling to mind Weber's observation that prosperous work eased spiritual anxieties, Cleaver urged workers to "be faithful in all things committed to them," knowing that ultimately "they are serving the Lord, not men; and not only have respect of the earthly reward, but because they know, and are assured, that of the Lord they shall receive the reward of inheritance, in as much as they serve the Lord Christ."[29]

Faithful maintenance of all these household duties and offices was the best guarantee of productive order within the broader commonwealths of church and state, Cleaver insisted, echoing early manualists like Thomas Becon. Indeed, properly functioning households were indispensable to civic flourishing: "[I]f masters of families do not practice at home catechizing, and discipline in their houses and join their helping hands to magistrates and ministers," social order and stability will soon give way to chaos and anarchy. "[I]t is impossible for a man to understand to govern the commonwealth, that doth not know to rule his own house, or order his own person, so that he that knoweth not to govern, deserveth not to reign."[30]

This was common lore among Cleaver's fellow English divines. "There was never any disorder and outrage, in any family, church, or commonwealth," when domestic offices were respected and domestic duties discharged, Robert Pricke insisted. For domestic duty and discipline allow persons "to rise up to the knowledge of the sovereign Lord, and to give unto him the reverence and honor due to his divine majesty." Duty and discipline also teach the personal virtues and civic habits that "upholdeth, and continueth all these estates, degrees, and orders" of the broader commonwealth.[31] Daniel Rogers wrote further that a stable household served as "the right hand of providence, supporter of laws, states, orders, offices, gifts, and services, the glory of peace, ... the foundation of countries, cities, universities ... crowns, and kingdoms."[32] Puritan divine William Gouge wrote in his massive, eight-hundred-page, eight-book treatise *Of Domesticall Duties* (1622), "A conscionable performance of household duties ... may be accounted a public

---

[29] Ibid., 372–73, 378–83.
[30] Ibid., Preface, A4; 4–5.
[31] Robert Pricke, *The Doctrine of Superioritie, and of Subjection, contained in the Fifth Commandment of the Holy Law of Almightie God* (London, 1609), B2.
[32] Daniel Rogers, *Matrimoniall Honour or, The Mutuall Crowne and Comfort of Godly, Loyall, and Chaste Marriage* (London, 1642), 17.

work." For "good members of a family are likely to make good members of church and commonwealth."³³

Gouge zeroed in on the master-servant relationship, devoting more than a hundred pages to describing their respective duties. Like Cleaver, Gouge called masters to serve as "prophets, priests, and kings" within their households and to cater to the soul, mind, and body of their servants and apprentices:

> Masters themselves reap great benefit by a faithful discharge of this duty ... by bringing their servants to do more faithful service to them. For there is no such means to stir up servants to do all good duty, as the fear of God planted in their hearts. That servant that shall find true grace either first wrought, or further increased in him by his master's means, will think himself so beholding to such a master, as he has never been able to make any sufficient recompense, and therefore will endeavor to do what good service he can in way of thankfulness: he will not only be faithful and diligent in his business, but he will call upon God to prosper his services for his master's good.... Servants well instructed in piety are likeliest to prove most profitable not only to the family, but also to the Church and the Commonwealth where they live.³⁴

Servants so trained will also be able to find their own "true calling" or "vocation," Gouge continued.

> God by his providence so ordereth men's affairs, that masters who from time to time train up and send forth many [ap]prentices well exercised and skillful in their trade, do hold on and yea increase their own dealing and gain which they get thereby; and yet withal their apprentices also come well forward.... This is an especial means to make everyone the more diligent and faithful. For when everyone hath his peculiar work, they know, that they in particular have to give an account thereof to themselves, to their fellow servants, to their master and family, and ultimately to God himself, who has called them to this vocation.³⁵

William Perkins (1558–1602)

Concern for the Christian vocation was a special focus of another Anglo-Puritan, William Perkins, fellow of Christ College, Cambridge, and rector of St. Andrew's Church in Cambridge. Perkins wrote a famous *Treatise of the Vocations,* published posthumously in 1605. His description of the well-ordered household was very much like Cleaver's and Bullinger's. "[M]arriage was made and appointed by God

---

33 William Gouge, *Of Domesticall Duties: Eight Treatises* (London, ca. 1622) (STC 12119), 17, 27.

34 Ibid., bk. 8, 21, using modern printing, William Gouge, *Of Domestical Duties*, ed. Greg Fox (Pensacola, FL: Chapel Library, 2006), 484.

35 Ibid., 495–96.

himself to be the foundation and seminary of all sorts and kinds of life in the commonwealth and the church," Perkins declared. "[T]hose families wherein the service of God is performed are, as it were, little churches; yea, even a kind of paradise on earth." In a well-ordered Christian household, worship of God must come first and undergird all family relationships, duties, and activities:

> Common reason and equity showeth it to be a necessary duty: for the happy and prosperous estate of the family, which consisteth in the mutual love and agreement of the man and wife, in the dutiful obedience of children to their parents, and in the faithful service of servants to their Masters, wholly dependeth upon the grace and blessings of God: and this blessing is annexed to his worship.

Like Cleaver, Perkins emphasized that the parent's and master's responsibilities to children and servants were not only to love, nurture, feed, and clothe them and protect them against hardship. They were also to "observe both the inclination and the natural gifts of body and mind, that are in the child, and accordingly to bestow it in some honest calling and course of life."[36]

Perkins homed in on the need for an "honest calling" for all members of the community. "Every person of every degree, state, sex, or condition, without exception, must have some personal and particular calling to walk in," Perkins wrote. And he or she must discharge that calling with diligence and zeal, and to the glory and honor of God and neighbor, church and state, family and self.

> Sloth and negligence in the duties of our callings, are a *disorder* against that good order which God set in the societies of mankind, in both church and commonwealth. And indeed, idleness and sloth are the causes of many damnable sins. The idle body, or the idle brain, is the workshop of the devil.

Each person must "shake off that spiritual drowsiness" and be constantly ready to answer the question *"What have I done? or How does it stand between God and me?"*[37]

Piling up biblical and classical verses that reflected this vocational ideal, Perkins took sharp aim at those who, in his view, betrayed it. The first were idle beggars and drunks, itinerant vagabonds and mendicants, and others who wrongly exploited the charity of others. These are the classic "undeserving poor," Perkins

---

[36] William Perkins, *Economy, or Household-Government: A Short Survey of the Right Manner of Erecting and Ordering a Family, According to the Scriptures*, in *The Workes of that Famous and Worthy Minister of Christ in the Universitie of Cambridge, M. W. Perkins* (London, 1631), 3:418–419, 669, 695. Ibid., 3:695.

[37] William Perkins, "A Treatise of the Vocations," in *Works*, 1:750–79, using modernized edition of William Gross (2015) (digitalpuritan.net), 9, 13, 17–18, 50.

wrote. They should be put to hard work to restore the charitable and diaconal coffers they emptied so these alms may properly serve the "deserving poor"—widows, orphans, the injured and disabled. The second were the "idle rich," who had inherited or earned "great livings and revenues, [and now] spend their days in eating and drinking, in sports and pastimes, not employing themselves in service for church or commonwealth." From those who have been given much, much is expected, Perkins argued, citing scripture. And those with wealth or time to spare are obliged to "set it in motion" to provide opportunities for others and to enhance the common good. The third and most egregious betrayers of vocational ideals, are "monks and friars" and other "popish votaries" who "live apart from the societies of men in fasting and prayer." Perkins wrote, "This monkish kind of living is damnable," for it is sloth and idleness masquerading as a spiritual vocation. In fact, "all monks a[re] thieves and robbers" living on the tithes of others, rather than as "good and profitable member[s] of some society and body."[38]

"Every man must judge that the particular calling in which God has placed him, is the best of all callings for him. I do not say simply *best*, but best *for him*." At minimum, this requires each Christian to "join the practice of his personal calling, with the practice of the general calling of Christianity…. [I]n his personal calling, he must show himself to be a Christian." Furthermore, a person has to pick a vocation that best suits his inclinations and gifts. Here, Christian parents and masters must play a key role, said Perkins. They must be attentive to their child's inclinations: "some are affected with music more than others; some with merchandise; some with a more liberal kind of learning." Their training must follow these inclinations. The parents must also discern the "natural gifts" of their children. "Those children who excel in the gifts of the body are to be brought up in callings performed by the labor of the body, as in mechanical arts. And those who excel in the gifts of the mind, are to be applied to those sciences that are performed by wit and learning." A parent's failure to encourage and prepare the child for his or her proper vocation "is a great and common sin," Perkins argued:

> For the care of most is that their children may *live*—not regarding at all whether they live *well*, and do service to God in a fit calling or not. And the truth is, parents cannot do greater wrong to their children, and to the society of men, than to apply them to unfit callings—as when a child is fit for learning, to apply him to a trade, or other bodily service; or contrariwise, to apply him to learning when he is fittest for a trade. For this is like a man applying his toes to feeling, and not his fingers; and to go about on his hands and not his foot; and to set the members of the body out of their proper places."[39]

---

[38] Ibid., 13, 16–17.
[39] Ibid., 14–19.

Perkins used this metaphor of the body and its members to argue further that when a person has properly prepared and pursued a vocation most suitable to his talents, that person must "keep himself within the compass, limits, or precincts of it," following the rules of his vocation. Much as a body needs each member to perform its own function, or an army needs each soldier to follow orders, so a properly running society and economy need workers in their places. If a man stays within his calling, he will be blessed, and all society with him. If he strays "outside the compass of his calling, he is out of the way, and by this means he bereaves himself of the protection of the Almighty; and he lies open and naked to all the punishments and plagues of God."[40]

Richard Baxter (1615–91)

The repeated emphasis on the Christian vocation and the orderly Christian household as an essential foundation for church, state, society, and economy was the starting point for Puritan preacher Richard Baxter, whom Max Weber used to illustrate the early modern Protestant spirit of capitalism. Baxter was a popular preacher in Kidderminster and London and a prolific author, leaving some 168 books. His five-hundred-page tome on *Christian Economics (or Family Duties)* [41] was but one of four huge volumes in Baxter's much-read manual of Puritan moral theology. The position of *Christian Economics* in this collection is instructive. Baxter placed it second, after a volume on *Christian Ethics (or Private Duties)*, and before the two volumes on *Christian Ecclesiastics (or, Church Duties)* and *Christian Politics (or, Duties to Our Rulers and Neighbors)*. The very arrangement of the volumes underscored Baxter's perception that the economic duties of the family comprised the critical fulcrum between private and public virtues, the preparation and proving ground for life in church, state, and society.

Max Weber emphasized Baxter's "ascetic" Puritan ethics at work in this and many other tracts. Typical of early modern Puritan manualists, Baxter insisted on discipline over laxness, frugality over sumptuousness, thrift over waste, hard work over idleness, efficiency over sloppiness, the priesthood of all believers pursuing their God-given vocations over the idle clergy luxuriously exploiting the laity to the detriment of economic advancement of all. This Puritan ethic, Weber believed, was conducive to the rise of early modern capitalism. "The worker with a vocational calling will pursue his work in an orderly fashion, while others are stuck in a situation of constant confusion; their businesses fail to operate according to time and place," Weber wrote, quoting Baxter.[42]

---

[40] Ibid., 8.
[41] Reprinted as Richard Baxter, *A Christian Directory, or, a Body of Practical Divinity and Cases of Conscience*, 5 vols. (London: Richard Edwards, 1825).
[42] Weber, *Spirit of Capitalism*, 103–09. See further Baxter, *Christian Ethics (or Private Duties)*, chap. 3, Grand Directive 10.

Ascetic ethics was clearly part of Baxter's worldview, and he laid out his ethical rules in mind-numbingly prolix prose. But it bears emphasis that Baxter saw this ascetic ethic as part and product of the family duties that he also outlined at great length in his book on *Christian Economics.* Much like Bullinger, Cleaver, Perkins, and a century of Protestant manualists before him, Baxter believed that these good work habits and economic virtues were cultivated first and foremost in an orderly marital household, where everyone learned to do their Christian duties to each other and to those around them. The "sanctified family" is the foundation of church, state, and economy, Baxter believed, the first school and seminary, the first church and commonwealth, the first workshop and retailer. "The holy government of families, is a considerable part of God's own government of the world," he wrote. It "is the preparative to a holy and well-governed church." And it serves "to make a happy state and commonwealth" featuring a humming economy and society. Indeed, the "good education" and vocational training that a child or servant receives within the orderly home "is the first and greatest work to make good magistrates and good subjects, because it tends to make good men." So, Baxter exhorted parents, masters, and mistresses:

> Train up your children in a life of diligence and labour, and use them not to ease and idleness when they are young. Our wandering beggars and too much of the gentry utterly undo their children by this means, especially the female sex. They are taught no calling, nor exercised in any employment, but only such as is meet for nothing but ornament and recreation at the best; and therefore should have but recreation hours, which is but a small proportion of their time. So that by the sin of their parents, they are betimes engaged in a life of idleness.

It is far better to "choose such a calling and course of life for your children, as tendeth most to the saving of their souls, and to the public usefulness for church and state."[43]

Baxter insisted that "the chief part of family care and government consisteth in the right education" not only of one's own children but also of servants and even slaves. "Servants being integral parts of the family, who contribute much to the holiness or unholiness of it, and to the happiness and misery of it, much concerneth masters to be careful in their choice." Among many other qualifications, Baxter argued, a good servant needs "strength, skill, and willingness," not "a fleshpleasing, lazy, or sluggish disposition." A good servant needs to have "fear of God, or at least be tractable and willing to be taught," and not be "ungodly, sensual, and profane," for then he will endanger the family, detract from the work, steal from the business, and lead others astray. Indeed, "impious," "fleshly," and "slovenly servants" lack discipline, honor, and order. They will do what pleases

---

[43] Baxter, *Christian Economics (or Family Duties)*, 66–74, 97–105, 186–89.

them, not what the job needs. They will start their work late and leave early. They will indulge their appetites and not set their sights on productivity and efficiency. And they will follow their own wills, not the will of God, their masters, even their fellow servants. Such servants must be "cast out" of jobs, homes, and shops, Baxter insisted, and replaced with those more properly disposed, if not already well trained.[44]

Those servants who meet and maintain high moral standards must be treated well and consistently taught the virtues and values of hard work and discipline, Baxter insisted. "Seeing the happiness of a servant, the safety of his soul, and the comfort of his life, depend very much on the family." Masters and mistresses must treat their servants first as fellow Christians, not as beasts of burden. They must give them vigorous and meaningful work commensurate with their vocational skills and reward them and advance them in accordance with their talents and accomplishments. Masters and mistresses must provide decent food and shelter. They must teach habits of Christian worship, piety, and morality and insist on proper use of Sabbath rest. They must encourage Christian discipline, punish sinful conduct, and separate good servants from bad company. And masters and mistresses must provide models and means of Christian integrity, wisdom, and patience.[45]

SUMMARY AND CONCLUSIONS

The Protestant household manuals that we have sampled mandated a form of rationalization and routinization of the home that would prove critical for the early modern economy. The Protestant home was to be a little church and state that provided much of the nurture, education, social welfare, and moral discipline historically furnished by the medieval Catholic Church and later provided by the modern welfare state. The Protestant home was also to be a little business, with the family farm, shop, estate, or service giving servants and laborers the space and time to learn their craft and earn their keep, ideally under the benign Christian rule of the master. And the Protestant home was to be a little school, where children and apprentices were first taught and disciplined to pursue the vocation that best suited their inclinations and gifts, and learned to excel in that vocation as a form of loving service to God, neighbor, and self.

Like Max Weber's famous thesis in *The Protestant Ethic and the Spirit of Capitalism*, the real impact of these household manuals is difficult to quantify with precision. Numerous scholars have challenged Weber's claim that Protestant ideals and anxieties played a significant role in the emergence of modern economies.

---

[44] Ibid., 40–44, 155.
[45] Ibid., 43, 209–11.

If theology affected this transformation at all, they say, its effects were secondary to other innovations in technology, law, and politics. Similarly, sociologists after Weber have shown that the early modern household was one of many new institutions that cultivated the norms and habits of market morality, not least the new public schools that emerged out of the Renaissance and Reformation. And it is doubtful that every Protestant household lived up to the ideals put forth in these manuals. The sheer prevalence of the manuals may indicate how often Protestants fell short of these norms that thus required constant repetition.

Despite these caveats, household manuals like the ones sampled above clearly illustrate the type of rationalizing impulse that Weber attributed to early modern Protestantism, and they represent one of the means by which this impulse took institutional form. Protestants' elevation of ordinary jobs to divine callings transformed the social and religious status of important economic roles and relationships; importantly, this transformation required a thoroughgoing reinterpretation of how ordinary people could fulfill these roles and relationships in practice. The household manuals served this interpretive function. Written for a lay audience, they defined the metes and bounds of household economies. They provided a detailed, scalable model of organizational hierarchy. They furnished a work ethic and value system and a corresponding moral argument for the well-being of the individual, the family, and the broader community: industry, discipline, frugality, and mutual care were sacred duties, while idleness and profligacy were unholy vices. The household manuals thus sought to structure domestic life and its constituent economies and values to the finest detail. To the extent that people implemented these instructions, households contributed to the tide of economic transformation that washed over Protestant lands in the early modern period. Protestant households alone do not explain the emergence of modern capitalism. But they are an important part of that story.

Are there lessons in this story for contemporary scholars and readers? How should we understand the roles in and of families in our own contexts, where we find vast disparities of wealth and income, new methods of mass production, growing levels of internet connectivity, dizzyingly dynamic global financial systems, unprecedented divorce rates, rising numbers of out-of-wedlock births, growing disdain for marriage, and much more?

We may start simply by observing the new depths of irony in Weber's observations about the iron cage of modern economic systems. Weber pointed out the paradox in Protestants' remaking of the economic order: new forms of economic insecurity replaced Protestants' spiritual insecurities, making a once-voluntary Protestant work ethic all but compulsory to survive in the new economic order. Once-meaningful work now took on the character of bald necessity or mere sport. An important corollary to this is the havoc that economic systems have waged on the institution that early Protestants viewed as prior to all others—the family household. I do not lament that the patriarchal authority prescribed in these manuals has been replaced with relatively benign and egalitarian gender norms, nor do I dismiss the moral importance of other recent changes to the laws of marriage, divorce, and childrearing. A simplistic return to the norms espoused in these manuals will not solve many challenges facing modern families, which now include a broader array of relationships and legal arrangements than our forebears could have imagined.

I do lament, however, that modern economies and cultural norms often impair the formation of strong and well-ordered households as such. For all but the most affluent families, the conscious formation of the household as a place of nurturance and care, of religious and secular education, of training in the virtues, practical wisdom, trades, and more has become an unaffordable luxury reserved only for the educated and well-to-do in the West. The household, for many, has become a mere way station between long shifts; a place where children receive more commercially mediated screen time than quality time with their parents and elders; where lines of short-term lovers stand shabbily in the place of steady love from a lifelong spouse; where intergenerational ties are weak or nonexistent; and where the relationships that matter most in life are afforded the least veneration and the fewest public and private resources. Even in affluent homes, where resources are not scarce, parenting and household management are relegated to an army of professional staff while the nominal heads of house work long hours away from home.

Weber's *Protestant Ethic* was, in part, a refutation of Marx's claim that material institutions and interests alone are decisive factors in economic history. It was also a subtle and profound critique of the modern economic order and its ethos. If today we live amid a complex of interlocking iron cages that demand vocational mania and foster familial atrophy, Weber reminds his readers that there was a time, at least, when ideas and ideal interests—theological ones, no less!—also mattered. "No one knows who will live in this cage in the future," he pondered, "or whether at the end of this tremendous development entirely new prophets will arise, or there will be a great rebirth of old ideas and ideals, or, if neither, mechanized petrification, embellished with a sort of convulsive self-importance."[46]

It is conceivable that our households can be reincarnated as incubators of a new social transformation and value formation. Modern households might one day be reimagined as basic, humane institutions that reflect and instill our best values. Communities large and small will perhaps begin to invest more resources and implement better laws to support strong and stable families—especially on the bottom rungs of the socioeconomic ladder. At any rate, I hope so. And if this hope is naïve, the story of Protestant household manuals should at least remind us that we are not the first to try. It should also encourage researchers to investigate more fully the ties between religious worldviews and economic orders today. For

---

[46] Weber, *The Protestant Ethic*, 182.

the family is one significant place to look for the ways in which religion and economy come together and shape one another. *Oikos* and *oikonomiká* still matter for one another, and religion runs through them both.

Part Three:
Contemporary Perspectives

Pushing New Frontiers
The (Im)Possibility of Character Formation through ICT Products and Services

Katrin Gülden Le Maire

This chapter concentrates on the information and communications technology (ICT) sector: two technologies that have increasingly converged. They build on electronic systems, the use of hardware such as computers or mobile devices, and programs and algorithms (software) to store, retrieve, transmit, process, and manipulate data. The first part of the chapter provides a short overview of the ICT sector. The second part deals with various approaches to character formation within that sector. Particular attention is given to the potentially different impacts on different parts of the population and the effect that ICT has on adolescents.

The ICT Sector

The International Monetary Fund estimates that, in 2018, the world economy was almost 85 trillion US dollars strong. The ICT sector accounted for almost 9 percent of this global economic market.[1] The so-called Third Industrial Revolution, that is, the development and advance of digital information and communications technology, has been variously described as having started in the 1950 s to 1970 s.[2] The use of digital logic circuits and their technologies, such as the computer, the cellular mobile phone, and the internet are now widespread. The home computer and video games were first developed in 1979, the first mobile phone was created in 1983, and the digital camera was invented in 1988.[3] Tim Berners-Lee built the

---

[1] International Monetary Fund, "World Economic Outlook, April 2019: Growth, Slowdown, Precarious Recovery," at https://www.imf.org/en/Publications/WEO/Issues/2019/03/28/world-economic-outlook-april-2019#Statistical%20Appendix. Haishan Fu, "World Development Indicators 2017," *World Bank Report* (2017), 4–5. N.A., "China's Economic Outlook in Six Charts," International Monetary Fund Country Report No. 18/240 (Washington, DC: International Monetary Fund, July 26, 2018), iv.

[2] The digital revolution comes after the mechanical and electronic analogue revolutions.

[3] The Finnish company Nokia created an analogue mobile phone.

World Wide Web in 1989; in the 1990 s, television became digital with HDTV (high-definition television) technology. The internet formed part of mass culture as of 1996; the Short Message Service (SMS) was first offered commercially to customers in 1994.[4] The cell phone came into existence in the 1970 s, and the sales of smart phones, with their extensive computing capabilities, mobile operating systems, and various software components, started to grow rapidly in the late 2000 s. The debut of the iPad in 2010 marked the overall mass-market entry of the device, even though Apple was not the first company to develop handheld tablets. The American social-media network Facebook was created in 2004 and now counts 2.38 billion active users monthly.[5] The microblogging internet service Twitter was constructed in 2006, and the photo- and video-sharing network service Instagram was launched in 2010. In fact, data is likely to develop into the most important asset class in the world.[6]

While humanity is still embroiled in this Third Industrial Revolution, a Fourth one has already quietly started. It was Klaus Schwab, founder of the World Economic Forum, who coined the term in 2016:

> There are three reasons why today's transformations represent not merely a prolongation of the Third Industrial Revolution but rather the arrival of a Fourth and distinct one: velocity, scope, and systems impact. The current speed of breakthroughs has no historical precedent. When compared with previous industrial revolutions, the Fourth one is evolving at an exponential rather than a linear pace. Moreover, it is disrupting almost every industry in every country. And the breadth and depth of these changes herald the transformation of entire systems of production, management, and governance.[7]

Furthermore, the sector enters an era of aggressive implementation (including advancements in execution, product quality, speed, and data) that is managed by

---

[4] The Finnish GSM (Global System for Mobile Communications) operator Radiolinja did so.

[5] N.A., "Number of monthly active Facebook users worldwide as of 1st quarter 2019 (in millions)," Statista web site, https://www.statista.com/statistics/264810/number-of-monthly-active-facebook-users-worldwide/.

[6] Michael Rose, "Data: Your Most Ignored and Valuable Asset in the World," *Forbes*, at https://www.forbes.com/sites/forbesagencycouncil/2018/02/12/data-your-most-ignored-and-valuable-asset/#3619c731715b. Robert K. Perrons and Jesse W. Jensen, "What the Oil and Gas Sector Can Learn from Other Industry about 'Big Data,'" *Energy Policy* 81 (2015): 117–122.

[7] Klaus Schwab, "The Fourth Industrial Revolution—What It Means, How to Respond," World Economic Forum web site, https://www.weforum.org/agenda/2016/01/the-fourth-industrial-revolution-what-it-means-and-how-to-respond.

China.⁸ The impact on the sector of this geographical shift from the Silicon Valley in the United States to the Asia-Pacific region, with its different conception of the human person and contrasting sociocultural and religious norms and ethics, has not yet been explored. What kind of anthropological assumptions underlie the construction of algorithms and software programs? What effect and impact are they likely to have for the individual user and compounded at the level of society?

ICT goods and services are profitable for investors and, so far, increase amenities in everyday life considerably. Yet it appears that the initial tech-optimism of the early 2000s is fading. The neuro- and cognitive sciences as well as increasing grass-roots efforts start to direct public awareness towards potential drawbacks.⁹ However, in this late modern pluralistic information economy, ICT is a sector that will shape the human future and existence significantly and to an extent that will vary depending on the country in which people live.

By 2025, 75 percent of all employees will be Millennials who have not known a life without digital devices and networks.¹⁰ This demographic change presents both challenges and opportunities. Four generations with different ICT affinities (Baby Boomers, Generation X, Generation Y/Millennials, and Generation Z/Post-Millennials) will be working together.¹¹ The intergenerational differences concerning the technological impact are little explored; yet it seems that ICT goods and services are utilized and experienced in different ways by these four generations. These differences can potentially result in intergenerational misunderstandings.¹² Mullen, Dowling, and O'Reilly highlight the cross-genera-

---

⁸ Kai-Fu Lee, "How AI Can Enhance Our Humanity," TED2018 web site, https://www.ted.com/talks/kai_fu_lee_how_ai_can_save_our_humanity.

⁹ Madeleine J. George, et al., "Concurrent and Subsequent Associations between Daily Digital Technology Use and High-Risk Adolescencts' Mental Health Symptoms," *Child Development* 89 (2018): 78-88. E. g.: Katherine Ormerod, *Why Social Media Is Ruining Your Life* (London: Octopus, 2018). Catherine Price, *How to Break up with Your Phone* (London: Trapeze, 2018).

¹⁰ Morley Winograd and Michael Hais, "How Millennials Could Upend Wall Street and Corporate America," *Brookings Report* (Washington, DC: Brookings Institution 2014).

¹¹ The article adheres to the revised classification of generational cohorts as outlined by the Pew Research Center: Baby Boomers (mid-1940s-1960/1964), Generation X (mid-1960s-early 1980s), Millennials (mid-1980s-mid-1990s/early 2000s), Generation Z (mid-1990s-mid-2000s). Michael Dimock, "Defining Generations: Where Millennials End and Post-Millennials Begin," The Pew Research Center web site, http://www.pewresearch.org/fact-tank/2018/03/01/defining-generations-where-millennials-end-and-post-millennials-begin/.

¹² Jean M. Twenge, "Have Smartphones Destroyed a Generation?," *The Atlantic* 161 (2018): 61. The article is adapted from: Jean M. Twenge, *iGen–Why Today's Super Connected Kids Are Growing up Less Rebellious, More Tolerant, Less Happy–and Completely Unprepared for Adulthood–and What That Means for the Rest of Us* (New York: Atria Books 2017).

tional gap that arises when adults are expected to provide younger people with guidance and support for a medium and online experiences they themselves are unfamiliar with.[13]

In view of these challenges, some preliminary theological reflections considering the size, impact, and paradigmatic shift that this whole sector exerts over the economy, the workplace, and everyday life seem appropriate.

The Impact of ICT on Character Formation

In order to assess the ICT sector's potential impact on character formation, it is important to define character. There are various scientific theories about the extent to which character is a combination of socialization (family, religion, school, and peer education) and genetic disposition.[14] Christian theology emphasizes that a person is "fearfully and wonderfully made in the image of God," the creation of a loving and creative God who seeks a personal relationship with human beings through Jesus Christ.[15] Ted Peters, for example, characterizes the Imago Dei through five models and outlines them as rationality, morality, relationality, created cocreator, and prolepsis; being truly human in Christian theology is to participate with Jesus Christ in the forgiveness of sin and the resurrection of the dead.[16] Indeed, Peters points out: "God calls each of us individually and the human race as a whole toward a divinely appointed end or goal, namely, our true humanity in participation with a redeemed and healed creation…. This anticipatory impulse built into human creaturehood becomes the foundation of ethics, the point of departure for pursuing a future which is better than the past."[17] The character of the creature is validated through the creator and thus receives an intrinsic value. Theologians mainly work with the notion of the human being as physically

---

[13] G. Mullen, C. Dowling, and G. O'Reilly, "Internet Use among Young People with and without Mental Health Difficulties," *The Irish Journal of Psychological Medicine* 35 (2018): 11–21.

[14] Despina Archontaki, Gary J. Lewis, and Timothy C. Bates, "Genetic Influence on Psychological Well-Being: A Nationally Representative Twin Study," *Journal of Personality* 81 (2013): 221–30. Robert C. Cloninger, "Completing the Psychobiological Architecture of Human Personality Development. Temperament, Character, Coherence," in *Understanding Human Development*, ed. Ursula Staudinger and Ulman Lindenberger (Berlin: Springer Science+Business Media, 2003), 159–81.

[15] Genesis 1:27, Psalm 139:14.

[16] Ted Peters, "Imago Dei, DNA, and the Transhuman Way," *Theology and Science* 16 (2018): 355–56.

[17] Ibid, 360.

and psychologically mature (*mündig*), leaving aside the neuronal and cognitive developmental particularities of children and adolescents.[18]

Whether an economic sector or a business operating in it can form the human character relies, then, on the conviction of what or who forms character. Scientific evidence indicates that character is largely developed and acquired in childhood.[19] Moral, mental, and distinguishing evaluative qualities are internalized at this human developmental stage through repeated actions until behavior becomes habitual. However, character can be deeply affected and changed through religious conviction and inspiration.[20] Christian theology, in contrast, admits the possibility of character change through faith in Jesus Christ.[21] Accordingly, a profound character transformation is possible at any point in human life. Interestingly, cognitive scientists such as Justin L. Barrett argue that children are intrinsically "born believers."[22]

Overall, there seem to be five approaches for companies and organizations to align employee behavior with character traits deemed ethically good. These approaches consist of penalizing, incentivizing, emulating, inspiring, and, in the age of ICT, programming employees and devices to manage people. A previously agreed and preferred good or bad ethical outcome can be reached by each of these. Penalizing and incentivizing employees is a way to reach a desirable result by either punishment or reward of behavior. This can take the form of a monetary, reputational, promotional, or even emotional response. It is not necessary for employees to hold on to their own "good" character values, so long as they agree to act in line with the organization's stipulated code of conduct. It is a mechanical option to achieve the kind of behavior typical of a fully developed character. Various employee-motivation theories try to explore these mechanisms.[23]

Somewhat differently, emulation is the effort to match or surpass a person or an achievement. It is typically accomplished through imitating a set of rules or somebody else's behavior. Again, this notion is mechanical, meaning that an employee acts appropriately but does not need to have internalized the foundational character traits on which a regulation is based. There can be various motives for

---

[18] Ingolf U. Dalferth, *Creatures of Possibility: The Theological Basis of Human Freedom* (London: Baker Academic, 2016), 191.

[19] Frances A. Campbell, et al., "Early Childhood Education: Young Adult Outcomes from the Abecedarian Project," *Applied Developmental Science* 6 (2002): 42–57.

[20] 2 Cor. 5:17; Eph. 4:22–24.

[21] John 1:12–13; John 3:3–8; 1 Pet. 1:3.

[22] Justin L. Barrett, *Born Believers: The Science of Children's Religious Belief* (New York: Free Press, 2012).

[23] Sunil Ramlall, "A Review of Employee Motivation Theories and Their Implications for Employee Retention within Organizations," *The Journal of American Academy of Business Cambridge* 5 (2004): 52–63.

emulating, including the penalizing or incentivizing options but also a fourth option: inspiration. This, in turn, is the process of being mentally stimulated by either a divine or human source to do or feel something. The definition already points to an internal process of habit formation that either precedes or accompanies the action a person is doing.

Programming is the process whereby a previously designed mathematical algorithm is encoded into a programming language (notation) in order to be executed by an electronic machine or device. The algorithm entails a certain set of instructions to perform a calculation or solve a problem. ICT companies search for targeted economic returns: they secure these through tailored advertising and the collection and sale of personal data. It is in their interest to approach their consumers as precisely as possible, to gather and evaluate their interests, and to maintain attraction to their products and services. Scientific insight concerning human behavior and the brain structure is therefore indispensable in their development of products and services.[24] Remarkably, IT programmers consider important scientific insights concerning the human brain, habit formation, and communications for the development of mathematical algorithms and social networks. Targeted digital content triggers responses in the adult, the adolescent, and the child's brain. Yet due to the way the human brain matures, content may trigger strikingly different responses. The brain and behavioral development are not yet fully formed in younger people—current consumers and future employees. A child's or an adolescent's brain is being molded through the early twenties as the grey matter at the back of the brain slowly subsides with changes continuing into adulthood.[25] The prefrontal cortex, in the front of the brain, continues to develop in adolescence, as adolescents rely more on the amygdala than adults in making decisions.[26] Neuroscientists have identified the amygdala as the part of the brain associated with emotions, impulses, aggression, and instinctive behavior. Interestingly, this part of the brain is especially activated when people engage

---

[24] Tesla and SpaceX CEO Musk created the company Neuralink in 2017, considering neural implants to harvest data: https://www.neuralink.com/. Kernel is a US start-up founded in 2015 that intends to build a platform to record and stimulate neurons: https://kernel.co/. Emotiv produces software products evaluating brain fitness: https://www.emotiv.com/. Moreover, former US President Obama initiated the BRAIN Initiative, in which the US military's Defense Advanced Research Projects Agency (DARPA) works in collaboration with private companies to develop implantable neural interfaces: https://www.darpa.mil/.

[25] Jay N. Giedd, et al., "Brain Development During Childhood and Adolescence: A Longitudinal MRI Study," *Nature Neuroscience* 2 (1999): 861–63.

[26] Sarah-Jayne Blakemore, "Development of the Social Brain in Adolescence," *Journal of the Royal Society of Medicine* 105 (2012): 111–16.

in social-media network activities.[27] The setups of social networks and their underlying mathematical algorithms entail triggers that provoke neuronal processes in the human brain's subcortical and cortical regions that are attributed to personal relevance and reward (for instance, making "friends" on Facebook, the "like" button, etc.).[28] Due to their differently formed brain structures, adolescents act in ways different from adults; they also engage in different ways and considerably longer in social-media network activities. Moreover, while the foundations for character development are laid in infancy and childhood, influencing factors such as the classic family unit can no longer be taken for granted. Could an adolescent's character therefore be more easily manipulated and programmed by ICT products and services as he or she seem more susceptible to character and behavior modification through technological manipulation? Could the use of technological networks become systemic, and, if so, with what effects for the individual and future society?

Thus far, the scope of the ethical, medical, religious, and overall existential implications of the current foundational technological paradigm shift has only been rudimentarily assessed.[29] Due to the novelty of the phenomena, the overall cost of scientific research, and the speed of the sector's developments, no conclusive longitudinal evidence has and could have been assembled to assess the potential impact and transgenerational effects for the workplace, let alone for humanity, by the ICT sector. Moreover, the focus on adolescent developmental particularities and the adolescent brain is only a recent phenomenon in neuroscientific research.[30] The British Psychological Society points out that, to date, the

---

[27] Lauren E. Sherman, et al., "What the Brain 'Likes': Neural Correlates of Providing Feedback on Social Media," *Social Cognitive and Affective Neuroscience* 13 (2018): 699–707.

[28] Björn Enzi, et al., "Is Our Self Nothing but Reward? Neuronal Overlap and Distinction between Reward and Personal Relevance and Its Relation to Human Personality," *PLoS One* 4 (2009): 1–12. Cameron Anderson, John Angus D. Hildreth, and Laura Howland, "Is the Desire for Status a Fundamental Human Motive? A Review of the Empirical Literature," *Psychological Bulletin* 141 (2015): 574–601. Simon McCarthy-Jones, "Social Networking Sites May Be Controlling Your Mind—Here's How to Take Charge," *The Conversation*, http://theconversation.com/social-networking-sites-may-be-controlling-your-mind-heres-how-to-take-charge-88516.

[29] Emily Frith, "Social Media and Children's Mental Health: A Review of the Evidence," *Education Policy Institute* (2017), 17–24. Chloe Barryman, Christopher J. Fergueson, and Charles Negy, "Social Media Use and Mental Health among Young Adults," *Psychiatric Quarterly* 89 (2017): 307–14. Marie Lamblin, et al., "Social Connectedness, Mental Health and the Adolescent Brain," *Neuroscience & Biobehavioral Reviews* 41 (2017): 57–68. Yuval Noah Harari, *21 Lessons for the 21st Century* (London: Jonathan Cape 2018), 72.

[30] Nandita Vijayakumar, et al., "Brain Development during Adolescence: A Mixed-Longitudinal Investigation of Cortical Thickness, Surface Area, and Volume," *Human Brain Map-*

majority of scientific evidence on this issue is cross-sectional. An overall causality limited to just one or several phenomena caused specifically by ICT products and services cannot be inferred. Differences in the scientific foci within cognitive scientific research further aggravate this problem.[31] Nevertheless, it has been shown that the time spent in ICT product and services consumption has considerably increased, especially among younger people.[32] In 2016, the US National Institutes of Health (NIH) instigated the first large-scale study to evaluate various factors that affect the brain and cognitive development. The study will follow more than ten thousand nine-to-ten-year-olds in the course of ten years. The goal is to determine the extent to which childhood experiences such as video games, social media, or unhealthy sleep patterns interact with each other and with a child's changing biology, and how they affect brain development.[33] To achieve this, the so-called ABCD project (Adolescent Brain Cognitive Development Study) performs functional brain MRIs (Magnetic Resonance Imaging) and conducts further comprehensive health assessments. Results are not expected before the mid-2020s.

"Programming" and mental manipulation by regimes and autocrats have long formed the human character and controlled and manipulated not just individuals but also large groups of people. On the whole, the ethical issues of the information

---

ping 37 (2016): 2027-38. Daniel J. Simmonds, Michael N. Hallquist, and Beatriz Luna, "Protracted Development of Executive and Mnemonic Brain Systems Underlying Working Memory in Adolescence: A Longitudinal FMRI Study," *NeuroImage* 157 (2017): 695-704. Lucy Foulkes and Sarah-Jayne Blakemore, "Studying Individual Differences in Human Adolescent Brain Development," *Nature Neuroscience* 21 (2018): 315-23.

[31] A. Galpin, G. Taylor, *Changing Behaviour: Children, Adolescents and Screen Use* (Leicester: The British Psychological Society, 2018), 4. For example: Elroy Boers, et al., "Association of Screen Time and Depression in Adolescence," *JAMA Pediatrics* 173 (2019): 853-59. Russell M. Viner, et al., "Roles of Cyberbullying, Sleep, and Physical Activity in Mediating the Effects of Social Media Use on Mental Health and Wellbeing among Young People in England; A Secondary Analysis of Longitudinal Data," *The Lancet Child and Adolescent Health* 3 (2019): 685-96. Ofir Turel, et al., "Delay Discounting Mediates the Association between Posterior Insular Cortex Volume and Social Media Addiction Symptoms," *Cognitive Affective & Behavioural Neurocience* 18 (2018): 694-704.

[32] N.A., "The Common Sense Sensus Media Use by Tweens+Teens 2015," Common Sense Media, https://www.commonsensemedia.org/the-common-sense-census-media-use-by-tweens-and-teens-infographic. For general information on individual social medial channels: Aaron Smith and Monica Anderson, *Social Media Use in 2018* (Washington, DC: Pew Research Center, 2018). Emma Louise Anderson, Eloisa Steen, and Vasileios Stavropoulos, "Internet Use and Problematic Internet Use: A Systematic Review of Longitudinal Research Trends in Adolescence and Emergent Adulthood," *International Journal of Adolescence and Youth* 22 (2017): 430-54.

[33] N.A., "The Adolescent Brain Cognitive Development Study (ABDC)," National Institutes Health, https://abcdstudy.org/.

age are not new. Various philosophical aspects have been highlighted: Richard Mason developed the "PAPA model" in 1986,[34] and Kathy O'Neil proposed the notion of a "moral imagination" to anticipate the effects of applied algorithms.[35] Jaron Lanier introduced the concept of "digital dignity," whereby individuals should own the commercial rights of their data.[36] Since the 1950 s, philosophers have grappled with potential systemic, autocratic, and controlling features of technology.[37] Dieter Mersch refers to the universal reach and potential fascist structures of technological systems, highlighting that, within systems, freedom and control hold a complicated balance that implies a dimension of real participation but effectively denies it.[38] Yet the strategic commercial effort to collect and sell personal data to trace and target individuals on a global scale by a select few tech companies is a novelty.

Interestingly, investors and social-media programmers are sensitive to potential mental and behavioral implications. They tend to shield their children from harming effects and do not expose them to digital activities until a certain age.[39] However, today's children and adolescents generally grow up in a profoundly *connected* society. The use of technical devices, social media consumption, video gaming, and online activities are no longer occasional *individual* or *family* activities, as watching television used to be just a generation ago. It is thus a valid quest to research whether the world is confronted with a quasi-autocratic system, governed by few investors, that potentially changes cognitive patterns on a global scale and of epidemic proportions.[40] How can and will characters be programmed in the future, and into whose image and at whose will? Never in human history

---

[34] The "PAPA model" consists of: Privacy, Accuracy, Property, and Accessibility. See Richard Mason, "Four Ethical Issues in the Information Age," *MIS Quarterly* 10 (1986): 6–12.

[35] Kathy O'Neil, *Weapons of Math Destruction: How Big Data Increases Inequality and Threatens Democracy* (London: Penguin, 2016), 204.

[36] Jaron Lanier, *Who Owns the Future?* (London: Penguin Books, 2014), 16.

[37] E.g., Günther Anders, *Die Antiquiertheit des Menschen*, Vol. 1, *Über die Seele im Zeitalter der zweiten industriellen Revolution* (Munich: Beck, 1956). Idem, *Die Antiquiertheit des Menschen*, Vol. 2, *Über die Zerstörung des Lebens im Zeitalter der dritten Revolution* (Munich: Beck, 1980). Karl Deutsch, *Politische Kybernetik. Modelle und Perspektiven* (Freiburg: Rombach, 1966).

[38] Dieter Mersch, *Ordo ab Chao-Order from Noise* (Zürich: Diaphanes, 2013), 52. Felix Maschewski, "Anna-Verena Nosthoff: Passivity in the Costume of Activity," *BEHEMOTH: A Journal on Civilisation* 11 (2018): 17.

[39] Alex Hern, "Never Get High on Your Own Supply—Why Social Media Bosses Don't Use Social Media," *The Guardian*, https://www.theguardian.com/media/2018/jan/23/never-get-high-on-your-own-supply-why-social-media-bosses-dont-use-social-media.

[40] Jaron Lanier, CEBIT/ d!talk Keynote Lanier Virtual Reality, Cebit channel YouTube, https://www.youtube.com/watch?v=XUU3DJO_juM.

has there been such a potential global mass-control system in place as in today's digital age, a system managed by a handful of tech companies in Silicon Valley, Nanjing, and Zhongguancun with a technical and digital reach into a family's home, their minds, and cognition. China has already outlined its vision in its "New Generation of Artificial Intelligence Development Plan": by 2020, its social-credit system will have standardized the assessment of its citizens and businesses to enforce certain stipulated behavior.[41] In another example, India, a democratic society, collects biometrical and biographical data of all its citizens at the Unique Identification Authority of India through its Aadhaar system, which repeatedly hits the headlines: in 2018, the personal data of more than one billion Indian citizens was hacked and offered for sale online.[42]

These are just some examples where ICT products are now systemically applied. The scale of the application and the effects for employees and people in general citizens has not reached countries like Germany yet. But in a globalized world with cross-border economic activities, these phenomena equally concern European citizens. What are the implications for future employees in terms of their character formation, resilience mechanisms, and autonomous decision making, let alone for the security of their personal data?

Conclusion

ICT is one of the fastest-growing sectors of the global economy. The challenges arising from the technological revolution are not just complex, they are global. Public awareness and insight regarding the potential effects of digital networks and services on people and, especially, on a younger generation growing up within an advanced technological society are slowly increasing.[43] Recent Asian and South Asian developments and trends—but also scandals—widen the perspective and raise questions concerning data security and individual freedom. Research-

---

[41] N.A., "China's New Generation of Artificial Intelligence Development Plan," Foundation for Law and International Affairs, https://flia.org/notice-state-council-issuing-new-generation-artificial-intelligence-development-plan/. cf. Danielle Keats Citron and Frank Pasquale, "The Scored Society: Due Process for Automated Predictions," *Washington Law Review* 89 (2014): 1–33. Duncan McCann, Miranda Hall, and Robbie Warin, "Controlled by Calculations: Power and Accountability in the Digital Economy, Part 3: The Rise of Algorithms," New Economics Foundation, 2018.

[42] N.A., The Global Risks Report 2019, World Economic Forum, http://www3.weforum.org/docs/WEF_Global_Risks_Report_2019.pdf, 16. Regarding the overall project: Vijay Sathe, "Managing Massive Change: India's Aadhaar, The World's Most Ambitious ID Project," *Innovations: Technology, Governance, Globalization* 9 (2014): 85–111.

[43] N.A., Six Charts, 22–23.

ers face the challenge of keeping up with ICT developments. Evidence concerning the long-term impact of ICT on adolescents and adults is still missing.

Contemporary historians like Yuval Noah Harari already paint dystopic visions of the future, in which "the very meaning of being human is likely to mutate and physical and cognitive structures will melt."[44] The larger theological and philosophical questions raised by developments in the ICT sector concerning the identity of the human being as made in the image of God, of human freedom, and the purpose of human life are to be explored further.

---

[44] Yuval Noah Harari, "Yuval Noah Harari on what 2050 has in store for humankind," *Wired*, https://www.wired.co.uk/article/yuval-noah-harari-extract-21-lessons-for-the-21st-century.

Can Character Formation Survive the Digital Economy?

William Schweiker

> For what does it profit a human being (ανθρωπον)
> to gain the whole world and forfeit his soul (ψυχην)?
> For what can one give in return for his soul?"
> —The Gospel of Mark 8:36–37 (RSV altered)

Introduction

Unless one believes that human character is completely formed by some sort of rigid determinism—say, by genes, social environment, or God—then it must be the case that human action, to a greater or lesser extent, is the engine of character formation. How, then, should we speak about the reflexive character of human action? That is, our actions—and choices—bend back, as it were, to shape the character of the agent and thereby to help direct any and all future action. Character and action are then interrelated in a complex way, even as they are related to reasons for actions, desires, motivations, values, perceptions, and a host of other human capacities.

In the long history of theological and philosophical ethics, the discourse of "virtue" has been used to speak about how, to what end, and to what extent human action can and does shape character. Indeed, for some forty years now there has been a revival of "virtue ethics" among philosophers and theologians, a revival that has found its way into many other disciplines concerned with social and individual conduct: political science, behavioral economics, psychology, and the like. And, in fact, while "labor" used to suffice when discussing character formation and value creation in economics, this is no longer adequate because of advances in economics and the rise of Big Data.[1] Individuals' contributions to the mar-

---

[1] Some definitions are in order. Big Data simply means the collection of large amounts of information in order to refine machine-learning algorithms to get as accurate an algorithm as possible (accurate as defined by recommending an action that is best informed

ket are simply their preferences in purchasing, preferences that are collected—for free—and then used to feed and shape further preferences through high-speed tracking of purchases. And, of course, such data can be used for almost anything ranging from product production to trolling on social media and the attempts to influence public opinion in political elections.

The upshot of the digital economy (DE), it would seem, is to decrease the range of our self-determination, since one purchase—as an action—can, because of the reflexive nature of human acts, shape future preferences.[2] This is why, for instance, once a consumer makes an online purchase, her or his email inbox as well as other online sites used are flooded with ads for similar products and recommendations for purchase. DE is the outcome of the transition from a manufacturing to a service and consumption economy and of the impact of information technology on economies around the world. It has been argued that within the DE the most important commodity is human attention.[3] And human attention is, of course, easily manipulated, as global politics in the twentieth century sadly showed through two world wars.

In terms of moral thought, we seem to be, conceptually speaking, in a conundrum not unlike the challenges facing environmental ethics. Old theories are outpaced by new realities. Put otherwise, the language of virtue and character formation seems inadequate to articulate, much less orient, the formation of human selves in the age of the DE. This is the case even though virtue theory tries to account for non-agential social forces that also help to shape character. Moralists have long granted that character is influenced by social and natural environments, the whims of fate, or the working of providence, genetics, and the like. Yet now non-agential forces not only place limits on and fund possibilities for action, as traditional virtue theory acknowledged, but, in the DE, supervene on human

---

by inputs). "A computer program is said to learn from experience E with respect to some class of tasks T and performance measure P, if its performance at tasks in T, as measured by P, improves with experience E." See Tom M. Mitchell, *Machine Learning* (New York: McGraw-Hill, 1997), 2. Put more simply, a machine-learning algorithm is an algorithm that becomes more accurate as it is fed more data. An algorithm is a system for deciding actions based on data. This can be as simple as long division or as complex as the programs dictating the movements of magnets in an MRI machine.

[2] There is a longstanding distinction in moral theory between human acts and acts of a human. Human acts require the use of intellect, will, desire, etc., whereas acts of a human are nonrational or instinctive acts, say, the normal blinking of the eyes. In this essay, I am exclusively concerned with human acts.

[3] See Günter Thomas, "The Cultural Contest for Our Attention: Observations on Media, Property, and Religion," in *Having: Property and Possession in Religious and Social Life*, eds. W. Schweiker and C. T. Mathewes (Grand Rapids, MI: Eerdmans, 2004), 272-95.

desires. The feedback loop between purchase and recommendation, action and digital reaction, is shaping attention and human consciousness itself.[4]

My task in this chapter is to ponder why this might be the case and how we might respond to this situation. At stake, I will argue, is the formation of consciousness and, importantly, moral conscience. The aim is to sketch an affirmative answer to the question of this essay: "Can character formation survive the digital economy?"[5] My argument thus goes beyond Katrin Gülden Le Maire's contribution in chapter 12 of this volume. But I am also undertaking a thought experiment on Mark 8:36–38 about the soul, its worth, and its possible loss.[6]

I hasten to add that I am not making this argument in order to rescue the language of virtue, which, in any case, I find inadequate to do all of the ethical and conceptual work its proponents claim for it. I certainly do not claim to be recovering the "labor theory of value"! Rather, I want *to balance* attention to economic and technical *social systems* in the formation of human preferences and a reasoned insistence on the dignity, freedom, and worth of individual persons—the "soul"—within those systems in order to enact the integrity of their own lives. Absent the capacity to deliberately shape our own lives to some important degree, human dignity is itself effaced. If we cannot "live our own lives in our own way," as J. S. Mill famously defined liberty, then we have become slaves or puppets to other forces.[7] Of course moral freedom is more than simple license, and because of this there must be some capacity for the apprehension of and acting on moral values and norms for conduct to be genuinely free. This requires, I will argue, a free exercise of conscience in the formation of one's character. Yet in my account, conscience is not, as it was for medieval thinkers, a specific faculty of the mind. Rather, it is the whole self acting on the whole self in order to integrate a life marked by

---

[4] For more details on the DE and this feedback loop, see Katrin Gülden Le Maire's contribution to this volume.

[5] I hasten to add—and to stress—that I am *not* an economist, and therefore I want my argument to be judged in terms of its adequacy to moral theory and its plausibility for and resonance with our experience of the Digital Economy. I take my knowledge of economics, little as it is, to be relevant for, but not determinative of, the ethics proposed. I thank, again, Jürgen von Hagen for his saving me from errors in my comments on economics. The problems that remain are mine. But thanks to him, they are, I trust, fewer in number than before his careful editing!

[6] By "soul" I do not mean some kind of "ghost" in the dynamics of the self but, rather, the dynamics themselves, insofar as we have some sense of the worth and freedom of our lives.

[7] J. S. Mill, *On Liberty* (n.p.: Simon & Brown, 2016).

responsibility with and for others. The concept "conscience" is used to denote the whole of our moral being. It is the soul morally active.[8]

My worry, to put it boldly, is that increasingly, people in economically advanced nations and globalized markets are more lived through than actually living their own lives. They have gained economic wealth at the loss of their soul, that is, the freedom and capacity to integrate their lives within systems that work upon and in them. Insofar as ethics is about how we can and ought to live, then the topic of this essay falls squarely into moral reflection, philosophical and theological, that is, how to counter a loss of self-determination and so freedom within the DE. Of immediate concern is, first, how economics in the past has attended to human action in the form of labor, and, second, how the DE erodes the freedom of human action and shifts the question of value-creation from labor to attention and preferences. Those topics will allow me to think about conscience as the virtue of virtues, if I can call it such.[9]

Consider this essay a thought experiment that moves through several planes of reflection in order to isolate the moral danger of the DE. My main concern is with the effacing of any distinction between moral and nonmoral value, that is, between worth and price.[10] Further, I contend that the use of the DE to acquire big data about people's preferences too easily shapes human consciousness via those preferences and thereby endangers our moral being. However, unlike some

---

[8] For this account of conscience, see William Schweiker, *Dust That Breathes: Christian Faith and the New Humanisms* (Oxford: Wiley-Blackwell, 2010).

[9] My argument has certain historical analogies to the thought of the great Anglican thinker Bishop Joseph Butler, John Wesley, and, more recently, Mary Midgley. I cannot explore those connections in this essay. The point is to see the self, or the soul, as Plato would put it, as a multidimensional and self-regulating, or self-destructive, whole emergent from the interaction of its parts. This is why I speak of conscience as the whole self acting on the whole self with respect to the demands and possibilities of responsible life. It is soul in its moral working. All of this can be seen as a moral hermeneutics of agency. This essay also has connections to previous work of mine on the meaning and formation of moral consciousness. See, for example, William Schweiker, "'God as Light' in the Christian Moral Imagination," in *Images of the Divine and Cultural Orientations: Jewish, Christian, and Islamic Voices*, eds. M. Welker and W. Schweiker (Leipzig: Evangelische Verlagsanstalt, 2015), 153–66, and "Trust, Risk, and the Moral Enhancement of Life," in *Risiko under Vertrauen/Risk and Trust*, eds. H. Springhart and G. Thomas (Leipzig: Evangelische Verlagsanstalt, 2017), 395–400.

[10] Importantly, it was Immanuel Kant who insisted on the distinction between moral worth found, he held, in rational freedom, and price. This distinction is easily elided in English through the use of the term "value" to cover both moral (worth) and nonmoral (price) goods. The distinction, I hold, is basic to any valid moral theory. One must insist on the moral worth of human beings not reducible to a price, that is, a nonmoral good. See Jürgen von Hagen, "Markets and the Human Character," chapter 1 in this volume.

theologians, I am not advocating an end to "Global Capitalism" based on the bounty of God's gift giving. We live in a world of scarcity, and consoling beliefs about God's beneficence cannot and ought not to relieve us of our moral responsibilities. Scarcity can also be an engine of creativity, the so-called mother of invention. Insofar as that is the case, we have a responsibility to respect and enhance our existence as moral agents. By reconstructive virtue theory through the idea of conscience—what I call the virtue of virtues—I aim in the following pages to protect our moral being.

Human Action and the Creation of Value

One longstanding strand of thinking about the meaning and creation of economic value—that is, value that can and ought to be assigned a price—argues that the true value of an object, be it a material good, an immaterial good, or a service, is objectively determined by the cost of the inputs required for its making. A just price then equals this true value rather than a price determined by the scarcity of the object compared to others and the utility and pleasure it provides to the buyer. One prominent example of this tradition is the *labor theory of value* (LTV). In terms of this theory, the economic value of an object is exclusively a product of human action, namely, the labor it takes to produce it, measured in terms of labor hours. Labor is the pouring-out of human time and efforts into the object's production. It follows that the just price of one object relative to another equals the ratio of the respective numbers of labor hours spent in the production of the two. Although it goes back at least as far as Aristotle's *Nicomachean Ethics*, modern LTV was developed in response to and superseded the value theory of the French Physiocrats, which held that the fertility of land was the only source of value creation. Adam Smith, David Ricardo, and Karl Marx, among many others, adhered to the LTV. Marx in particular used the theory to critique capitalism. In capitalist economies, labor is bought from the worker in terms of a wage, and the economic value of the object (which, as a commodity, is then alienated from its maker) resides with his capitalist employer. Marx claimed that the capitalist must pay the worker less than the objective value, while the worker spends her or his lifetime alienated from his or her labor through the capitalist system of value. Today, the LTV continues to influence debates about fair trade, just wages that suffice to sustain the life of the worker (and family), the number of hours to be worked in a day or week, and, on the capitalist's side, the need always to increase the speed, and thus decrease the time, of production.

Modern mainstream economics agrees that labor is a source of value, but there are other sources, too: knowledge (important for the DE), capital, and land. Recognizing these additional sources of value merely generalizes the idea that the value of an object is determined objectively by the cost of the inputs into its production, the objective value being the value of the amounts of labor, knowledge, capital, and land used in its production.

In contrast, the so-called subjectivist revolution of the late nineteenth century argued that the economic value of an object is determined by the preferences of its potential buyers in the market.[11] Economic value thus emerges from human perceptions of desirability, and it is realized only in the process of exchanging the object against another.[12] Voluntary exchange takes place only when both trading partners subjectively value each other's object more than their own. Prices—and wages—are thus determined by subjective valuations and can fluctuate driven by changes in people's preferences.[13] When it comes to the determination of market prices, current mainstream economics (ME) rests on this subjectivist revolution. ME focuses particularly on people's rationality, that is, the processing of all information, cost, and objective determination aimed at maximizing utility and happiness.[14] Action or choice is rational with respect to what is determined to be the person's subjective utility. There is, thereby, no objective standard of value.

It is well-known that there are extensive debates about the adequacy of ME's conception of rationality, especially when applied to the real world in which agents do not and cannot meet the demands of rationality and seem to act, at times, otherwise than maximizing their utility. As I understand it, developments in behavioral economics try to address these problems. Yet for the sake of this thought experiment, it is more important to note that the ME's focus on "rational" subjects undergirds the DE insofar as what is sought is data on consumer preferences in the real world with increasing speed, efficiency, and scope. In other words, the drive is to increase knowledge as one key factor in producing economic value. Gigantic economic forces like Amazon can easily track a customer's preferences, and we all have probably received suggestions from them about products we might want.[15] The upshot is the creation of data, which can be used to various

---

[11] More specifically, the price realized in the exchange depends on the desirability of the last unit of the object exchanged.

[12] On this, see Samuel Gregg's essay in this volume, chapter 11.

[13] Earlier economists knew, of course, that the market price of an object could deviate from the just price. Lacking a theory of consumption demand, however, they could explain the difference only in terms of fairly crude notions of scarcity and abundance.

[14] Economic rationality is defined simply as having well-ordered preferences: that is, having preferences for one thing or another and having the ranking of those preferences relative to each other stay consistent. For example: if one prefers oranges to apples and apples to bananas, then, if presented with an orange or a banana to eat, it would be rational to select the orange.

[15] I am intensely mindful of the irony of my argument, since I am relying on information obtained online and thus am part of the very phenomenon I am exploring. As noted above, as soon as I place an order for, say, tickets to a soccer game or purchase a pair

ends. It also means that the DE is increasingly fast and seeks to reduce risk in the market, which means, conceptually at least, a priority of the future untethered from the time of labor, which LTV had always assumed was crucial in the production of economic value. The conjunction of data and speed to reduce risk is also bound to the need to secure market preferences and thereby to evoke and fulfill specific human preferences.

Thus, we return to the question of human action not in terms of labor-time, but, rather, in terms of the flow of data about the preferences that motivate human conduct. Whereas Marx thought that workers sold their lifetime to the capitalist through production and wages, now the human desires and preferences that help to drive economic action are at stake. And we should see that the claim about the reflexive nature of action assumed in classical virtue theory is at work in the DE. That is, a customer's actions motivated by her or his preferences are reflexively fed back to her or him through ads, emails, and the like, even as they are stored in order to understand larger movements in the market. All of this has gone global, where massive companies generate immense wealth. And these companies thereby exert tremendous power on the daily lives of millions of people around the world. If the DE is *a* crucial, if not *the* crucial, feature of the moral space in which we live in global times and pluralistic societies, how, if at all, should we speak about the formation of character?

The Digital Economy and Moral Consciousness

One crucial assumption of traditional virtue theory is that human beings have the capacity to understand, feel, and monitor the desires and passions motivating their actions. It is for this reason that thinkers from Aristotle and Thomas Aquinas onward held that virtue is putting reason into our passions, and, further, that a virtue is an excellence of character that is a mean between excess and deficiency with respect to the person in her or his circumstances.[16] But reason, for the ancients and medieval thinkers, had ontological reach; it was locked into the ration-

---

of shoes, I immediately receive ads in my email and on other websites for more tickets, other shoes. This merely shows the ubiquity of the Internet and the DE.

[16] The literature on virtue and these figures is monumental. For a fine recent work, see David Decosimo, *Ethics as a Work of Charity: Thomas Aquinas and the Pagan Virtues* (Stanford, CA: Stanford University Press, 2014). It is important to note that Thomas distinguished moral and intellectual virtues, and that moral virtues concern the passions. In my claim that conscience is the virtue of virtues, I am fudging his distinction and also understanding conscience in a more robust sense than Thomas, for whom it was a habit. This is where, if one wants to note it, the moral psychology I am presenting is more Protestant than Catholic.

ality of reality conceived as *Logos*, God's mind, or, in Aristotle, the Unmoved Mover. What does it mean to put reason into passions when (1) reason is redefined in terms of utility maximization, and (2) passions, or preferences, are seen as the proper motivators of action, while at the same time they are reflexively manipulated by technological means?

In the mid-twentieth century, a host of theologians and philosophers (e.g., Paul Tillich, Martin Heidegger, Hannah Arendt, Hans Jonas, and others) saw a profound shift rooted in the rise of modern science. The shift was from previous ideas about ontological reason, able to define and evaluate the reality and moral worth of ends or goods, to that of technical reason, concerned only with the means to desired ends, whatever those happen to be. From this perspective, the DE is the triumph of technical reason, whose aim or ends is simply utility value, that is, what is preferred in the market. It seems difficult, by this logic, to explain why people should read the Bible rather than comic strips, value a good soul rather than greedily seek wealth, or see a human being as having intrinsic moral worth, or dignity, rather than as a source for big data on market trends. This means, at the level of concepts, conflating moral and nonmoral ideas of value in ways that endanger the worth, the dignity, of the acting human being. It is not just labor that is threatened with alienation; it is also our consciousness as moral agents.[17]

However, it is precisely at this level of reflection on the nature of human agency that one can find an opening, admittedly small, to recall a more robust conception of the acting person. And this is because the DE assumes, but does not conceptualize, that human beings are agents *who can be formed in terms of wants, preferences, and utilities.* The rational agent is precisely the one who puts reason into his or her decisions, such that knowledge is one of the sources of economic value. Of course, such a conception of reason is admittedly ideal. What is at issue, then, for the ethicist is not the idea of character formation as such, but who or what is the agent of that formation within the real world of manifest and inchoate social forces. In terms of the history of ethics, that agent has been conceived as reason (ontological rationality), conscience, or, among ethical hedonists, passions and interests. That is to say, we can talk about the capacity to form character in any of these ways, as thinkers have done from ancient times.

Among these candidates to conceptualize the capacity for self-formation, conscience holds, I contend, distinctive advantages over other ideas for our digital age. Conscience has long been a means to conceive of how, at a fundamental level of human existence, persons cannot be coerced about their most basic beliefs, loves, and valuations. This makes the idea of "conscience," reconstructed, and its freedom the best concept to speak about the agent of character formation. This is

---

[17] Marx, of course, would say that labor also alienates consciousness within a capitalist system, but this is due to his materialist conception of the emergence of consciousness, a theory I reject while unable, in this essay, to defend my own conception.

so even within the forces of the DE and diverse other social forces. To reconstruct the concept, as I have already hinted, is to grasp it in the experience of our whole selves acting on ourselves within complex social systems. This experience is something, I have intimated, that cannot be coerced, and so is the appearance of moral freedom in the actual world. Put differently, conscience is a concept for our apprehension of ourselves as moral beings whose condition of possibility is freedom, the freedom to integrate our lives.

Now, to be sure, one can coerce belief, confession, and fidelity. And it seems the case that the DE seeks to shape preferences, and so motives for action, with respect to nonmoral goods, and in doing so to efface the human self as a self-determining agent. But conscience, the whole self acting on the whole self, cannot and ought not be so coerced. To do so is to violate human dignity. This means that the formation of character requires, but is not limited to, honing of moral perception and the rehabilitation of the fallen conscience, which, to varying degrees, is a failing of every human being. Theologically, all have sinned and fallen short of the glory of God (Rom. 3:23). Still, this conception of conscience, insofar as it articulates a transcendent good of human worth that must and may be lived in the turmoil of actual life—what I have called elsewhere the integrity of life—is a daring act of hope and trust. Religiously, this entails an act of faith, insofar as one trusts that a life so lived, a life of moral integrity in individual and communal existence, will indeed relate the goods of human flourishing through the claim of conscience.[18]

Conscience, most robustly understood, is, then, a free action of the whole self on the whole self, seeking to resolve conflicts of moral and nonmoral convictions within the self and between conscientious people.[19] And if moral virtue is putting reason into the passions, then conscience, so conceived, is putting moral reason into the whole of life. It is, as said above, the virtue of virtues. Without the rightly formed conscience, all of our desires, passions, and preferences can run amok and be manipulated by market forces. The formation of conscience is the most basic task of moral formation facing people; it is a way of conceiving of persons qua persons as moral beings, beings of worth, not reducible to price. Moral failure, then, is to allow one's conscience to be deformed by bequeathing oneself to forces that reduce one's worth to that of price. It is to lose one's soul.

While much could be said about conscience, I return now to the guiding question of this thought experiment, that is, "can character formation survive the digital economy?" I have tried to isolate the moral danger in the DE with respect to

---

[18] Put in classical terms, the highest human good is the unity of happiness and morality (Immanuel Kant) or, the same thing, happiness and holiness (John Wesley). On this, see William Schweiker, "God and the Human Good," in *God and the Moral Life*, eds. M. Renaud and J. Daniel (New York: Routledge, 2018): 47–62.

[19] Mary Midgley, *The Ethical Primate* (London: Routledge, 2002).

three developments of thought, namely, (1) the difference between the inherent value of an object and its market price, which depends on forces external to it—preferences and market conditions—and is therefore subjective and changing over time;[20] (2) the eliding of the distinction between worth and price, moral and nonmoral value; and (3) the ability of the DE to acquire, often for free, big data about people's preferences that too easily shape human consciousness via those preferences. In light of these developments, I have argued that any simple virtue theory, if taken alone, is inadequate to talk about the formation of character since (1) it cannot address the complexity of systems within which we actually live, especially global communications and the DE, and (2) its moral psychology, especially talk about mental faculties, is not robust enough to capture the challenge we face. Given this, I have tried to reclaim and reconstruct the discourse of conscience in its freedom and noncoercible character as the basis for distinguishing worth and price in its capacity to *give form* to life. Even granting the power of the DE to form preferences, human beings can and must understand themselves as the form-giving agents with respect to the integrity of their lives with others and within systems and institutions that constitute the moral space of contemporary pluralistic societies.

Conclusion

In the reflections above, I have focused on the question of character formation within the DE, but, it should be noted, I have done so in a way that touches on the other aspects of the consultation that led to this book. That is, I have tried to show (1) how educating conscience, that is, interpreting and understanding ourselves within the moral space of the present and the scope of responsibility, is necessary for any character formation. Further, the moral space of late modern pluralistic societies is (2) defined in good part by the DE, which itself is a communication about nonmoral values and preferences but also threatens a reduction of moral to nonmoral value. Given that possibility, the reclaiming and reconstruction of conscience is (3) one way to secure the distinction between moral and nonmoral value so basic to human rights and economic justice without thereby negating the advances of the DE. So taken, this thought experiment could be seen, as noted before, as a meditation on Mark 8: 36–37: "For what will it profit a human being, to gain the whole world and forfeit his soul? Or what shall one give in return for his soul?"

---

[20] I want to thank Jürgen von Hagen for this formulation of the issue.

Rational Choice Theory and Virtuous Economics?

Problems and Possibilities

Steven Pickard

Homo Economicus

"Economics is in essence a modernist subject, a product of the Enlightenment project to free the individual from higher moral authority or external teleology. It retains very firmly a distinct meta-narrative, derived from the notion of *homo economicus*, the rational economic individual."[1] The rational economic individual (REI) has its origins in the utilitarian view of human behavior proposed by Jeremy Bentham, namely, that human beings are motivated by pleasure and avoidance of pain, where pleasure is equated with self-interest. Over the course of the nineteenth century and the first half of the twentieth, the REI underwent a number of modifications. First, theorists soon recognized that human beings evaluate the possible options available with the intention of identifying the outcomes by which utility is maximized. Second, they realized that it was not in fact possible to know when or if utility had been maximized, and hence the REI criterion failed as an indicator of human well-being. Third, it became apparent that all that was necessary for human beings to make choices among the set of possible options was to identify "the one that best satisfies that consumer's preferences, given the disposable income available."[2] The criterion for choice was that it must be rational,

---

[1] Andrew Henley, "Economics and Virtue Ethics: Reflections for a Christian Perspective," in *Economics and Theology: A Christian Vision of the Common Good*, ed. J. Kidwell and S. Doherty, 109-26 (Basingstoke, Hampshire: Palgrave Macmillan, 2015), 109. It is legitimate to ask how central a role *homo economicus* plays in economics as a discipline. The point is that for many economists, the main game of economics is not exhausted by its peculiar psychological assumptions about motivations for economic behaviors as such, even though such motivations and interrogation of notions of self-interest occupy the concerns of those outside the discipline.

[2] Donald Hay and Gordon Menzies, "Is the Model of Human Nature in Economics Fundamentally Flawed? Seeking a Better Model of Economic Behavior," in Kidwell and Doherty, *Economics and Theology*, 183-98, at 184.

which basically equated with being consistent.[3] The result was that the notion of REI was transformed into rational choice theory (RCT).

Rational Choice Theory and its Limits

RCT offers a powerful explanatory method to account for economic behavior. It assumes that human agents maximize utility, have stable preferences, and accumulate an optimal amount of information in a variety of markets. The underlying driver is self-interest, such that "individuals who allow themselves any goal or motivation other than single-minded pursuit of their own welfare are violating the demands of rationality."[4] It appears that RCT "has retained a strangle hold on economic theorizing," even as it has been adapted and modified. For everyday transactions and contractual arrangements in commercial society undertaken by rational autonomous agents, RCT has high predictive value.

RCT has been subjected to significant critique and modification. The strict application of acting rationally in one's choices according to self-interest cannot account for a great deal of the everyday social world in which human beings function. In this regard Hay and Menzies draw attention to Amartya Sen's observation that the complexity of human life is such that we may not unusually act in ways that are contrary to self-interest and which may be detrimental to our welfare.[5] Strictly speaking this is not rational in terms of RCT. Hay and Menzies comment that while RCT may provide high predictive value "for production and trade, and for consumer behavior in relation to the purchase of goods and services, but it is unconvincing when applied to other areas of human life, such as marriage and the family, service to neighbor and community, work and its motivations, and religious commitment and observance."[6]

A case in point is marriage, which is seriously diminished when it is reduced to a contractual arrangement and shorn of any covenantal dimension by which partners commit to each other "for richer, for poorer; for better for worse; in sick-

---

[3] It is as well to note that economic analysis involves a distinction between two aspects of *homo economicus*—the rationality aspect and the self-interest aspect. While related, they are not coterminous. This means that defining rationality in terms of maximizing one's own welfare/well-being may not accord with best practice conceptually.

[4] Hay and Menzies, "Is the Model of Human Nature in Economics Fundamentally Flawed?" in Kidwell and Doherty, *Economics and Theology*, 184.

[5] Ibid., 184–86, Hay and Menzies commenting on Amartya Sen's critique of the behavioral foundations of economic theory in "Rational Fools: A Critique of the Behavioral Foundations of Economic Theory," *Philosophy & Public Affairs* 6/4 (Summer,1977): 317–44.

[6] Ibid., 192.

ness and in health; until death us do part."[7] Sen argues for an expanded sense of what constitutes rational choice and reminds us that Adam Smith referred to multiple motives for choice beyond "self-love," including, notes Hay and Menzies, "sympathy, generosity, and public spiritedness."[8]

Homo economicus Reconsidered

The critique of *homo economicus* by Sen and others raises a fundamental issue at the heart of RCT about what it means to be a human being. A problem arises when *homo economicus* is too closely identified with and circumscribed by RCT. The rational, relentlessly calculating, choice-driven consumer of benefits—*I calculate, I choose, I consume, therefore I am*—determined by self-interest may be a useful abstraction for the purposes of prediction within modern commercial society. But does this adequately capture the complexities of *homo economicus?*

Perhaps this was never the intention. Economists would probably be the first to admit that the rather abstracted notion of the human agent associated with RCT is an analytical abstraction for a very specific purpose. For this reason, it is inadequate for a rounded and accurate depiction of the human behavior and motivations in commercial society. At best it is a blunt but useful instrument to predict choices and consumption.

The late economist and ethicist Paul Heyne offered a broad and nuanced account of *homo economicus* in his essay "Can *Homo Oeconomicus* Be Christian?"[9] Heyne is critical of economists for failing to distinguish between self-interest and selfishness; or between rational behavior and greedy behavior (58). He notes that Adam Smith was careful to distinguish between these "and insisted ... that self-love could be a virtuous motive of action" (58). Heyne points us back to Adam Smith's "realistic anthropology." According to Heyne, people in Smith's world are motivated by self-love or self-interest, which is to be distinguished from selfishness (60). Heyne suggests that self-love and self-interest are "morally neutral, embracing acts of laudable generosity as well as acts of despicable greed" (60). He concludes that "to condemn self-interested behavior, as Smith uses the concept, amounts to condemning purposive behavior" (60).

For Smith, it seems that what people want more than anything else is, in Heyne's view, to "better their condition"—a desire that Smith says "comes from

---

[7] Ibid., 185.
[8] Ibid., 187. Sen as commented on by Hay and Menzies.
[9] Paul Heyne, *"Are Economists Basically Immoral?"and Other Essays on Economics, Ethics, and Religion,* edited and introduction by Geoffrey Brennan and A. M. C Waterman (Indianapolis, IN: Liberty Fund, 2008), 49–80. Hereafter page numbers in text.

the womb, and never leaves us till we go into the grave"[10]. This primal desire ought not to be reduced to desire for monetary wealth or income, which appears for Smith to be the "most vulgar and obvious" means of fulfilling it. Yet Heyne states that for Smith "wealth without limit is not the goal of life" (61). Rather, for Smith, it seems to be enhancement of one's reputation. While this goal also admits of vanity, Heyne, following Smith, states that it "prompts us toward behavior that genuinely merits praise" (61). Indeed, Heyne notes that even mere vanity will, in Smith's words "naturally, or even necessarily" lead to the pursuit of true glory (61). Perhaps here we face one of those fundamental ambiguities of the human condition whereby the road to the formation of a truly praiseworthy character might involve a route via vanity! Heyne suggests that the concern for reputation (which admittedly is not the same as character) brings into play the importance of self-respect as "a primary objective in self-interested behavior" (61). Associated with this is Smith's view that "self-interested behavior ought not violate the laws of justice" (62).

Heyne concludes that Smith "remains an instructive guide for those who want to construct an economics that is relevant to public policy decisions" (63). Heyen concludes that for Smith *Homo economicus* "is completely capable of being a moral and public-spirited person" (63). Heyne notes that this same view was taken up and expounded in the modern period of economic theorizing by Philip Wicksteed in *The Common Sense of Political Economy*.[11] Heyne draws attention to Wicksteed's distinction between the two aspects of *homo economicus*, that is, the "economizing aspect and the exchange aspect" (64). With regard to the former aspect, Wicksteed broadened the notion of the rational calculating agent seeking to maximize personal benefit. Human beings engage in economic transactions for a whole range of reasons and purposes that cannot be circumscribed by "egoistic or self-regarding basis" (68). Importantly, Wicksteed identifies the principle of exchange as central to Smith's vision of the commercial society. This necessarily required division of labor and importantly required cooperation and trust as fundamental constituents of economic behavior, such that there is nothing in the makeup of *homo economicus* "to keep him from being a public-spirited and thoroughly moral citizen" (71).

Heyne sums up his excursus into Smith and Wicksteed thus: "*Homo oeconomicus* as described by Adam Smith and Philip Wicksteed can be a thoroughly moral and public-spirited citizen. It remains to be asked whether he can also be a Christian" (71). This somewhat surprising twist in Heyne's argument arises from

---

[10] Heyne, "Are Economists Basically Immoral," is quoting from Smith's *The Wealth of Nations*, book 2, chapt. 3, first published in 1776 (Indianapolis: Liberty Fund, 1981), 330–49.

[11] Philip Wicksteed, *The Common Sense of Political Economy* (London: Routledge and Kegan Paul, 1910). Heyne's discussion is based on the 1933 edition of Wicksteed's book.

his recognition of the socially radical nature of the message of the Gospels. It leads to a fundamental tension "between the message of the New Testament and the character of *Homo oeconomicus*" (72) in relation to the economizing and exchange aspects of the behavior of economic agents. For example, Matthew 6:19-21 draws a sharp distinction between "the calculating, prudential attitude of *Homo oeconomicus* and the Gospel imperative" (72): "do not lay up for yourselves treasures on earth ... for where your treasure is there will your heart be also" (Matt. 6:19, 21). Heyne examines a number of other such examples of this tension and concludes that the Gospels "advocate a trusting dependence on God that coexists uneasily with the desire of *Homo oeconomicus* to make adequate provision for his own future. The determination to provide for oneself reveals a lack of faith, a lack of faith that in turn prevents people from practicing the mutual concern that will characterize the Kingdom of God" (73). This is most sharply and clearly apparent in Luke's concern for the poor. In short, for Heyne "the ethos of the New Testament is radically communitarian" (74), and scholars have offered various ways to understand this trajectory in such a way as to not undermine a realism about how social order actually works.[12]

Yet in the end, Heyne is a defender of commercial society and *homo economicus*. He argues against the simple depictions of the market as totalitarian and savage and highlights the essentially persuasive rather than coercive character of commercial society (77). Heyne argues that there is no position above the cut and thrust of ordinary commercial and social life—no rarefied site from which, for example, church pronouncements might be made. Heyne's portrait of *homo oeconomicus* is of a complex character capable of great good, necessarily enmeshed in the everyday complexities and ethical challenges of the life of exchange and distribution of resources with "limited knowledge" and "partial interests" (80).

Heyne concludes with a question and an answer: "Can *Homo oeconomicus* be Christian? It's always a possibility" (80). From a theological point of view, a more positive assessment is surely possible. The fundamental reality of the human condition articulated so crisply and famously by Luther recognized that under God, the justified person is simultaneously righteous and a sinner (*simul iustus et peccator*) and, just as importantly, always penitent. Minimally this suggests that notions of self-interest and self-love as discussed above retain an open-textured character for *homo economicus* that is at least consonant with an inquiry into the possibility of virtue within RCT.

---

[12] Heyne points to distinctions between the "ideal" and reality; between "counsels of perfection" and the ethics of the immediate household of faith.

The Possibility of Virtue within RCT

Should an economist be interested in virtue? This is an important question, especially when virtue "is not a standard term in the mainstream economist's lexicon."[13] Michael Baurmann and Geoffrey Brennan offer three possible grounds for a virtue economics: (a) that virtue is of intrinsic value; (b) that "virtue is normatively important but not intrinsically so,"[14] in so far as certain virtuous dispositions may be productive in utility terms; and (c) that in point of fact, virtuous behavior is an empirical reality that informs choices and complicates more usual expectations of an agent's motivations based on an abstracted account of self-interest. These two economists conclude that "a sensitivity to virtue can enrich the capacity to explain and predict human behavior and contribute insights relevant for policy analysis and institutional design that are important and largely overlooked within the discipline [economics] as it stands."[15]

Andrew Henley asks if there is an implicit conception of virtue within (neo) classical economics.[16] He concludes that "for the economist, virtuous behavior is behavior that satisfies the axioms of neoclassical consumer preference theory since that will, by construction, result in the greatest good for the greatest number" (113). This has been explored sympathetically by Deirdre McCloskey, who argues according to Henley that "market-based capitalist economies can be regarded as promoting virtuous behavior, in the Aristotelian sense that this promotes *eudaimonia*" (113). Such behavior may not necessarily be "solely self-interested." Henley suggests that for the neoclassical economist, self-interest can be virtuous (not the same as selfishness or self-serving): "The 'private vice' of self-interested behavior is virtuous because, through the mechanism of the Smithian 'invisible hand,' such behavior promotes the 'public virtue' of the common good" (113). In the well-known words of Adam Smith from *The Wealth of Nations*: "It is not from the benevolence of the butcher, the brewer, or the baker that we expect our dinner, but from their regard for their own interest. We address ourselves, not to their humanity, but to their self-love, and never talk to them of our own necessities, but of their advantages" (quoted in Henley, 113). According to this form of economic virtue, failure to focus on outcomes can generate misallocation of resources, which needs to be corrected by returning to the "virtuous"

---

[13] Michael Baurmann and Geoffrey Brennan, "On Virtue Economics," in *Economics and the Virtues: Building a New Moral Foundation*, ed. Jennifer A. Baker and Mark D. White, 119–40 (Oxford: Oxford University Press, 2016), 119.
[14] Ibid., 123.
[15] Ibid., 138.
[16] Andrew Henley, "Economics and Virtue Ethics," in Kidwell and Doherty, *Economics and Theology*, 110. Hereafter page numbers in text.

pursuit of self-interest and "propel[ing] the economy toward optimality." The virtue of self-interest can also be the means for correcting market failures.

The discussion about the status of self-interest and the possibility of acting virtuously in economic life continues. The matter has been helpfully put by economist Jason Brennan in the form of a basic question, do markets corrupt?[17] Brennan argues that empirical evidence "support[s] the arguments of institutional economists, who often argue that market exchange does not rely upon self-interest alone, but also upon—and at the same time tends to reinforce—mutual trust, reciprocity, and trustworthiness."[18] Brennan notes that there are a great number of empirical studies "to test what effect, if any, exposure to markets or living in a capitalist society has on people's character."[19] He concludes that the claim that markets generate selfishness may well be true, but that further testing is required to justify such a conclusion. Brennan examines the claim (by, for instance, Benjamin Barber and earlier Rousseau) "that market societies tend to draw people away from public, civic life, inducing citizens to be more concerned with procuring consumer goods for themselves."[20] He tests this claim by analyzing political participation rates in marketized societies and finds a "weakly positive" correlation contrary to what others had predicted. Brennan does not claim finality regarding his and others' empirical studies, but he does conclude that "as things now stand, the charge that markets are corrupting is not only ungrounded or unsupported by evidence—instead, the evidence shows that markets improve our character."[21] From another perspective, markets "do not cure all vices, but they tend to help."[22] Brennan appears to equate self-interest with selfishness. Moreover, he focuses on market societies, though his discussion is not equipped to interrogate the "trickle-down" economics of neoliberalism. In other words, there are different kinds of market societies in which self-interest and civic participation are skewed in different ways with different assumptions about optimizing distribution for the purpose of the common good. To identify, track, and assess degrees of corruptibility of market societies is an inherently complex task.

Yet as Andrew Henley notes we also have to reckon with virtuous self-interest (a) "being pursued in ignorance (willful or otherwise) of the costs imposed on oth-

---

[17] Jason Brennan, "Do Markets Corrupt?" in *Economics and the Virtues: Building a New Moral Foundation*, ed. Jennifer A. Baker and Mark D. White, 237–55 (Oxford: Oxford University Press, 2016).

[18] Ibid., 241.

[19] Ibid.

[20] Ibid., 249.

[21] Brennan, "Do Markets Corrupt?," 253.

[22] Ibid.

ers (e.g., pollution)"[23] and (b) being associated with excessive risk-taking, where the risks have been outsourced to third parties (insurance contracts). One result of this according to Henley is the concept of moral hazard, because self-interest without consideration for the well-being of others can promote less-than-virtuous behavior.[24] Henley concludes that overall, it is very difficult to interpret economic behavior in terms of virtue within the framework of RCT. The point is, virtuous action may in fact occur precisely because human agents do not act in strict accord with RCT. This conclusion seems to be in keeping with the earlier comments and discussion of Sen and Heyne that draw attention to the broader concerns and motivations for human behavior in commercial society.

Henley notes the subtle shift from Aristotle's originative notion of eudaemonia, which was concerned to *optimize* the good, where the optimum "is not the maximum but a behavioral 'mean' tempered by virtues such as temperance and continence (moderation)".[25] In the modern period, eudaemonia was interpreted as the utilitarian notion of the greatest good (utility) for the greatest number, and the *optimum* became *maximization.* In this way a blind eye was turned "to questions of the quality of behavior or actions that might lead to human well-being"; any conception of what virtuous behavior might entail gave way to a "sole focus on consequence".[26] This move from optimum to maximum significantly skewed considerations of virtue informing character formation and ethics in modern economic behavior.

THE PROBLEMATIC NATURE OF VIRTUE WITHIN RCT

Wherein lies the possibility for a virtuous economics? And for what purpose should economic behavior be directed? Minimally, such questions involve a teleology—that is, a vision of what the human being could be, a vision associated with a historical perspective on human life. This is quite different from economic analysis based on human nature "as it is" and acting according to immediate dictates of rational choice without recourse to past wisdom or narrative. It seems that within a strict account of RCT, the possibility of a virtuous economics is problematic given (a) the priority of self-interest (albeit with some provision for altruistic behavior), (b) the narrow conception of what constitutes rational choice, (c) preoccupation with the condition of human being "as is," and (d) an associated utilitarian teleology. On this account, virtuous outcomes can never be presumed or finally

---

[23] Henley, "Economics and Virtue Ethics" in Kidwell and S Doherty, *Economics and Theology,* 114.
[24] Ibid.
[25] Ibid.
[26] Ibid.

established, but operate to some extent as alien intrusions that from time to time may offer societal benefit and contribute to the common good. *Homo economicus*, circumscribed by the requirements of RCT, will most likely deliver a truncated version of the virtuous human agent operating within a complex life world—forever in danger of being embroiled in competitive and rivalrous behaviors driven by cycles of greed. What this minimally means is that economics construed according to RCT is insufficient to generate the optimal conditions for the nurture of virtue and the formation of character that might contribute to the well-being and good of society and the planet. This conclusion is unsurprising but nonetheless of high importance. However, it returns us to the earlier discussion of the character of *homo economicus* and the potential within the dynamics of economic and commercial life for the formation of character and ethical education in late modern pluralistic societies.

Reconstituting the Self as Economic Agent

For a recent interesting, provocative, and at times fanciful attempt to map out a new economic paradigm, see Charles Eisenstein's *Sacred Economics*.[27] An earlier important (both theoretically and practically) series of essays on the economy of communion and more recent material offer a very different philosophical/communitarian approach to matters of economics and economy.[28] The underlying theological anthropology of these writers challenges current notions of self-interest which are skewed by reason of their embeddedness within a highly individualized and atomized conception of society and human agency. In this context, the real problem regarding self-interest is not interest as such, but the manner in which the self is assumed to function as an autonomous, independent center of authority. Against this backdrop, notions of altruistic behavior are the exception and difficult to justify.

A more realistic anthropology, with roots in the Christian theological tradition, regards human beings as persons-in-relation. On this basis, the self is not an isolated and self-constituting agent. Rather the self is necessarily relational. While notions of utility may be personal, they are never without a communitarian dimension. Human beings are necessarily embedded in dynamic forms of sociality that are constituting of the self without threatening personal autonomy. As

---

[27] Charles Eisenstein, *Sacred Economics: Money, Gift and Society in an Age of Transition* (Berkeley, CA: North Atlantic Books, 2011).

[28] Luigino Bruni, ed., *The Economy of Communion: Toward a Multi-Dimensional Economic Culture*, trans. Lorna Gold (Hyde Park, NY: New City Press, 2002); Andrew Lightbrown and Peter Sills, eds., *Theonomics: Reconnecting Economics with Virtue and Integrity* (Durham, UK: Sacristy Press, 2014).

observed in the earlier discussion, this more nuanced and socially engaged concept of the self is not entirely absent from original conceptions of human behavior within economic and commercial life as espoused by Adam Smith. In this broader social anthropology, matters of virtue and character formation are simultaneously both personal and communitarian. What is often forgotten is that concern for the common good and concern for personal well-being are co-related.

In short, *homo economicus* subsists within an anthropology of the social self. As such, an ethic of cooperation lies at the very core of economic life. Human society is geared toward cooperative ventures. In this respect, the philosopher Raimo Tuomela states: "Cooperation seems to be innate, a co-evolutionary adaptation based on group selection, the basic reason for this being that human beings have evolved in a group context."[29] Minimally, this means that self-interest is inherently a cooperative activity in relation to other selves-in-relation. This fundamental dynamic endures notwithstanding the fact that people also seem disposed to "defect, act competitively, or even act aggressively."[30] A realistic anthropology will give due weight to the cooperative spirit (as identified by evolutionary psychology) that sustains *homo economicus* and functions as a counter to competitive and rivalrous behavior. The latter may in fact have the unintended consequence (through the workings of Smith's "invisible hand") to improve society as a whole. However, it becomes a destructive force to the extent that it overrides the cooperative mode of behavior.

An issue arises in this depiction of the human agent about the status of competitive behavior. From the perspective of *homo economicus*, competition is to be expected and, indeed, might be precisely the way in which positive outcomes regarding choice and consumption are optimized. From this perspective, the basic threat to competition is not cooperation as such but rather monopoly behavior, which exercises control over goods and services and excludes possibilities of choice. This observation generates a question about the nature of competition. Is it possible to differentiate nonrivalrous forms of competitive behavior from other kinds of competitive behavior that are fundamentally rivalrous and tend toward the undermining of the common good? Nonrivalrous competition may well have resonance with forms of cooperative behavior and accord with an understanding of the human agent as a relational self.

---

[29] Raimo Tuomela, *The Philosophy of Sociality: The Shared Point of View* (Oxford: Oxford University Press, 2007), 149–81, at 150.

[30] Ibid., 150.

The Shape of a Virtue Economics

The foregoing begs the question of how to conceive economics within the purposes of God as the locus for the inculcation of virtue and character. This question necessarily includes a double focus on the end or telos of economics and its practice. Such a project is indeed quite major. From a theological point of view, what is required is the relocation of economics and economic behavior within a doctrine of creation. As such, economics can be identified as one of those primary ways through which God's presence and action in the world are mediated. Of course it is only one of a number of critical intermediate categories for the active work of God alongside other important domains, including interpersonal relations, communications, place, and polity.[31] Economics includes mediums of exchange, production, and distribution. The importance of beginning with creation—which includes materiality and its interwovenness with human and other life—is that it calls attention to the fact that in a critical way, economics (and market behavior) represent a fundamental way by which humans live and relate to the world. As such, it is an indispensable way for human beings to become bonded to each other and the world. This theological account of the location and function of economics as a medium for exchange, distribution, and consumption of resources means that the domain of economics has an appropriate and legitimate place within the good ordering of the world. Indeed, on this account economics is a critical means by which exchange and distribution might contribute to the raising of such activities to their true and proper place within the economy of God and life in the world. The tendency to separate economics from other disciplines and societal practices and their attendant systems of accountability needs to be vigorously resisted, because it falsifies the organic way in which our lives as human agents actually function and flourish in the world.

From the earlier discussion, I would highlight the following features of *homo economicus* that suggest a richer platform for character formation and ethical education in modern Western pluralistic societies. First, exchange and distribution of necessary and desired resources for human life and well-being operate within increasingly complex cultural and commercial settings. Second, modes of exchange and economic behavior necessarily become highly sophisticated and display increasing levels of intensity. Third, one critical feature of such environments is unpredictability, notwithstanding significant investment in modeling designed to enhance predictability of outcomes. Fourth, given this situation, optimizing personal and community well-being will be best achieved through cooperative behavior. Fifth, given the intensity and extent of the impact of economic

---

[31] Daniel W. Hardy, "Created and Redeemed Sociality," in *On Being the Church: Essays on the Christian Community*, ed. Colin Gunton and Daniel W. Hardy (Edinburgh: T & T Clark, 1989), 44–77.

life on people and cultures, it should not be surprising that the cooperative spirit of *homo economicus* provides a foundation and impetus for the positive and intentional nature of virtue and the formation of personal and communal character.

That we find dynamics which are destructive in the very place where cooperative (nonrivalrous) competition ought to be expected raises serious questions for contemporary society about its values and aspirations. Repair and renewal of economic life and commercial society are thus fundamental for human well-being. How this renovation might be achieved and communicated is a major task that involves policy development and regulatory frameworks at governmental and national levels. The challenge is to find that delicate interaction and, indeed, cooperation between freedom for bottom-up emergent modes of economic decision-making and distribution of resources, on one hand, and top-down influence on the other. The dynamic that informs this interaction becomes critical for the communication of values in late modern pluralistic societies.

Two Bodies: Christ and Economy

The church is called to display, through its life and action, what the renewal of economics might actually look like. The presupposition here is that God's work in the life, death, and resurrection of Jesus Christ through the eternal Spirit initiated the conditions for the reconstitution of the basic forms of human society, including economic activity and purpose.[32] But what clues do we have to identify what that reconstituting work of God entails? I suggest that we can begin to discern the dynamic at work in this renewal of life in the market economy through attention to that central act of Christian worship, the Eucharist. Here we have an instance of a concentrated and energy-releasing celebration of the generosity of God.[33] This celebration points to and enacts in liturgical form the purpose of God to provide a just distribution of the divine resources for the world.

How so? This reconstitution—indeed, transformation—occurs through an exchange between God and creation. It is marked by blessing and enrichment. In this divine economy, scarcity—which arises from finitude and limit—is brought into relation with the abundance of God's self-giving love. However, this enrichment comes by way of divine *kenosis*, or self-emptying. This is symbolized in the

---

[32] See Hardy, "Created and Redeemed Sociality." Importantly, Hardy argues that the forms through which human society emerges and flourishes—including the domain of economic activity, e.g., production and distribution—constitute the "primary themata" of what he terms "the social transcendental," which is itself a manifestation of the Divine Trinity (45).

[33] I have discussed this in *Seeking the Church: An Introduction to Ecclesiology* (London: SCM Press, 2012), 202–07.

broken bread and wine outpoured—the pattern and the cup of salvation. The movement toward humanity through God's Spirit in Christ has a redistributive quality that generates a practical and spiritual benefit for all without favor or entitlement. The Holy Spirit does this by drawing all things toward a deeper purpose within God's life and economy.

The key theological themes here are justice and generosity. Moreover, as we have received, so we are called to give and live. Herein lies the deepest resource for the generation, nurture, and expansion of the virtues (e.g., compassion, friendship, and justice) and the consequential forming of character, both individually and for society. The human being as economic agent is a critical participant and contributor to a society marked by such virtues.

A Conceptual Analysis of "Value" in Select Business Literature and Its Implications for Ethical Educations

Piet Naudé

The values underlying and present in current management education have been informed by debates about the purpose of business in the literature on management and applied ethics. This exploratory chapter presents an abstract from the shifting debates between 1970 and 2015 about what kind of value business does and ought to create. Instead of a detailed historical account of the developments during this period,[1] the aim is more modest: to determine what can be inferred about values from a close reading of four significant "markers" in the values-debate–works by Milton Friedman;[2] Ronald Freeman;[3] Michael Porter and Mark Kramer;[4] and Thomas Donaldson and James Walsh.[5]

The limitation of this chapter lies in the narrow selection of what are deemed influential texts as far as management education is concerned, omitting both associated literature by the same authors as well as many important contributions by others in secondary literature. The idea is to develop a values trajectory in the

---

[1] See Bradley R. Agle and Craig B. Caldwell, "Understanding Research on Values in Business," *Business and Society* 38/3 (1999): 326–87; World Economic Forum, *Values and the Fourth Industrial Revolution: Connecting the Dots between Value, Values, Profit and Purpose* (Geneva: WEF, 2016).

[2] Milton Friedman, "The Social Responsibility of Business Is to Increase Its Profits," *The New York Times*, Sept. 13, 1970, 1–8., retrieved from https://www.nytimes.com/1970/09/13/archives/a-friedman-doctrine-the-social-responsibiity-of-business-is-to.html. Reprinted in *Business Ethics: A Philosophical Reader*, ed. Thomas T. White, 162–67 (New York: Macmillan, 1991). Cited hereafter parenthetically in the text.

[3] Ronald Edward Freeman, *Strategic Management: A Stakeholder Approach* (London: Pitman, 1984). Cited hereafter parenthetically in the text.

[4] Michael E. Porter and Mark R. Kramer, "Strategy and Society: The Link between Competitive Advantage and Corporate Social Responsibility," *Harvard Business Review* (Dec. 2006): 1–13. Cited hereafter parenthetically in the text.

[5] Thomas Donaldson and James P. Walsh, "Toward a Theory of Business," *Research in Organizational Behavior* 35 (2015): 181–207. Cited hereafter parenthetically in the text.

narrow channel provided by the selected works and infer some ideas about (moral) education commensurate with the views expressed in the respective writings. The chapter will demonstrate that there was an apparent expansion of the values concept from narrow shareholder benefit (Friedman) to broader stakeholder value (Freeman) and, more recently, to "creating shared value" (Porter and Kramer[6]) with an advancement toward stating the purpose of business as "optimized collective value" (Donaldson and Walsh).

Milton Friedman: Increasing Shareholder Value

In his famous article "The Social Responsibility of Business Is to Increase Its Profits," included in virtually every business ethics reader, Milton Friedman, makes a number of important ethical claims: moral values make sense only if used in relation to people and are not to be applied to business entities like corporations. "Only people can have moral responsibilities. A corporation is an artificial person and in this sense may have artificial responsibilities, but 'business' as a whole cannot be said to have responsibilities" (1). In a classical statement of individualism ("society is a collection of individuals" [7]), Friedman denies the existence of social values beyond the individual. In his view, "(T)here are no 'social' values, no 'social' responsibilities in any sense other than the shared values and responsibilities of individuals" (7). Based on this distinction, Friedman argues for a strict role differentiation: a business person "in his own right" can surely assume voluntary ethical responsibilities to family, church, club, city, and country according to his conscience, but "in his capacity as a businessman" or corporate executive, he has no "social responsibility," because "the executive is an agent serving the interests of his principal," and that interest is to increase profits for stockholders (4).

This view in fact defeats the impression created by the title of the article (derived from Friedman's book *Capitalism and Freedom*)[7] that to "increase profits" (value in the monetary sense devoid of moral responsibility) is a "social responsibility" (value in the moral sense, including responsibility), unless one reads the title as an ironic rhetorical strategy against those who express an aversion to capitalism and profits as a matter of principle and view corporations as "soulless" (6).

A further distinction divides the political principle of unanimity, which underlies the free-market mechanism of voluntary cooperation, and the political principle of conformity, which unavoidably governs the political sphere of soci-

---

[6] Michael E. Porter and Mark R. Kramer, "Creating Shared Value, *Harvard Business Review* (Jan.-Feb. 2011): 1-17.

[7] Milton Friedman, *Capitalism and Freedom* (Chicago: University of Chicago Press, 1962), 133-36.

ety. The imposition of moral values (via the call for the social responsibilities of business) harms the foundations of a free society based on a free-market system. The harm stems from the confusion of conformity to promote social interests under the political mechanism of majority rule with the noncoercive character of the market, where the increase of profits is the "one and only" responsibility of business (8).

An important part of Friedman's argument is that the principle of self-interest (to increase monetary value) should guide actions that may be seen by the public as socially responsible (moral value): tax-deductible charitable giving or providing resources to upgrade local community amenities are entirely justified if they serve the long-run self-interest of a corporation. If the public opinion at a given time requires corporations to generate goodwill as a byproduct of such social expenditures, it may be in their self-interest "to cloak their actions" as "social responsibility" (albeit such action is approaching fraud, and Friedman expresses his admiration for business people who hold this in disdain: 6).

Friedman—while denying a social conscience for business as such—does acknowledge that the striving "to make as much money as possible" (2) is subject to the ethical constraints contained in the basic rules of society, "both those embodied in law and those embodied in ethical custom" (2). The only guiding principle for the actions of a corporation in a free market is promotion of self-interest—that is, to increase profits. But that principle is subject to the moral authority of law and custom exterior to the corporation, which will adhere to them exactly because it is in its self-interest to do so.

Michael Porter and Mark Kramer: Creating Shared Value

In their hugely influential article "Creating Shared Value," published in *Harvard Business Review* in 2011, Michael Porter and Mark Kramer claim to "reinvent capitalism." In their view, business has lost its social legitimacy and experiences diminished levels of trust, aggravated by the 2008 subprime banking crisis.

Part of the problem is that the "the old, narrow view of capitalism" (6) put forward by Friedman limits the contribution of business to society to the making of profits. According to this narrow view, the authors argue, the social benefit of a business lies exclusively and sufficiently in the employment it creates, the wages and taxes it pays, and the investment it makes. In short, "Conducting business as usual is sufficient social benefit. A firm is largely a self-contained entity and social or community issues fall outside its proper scope" (6). This narrow view of capitalism led to a zero-sum relation between business and society, with profits perceived as coming at the expense of society. The response of the corporate social responsibility movement[8] has two weaknesses: it constructs a business's contribution to addressing a social need as a necessary expense to improve reputation (5), and such social involvement remains at the periphery, and not the core, of the business enterprise itself (4).

The solution lies in a new approach which redefines the purpose of the corporation as "creating shared value" (CSV). The key definition of CSV is "creating economic value in a way that *also* creates value for society by addressing its needs and challenges" (4, original emphasis). Porter and Kramer are quick to add that CSV is not about social philanthropy (social value) or personal ethics (moral value) or an approach to share company profits (redistributive value) (5). CSV incorporates social needs into the core business function so that a new way to achieve economic success (monetary value) becomes possible.

The article explains that there are three distinct ways in which "companies can create economic value by creating societal value" (7), namely, to reconceive markets and products (7-8), to redefine productivity in the economic value chain (8-11), and to build thriving supporting industry clusters at the company's location (12-15).

My interest is not in the actual business proposals contained in the three recommendations, but in the conceptualization of economic value and social value—plus their interrelation—as it emerges from these proposals. It is clear that economic value is constructed in the traditional capitalist way as financial success that flows from an efficiency approach, in which profits are increased relative to cost. Social value is seen as the benefits for society when social needs, social weaknesses, or social challenges are addressed by approaching them in a more efficient and productive manner. Due to their firm belief that "capitalism is an unparalleled vehicle for meeting human needs, improving efficiency, creating jobs and building wealth" (4), the authors make a number of significant claims.

First, as is evident from social entrepreneurial businesses (10), the productivity methods of private enterprise are better at solving social problems than the methods of traditional public policy and spending. In this manner, Porter and Kramer are able to frame social problems and the creation of social value as, in principle, an economic problem and opportunity best solved and exploited by applying economic value-creating principles. In this vein, "disadvantaged communities" are reconstructed as "new viable markets," and "poor urban areas" constitute often overlooked "substantial concentrated purchasing power" (8). This kind of framing extends to "immense human needs" that are restated as constituting "internal costs," as representing new markets, and as opportunities for competitive advantages (15).

Second, the idea of creating shared value is viewed as valuable only if economic value is realized. This is an important point: "The concept of shared value

---

[8] Porter and Kramer, "Strategy and Society."

can be defined as policies and operating practices that enhance the competitiveness of a company while simultaneously advancing the economic and social conditions in which it operates" (6). The key idea throughout the article, reinforced time and again via business examples, is that the sharing of value does not happen between two equal partners with a common goal of creating value: if economic value (profit) is not or cannot be realized in the creation of social value, the latter drops from the business agenda.

The so-called new connection between business and society is predicated on the financial success of business. The aim is not to address societal problems but to frame them as productivity challenges and economic opportunities, and to address them only if companies are more successful because they are able "to serve new needs, gain efficiency, create differentiation, and expand markets" (7). Despite the impression created by the CSV concept, the concern that drives the idea of creating shared value is not a societal concern (that is, creating social value) but a concern for corporate success (that is, economic value), which both frames and measures social value in terms of the economic value's internal logic of efficiency, productivity, and market penetration. Behind this lies the dogma of trickle-down economics, that is, "if all companies individually pursued shared value ... society's overall interests would be served" (17).

Toward the end of the article, the authors make clear that social value is only a subsidiary, instrumental idea in service of creating economic value: "The opportunity to create economic value through creating societal value will be one of the most powerful forces driving growth in the global economy" (15). In clever rhetoric, they make a brave ethical claim: "Not all profit is equal." The pursuit of narrow, short-term profit should be replaced by "the right kind of profits." What are these? "Profits involving a social purpose represent a higher form of capitalism." The primacy of economic value is, however, clear, because this higher form of capitalism "will enable society to advance more rapidly while allowing companies to grow even more. The result is a positive cycle of company and community prosperity, *which leads to profits that endure*" (15, my emphasis).

Despite their criticism of Friedman, Porter and Kramer operate fully within the same paradigm. "The social responsibility of business is to increase its profits" is simply restated as "the responsibility of business is to increase its profits through selective social engagement." And their hand was forced. The world of 1970 was quite different from the one in 2011. The expectations of business to respond to environmental and social challenges were now much higher.

Porter and Kramer realize two things. First, markets are affected by these challenges, which should, therefore, be incorporated into the purpose and strategy of business by turning them into economic value propositions. Second, business requires a social license to operate, and for that, trust and legitimacy are preconditions. Creating shared value therefore serves the double purpose of advancing profits through addressing social problems and, along the way, earning the trust of society by claiming a "reinvention of capitalism," which is "imbued with a social purpose." Despite the rephrasing, the proposal is firmly entrenched in capitalism: "But that (social) purpose should arise not out of charity, but out of a deeper understanding of competition and economic value creation. The next evolution in the capitalist model recognizes new and better ways to develop products, serve markets, and build productive enterprises" (17).

What are the implications for ethical education? Porter and Kramer construct some implications of CSV for education. Public-sector students should be exposed to more managerial training, which—in terms of character formation—should instill an entrepreneurial mindset. Business schools should cease teaching "the narrow view of capitalism" in response to students' "hunger for a greater sense of purpose" (17). That purpose is best served when the curricula are broadened in line with the preceding exposition of CSV: value chains should include the efficient use of resources; marketing should address "deeper human needs" and include nontraditional customers; the economic impact of societal factors on business must be studied; and finance courses should move beyond financial market participants to include questions of how capital markets can support true value creation in companies (17).

The sting of these proposals lies in the tail. Porter and Kramer—in typical business school fashion—say defensively (or defiantly?): "There is nothing soft about the concept of shared value. These proposed changes in business school curricula are not qualitative and do not depart from economic value creation. Instead, they represent the next stage in our understanding of markets, competition, and business management" (17). Despite the impression of shared value, the formation of character and the shaping of purpose via business education are constructed solely in terms of economic value. Despite their claim that CSV has nothing to do with ethics and shaping of personal values (5), CSV is in fact a powerful ethical statement that one's greater sense of purpose is aimed at and determined by increasing economic value, predicated upon the key moral principle of self-interested behavior.

As demonstrated above, Porter and Kramer hold a fundamentally instrumentalist view on social value, insofar as both its framing and its advancing depend on its contribution to economic value. This is typical of constructing value in a derivative sense—that is, something has value for the sake of something else to which it is related. In this view, solving social problems is not a good in itself and is valued only because it contributes to economic value. From a moral perspective, the implication is quite dire: those human needs or social problems that cannot be framed as and used for advancing economic value will simply fall off the radar screen of business. This is partially attributed to an inability to view solutions to social questions as good in themselves, like assisting poor people for their own sake as human persons, or to formulate personal/business purposes via virtues like care, honesty, and responsibility that are good in their own right, without reference to some derivative (in this case, economic) value.

EDWARD FREEMAN: INCREASING STRATEGIC STAKEHOLDER VALUE

The publication of *Strategic Management: A Stakeholder Approach*, by R. Edward Freeman, in 1984 marks the transition from a narrow Friedman-style shareholder focus to a broader, inclusive stakeholder approach to business. In short, Freeman holds that the success of a business enterprise relies on many more stakeholder groups than only those who hold a direct financial interest in it. These groups vary in kind—suppliers, local and national governments, local communities, consumer advocates, global institutions—and their effects on a corporation may vary from direct economic ones to technological, political, managerial, and social ones (94).

Freeman argues that for a corporation to set its strategic direction in relation to different stakeholders, it requires an enterprise strategy. This strategy in turn consists of three related analyses, namely, stakeholder, values, and social-issues analyses (92). Stakeholder analysis assists in gaining an accurate and detailed account of significant actors in the external environment, whereas societal analysis aims at understanding major issues facing society now and over the next decade (99). Values analysis asks the questions of "who we are" and "what we should do in relation to our context." This analysis "represents the moral or ethical component to strategic management ... which has been largely ignored, except as an addition to the 'business' concerns of the firm" (90). Understanding internal organizational values and those of the stakeholders will assist in a closer alignment of "social and ethical concerns" with "traditional business concerns" (90) and overcome the divide between business and ethics.

Freeman then makes three important distinctions in his discussion on values. First, the word "value" refers to different kinds of values like aesthetic, social, religious, and moral values. Therefore, "all questions of values are not questions of moral values," and "while a concern for ethics is necessary ingredient" of an enterprise strategy, "it is it not in itself sufficient" (96).

Second, intrinsic values are basic values in the sense that they refer to things which are "good in and of themselves," and they represent the bottom line of life and its pursuits—for example, the freedom to act, belief in a supreme being, or the pursuit of personal/family happiness. Instrumental values are means to realize intrinsic values. "We place instrumental value on those things which lead us toward the attainment of things, actions or states of mind which are intrinsically valuable" (96).

Third, personal values are distinct from organizational values, and the ideal situation is obviously when there is "high degree of congruence" between the two value sets.

When the three analyses of stakeholders, values, and society are brought together, a typology of the relation between business and society emerges. Freeman proceeds to construct such typologies, beginning with a Friedman-type stockholder orientation (maximize benefits to financial stakeholders) and adding a utilitarian orientation (maximize benefit to all stakeholders), a Rawlsian orientation (raise the welfare of the worst-off stakeholder), and a social-harmony orientation (aim at consensus and social harmony).

In an enlightening section on "the necessity of enterprise strategy" (107–10), Freeman writes:

> It is very easy to misinterpret the foregoing analysis as yet another call for social responsibility or business ethics. While these issues are important in their own right, enterprise strategy is a different concept. We need to worry about enterprise level strategy for the simple fact that the corporate survival depends in part on there being some "fit" between the values of the corporation and its managers, the expectations of the stakeholders in the firm and the societal issues which will determine the ability of the firm to sell its products. (107)

In short: "Enterprise strategy is concerned with the question of 'consistency' among the key elements of the firm's relationship with its environment" (107).

The implication is clear: in Freeman's stakeholder approach, value analysis has only instrumental and no intrinsic value, because the actual intrinsic value he proposes is enhancing economic value. He accords to ethics and social responsibility the status of intrinsic values, that is, as "important in their own right." But when a specific firm develops changes in its strategy based on stakeholder and societal expectations, the question "whether such changes are socially responsible or morally praiseworthy is an important question, but it is yet a further question which an analysis of enterprise strategy does not address" (107). In other words, the initial aim to integrate traditional business concerns with ethics (89, 90) is dropped from the agenda of enterprise strategy, and the inclusion of moral values, worthy of pursuit in themselves, is merely a strategy to—ultimately—increase shareholders' economic value.

Freeman is very critical of Friedman and calls the exclusive focus on maximizing owners' interests the "original pathology of the stockholder strategy" (109). One could, however, translate Freeman's approach into Friedman language: the purpose of the firm is to increase shareholder (economic) value by a strategic management of relations with stakeholders, attention to values (including moral ones), and reading the societal context correctly.

Freeman in 1984 simply skipped a key values question that he himself implicitly raised: is it desirable in some cases that a firm reduces its economic value (the traditional bottom line) for the sake of achieving a more basic intrinsic value (what he terms "the bottom line of life")? He states almost in passing that intrinsic values are held because they are good in themselves, "and it does not matter if they lead to the original outcome" which one might have pursued. But because economic value is for Freeman the ultimate intrinsic value, such possibility does not even arise in this theory, as he neatly moves moral questions to the realm "which an analysis of enterprise strategy does not address" (107), despite claiming the opposite.

To his credit, Freeman did in 1984 expand the values concept by expanding the accountability of business beyond shareholders to a broader range of stakeholders and transcending at least in theory the notion of values beyond narrow profit-seeking to include normative, aesthetic, and intrinsic values. But when he claims that enterprise strategies lead "towards a unified purpose that both produces bottom line results and serves the purposes and values of executives and other organizational members and stakeholders," the only inference is that "bottom line results" are in fact the real purpose, and other purposes and values are mere strategic instruments in its realization.

Freeman attempted to correct this impression by coauthoring *Corporate Strategy and the Search for Ethics* with Daniel R. Gilbert in 1988.[9] Freeman later made a substantive contribution toward an integration of ethics in business in his article "The Politics of Stakeholder Theory."[10] The genie, however, had left the bottle, and the 1984 book became the guiding foundation for a stakeholder approach with an enduring influence on research, practitioners, and ethics educators.[11]

THOMAS DONALDSON AND JAMES WALSH: OPTIMIZING COLLECTIVE VALUE

I now turn to the last and, in my view, most sophisticated example of how the value-concept evolved in business-and-ethics literature. Donaldson and Walsh, in their article "Toward a Theory of Business," published in late 2015, addressed the key question about the purpose of business.

---

[9] R. Edward Freeman and Daniel R. Gilbert, *Corporate Strategy and the Search for Ethics* (Englewood Cliffs, NJ: Prentice Hall, 1988). See especially chapters 3 and 4.

[10] R. Edward Freeman, "The Politics of Stakeholder Theory: Some Future Directions," *Business Ethics Quarterly* 4 (1994): 409–22.

[11] A. Wicks, "Overcoming the Separation Thesis? The Need for a Reconsideration of Business and Society Research," *Business and Society* 35/1 (1996): 89–118, at 90–91.

They argue that the neoclassical theory of the firm, which sees individuals as primarily self-interested economic agents, is for two reasons not adequate to answer the question of the purpose of business. First, the theory, *inter alia* because of its underlying anthropological assumptions, is incapable to accommodate other, more intangible purposes like a good society, social harmony, or environmental stewardship which go beyond economic prosperity (184). Second, it is a theory of the firm—a specific type of organization—and it would be "a fallacy of composition" to transfer the purpose of an individual firm to business in general. "We should take great care before we conclude that the purpose of business is to maximize shareholder return or to delight customers. The composition fallacy alerts us to the possibility that the attributes of a successful firm may not be the same as the attributes of successful business in general" (187). That is why "we need a theory of business" (187) in which—as will be evident below—the authors include a significant normative element for business success.

The authors view moral values as motivators of intentional behavior.[12] They write that a positive value is "a reason for acting when the object of the act is seen as worthy of pursuit" (189). Furthermore, "When something that is 'worthy of pursuit' does not have its own value derived form a higher-order value, it counts as an intrinsic value." Such intrinsic values provide "a final reason for acting" and they possess "an 'objective' normative status" (190). In their theory of business, Donaldson and Walsh then introduce human dignity (and later, on page 199, the dignity of other species) as "a central and even sacred intrinsic value to guide Business activity" (192).

The purpose of business cannot be expressed in normative terms only. The empirical dimension of a business theory should also give account of other values, so that the value monism underlying a neoclassical understanding of the firm is—reminiscent of Freeman—expanded to "multiple values of differing character" (191). Here Donaldson and Walsh develop a notion of "Collective Value," which they describe as "the agglomeration of the Business Participants' benefits, net of any aversive Business outcomes" (191).

The authors avoid stakeholder language because of its association with firm-theory and rather refer to "Business Participants" as an expansive term including "anyone who affects or is affected by business" (188). "Benefits" refer to "the contributions made by Business to the satisfaction of a Business Participant's Values, including his or her Intrinsic Values" (190). These benefits are not numerically

---

[12] See Stefan Hradil, "Der Wert von Werten: Wozu sind sie gut und wie entstehen sie?," in *Werte—und was sie uns wert sind. Eine interdisziplinäre Anthologie*, ed. Randolf Rodenstock and Nese Sevsay-Tegethoff, 20-36 (Munich: Roman Herzog Institut, 2016), 27; Clyde Kluckhohn, "Values and Value-Orientation in the Theory of Action: An Exploration in Definition and Classification," in *Toward a General Theory of Action*, ed. Talcott Parsons and Edward Shils, 388-433 (Cambridge, MA: Harvard University Press, 1951), 395.

aggregated but *agglomerated* in a clustering of different kinds of benefits. Collective Value should be optimized, expressing an aspiration to bring about as much value as possible, enabling people to flourish, subject to the normative guide of dignity: "We invoke a world where collective value is optimised. Where the dignity of every business participant is recognized and honored, where every act and decision in the world of business clear the Dignity Threshold" (202).

It is important to note that the word "value" in the term "Collective Value" has an expanded meaning beyond moral or intrinsic value. It includes economic value as but one of many motivations why people participate in Business (with a capital B) and one of the many ways in which participants benefit from Business. This theory of Business therefore addresses two recurring concerns that emerge from the earlier discussion of values: By subsuming participants' varied benefits under a "value" term, it is able to include a variety of values not expressly present in economic theory. And by explicitly requiring a dignity threshold as an integral part of business, it is able to bridge the divide between business and intrinsic value that plagues a narrow economic value-conception. The theory is therefore able to merge the satisfaction of an intrinsic value like dignity with other values while maintaining the normative primacy of the former. Because an intrinsic value like dignity is inviolable in principle, this theory avoids the instrumentalization of moral values in service of economic gain.

This theory of business is at the same time a theory of business success. No matter which and how many benefits are derived from participation in business, if it does not satisfy the criterion of dignity, a business cannot be deemed successful. If accepted (assisted perhaps by a "dignitarian social movement in business," 201), this theory could require business to forgo economic value when faced with a dignity deficit, as the latter overrides the former in this normative conception of business success. Donaldson and Walsh start their article with a riddle: "Law is to justice, as medicine is to health, as business is to ...," and leave the answer open until the end. The purpose of business and the mark of business success is "optimized collective value" (202).

What are the implications of this business theory for understanding an individual firm's purpose? The authors suggest a distinction between the focal purpose of a firm that addresses traditional economic value creation and the simultaneous contextual purpose that expresses the firm's societal role. The dignity threshold, however, holds for business in general and for particular firms: "Each decision maker should honor the dignity of those who affect and are affected by that decision maker's work" (200).

It lies outside the scope of Donaldson and Walsh's article to address implications for business education. One could, however, infer certain guidelines: the paradigm of business education as serving the interest of private and firm-level economic value maximization must be challenged. This is no easy task, as it requires a critical examination of dominant neoclassical thinking that held and still holds sway in business schools around the globe, as expressed, for example, in the fact that influential rankings of business schools are, to a large extent, based on a comparison of salaries before and after the completion of studies.[13]

Business education should move beyond the value-monism of economics and engage in a complex process of clarifying and expanding the notion of values, which should include the nature of intrinsic values and their status as normative criteria for business behavior and success.

Summary and Conclusion

This chapter has undertaken a focused journey through a small selection of key texts analyzing the meaning of "value" in business as it emerges in relation to the question of the purpose of business. Four examples were selected: maximizing shareholder value (Friedman); creating shared (business and social) value (Porter and Kramer); creating, trading, and sustaining stakeholder value (Freeman); and optimizing collective value (Donaldson and Walsh).

The first three examples operate squarely within a neoclassical capitalist framework (supply and demand relate to an individual's rational ability to maximize utility and profit) and do not distinguish between individual businesses and business in general. An attempt to make a transition toward including noneconomic values, including moral values, into stakeholder capitalism is detected in Freeman's later work. A more nuanced view emerges from Donaldson and Walsh, who set forward a theory of business in general which includes multiple values while being subject to intrinsic value (in their case, dignity) as a normative threshold for business success.

This trajectory demonstrates that moral education and character formation in business schools was (and still is?) fundamentally shaped by advancing the private good, maximizing shareholder returns, and defining personal and organizational purpose in maximizing economic value. When the expectations of society from business and business schools rose to include additional forms of value-creation, such as good corporate citizenship and adding societal value, Porter and Kramer demonstrate the response: while maintaining the underlying neoclassical assumptions, these legitimate external concerns are framed from the perspective of economic value advancement, and the solutions provided are drawn from the traditional strengths of business like efficiency and market penetration. The influential stakeholder theory in its early forms includes a variety of values-creation as perceived by different stakeholders, but it is still locked into economic value as the determining, actual goal. It is thus possible to include courses on social re-

---

[13] David Pitt-Watson and Ellen Quigley, *Business School Rankings for the 21st Century* (New York: United Nations Global Impact, 2019), 13-14.

sponsibility and even business ethics in business education in order to regain social trust, but unless the underlying paradigm itself is challenged, there is no actual shift beyond a monistic economic value perspective, despite an appearance to the contrary.

We have seen that the litmus test lies in how intrinsic values are dealt with. Is it thought desirable to forgo economic value-maximization not merely for realizing such value as a postponed self-interest or as part of a public-relations exercise, but for the sake of realizing an intrinsic value for its own sake? Friedman as well as Porter and Kramer would not accept this possibility, because for them the purpose of business is increasing profits in a direct manner or via the inclusion of social-value creation. The early Freeman acknowledges the importance of intrinsic values but deals with them in an ambiguous way: On one hand, they are included in stakeholder management, but in an instrumental way which subjects their normative function to successful stakeholder negotiations. On the other hand, he simply states that normative questions lie outside the scope of stakeholder management. The strength of Donaldson's and Walsh's proposal is that they include intrinsic values as part of the business participants' benefits and as normative criteria for business success.

It would further refine their theory if good-related intrinsic values (e. g., health, social cohesion) remained in the basket of collective benefits while principle-related intrinsic values (dignity, promise-keeping) were accorded "adjudication" status of benefit realization in a more objective sense. The reason for this proposal lies in the fact that an intrinsic value like dignity is different in kind than other values (aesthetic, cognitive, economic, social) because it is both a benefit to be optimized (part of the collective) and the normative threshold against which all other value realization is to be tested (beyond the collective).

Donaldson and Walsh do demonstrate the difficulty of transcending and augmenting economic value so as to design a theory of business with a constitutive, normative character. This effort can be explored in relation to the theme of this book. Let us accept that late modern societies are pluralistic in the sense that they are made up by distinctive social systems like religion, family, education, economics, media, and law. Insofar as each of these social spheres has distinct and overlapping internal value systems and institutionalized rationalities that create normative expectations and shape individual and institutional character, the exposition of "economic value" above raises a pertinent question, which is also discussed in Klaus Leisinger's contribution to this volume: what happens when the normative code of one social sphere (the economic market) is transferred into the other social spheres by displacing their moral codes and rationalities, while at the same time claiming to be beyond the reach of moral consideration itself?

The economic market has become one of the key social systems shaping the values of late modern pluralistic societies. In fact, it has been argued that the Market (with a capital letter) has assumed divine status and has become the predominant social system whose values of competition, commodification, and ever-increasing consumption have permeated other systems like religion, law, family and media and changed their nature and inner normative codes.[14] What happened in business education is the uncritical adoption of neoclassical economic thinking on the assumption that such thinking is itself an amoral position while serving as default position from which the content, character formation, and purpose of the education process are derived.

The question in management education is, however, not how to include non-economic values in the curriculum as an add-on, but how to embed an array of values in the curriculum itself and provide a normative framework for this education as whole. Business education has never been value-neutral. It is philosophically unsound to suggest that one can separate business and business education from their underlying (implicit) values (Donaldson and Walsh, 195) as is claimed in the so-called separation thesis.[15] The choice for the priority of economic value is based on specific views about the human person and motivations to act. These are in themselves significant moral choices already. The assumptions underlying such a choice must be questioned and not accepted as a given, then afterward "moralized" by "applying" ethical thinking to them.

A body of credible research suggests that business school students exposed to economics and finance coursework based on the view of human nature underlying *homo economicus* "tend to change their own beliefs and behavior toward the self-interest model under experimental conditions." This attitudinal shift toward a greater "free riding" tendency, diminished prosocial openness, and justification of self-interested behavior are "exacerbated by the competitive socialization endemic to business schools' programs."[16] The combination of educational content with the social conditions under which this education is presented forms a powerful force in character formation and communication of values with—as we now know—disastrous consequences for financial markets, international cooperation, and the natural environment. A reconceptualization of the purpose of business and the values imparted via management education remains an unfinished and urgent project.

---

[14] Harvey Gallagher Cox, *The Market as God* (Cambridge, MA: Harvard University, 2016).
[15] Wicks, "Overcoming the Separation Thesis?"; R. Edward Freeman, et al., *Stakeholder Theory: The State of the Art* (Cambridge: Cambridge University Press, 2010).
[16] Pitt-Watson and Quigley, 9.

Part Four: Applications and Explanations

Economics, Character, and Values
Vital Questions in Society

Manfred Lautenschläger

I am delighted to be here with you today and to make my own contribution to the discussion of the extremely important topic of this conference.[1] To be honest, when I was invited to speak here, I initially wondered whether I would be able to make an adequate contribution to such an important issue, and whether, as an outsider, I would be able to hold my own in the presence of so many distinguished scholars. Ultimately, however, I concluded that I might be able to contribute something of substance. After all, the topic of the impact of markets on character formation—which is really the question about the extent to which the economy and character formation are related—has haunted me repeatedly throughout my life and in numerous different roles as a student, a businessman, a father of five children, and a donor.

I should clarify right away that I will not offer you any concrete answers. In fact, I will pose questions. I would then like to leave the search for answers to your academic discourse. Important ethical questions require a multifaceted discussion with interdisciplinary and potentially transdisciplinary approaches. A discussion about values needs to incorporate many disciplines and traditions. Consider the following examples of ethical problems we face today: genetic engineering and "gene scissors"; euthanasia, living wills, and palliative medicine; stem cell research and the question of when life actually begins; securing the world's food supply by potentially carcinogenic crop-protection agents. All of these examples show how various disciplines today need to communicate and interact. I quite intentionally chose examples that have a direct connection with departments and institutes at the University of Heidelberg, my alma mater.

Particularly in pluralistic societies, we must ask these questions and engage in broader and more profound debates. The academic world needs to work on these questions for the good of our society. That is exactly what you are doing.

---

[1] Presentation to conference on the impact of the economic market on character formation, University of Heidelberg, April 2018.

We also need a kind of institutional umbrella for dealing with these far-reaching questions. These problems are not easy to solve. They require a subtle discussion of informed hypotheses. The Forschungszentrum Internationale und Interdisziplinäre Theologie (Research Center for International and Interdisciplinary Theology) at the University of Heidelberg (FIIT) offers such an institutional umbrella. This is one reason why I have been supporting this institution and its ongoing discourses for many years.

From my perspective, modern ethics as a scholarly discipline must remain connected to the problems of everyday life. However, as I've mentioned, we need a structured discussion. We must seek a dialogue among the sciences, life sciences, and humanities. To my mind, this puts the world's leading universities, including Heidelberg, at the forefront of our societies' larger debates. And the FIIT is an ideal environment for such structured discussions. It is a beacon of scholarship recognized all over the world.

Following this declaration of love for my university, with which, as you may have noticed, I feel deeply connected, let us move to the interdisciplinary exchange regarding values, ethics, character formation, and *economics*. Really, there can be no discussion of such matters without mentioning a famous Heidelberger: the sociologist and economist Max Weber, who in 1896 took over the prestigious chair from Karl Knies at Ruprecht-Karls-Universität. It is hard to think of another sociologist anywhere in the world whose philosophy is more closely linked to the issues and questions of this conference. You are all familiar with Max Weber's famous thesis that a work ethic rooted in Calvinism and a pietistic worldview were the ultimate prerequisites for the success of the capitalist system in Central Europe, especially in Germany. Put simply, for Weber the spirit of capitalism is based on two virtues—a tremendous will to work and ascetic abstention from consumption.

His great work, *The Protestant Ethic and the Spirit of Capitalism*, is highly relevant to this day. In his book he offers causal relations between an (increasingly secularized) tradition of Protestant work ethics and the targeted reinvestment of profits earned, the subsequent accumulation of capital, and, as a result, the industrialization of Western Europe. The question of whether the inner-worldly asceticism of the restless entrepreneur and his worldly success can be interpreted as an indication of divine grace is better answered by theologians. For me, a lot of what Weber addresses in his work remains very reasonable to this day. In fact, I can say that, although I am not a religious person, the way of thinking described by Weber has definitely shaped my life—albeit unconsciously, perhaps.

I was not born to wealthy parents but was brought up at the lower end of the middle class. However, I was always able to understand the ethic of hard work that my father and mother pursued after the Second World War, when they were quite literally forced to rebuild their existence from ruins. This work ethic they shared with their contemporaries. It characterized the West German society during the reconstruction period: "Achieve, achieve, and achieve more!" There was simply no time for other things. I internalized this ethic, despite living a very different lifestyle as a student in Heidelberg's Old Town. Once I had escaped the strict restraints of my parental home, I enjoyed the total freedom that student life offered at the time. Back in the 1960s, we lived the kind of free life described by Henry Miller in his *Nights of Love and Laughter.* Night after night, we had discussions on whether the absolute value of achievement held by the reconstruction generation of our parents could be the only true meaning in life. These student years influenced me for the rest of my life, including my openness toward the nonprivileged classes of our society.

My later success as a businessman is largely the result of this notion of achievement. Yet the ideal of meritocracy, of an achievement-based society, does not suffice! For only those that make their achievements with passion and enjoyment will enjoy long-term success. For many people, myself included, finding pleasure in achievement also requires sufficient freedom to shape one's circumstances. The idea of working only according to established rules or norms (in German: *Dienst nach Vorschrift*) has never been my thing. This philosophy of achievement through passion and freedom is something I have always instilled at my company together with my employees, who were given the space they needed to develop their full potential. Our success, which naturally also involved a good deal of good luck, has confirmed this and thereby reinforced the principles that my parents taught me. I have experienced firsthand how ambition, knowledge, and achievement can pay off directly. The motivational boost that results from this is huge. I am convinced that a significant part of business success is based on actively living according to the Protestant work ethic. It is actually rather surprising for me that I can express this concept in these words standing here today. However, it was important and truly defining for me that the years of freedom I enjoyed as a student were what I would like to describe as a filter and a check on the ideology of achievement.

So far, I have focused on how an underlying set of values influences market activity. However, the title of your conference—if I am interpreting it correctly—sees this relationship entirely the other way around: To what extent does the market influence our values, and our ethical perceptions? How do we incorporate values into our lives today? I consider this inverted concept particularly exciting, as all great economists have actually asked themselves these and similar questions over and over again.

Walter Eucken, father of Germany's modern social market economy, never made a secret of his Christian convictions. Wilhelm Röpke—author of *Maß und Mitte* (Measure and center) and another of the great liberal economists of the Freiburg School—also wrote *Civitas Humana*, in which he addressed fundamental questions regarding social and economic reform. Even the founding father of modern economics, Adam Smith, wrote not only *The Wealth of Nations* but also *A Theory of Moral Sentiments*.

The question of how humane an economic system can be—or indeed must be—and how to achieve increased prosperity for all or for as many social classes as possible, is something that economics and its protagonists have addressed from the beginning. Today, it is a hotly contested issue in all industrialized societies. As I've mentioned, I devoted myself to questions of this kind particularly in my twenties, during my many late nights as a student working and enjoying life as a barkeeper, doorman, and DJ at Tangente, which was then *the* student club in Heidelberg. Bügelbrett, an award-winning student cabaret group, performed there several times a week. After their performances, we would discuss sociopolitical matters such as sexual liberation—the birth-control pill had just been invented—ethical indication for abortion, and many more.

In short, I was pretty far to the left on the political spectrum. This is nothing I regret, as we asked the right questions. The 1962 *Spiegel* Affair affected us, when Germany's defense minister, Franz-Josef Strauß, used his relationships with right-wing radicals in Franco's Spain to contravene existing laws and to have the *Der Spiegel* journalist Conrad Ahlers arrested while on holiday in Spain. Many judges in Germany were still the same ones who had suspended the rule of law and practiced injustice under the Nazi regime. Commenting on a blatant breach of the law—the detention of the *Spiegel* editor-in-chief Rudolf Augstein was nothing less—the then minister of interior of the Federal Republic of Germany simply stated: "You can't always be running around with a copy of the constitution under your arm." Bügelbrett wrote about this: "Again, it has happened again, yet another knock on the door, yet another constitution has collapsed."

Many years later, former Deutsche Bahn CEO Hartmut Mehdorn, at the time still CEO at Heidelberger Druckmaschinen, introduced me to former German Chancellor Helmut Schmidt during an event with these words: "This is the founder of one of the largest financial services providers in Europe and a former member of the '68 movement." Schmidt immediately responded with the question: "So when did you become reasonable?" I still smile when I think back to this meeting. Maybe I really became more reasonable when facing the realities of life. It led me to the insight that age always has an impact on values when it comes to economic thinking. In other words, your age affects the way you think. As I will be celebrating my eightieth birthday soon, I feel free to make comments like this. I also like the insight attributed variously to John Adams, Clemenceau, and Churchill: "Whoever is not a liberal at twenty has no heart. Whoever is still a liberal at thirty has no head." Yes, developments in the market and economic thinking shape our character, our set of values, and the way we live together in society. I believe this relationship to be something we can all understand.

I think I can justifiably claim to be a successful businessman. This is something I achieved despite, or perhaps because of, not spending my university time focusing on a career. I never pursued a streamlined career. After completing my state exam in law, I started working as an independent insurance broker, which at that time was regarded as a step down the social ladder compared to a career as a lawyer. I did it because I wanted to be independent. I hated hierarchies, because I was pursuing a new business idea, and because I enjoyed the advisory work itself. My free, politically left-wing student years had left their mark. I very quickly introduced a program of participation for my employees, so that they, too, could enjoy the fruits of our joint labor.

In 2000 I set up a foundation. I never forgot that my success and my prosperity were not just the result of my own competence but due also to the fact that I grew up here in the Federal Republic of Germany, one of the biggest success stories in history. I feel obliged to offer help where the state cannot help or is unable and unwilling to do so. I therefore use the means available to me to provide selective support to the socially deprived, to minorities suffering from persecution, both past and present, including Jews, Roma, and Sinti. I promote education for children and young people, sports and physical education, international cooperation and intercultural understanding, culture and art. These involvements, which I select and pursue personally, are no doubt a long-term effect of my unpretentious years as a student. Moreover, I always enjoyed interesting and rewarding meetings with people from completely different walks of life that truly transformed me.

As you may have noticed, and as I stated at the beginning, my talk today is not one that provides answers. It is not intended to do so. Therefore, allow me to share with you another thought as a proposal for discussion: What will happen to our society when the Protestant work ethic no longer holds us together? What will happen when this modern, pluralistic society, as we call it, no longer feels an obligation or commitment to this principle of achievement? What effect will this have on the Western world? What will be the impact on global understanding? In what way will this influence our position in the global markets?

I pose these questions as a way of stimulating discussion and further interdisciplinary research. As I mentioned at the start, I consider it essential to address important ethical questions from an interdisciplinary perspective. How can economic theory and theology be reconciled? Thomas Duve, director of the Max Planck Institute for European History of Law, in Frankfurt am Main, wrote about the minimum obligations that accompany the opportunities of globalization, making reference to the poverty crisis experienced in Spain in the sixteenth century. In 1545, Dominican Friar Domingo de Soto published a work titled *In causa pauperum deliberatio*—a deliberation in behalf of the poor. The theological school from which de Soto came is the famous School of Salamanca, which is of central importance to the history of law. Its influence can be seen to this day in international law. De Soto's focus is on poverty. The publication is based on the conviction that the poor are entitled to an income, and that this should be achieved practically. On one hand, those in need should have the right to receive everything they require in order to survive, while, on the other hand, we also have the duty to go further and provide the poor with decent life opportunities.

Nota bene: Domingo de Soto derived these concepts from the same reasons both he and others used to legitimize the free movement of goods. This is where our set of values and economics meet, where character and developments in the market come together—all on the basis of law and the interpretation of law. The key issue is this: in the age of the first conquests of new continents, the School of Salamanca assumed that there was a world community which was connected via *ius gentium*, a set of fundamental standards. This led to the idea of freedom of mobility, trade, or even defense of one's own religious convictions, that is, to do missionary work. Back then, the theologians used this *ius communicationis* to legitimize the Spanish presence in America. Imperialism, the colonialism of the modern era, is based on this body of thought. And it also serves as justification of the free movement of goods across the globe.

In this context, Thomas Duve correctly argues: "You do not need to be a scholastic from the sixteenth century to pose questions such as: What is the justification for giving companies the right to make money throughout the world when individuals cannot? Why do we demand the former as a right, yet ultimately view the latter as a discretionary act of humanity?" These are exciting and, for me, also truly central questions of an increasingly global (and in any case very mobile) society.

Dear participants of this conference: this leads us to a key point of all discussions in the context of theology, law, and our global understanding of economics—a key point at which we can redefine ourselves and our values between market, individual character, and ethical and moral positioning in an increasingly pluralistic society. This includes the question of how we handle the current realities of poverty-driven migration. What can we learn from the *ius gentium* of the scholastics?

Allow me to end with the following observation: we need a broad academic discourse; we need to come together and discuss the issues. We constantly need to ensure that we can find intelligent answers to the truly *big* questions of our diverse, colorful, modern, and pluralistic society that can be accepted by the majority.

At this point, I remind you of Max Weber, who differentiated between the ethics of conviction and the ethics of responsibility. After all, a spontaneous "we'll make it" without setting the conditions for doing so, for answering the question of *how* we'll make it, is unlikely to achieve anything meaningful. If we fail to discuss or to engage in intellectual discourse, there will be a greater risk that we will simply accept easy answers, allow populist assaults, and waste opportunities to help our society move forward. My request is, therefore: Please, let us strive to talk about these issues. Bring both questions and findings to the public arena.

I am genuinely delighted to have been invited to speak at this conference. I am pleased because there are so few opportunities to discuss and reflect on central questions. I am very grateful to have been given such an opportunity here today. This conference poses important, relevant, decisive questions. Let us now work together to find answers.

NICE WORDS ARE FINE, BUT HENS LAY EGGS
COMMUNICATION ABOUT VALUES LEADS TO EXPECTATIONS OF PRACTICAL CONSEQUENCES

Klaus Leisinger

The term "value," it seems, is in high demand. Particularly in turbulent times, political, corporate, and other communication on values takes off. This is a gratifying development, because values are important poles on which to base the compass of action. A discourse on values can help to weigh benefits and risks of different courses of action in dilemma situations, whether in business, politics, or elsewhere.

- There is currently a widespread uneasiness if not discontent about the practical responsibility of business leaders and senior government officials in practically all industrial countries.[1] The common reaction is a lot of talk about values—talk seldom followed up, if measured by key performance indicators.
- When talking about core values (*Grundwerte*) the German Social Democratic Party (SPD) refers to the ideals of the French Revolution: Liberty, Equality, and Fraternity. They claim that these values are their criteria for assessing political reality, a benchmark for a better society, and an orientation for the actions of social democrats.[2]
- The Christian Democratic Party (CDU) goes on record that it is aware of its responsibility before God and humankind and is guided by the Christian image of humanity and inviolable human dignity, and thus by the fundamental values of freedom, solidarity, and justice.[3] Looking at the current polls in Germany, people do not have the feeling that key personnel of the political parties are living up to their proclaimed values.

Values talk also has become fashionable in the business sector—particularly if something has gone really wrong.

---

[1] Edelman Trust Barometer 2018, http://cms.edelman.com/sites/default/files/2018-02/2018_Edelman_Trust_Barometer_Global_Report_FEB.pdf–and the picture barely changed in 2019.
[2] SPD Grundwerte: https://grundwertekommission.spd.de/grundwerte/.
[3] CDU Grundsatzprogramm: https://www.cdu-much.de/partei/wertekatalog/.

- Presumably as a result of the public naming and shaming after reports relating to higher-than-reported emissions from diesel engines, the Volkswagen Group announced the development of six "new values": "We are customer-oriented, efficient, and courageous. We act sincerely, treat each other with respect, and achieve our goals together."[4]
- Audi stipulates in its management concept (*Führungsleitbild*) that "We are aware of our role model function. We are responsible and credible—we walk the talk and live our management model. We treat others with respect and appreciation."[5]
- When visiting the Code of Conduct and Ethics Code of Deutsche Bank—the bank that appeared prominently in the news in the context of interest-rate manipulations—one finds wonderful sentences such as, "We always adhere to the highest standards of integrity—in words and in deeds. We do what is not only legally permissible but also correct. We speak openly. We encourage, express, and respect constructive criticism. We abide by rules and stand by our promises without ifs and buts."[6]
- Last but not least, the German Soccer Association (DFB), looking for a scapegoat for the lack of success at the FIFA World Cup tournament, criticized one of their technically best players for agreeing to be photographed with the president of Turkey, the country of his ancestors. The association thus clearly violated his right to freedom of opinion. The DFB website contains a code of ethics which lists values such as "Respect and diversity, fair play on and off the pitch, integrity in sporting and economic competition, transparency as the basis for trust, solidarity as well as health and environment as a commitment and opportunity."[7]

We could go on quoting value statements of political, commercial, and civil society institutions, compare their content with selected examples of practical behavior, and burst into criticism and cynical comments. Instead, however, we will draw a *first conclusion: it is much easier to formulate values and publish them in a professional manner than to live up to them consistently and coherently in a complex world full of dilemmas.*

And yet, the commitment to values is certainly important for business enterprises: being profitable in a global marketplace necessitates wise management of ambiguities, trade-offs, and moral dilemmas—tasks that can be handled consis-

---

[4] http://inside.volkswagen.de/Unsere-neuen-Werte.html.

[5] AUDI Führungsleitbild (my translation), https://www.audi.com/content/dam/com/DE/careers/Fuehrungsleitbild_deutsch.pdf.

[6] Verhaltens und Ethikkodex Deutsche Bank: https://www.db.com/ir/de/download/Verhaltens-_und_Ethikkodex_09_2015.pdf.

[7] Ethik-Kodes DFB: https://www.dfb.de/fileadmin/_dfbdam/128752-04_Ethik-Kodex.pdf.

tently only by a values-based management. There is no template for being sustainably successful in an ever-changing commercial environment, but for managers doing business with integrity there is a nonnegotiable will to stay within a corridor of normative rules in everything they do. A coherent corporate culture is needed in order to live up to such good intentions consistently. This again requires that the financial, social, and ecological objectives and targets, the performance appraisals, promotion criteria, and incentive and bonus systems must be enriched by values and operationalized by principles that encourage consistent values-based management.

VALUES-BASED MANAGEMENT

There are several ways to define values-based management, but they have an important common denominator: the understanding of *value* created by a business enterprise is not restricted to financial and other economic indicators but includes indicators of natural capital and social capital as well as normative considerations with regard to achieving the desired financial results in a sustainable way. Corporate leadership selects from the multitude of potentially possible courses of action and behavior those achievable in accordance with the core values and normative principles defined. In this way, management strives to achieve sustained value-added for shareholders and stakeholders—a strategy that was backed in the summer of 2019 by the US Business Roundtable[8] and supported by the new Davos Manifesto formulated by the president of the World Economic Forum, Klaus Schwab.[9]

A short remark on the subject of stakeholders: If we define a company's stakeholders as individuals or groups who are or are perceived to be affected by a company's decisions, policies, and practices or are able to affect them, corporate leadership will have to know and prioritize those stakeholders according to strategic importance, be in regular dialogue with them, and be responsive to their demands.[10] Decisively important in this regard are awareness of and sensitivity

---

[8] Business Roundtable: "Business Roundtable Redefines the Purpose of a Corporation to Promote' An Economy That Serves all Americans,'" Washington, DC, August 19, 2019: www.businessroundtable.org/business-roundtable-redefines-the-purpose-of-a-corporation-to-promote-an-economy-that-serves-all-americans.

[9] World Economic Forum: Davos Manifesto 2020: "The Universal Purpose of a Company in the Fourth Industrial Revolution" (Cologne/ Geneva, December 2, 2019), www.weforum.org/agenda/2019/12/davos-manifesto-2020-the-universal-purpose-of-a-company-in-the-fourth-industrial-revolution/.

[10] For more, see R. Edward Freeman, et al., *Stakeholder Theory: The State of the Art* (New York: Cambridge University Press, 2010).

to the fact that different stakeholders value different things in different cultural and socioeconomic settings, and that a VUCA[11] world makes corporate strategy more complex.[12]

VALUES-BASED MANAGEMENT STEP 1: WHAT VALUES ARE IMPORTANT TO US AS CORPORATE LEADERS?

Since the early 1970s, conferences have been held and countless articles and books published on the ethical state of affairs of business.[13] Corporate actions are analyzed from a *moral point of view* with the tools of moral philosophy. A nondelegable part of the responsibility of business (and other!) leaders is the *reflection of and decision on the specific values and norms which should guide, encourage, and limit the scope of action and behavior* in everyday business life. For a variety of reasons, this is easier said than done, as there are multiple ethical schools recommending different concepts of right and wrong, and people with integrity can choose to apply different ways and methods to determine the desirable path of action. Business leaders following, for instance, Francis Hutcheson's maxim to create "the greatest happiness of the greatest number"[14] will judge available strategic options differently than those who perceive John Rawls's "MaxiMin principle" as the most appropriate path to follow.[15]

Nevertheless, the top management's answer on the question *"What is important to us?"* must be the first step. This step must ideally be prepared and accompanied by experts. Employees and customers ought to be invited to propose values from their perspective. Business leaders doing business with integrity as well as leaders in the political or religious sector will acknowledge the importance of ethical values such as *honesty, truthfulness, respect, transparency, and tolerance.* But then, different subsystems of society will emphasize different value priorities.

In his encyclical letter *Laudate Si'*, Pope Francis emphasizes values such as a *strong sense of community, readiness to protect others,* and a *deep love for land* (LS 179) as well as *profound humanism* (LS 181). He condemns *short-term gain*

---

[11] VUCA is the acronym for Volatility, Uncertainty, Complexity, and Ambiguity; see N. Bennett and G. J. Lemoine, "What VUCA Means for You," *Harvard Business Review* (Jan.-Feb. 2014).

[12] See K.M. Leisinger, "Corporate Responsibility in a World of Cultural Diversity and Pluralism of Values," *Journal of International Business Ethics* 8/2 (Beijing 2015).

[13] See as an excellent summary G.G. Brenkert and T.L. Beauchamp, eds., *The Oxford Handbook on Business Ethics* (Oxford: Oxford University Press, 2012).

[14] See https://www.iep.utm.edu/hutcheso/: "that action is best, which procures the greatest happiness for the greatest numbers; and that, worst, which, in like manner, occasions, misery."

[15] John Rawls, *A Theory of Justice*, rev. ed. (Cambridge, MA: Harvard University Press, 1999).

and *private interest* (LS 184). He warns that ecological and social values are "absorbed into the categories of finance and technocracy" (LS 194) and that "social and environmental responsibility of businesses often gets reduced to a series of marketing and image-enhancing measures." Economic and technological progress, unless accompanied by authentic social and moral progress, says Pope Francis, "will definitely turn against man" (LS 4).

Business leaders will first and foremost emphasize performance values such as *efficiency, effectiveness, competence, quality,* and *diligence.* Enlightened business leaders will also mention values such as integrity, fairness and tolerance. This is not a question of either/or but one about how to embed performance values in ethical values. In other words, if and when business leadership is confronted with a conflict of values resulting in a conflict of interest, which value has the higher priority for solving the dilemma? To give an example: the oil company BP defines five values, providing "a fixed point of reference for the way we operate and behave." These values are *safety* ("We care about the safe management of the environment"); *respect* ("We hold ourselves to the highest ethical standards and behave in ways that earn the trust of others."); *excellence* ("We commit to quality outcomes."); *courage* ("We always strive to do the right thing."); and *being one team* ("Whatever the strength of the individual, we will accomplish more together.").[16] Comparing these value statements and analyzing the consequences of the Deepwater Horizon oil spill[17] will leave even well-meaning observers in distress.

A *second conclusion: while it is important that business leadership (or leadership of other institutions) reflects about values and defines those they strive to be accountable for, each and every institution consists of human beings—and human beings are fallible. Leaders of different institutions may feel committed to the same abstract values, but since they have different tasks, they will understand and contextualize these values in different ways and complement them with values that are important in their work settings.* So one has also to put value statements in perspective.

VALUES-BASED MANAGEMENT STEP 2: PUTTING THINGS IN CONTEXT

Who is responsible for what?

Operationalizing and contextualizing values is as complex a step as the first. The application of defined core values derived from a specific school of philosophical thought in a real-life situation like doing business is implicitly based on a presupposition of what constitutes a fair division of duty and responsibility. Different

---

[16] BP: Our Values and Code of Conduct: https://www.bp.com/en/global/corporate/who-we-are/our-values-and-code-of-conduct.html..

[17] See https://en.wikipedia.org/wiki/Deepwater_Horizon_oil_spill.

assumptions in this regard result in the determination of different rights and duties—for example, between the political sector and the economic sector, between the legal system and religious systems, and among art, education, and other spheres of activity.

Depending on how an *impartial spectator* (a concept used by Adam Smith) defines the proper division of responsibility and duty in a society, he or she will come to different judgments about the "job description" of actors in the economic subsystem, that is, business managers. Modern societies are shaped by a pronounced *functional differentiation*. They organize their economic, social, cultural, political, and other processes by delegating specific tasks to specific subsystems.[18] Different subsystems have different functions, and, as a consequence, actors in the different subsystems have different roles, competences, skills, and responsibilities. They also avail themselves of specific knowledge, skills, resources, and interests—and pursue specific objectives. Anyone who lives in a small village knows that one can expect different services from the pastor than from the mayor, the village policeman, or the shopkeeper.

Actors in the different subsystems work to a certain extent self-referentially and evolve within applicable law. They are to a certain degree decoupled from other societal subsystems and thus from their specific rules, processes, objectives, and interests. Running a corporation implies having different interests and necessitates different professional knowledge and skills than, for instance, being in charge of a parish, a magistracy, or an orphanage. However, as long as people act in the different subsystems within a corridor of widely shared values safeguarding the dignity of the human person, the differences in interests, skills, and objectives are not an ethical issue. But even if this question is answered, expectations of what business enterprises are supposed to deliver vary.

In the understanding of what corporations are responsible for, the European Commission mentions

> human rights, labor, and employment practices (such as training, diversity, gender equality, and employee health and well-being), environmental issues (such as biodiversity, climate change, resource efficiency, life-cycle assessment, and pollution prevention), and combating bribery and corruption. Community involvement and development, the integration of disabled persons, and consumer interests, including

---

[18] N. Luhmann, *Die Gesellschaft der Gesellschaft* (Frankfurt am Main: Suhrkamp, 1997); also Talcott Parsons, *The System of Modern Societies* (Englewood Cliffs, NJ: Prentice-Hall, 1971).

privacy, are also part of the CSR agenda. The promotion of social and environmental responsibility through the supply-chain, and the disclosure of nonfinancial information, are recognized as important cross-cutting issues.[19]

An alternative view that still guides the moral compass of many US-American and Anglo-Saxon managers was voiced by Milton Friedman in an essay to the *New York Times* in September 1970. Based on his book *Capitalism and Freedom*, he went on record that "there is one and only one social responsibility of business—to use its resources and engage in activities designed to increase its profits so long as it stays within the rules of the game, which is to say, engages in open and free competition without deception or fraud."[20] To be fair, Friedman qualified his statement with "so long as it stays within the rules of the game," and the rules of the game are different in pluralistic societies in a globalized economy than they were in the Cold War era when he was writing. But even after considering a change in public expectations, Friedman's understanding is clearly narrower than that of the EU Commission.

Only if and when business leaders create transparency and communicate what they perceive to be a fair societal division of duty and responsibility and what values have compass function for them will they be able to explain their view of the world with regard to the basics of their corporate-responsibility philosophy. Even then, there is a lack of specificity.

Values Have a Thick and a Thin Meaning

In 1989 Michael Walzer, like many others, saw television pictures of people marching in the streets of Prague, carrying signs, some of which were simply saying "truth" or "justice." He remembers having understood immediately what the signs meant and—like everyone else who saw the pictures—recognizing and acknowledging the values that the marchers were defending: "I could have walked comfortably in their midst. I could carry the same signs."[21] The following reflection of Walzer is of great importance to the corporate value discourse:

---

[19] European Commission: "A renewed EU strategy 2011–14 for Corporate Responsibility," Brussels, 2011: http://www.europarl.europa.eu/meetdocs/2009_2014/documents/com/com_com(2011)0681_/com_com(2011)0681_en.pdf.

[20] Milton Friedman, "The Social Responsibility of Business is to Increase its Profits," *The New York Times*, Sept. 13, 1970, http://graphics8.nytimes.com/packages/pdf/business/miltonfriedman1970.pdf.

[21] Michael Walzer, *Thick and Thin: Moral Argument at Home and Abroad* (Notre Dame, IN: University of Notre Dame Press, 1994), 1.

> They were not marching in defense of the coherence theory, or the consensus theory, or the correspondence theory of truth. Perhaps they disagreed about such theories among themselves; more likely, they did not care about them. No particular account of truth was at issue here. The march had nothing to do with epistemology. Or, better, the epistemological commitments of the marchers were so elementary that they could be expressed in any of the available theories—except those that denied the very possibility of statements being "true." The marchers wanted to hear true statements from their political leaders; they wanted to be able to believe what they read in the newspapers, they didn't want to be lied to anymore…. [U]ndoubtedly, they would have argued, if pressed, for different distributive programs; they would have described a just society in different ways; they would have urged different rationales for reward and punishment; they would have drawn on different accounts of history and culture. What they meant by "justice" inscribed on their signs, however, was simple enough: an end to arbitrary arrests, equal and impartial law enforcement, the abolition of privileges and prerogatives of the party elite—common, garden variety justice.[22]

Walzer described a fact that is most underrated in the modern discourse about corporate values: "Moral terms have minimal and maximal meanings; we can standardly give thin and thick accounts of them, and the two accounts are appropriate to different contexts, serve different purposes."[23]

My forty years' professional experience are full of evidence of identical normative terms being used in stakeholder dialogues by corporate spokespersons and representatives of nongovernmental organizations. The problem, however, was and is that agreement on the values discussed was on both sides abstract and general—in Walzer's terms, "thin." Applying the abstract values to a specific context—in Walzer's terms making them "thick"—led to totally different conclusions. The underlying reasons were in most cases not bad will or evil tactics, but the result of different worldviews and axiomatic assumptions. Human beings perceive the world around them through filters made up of personal preferences, judgments, worldviews, and lessons learned from past experience. Together, these determine the way they construct "reality."[24]

Our individually constructed reality is not an objective representation of measurable facts and existing issues, but the subjective result of the assimilation,

---

[22] Ibid., 1–2.

[23] Ibid., 2.

[24] For an introduction to constructivism, see Paul Watzlawick, ed., *The Invented Reality: How do We Know What We Believe We Know?* (New York: W.W. Norton, 1984); Heinz von Foerster, *Understanding Understanding* (New York: Springer, 2003); and Ernst von Glasersfeld, *Radical Constructivism: A Way of Knowing and Learning* (London: Falmer Press, 1995). See also Rupert Lay, *Die Zweite Aufklärung. Einführung in den Konstruktivismus* (Frankfurt 2015), http://www.karl-schlecht.de/fileadmin/daten/Download/Buecher/Rupert_Lay_-_Die_Zweite_Aufklaerung_-_2._Auflage_2015.pdf.

accommodation, and adaptation processes we undergo in our lives. Once human beings in all subsystems of society are convinced that their definition of the problem is accurate and their solution the best under the prevailing circumstances, they stop searching for alternative ways to address a problem. Self-referential simplification ("the problem is very simple, you only have to...") is the mode of doing business as usual, not the willingness to evaluate the pluralism of perspectives.

Therefore, a general support of global values, such as justice and fairness, does not mean that well-meaning people all over the world understand the same normative content and act coherently—neither in private nor in business life. If, for example, a corporate-responsibility guideline articulates that "we treat everyone just and fairly," the interpretation of its implicit "must do" or "ought to do" will differ among an Indian, a Chinese, and a Swiss businessman or businesswoman and their counterparts in specialized NGOs. Reasonable people all over the world and in all subsystems of society will agree that justice, integrity, and fairness as well as truthfulness and freedom *are* important values. However, this abstract acknowledgment has to be contextualized. It must be made thick, in Walzer's terms: moral deliberations must be done "in a thick manner, accounting for the specificities of the actual situation in which a decision has to be taken.... The claim that we must all be heading in the same direction since there is only one direction in which good-hearted (or ideological correct) men and women can possibly march is an example of philosophical high-mindedness. But it does not fit our moral experience."[25]

The problem that arises here is that, on one hand, any business operating in different countries must not only comply with local law and regulation but also, to be successful in the local market, become to a certain extent part of the local culture. On the other hand, internationally the business has only one reputation. Too much adaptation to the locally recognized customs and traditions creates international reputational risks.

A third conclusion: when communicating on values, make sure that they are contextualized so that resulting expectations can be managed.

VALUES-BASED MANAGEMENT STEP 3: CHANGING THE UNDERSTANDING OF "BUSINESS AS USUAL"

To shape business practice in a way and to an extent that a *values-driven responsibility culture* develops in which the appropriateness of certain courses of action and behavior is self-evident for all, while other courses of action and behavior are naturally excluded by all, requires a leadership decision on values—but only as a first step. After defining the corporate values against which business leaders want to be held accountable, a comprehensive ethics program has to be installed.

---

[25] Walzer, *Thick and Thin*, 9.

Insights from the London-based Institute of Business Ethics[26] suggest that, on one hand, pressure to compromise ethical standards has risen; on the other hand, there is clear evidence, that measures to support ethical behavior by comprehensive ethics programs[27] make a measurable positive difference: organizations with ethics programs act more responsibly. In organizations with comprehensive ethics programs, 86 percent of employees say their organizations act responsibly in all their business dealings. This compares with 57 percent in organizations without an ethics program.

- Employees in organizations with ethics programs are more likely to speak out about misconduct: 73 percent of employees in organizations with comprehensive ethics programs who were aware of misconduct spoke out, as opposed to 42 percent in organizations without ethics programs.
- Organizations with ethics programs are better at dealing with ethical issues raised by employees: 78 percent of employees in organizations with comprehensive ethics programs who were aware of misconduct and spoke out are satisfied with the result of doing so, as opposed to 28 percent in organizations without ethics programs.
- Line managers in organizations with ethics programs set better examples: 83 percent of employees in organizations with comprehensive ethics programs say their line manager sets a good example of ethical behavior, in comparison with 46 percent in organizations without ethics programs.

CREATING A NEW UNDERSTANDING OF "BUSINESS AS USUAL"

If and when corporate leadership wants to change what is perceived to be *business as usual*, additional steps are recommended.[28] Leadership should be clear about the business's purpose—reflecting on and deciding why they are doing what they are doing and what is the end-means relation—and then should align corporate products and services as well as the whole portfolio of corporate action with the purpose. If, as the Davos Manifesto 2020 suggests, the purpose of a company in its specific core competence is to engage all its stakeholders on shared and sustained

---

[26] Institute of Business Ethics, G. Dondé, "Ethics at Work. 2018 Survey of employees " (London, 2018), https://www.ibe.org.uk/userassets/publicationdownloads/ibe_survey_report_ethics_at_work_2018_survey_of_employees_europe_int.pdf.

[27] Defined as the package of having written standards of ethical business conduct; providing a means of reporting misconduct confidentially; offering advice or an information helpline about behaving ethically; and providing training on ethical conduct.

[28] See as an introduction The Leipzig Leadership Model, https://www.hhl.de/en/about/leipzig-leadership-model/; see also D. Grayson, C. Coulter, and M. Lee, *All In: The Future of Business Leadership* (New York: Routledge, 2018).

value creation, if fair competition and a level playing field are accepted and supported and people inside and in the supply chain are treated with dignity and respect, then a special kind of people is necessary—top leadership has to choose the right people when hiring and promoting.

What is needed are human beings "characterized by respect for the dignity of fellow human beings and their entitlement to freedom and participation" (Leipzig Leadership Model). They are leaders who practice *love* in Erich Fromm's understanding of *care, sense of responsibility, respect for others, and knowledge*.[29] The personality of the people hired and promoted is the single most important success factor for values-based management. The reason is obvious. Business reality is far too complex to be governed by codes of conduct and corporate guidelines. Many problems that responsibility bearers have to deal with are *wicked problems*. "Tame problems" are clearly definable and can be solved under all circumstances with preexisting modes of data research pathways, decision preparation, and decision making. "Wicked problems," in contrast, often have no *right or wrong* solutions but only *better or worse* ones—particularly as judgments of stakeholders with different values, interests, and cultural background are likely to differ.[30]

Mature personalities in such situations must act like situation ethicists. They must focus on the outcome of their decision in relation to the values they are committed to and the goals they aspire to achieve. The corporate guidelines and codes of conduct must be used as compass and signposts, but the right thing to do in a critical situation or moral dilemma, according to Joseph Fletcher, depends on the case.[31] But as the "good people" chosen should not suffer materially from acting responsibly, treating people in a respectful way and inviting stakeholder dialogue, the whole corporate responsibility portfolio must reflect the spirit of the values chosen. Furthermore, since good people are likely to be particularly sensitive to what is measured and rewarded, codes of conduct, corporate guidelines for sensitive areas, target setting, incentive systems, performance appraisals, and bonus systems must be enriched in the light of the purpose defined and the values committed to.

---

[29] K.M. Leisinger, *Die Kunst der verantwortungsvollen Führung* (Bern: Paul Haupt, 2018).
[30] H.W.J. Rittel and M.M. Webber, "Dilemmas in a General Theory of Planning," *Policy Sciences* 4 (1973): 155–69.
[31] Joseph Fletcher, *Situation Ethics: The New Morality* (Louisville, KY: Westminster John Knox Press, 1966).

Serious Values-Based Management Is No Easy Undertaking

Doing all this is a very challenging, even strenuous effort which absorbs considerable resources and management attention. A pharmaceutical company, for example, would have to implement all of this across research and development, production, marketing, finance, and supply chain as well as in all detailed work streams within these departments. Within the different departments, all activities would have to be analyzed and their ethical quality judged in the light of the corporate values commitment. In addition, such a company would have to develop business models that "leave no one behind," as the preamble of the Agenda 2030[32] articulates. Moreover, as this work is for the most innovative medicines, the company would have to organize clinical trials in a way that protects the dignity of the trial participants and respects their entitlements.[33]

The implementation of value-based management helps to avoid the risk of reputation-damaging misconduct in the medium and long term and thus contributes to a good reputation. In the short term, however, it is associated with additional costs and management time. This creates a dilemma for financial analysts, as their focus is on short-term financial results. There is empirical evidence that "good" companies that take sustainability and other values seriously—and therefore follow a strategic approach and invest in policies and compliance measures to guide their impact on society and on the environment—outperform companies that don't.

But then: this outperformance occurs only in the longer term.[34] A values-based management culture that measures corporate success in financial, social, and ecological terms, but is engaged in a global competitive environment in which main competitors couldn't care less about people and the environment, is likely to have short-term competitive disadvantages. Corporate managers that base their strategic considerations exclusively on the signals sent out by the financial market are likely to run a higher risk of causing social and ecological collateral dam-

---

[32] See Agenda 2030 for Sustainable Development, https://sustainabledevelopment.un.org/post2015/transformingourworld.

[33] See in this context the Global Conduct for Research in Resource-Poor Settings, developed by the TRUST project, http://www.globalcodeofconduct.org; see also K.M. Leisinger, "Using the World Ethos Body of Thought as a Compass for Managers: Some Thoughts on the Practical Application of a Philosophical Concept," in *Weltethos für das 21. Jahrhundert*, ed. Ulrich Hemel (Freiburg: Herder, 2019).

[34] R. G. Eccles, I. Ioannou, and G. Serafeim, "The Impact of Corporate sustainability on Organizational Processes and Performance" (Cambridge, MA: National Bureau of Economic Research, 2012), https://www.hbs.edu/faculty/Publication%20Files/SSRN-id1964011_6791edac-7daa-4603-a220-4a0c6c7a3f7a.pdf.

age, even if this is not intentional—but share prices usually do not reflect such risks. This makes "good" companies vulnerable to hostile takeover attempts by companies who are more profitable in the short-term and have a higher shareholder value.[35]

Outlook

Values-based management is a marathon, not a short-distance race. It therefore needs deep convictions on the side of corporate leaders, corporate stamina, and a growing support by customers and the financial community. But the social, environmental, and political challenges of our time, in particular the implementation of Agenda 2030 for sustainable development, cannot be met if all societal actors continue to use *the business as usual approach of the past 25 years*. Balancing the different economic, social, and ecological requirements while avoiding collateral damage to the detriment of people living in the future necessitates reforms for all societal actors. Business corporations, however, have a special responsibility to manage the necessary change—and value-based management is the most promising way to achieve that.

Since reform processes of the kind outlined here are complicated and take time to succeed, business leaders must invest much more time and effort in communication than ever before. Not only do they have to communicate about purpose and values, but they also have to explain in an easily understandable manner:
- what they are doing differently, with what kind of impact and why;
- where they meet the obstacles in their endeavors and with what costs implications; and
- where they perceive the business case of values-based management to be (e.g., higher employee satisfaction and better motivation, less fluctuation, higher customer loyalty, investment of ethical investment funds, etc.).

The discourse on values in business is not a top-down matter. Successful communication programs include businesspeople, business ethicists, and civil society representatives. And they must transcend ideological and partisan divide. A societal values discourse must be based on the honest willingness to acknowledge that one side alone neither holds all the answers nor has the necessary resources to transform theoretical solutions into practical policy. Genuinely listening to other views opens up sources of different worldviews and new knowledge.

---

[35] P. Polman, "How I Fended off a Hostile Takeover Bid," https://www.ft.com/content/76cddc3e-d42e-11e7-a303-9060cb1e5f44.

Corporate communication about values and ethical issues is likely to result not only in better understanding but also in higher expectation and more intense scrutiny by media, NGOs, employees, and customers. Not only is complete truthfulness necessary, but strategies of *underpromise and overdelivery* are also advisable. The fundamental precondition for sustained credibility is walking the talk and delivering action that is beneficial to all corporate stakeholders, including the stakeholders.

Entrepreneurs' Ethics in South East Asia

Some Insights from Expert Interviews

Michael Welker

In 2015, the Karl Schlecht Stiftung invited us to develop a research project on the topic "Traditional Norms and International Corporate Responsibility and Integrity in Southeast Asian Contexts." The question was how traditional norms—not only Confucian or Buddhist ones but also those of other religions, secular-ethical norms, or nationally conditioned norms—and international corporate responsibility and integrity are related in Southeast Asian contexts. We invited several, mostly young scholars (most of them with a European doctoral degree) from universities in South Korea, the People's Republic of China, Hong Kong, Taiwan, and Japan to cooperate in this project. Each scholar was asked to address two or three internationally operating corporations in his own country, and to conduct and evaluate expert interviews with representatives of those corporations.

The interviews were to be concerned with the presentation of the profile of the corporation in question and the profile of the person interviewed. They should contain differentiated questions regarding normative ethical (both religious and secular) foundations in the company's management and their concrete effects on the corporation's entrepreneurial conduct:
- Are the values mediated to the employees, and—if so—in which ways?
- Are the values also mediated to further national or international publics?

We wrote a sixty-six-page evaluation of the interviews and brought six Asian experts from the business sector (chosen on the basis of the interviews) and six Asian scholars to a consultation at the FIIT in the spring of 2016. In the following, I present some of the results of the interviews and our discussions in Heidelberg. The project continues to aim at expanding the perspectives into the realms of religion and culture in a dialogue between South Korean and German experts in theology, ethical studies, and diaconal research, for which we selected the general title "Justice and Righteousness: Divine and Human."

Business and Daoist Religion

A highly profiled conversation partner was Ke Shu Shuquan, the owner and chairman of Guangdong Tai-an Tang, a Shanghai-based producer of traditional Chinese medicine, with five thousand employees at eleven locations. The firm has been owned by a family through thirteen generations since 1567. The head of this firm emphasized the strong connection to and cultivation of traditional value systems (Daoism, Yin-Yang, and the theory of the Five Elements) with modern technology in production and marketing. The firm has established and maintains several research centers and centers for the promotion of cultural values. The owner repeatedly emphasized the values of modesty, gratitude, attempts to benefit humanity, and avoidance of aggressive competition and fights.

It was not easy for the Westerners and the Asian colleagues educated in Western institutions to understand the translation of Daoist value systems and other Chinese classics into technical and economic processes. The Chinese firm, however, is building a center for traditional Chinese medicine (TMC) in Los Angeles and intends to build more centers in England and Germany.

Very important for them is the cultivation of a corporate culture. The firm is seen as a big family, and each morning at 8 o'clock there is a joint declaration of common values. Training programs, intended to enhance the well-being of individuals, make sure that this is not just a rhetorical enterprise. The firm's outreach into the society as a whole is important. Active support for poor, physically disabled, and lonesome old people, as well as relief activities in pressing catastrophes (for example, earthquakes) is strong. Equally important is the company's support of general education and the dissemination of medically relevant knowledge—in libraries, museums, and electronic media. Not only the economic success of the company but also communicative success in the form of feedback from employees and customers (pharmacists, doctors, and patients) are of high relevance.

Another participant with a Daoist background from Taiwan was present. Joseph Roan is the deputy chairman of China Commodity Exchange, Co., a globally active corporation connected with the Chinese Ministry of Foreign Trade. The corporation (CCE) accompanies and steers credit-based transactions all over the world. Chairman Roan, who lives in Taipei, is not only an entrepreneur but also a Daoist priest of the third grade. He estimates that the CEOs of 50 percent of the 100 largest firms in Taiwan follow a Daoist orientation, while 40 percent have a Christian background. In the Daoist orientation, the rhythms of nature and the seasons are of particular importance, as are the rules and rhythms of religious rituals. These rhythms are thought to contribute to the harmony and balance of both personal life and business life.

A complex pattern of relations guarantees this harmony, first in the relations of the family, then in the professional relations to colleagues and coworkers in order to balance professional success and social responsibility. Modesty, tranquility, self-discipline, and the search for good order are to be cultivated over against aggressive political and economic attitudes. The Daoist orientation offers a blissful impetus and counterbalance by emphasizing the value of trust, first in relation to the gods, then in the cycles of nature, and finally in other human beings, as in loyalty towards one's leaders and one's corporation.

In his own firm, Chairman Roan tries to create trust in the midst of economic and political relations of distrust. He sees good models in the Japanese culture and expresses a certain skepticism about the Chinese and the Russians. His corporation invests 10 percent of its income in the education of its employees, as an endeavor to create familiarity with good philosophical and ethical principles and models. He sees difficulties in the attempts to mediate United Nations values (Global Compact, CSR) in Asian countries.

Business and Confucian Values

Confucian values and the experience of the Chinese Cultural Revolution and the reforms of Deng Xiaoping inspired the entrepreneurial Wang Xu Ning of the Joyoung Company, who invented a soymilk machine and created and shaped a whole new consumer market, changing the breakfast and nourishment habits of millions of Chinese families. Four thousand employees, mostly young people, work for the firm, which is now centered in Hong Kong.

The Confucian values of altruism, honesty, and family piety are emphasized, and the climate of solidarity and fraternity in family and in the business are underscored. Again, the practice of incorporating these values is important for the social and cultural life in the firm and extends into consultations in the choice of partners and the foundation of families.

The striving for economic success of the firm is connected with work for a healthy lifestyle in general. Active support for the poor and the needy is organized under the name of Project Hope. In poor parts of the country, schools are built, and poor children are supported. Exemplary kitchens and canteens have been built in fourteen provinces, so that the living conditions of 150,000 children from poor regions have been improved.

Business and Buddhist Values

After studying in Taiwan and Japan and working as the CEO in the Sony Group for eighteen years, managing director Andy Cheng founded his own company in 2011–AZIO Electronics Co., a small company with fifteen employees and annual net revenues of 2.5 million US dollars. Mr. Cheng regards himself as a Buddhist and tries to keep a Buddhist orientation in his entrepreneurial activities. The religious traditions help him to find and keep inner and outer peace, to abstract from evil conditions, and to block impulses of hate and anger. They promote a successful life, which is accompanied by happiness and health. Most important for this successful life are good relations within the family. Mr. Cheng values his life with his Japanese wife and their three daughters most highly.

He is convinced that in public life and in economic processes, value-orientation is crucial, above all the value of loyalty. A friendly, honest, and reliable communication with customers and coworkers has to be cultivated. The success model of his firm is one of reliable service and long-term stability rather than undercutting of prices of competitors. He points to Japanese and British business strategies as good examples. He is convinced that the imperialistic background of these countries helps them develop cultural stability, maturity, and patience, and the betting on slow and long-term oriented processes of growth. He does not think that these mentalities are as strongly developed in the United States and China. In his own context, he complains of the pressure toward conformity over against the support of creativity.

With respect to his employees, he developed the so-called PURE approach—nurturing the values of "passion, unity, respect, and enjoyment." Small practical and symbolic actions in his firm have helped to implement these values: a spirit of commitment and dedication; community spirit and solidarity; the will to cooperate and be fair; and personal satisfaction and joie de vivre. Examples of these actions are the installation of waste disposals at beaches, blood donations, help after catastrophes, and support of local schools. Like other entrepreneurs, he sees difficulties in implementing regulative ideas of the United Nations Global Compact (for example, fighting corruption and caring for the environment).

Three managers took part in the interview with All Nippon Airways Holding, Inc. (ANA, Japan): senior manager Noguchi (studied economics), manager Sugimoto (political science), and Ben Terasaki (law). They showed familiarity with the ethical principles of the United Nations Global Compact and emphasized that Japan has embraced these principles in politics and economic ethics over centuries. Nevertheless, they admitted that it would not be easy to implement ideas of human rights and active social and political involvement "from below" in Japanese contexts. ANA is very much interested in increasing the number of female employees in leading positions. It is willing to intensify activities for environmental care and to control the cooperation with developing countries with respect to fighting child labor and discrimination.

ANA wants to support the development of a "sustainable society with honesty and integrity." Religious values are not perceived as highly relevant in these contexts. Only in connection with a topic central to airlines—security and safety—are religious components brought up. Once a year, a Buddhist ritual for casualties and injuries among passengers and airline personnel is conducted, although ANA has had only one plane crash, decades ago. At the beginning of each year, there is a prayer for safety and security in a Buddhist temple on Mount Narita. Each office and each airport possess a family altar, and there are rooms for meditation for people with different religious backgrounds. The Olympics Games originally scheduled for 2020 present a particular challenge to Japan to demonstrate ecological sensitivity and social responsibility.

BUSINESS, CONFUCIAN VALUES, WESTERN MANAGEMENT PHILOSOPHY, AND FAMILY VALUES

Shanghai DragonNet Technology Co. (DNT) is a young company which was founded in 2001 and has been listed in the stock market since 2011. With thirty branches and offices and one thousand employees, it is now a "leading IT service and solution provider in China." Vice president Wu Xuesong, born in 1975, received his BA degree from Beijda University and then worked for international corporations (British American Tobacco, SB China Capital, and China Hewlett-Packard). Besides his fast career, Wu took part-time graduate studies at the National School of Development of Beijda University. Central values of the Confucian tradition (taking action; making money in a proper way; striving for moral merits and virtues; being benevolent and forgiving) are important for him and have shaped his performance in his company. He also emphasizes his strong appreciation of Chinese calligraphy.

The climate of the firm is shaped by "trust and respect." Their employees should aim at a strong reputation of the firm regarding the care for its customers. They should deal with conflicts among values (customer benefits, profit interests of the firm, and ethical concerns) in a responsible way. Social activities are concentrated on supporting education in the country. Talented students are placed in structurally poor environments of the country for two years after their graduation.

John Chan Cung Cung comes from a family with roots in China and Peru. His father was a professor at the famous Beijda University in Beijing. The Cultural Revolution made them leave the People's Republic and move to Hong Kong. Chan received his academic and professional education in Hong Kong, in the People's Republic of China, and in Tokyo. He first worked for a Japanese firm for quite some time, then for China Resources, Ltd., a private firm financed by the Chinese government to support trade with European and Japanese partners. Finally, Chan set up his own business. Being self-employed allowed him to suspend his economic activities for a while in order to care for his mother when she had fallen ill. His ethos is very much shaped by Chinese cultural family loyalty. He was in constant exchange of letters with his father, including about questions of morality and values.

The sensitivity for a broad social responsibility beyond the family did not play a significant role in Chan's professional development. National interests and the success of his corporation dominated the orientation. However, international experiences finally led to an appreciation of a culture of equality and care for the weak. Several corporations and companies are shaped by this spirit and participate actively in the Project Hope mentioned above, supporting poor people, especially children in underdeveloped areas.

Business and Christian Values

Claudius Tsang Sze Wai works for Franklin Templeton, Inc., in Hong Kong. Founded in 1947 in New York, Franklin Templeton is one of the largest investment societies in the world, with 22 million customers and a volume of 800 billion US dollars. Tsang went to an Anglican school in Hong Kong and studied at the Chinese University of Hong Kong and the Tsinghua University in Beijing. He is the first Christian in his family, and he and his family belong to a Christian church. Combining Confucian and Christian values, he highly treasures his personal integrity and the connected inner peace of mind and avoidance of all legally dubious activities.

Although he regards Confucian and Christian value systems as good neighbors, he prefers the Christian teaching. The very strong Confucian emphasis on connections and duties toward family and relatives can easily lead, in his opinion, to complicated and corruptible relations. He is skeptical that the value systems of classic Chinese culture and the moral powers of modern Western subjectivity can counterbalance the power of global economic developments. He therefore puts his trust in an international legal system and a transparent regulation of the markets.

The forty-year-old Tanhay Corporation, in South Korea, a company with thirteen subsidiaries in the United States and China, produces pneumatic and environmental pollution-control systems, filter systems, transport systems, automatization systems for other firms, hydraulic machines, 3-D printers, etc. It has 750 employees and an annual turnover of 150 million euros. The first expert interview was conducted with the president and founder of the company, Ju Seph Uhm. Born in a rural environment and raised without his father under Japanese dictatorship, president Uhm served in the military for thirteen years, then worked for five years as an employee in a Japanese firm before he founded his own company in 1973.

The leading values of the founder and his company, constantly mediated to his employees, are creativity (the search for what is new); discernment (the attempt to gain good ethical and pragmatic power of judgment); and activity (the quick endeavor to seek implementation and realization of new ideas). The loyalty of all employees to the corporation should serve their own well-being and should have an impact on the broader public. The good behavior of all employees and the good order of the firm win and strengthen the trust of their customers and—at least indirectly—the value of the produced goods.

The entrepreneur is very much interested in the academic and scientific exploration of an "ethical economy," which in his opinion is grounded not only in human morals and reason but also in the orientation toward a theology of creation. He regards the spiritual basis of the economic and technical development of his enterprise as being of the same relevance as the material condition. The same is true, he thinks, of the furthering of the larger social and societal conditions of life. He suggests that all people should aim at a cultural peace in which solidarity, honesty, and modesty are the moving powers.

The ethical economy which president Uhm envisions is implemented in his company in: (1) educational projects for gifted employees; (2) an ethos of the model taxpayer and the conscious support of the work of the state; (3) a project developed to stop the rural exodus in a small village in a very beautiful but poor country environment. (For this purpose, a small part of the company was placed in that village and now offers work for one hundred people. This branch of the firm is also concerned with an ecologically superior agriculture and organic farming, especially fruit orchards and storage and distribution systems, and it also provides general education and offers room for religious communication.) The ethical economy also includes (4) the renunciation of unconditionally maximizing profits and at the same time securing stable incomes for all employees, even in times of unstable market conditions, and (5) the avoidance of potentially profitable economic partnerships if there is the least suspicion of ethical dishonesty on the other side.

The interview with CEO Jay Uhm, the son of Ju Seph Uhm, related to the firm Tanhay Pneumatic Engineering (TPC Mechatronics AG), founded in South Korea in 1980 and listed since 2001 on the South Korean stock market. CEO Uhm received a high school education and studied at the University of Southern California. His father's ethical honesty and entrepreneurial vigor shaped his own character.

According to CEO Uhm, Asian discipline on one side and the typically American appreciation of individualism on the other generate for him the creativity which he needs as a dynamic entrepreneur. At the same time, he sees himself rooted in the Christian faith. He belongs to a Methodist community and embraces the Christian values of love and mercy, of honesty and truthfulness. Honesty and truthfulness are also important for his relations to employees and customers. This is in line with his father's example.

His company developed an educational program for new employees so that they would internalize these key values. The mission of the company reads: "We satisfy the demands of our customers in innovative and differentiated ways in order to maximize the satisfaction of our customers, and at the same time we want to contribute to the enhancement of national competence." Two key values of the company are (1) "rightness" and (2) "strong mentality." The first concerns harmony of justice and honesty. This value should shape the relation of the entrepreneur with his employees, the relations among the employees and with the company, and the relation of the company with the customers and the broader public, the state, and international partners. The second value supports an ethical education that is not only offered to new employees but also further cultivated in monthly meetings. It has an impact on the spirit of the company and the good inner climate and enhances the firm's reputation in its country and internationally.

The perceived service to the community is above all the securing of safe jobs and occupations and the support of the state through honest payment of taxes. In addition, a church has been built, and the religious community of the "model village" receives support. There is also a plan to establish an academy in the rural environment to explore the opportunities and the dangers of cyberspace.

Yamaha Corp., Japan—the famous maker of pianos, other musical instruments, and sports and car equipment—was represented by Tsutomu Takizawa. Takizawa studied measurement technology and served Yamaha in many functions in Japan and the United States. He is now manager for planning and public relations in Tokyo. He first talked about the company's history and the development of the founder, Torakusu Yamaha, who was a watchmaker and producer of medical instruments in Nagasaki, a city shaped by Roman Catholicism. When the founder was asked one day to repair an imported organ, he decided to manufacture organs himself. In 1887 he produced the first Japanese organ, and other musical instruments followed.

In the middle of the twentieth century, Yamaha largely extended its scope of products. At the same time, the firm intensified its support of public music lessons, music festivals, and the development of cultural sites. When traditional European firms stopped the production of high-quality wind instruments, Yamaha filled this gap in the market. In Europe, China, and Indonesia, new markets were created, and new branches were established. In the 1970 s, more and more electronic musical instruments were produced.

Although it did not pursue specific religious and political interests, Yamaha contributed significantly to the introduction of Western culture to Japan. The entrepreneurial spirit of the city Hamamatsu—the central location of Yamaha as well as the initial home of Toyota, Honda, and Suzuki—contributed to the success story. A strong and complex connection to the religious traditions of the West became unavoidable, since its great classic music generally has a religious background, and many music-loving customers are religious people and live in religious groups and organizations.

Yamaha is very successful in many Asian cities, where the middle class is growing. The company connects the selling of its instruments with the establishment and cultivation of music schools. Yamaha music schools have fifty thousand students in Indonesia and ten thousand students in China, and also exist in Malaysia and Thailand.

As a globally active corporation, Yamaha supports the ethical activities of the United Nations Global Compact. The concept of human rights admittedly does not play a great role in the Japanese business world. For ethics and morals, the values of compliance und corporate philosophy are most relevant. Forced labor and child labor are taboo. The number of women in the workforce is steadily increasing. The production of musical instruments with environmentally friendly materials, and the company's contribution to the reforestation of Indonesia and to water recycling systems in China and Indonesia are mentioned as examples of morally worthy activities together with the fight against corruption and for humane and socially sensitive regulations of work time.

Concluding Comment

We added this chapter to this volume to offer a set of examples from Asian countries, indicating that even modest religious impacts from diverse traditions can shape ethical orientations and the communication of values in basically economically oriented corporations and their business operations. In no case did religious values override the leading maxims, namely customer satisfaction, coworker satisfaction, trust-building by long-term planning, and quality maintenance of products and professional performance. But they offered a specific tone and climate that supported the economic and ethical orientation.

Contributors

Jason Brennan
Robert J. and Elizabeth Flanagan Family Term Professor of Strategy, Economics, Ethics, and Public Policy, McDonough School of Business, Georgetown University, Washington D.C., USA

Michael J. Broyde
Professor of Law, Emory University School of Law, Atlanta, Georgia, USA

Ginny Seung Choi
Senior Fellow, F. A. Hayek Program for Advanced Studies in Philosophy, Politics, and Economics, Mercatus Center, George Mason University, Arlington, Virginia, USA

Samuel Gregg
Research Director, Acton Institute, Grand Rapids, Michigan, USA

Katrin Gülden Le Maire
Consultant, Paris

Peter Lampe
Professor of New Testament Theology, Ruprecht Karls University, Heidelberg, Germany

Manfred Lautenschläger
Founder, MLP Financial Consultants, Wiesloch, Germany

Frank J. Lechner
Professor of Sociology, Emory University, Atlanta, Georgia, USA

Klaus M. Leisinger
Professor Emeritus of Sociology, University of Basel, and Founder and President of the Global Values Alliance Foundation, Basel, Switzerland

Piet Naudé
Director, University of Stellenbosch Business School, Stellenbosch, South Africa

Paul Oslington
Professor of Economics and Theology, Alphacrucis College, Sydney, Australia

Stephen Pickard
Bishop in the Diocese of Canberra and Goulburn and Executive Director of the Australian Center for Christianity and Culture, Charles Sturt University, Canberra, Australia

William Schweiker
Edward L. Ryerson Distinguished Service Professor of Theological Ethics, University of Chicago Divinity School, Chicago, Illinois, USA

Virgil Henry Storr
Associate Professor of Economics, George Mason University, and Don C. Lavoie Senior Fellow and Director of Academic and Student Programs, Mercatus Center, George Mason University, Fairfax, Virginia, USA

Jürgen von Hagen
Professor of Economics, Rheinische Friedrich-Wilhelms University of Bonn, Germany

Michael Welker
Senior Professor of Theology and Director of the Research Center for International and Interdisciplinary Theology (FIIT), Ruprechts Karls University, Heidelberg, Germany

Kaja Wieczorek
Researcher, Institute for New Testament, University of Hamburg, Germany

John Witte Jr.
Robert W. Woodruff Professor of Law, Alonzo L. McDonald Distinguished Professor, and Director of the Center for the Study of Law and Religion, Emory University, Atlanta, Georgia, USA

Michael Welker | John Witte
Stephen Pickard (Eds.)
The Impact of Religion
on Character Formation, Ethical Education,
and the Communication of Values
in Late Modern Pluralistic Societies

288 pages | paperback | 15,5 x 23 cm
ISBN 978-3-374-06410-6
EUR 30,00 [D]

Pluralism has become the defining characteristic of modern societies. Individuals with differing values clamor for equality. Some see in this clash of principles and aims the potential for a more just human community, while others fear the erosion of enduring culture. Yet beneath this welter stand powerful and pervasive institutions, whose distinctive norms profoundly shape our moral commitments and character—notably the family, the market, the media, and systems of law, religion, politics, research, education, health care, and defense. Globalization carries the shifting dynamic between individuals and institutions into every part of the globe.

Drawing on scholarship from five continents, many disciplines, and diverse religious perspectives, this series examines the impact of these various institutions. The contributors hope that this conversation will help address the increasing challenges confronting our pluralist societies and our world.

The overwhelming majority of the contributions in this volume deal with the Christian religion, as pluralistic societies today thrive substantially in Christian environments.

EVANGELISCHE VERLAGSANSTALT
Leipzig   www.eva-leipzig.de

Tel +49 (0) 341/ 7 11 41 -44   shop@eva-leipzig.de

Forthcoming

John Witte | Michael Welker | Stephen Pickard (Eds.)
The Impact of the Law
on Character Formation, Ethical Education, and the Communication
of Values in Late Modern Pluralistic Societies
approx. February 2021

William Schwelker | Michael Welker | John Witte | Stephen Pickard (Eds.)
The Impact of Academic Research
on Character Formation, Ethical Education, and the Communication
of Values in Late Modern Pluralistic Societies
approx. February 2021

John Witte | Michael Welker | Stephen Pickard (Eds.)
The Impact of the Family
on Character Formation, Ethical Education, and the Communication
of Values in Late Modern Pluralistic Societies
approx. 2021

Stephen Pickard | Michael Welker | John Witte (Eds.)
The Impact of Education
on Character Formation, Ethics, and the Communication
of Values in Late Modern Pluralistic Societies
approx. 2021

The Impact of Military/Defense
on Character Formation, Ethical Education, and the Communication
of Values in Late Modern Pluralistic Societies
approx. 2022

The Impact of Media
on Character Formation, Ethical Education, and the Communication
of Values in Late Modern Pluralistic Societies
approx. 2022

The Impact of Healthcare
on Character Formation, Ethical Education, and the Communication
of Values in Late Modern Pluralistic Societies
approx. 2023

The Impact of Politics
on Character Formation, Ethical Education, and the Communicatio
of Values in Late Modern Pluralistic Societies
approx. 2023

Tel +49 (0) 341/ 7 11 41 -44   shop@eva-leipzig.de

Andrea Bieler | Isolde Karle
HyeRan Kim-Cragg | Ilona Nord (Eds.)
Religion and Migration
Negotiating Hospitality,
Agency and Vulnerability

264 pages | paperback | 15,5 x 23 cm
ISBN 978-3-374-06131-0
EUR 38,00 [D]

This volume explores religious discourses and practices of hospitality in the context of migration. It articulates the implied ambivalences and even contradictions as well as the potential contributions to a more just world through social interconnection with others.

The book features authors from diverse national, denominational, cultural, and racial backgrounds. Their essays explore the dichotomy of hospitality between guest and host, while tackling the meaning of home or the loss of it. By interrogating both the peril and promise of the relationship between religion, chiefly Christianity, and hospitality, special attention will be given to the role of migrants' vulnerability and agency, by drawing from empirical, theological, sociological and anthropological insights emerged from postcolonial migration contexts.

EVANGELISCHE VERLAGSANSTALT
Leipzig   www.eva-leipzig.de

Tel +49 (0) 341/ 7 11 41 -44   shop@eva-leipzig.de

Matthias Grebe | Jeremy Worthen (Eds.)
After Brexit?
European Unity and
the Unity of European Churches

160 pages | paperback | 15,5 x 23 cm
ISBN 978-3-374-06157-0
EUR 28,00 [D]

The political, social and cultural dimensions of European unity are going through a period of unsettling change and challenge. Whatever direction it takes, Brexit marks a crossroad from which there is no easy return to the way things were before.

How do the churches of Europe make sense of what is happening, and how should they respond? Is the unity between them, the focus for a century of ecumenical endeavour, a strength on which they can draw, or does that unity itself face new threats?

"After Brexit" is a vital resource for all those interested in these questions, bringing together contributions from scholars and church leaders. It reviews the role of the churches in European integration as a post-war project, analyses the current political and social landscape, and identifies key issues for the future of ecumenism in Europe.

EVANGELISCHE VERLAGSANSTALT
Leipzig   www.eva-leipzig.de

Tel +49 (0) 341/ 7 11 41 -44   shop@eva-leipzig.de

www.ingramcontent.com/pod-product-compliance
Lightning Source LLC
Chambersburg PA
CBHW071237230426
43668CB00011B/1472